Perl Power!

Glenn
Husk

Mohammad Haerian

10630 Pot spring

Perl Power!

A jumpstart guide to programming in Perl 5

Michael Schilli
America Online, Inc.

 **Addison-Wesley**

Harlow, England • Reading, Massachusetts • Menlo Park, California • New York
Don Mills, Ontario • Amsterdam • Bonn • Sydney • Singapore • Tokyo • Madrid
San Juan • Milan • Mexico City • Seoul • Taipei

Originally published in German by Addison Wesley Longman Verlag (Deutschland) GmbH as *GoTo Perl 5*.

English edition © Addison Wesley Longman Limited 1999

Addison Wesley Longman Limited
Edinburgh Gate
Harlow
Essex CM20 2JE
England

and Associated Companies throughout the World.

Cover image: Pearl in an Oyster, by John Shaw. Reproduced courtesy of Telegraph Colour Library.
Translated and typeset by 46.
Printed and bound in the United States of America.

First published 1999

ISBN 0–201–36068–3

British Library Cataloguing-in-Publication Data
A catalogue record for this book is available from the British Library

Library of Congress Cataloging-in-Publication Data
Schilli, Michael.
    Perl power!: a jumpstart guide to programming in Perl 5 / Michael Schilli.
        p.   cm.
    Includes bibliographical references (p.   ) and index.
    ISBN 0-201-36068-3
    1. Perl (Computer program language)   I. Title.
QA76.73.P22S366   1999
005.1'33--dc21   98-44427
                                                                          CIP

Preface

About the book

After the two successful years that this book has been available in German-speaking countries, the publishers decided to translate it into English and allow me the opportunity to address not only my German countrymen but savvy Perl programmers throughout the world!

This book has come a long way since it was first published: it was originally called *Effektives Programmieren mit Perl 5*, but when, about one year after the first edition was published, Joseph N. Hall's excellent *Effective Programming with Perl 5* entered the international arena, this book was renamed *GoTo Perl 5* – and now for the English edition, it has become *Perl Power!* – a happy coincidence, as everyone who works with me at aol.com is well aware of my constant bragging that 'Nothing's impossible, if you got the power of Perl!'

In order to comply with international rules, we have adapted all of the examples to British and American standards.

What this book covers

This book is intended to introduce Perl to the huge number of beginners and intermediate developers who need to use Perl to develop Internet applications, and who want to get up to speed quickly.

The comprehensive introductory chapter provides a quick start for all users new to Perl. The detailed description of object-oriented programming with Perl which follows then allows intermediate Perl programmers to get up to speed with the latest features of the language. Exercises demonstrating commonly encountered problems and providing ready-to-use solutions encourage the reader to actively write programs and to speed up the learning process.

As the use of freely available modules (included on the CD that accompanies the book) dramatically accelerates the development of Perl applications, the book provides guidance on locating the most relevant modules for common programming tasks and illustrates the use of many of these in detail. The book covers a wide variety of practical topics, including Utilities (calendar calculations, drawing charts), Internet Clients (retrieving pages from the Web, extracting HTML information, polling newsgroups and mail hosts, FTP/Telnet clients), CGI Programming (shopping carts) and graphical user interfaces with Perl/Tk.

Acknowledgements

First and foremost, I would like to thank Larry Wall for creating Perl, and to state my admiration for all of the dedicated people in the Perl5 Porters group, who are doing a great job in constantly improving its implementation.

I'd like to thank Steve Temblett, Fiona Kinnear, Julie Knight, and the entire Addison Wesley team in the UK for pulling this off, Hans-Dieter Rauschner for his great work and for his efforts to have me convert everything to international standards, and, of course, Thomas Wehren from Addison-Wesley Germany, who contacted me originally to write a book about Perl.

And, naturally, none of the success I have recently experienced would have happened without the tireless support of my loving wife Angelika. Yeah, Baby!

Michael Schilli
San Francisco, October 1998

If you find this book useful or want to send in suggestions for further updates, feel free to contact me at `michael@perlmeister.com`.

My website is `http://perlmeister.com`.

Introduction

Many years have gone by since a rumor leaked out of the magic circles of system administrators that a new language had seen the light: incredibly fast, elegant, and yet powerful, it was said to be able to solve the typical everyday problems: search text files, extract information, elaborate results. The name of this language was Perl.

The acronym stands for *Practical Extraction and Report Language*, and indicates the original conception of the language. But today, Perl can do much more – or vice versa: there is practically nothing that could not be written in Perl, and often more accurately and faster than in any other language. Tasks which cost days of concentrated programming in C, or become all too cryptic by using tools such as `sed`, `awk`, and a shell script, are in Perl a matter of minutes and a few lines of readable code.

With Perl Release 5, a true deluge of novelties was added. 'Object-oriented programming' was the new shibboleth, and some major projects initiated in the international Perl community, such as modules for graphical interfaces and programming in the Internet. Moreover, hundreds of other Perl enthusiasts braced themselves to create piece by piece a rich choice of mini-modules for everyday use which are today freely available in the CPAN (*Comprehensive Archive Network*, see page 381). In this way, Perl has today become a powerful multi-purpose tool.

In the World Wide Web, Perl has for years been playing the leading role for dynamic documents. Perl scripts are hidden behind online order systems, chat forums, or documents that contain dynamic components (such as changing advert pictures or counters). Recently, the CGI approach received a new stimulus through Perl because of a significant increase in speed.

Today, Perl is no longer a programming language for the initiated. Whether you implement a small test script or an application equipped with a fully fledged graphical interface – Perl is the right means for the purpose.

It is not the aim of the present book to provide a complete reference to the Perl language – here, others have already set unreachable standards (see Wall, Christiansen and Schwartz, 1996). It is instead intended to lead the reader to a practice-oriented use of Perl and its fantastic possibilities.

The book is divided into five chapters. Chapter 1 provides a brief introduction to basic Perl functionalities. Chapter 2 shows the object-oriented programming methods introduced with Perl 5. Equipped with these basic tools, the reader is shown in Chapters 3, 4, and 5 how Perl and several ready-made modules can be used to solve everyday problems, create Motif-like graphical interfaces, and conquer the Internet the programming way.

The Appendices include technical advice for Perl installation and trouble-shooting, together with a collection of subject-related Internet addresses and some information on practical uses of Perl. Appendix H gives a contents description of the CD-ROM enclosed with the book. Besides the sources of the printed sample scripts, it contains the Perl distribution, together with the Perl modules used in the book for successful installation.

Perl has grown in the UNIX universe. However, since it has recently also become quite popular in the Windows world, the second edition of this book includes the Perl distribution for Windows 95 and NT on the enclosed CD-ROM, and the text has been extended with the appropriate references to Windows peculiarities.

Contents

5 Perl programming on the Internet 249

Introduction to Perl

This chapter intends to provide the reader with some Perl craftsmanship. To the beginner, also known as a *Perl rookie*, it offers a concise introduction to the language, but advanced users too will – hopefully – find a few useful suggestions, especially because the book also discusses extensions that have only recently been incorporated into Perl.

It is not the aim of this chapter to explain Perl completely, but rather to lay the cornerstone for understanding the subsequent chapters on 'Object-oriented programming,' 'Prêt-à-porter modules,' 'Graphical interfaces with Tk,' and 'Perl programming in the Internet.'

1.1 Which Perl?

Frequently, one hears the question: 'With which version of Perl should I work? OK, Perl 5 is new and omnipresent. If it weren't for all my Perl 4 scripts ...'. Someone posting similar contributions to the attention of the frequently visited newsgroup `comp.lang.perl.misc`, the Internet forum for Perl-related questions, will reap either Homeric laughter or the answer:

> *Perl 4 is dead dead dead.*

And this is it: Perl 5 is the standard, Perl 4 totally obsolete. Next to none of the examples in this book is happy with Perl 4; some of them even run only with version `5.004_04`, the current version when this book went to print (in Summer 1998). If old Perl 4 scripts do not run with Perl 5, they have not been properly programmed and should be disposed of as quickly as possible.

Thus, the motto is: it does not always have to be the latest beta patch, but major release upgrades should definitely be followed by any serious Perl programmer. Appendix A describes the necessary steps for an installation or a successful update.

1.2 Additional modules

The sample scripts in this book make extensive use of external Perl modules, which in part are not included in the standard distribution. Please note, however, that Perl version 5.004_04 included on the enclosed CD already contains all the important modules. They can be found in the CPAN directory and are also freely available on the Internet from the CPAN archive (Appendix A.4). Appendix A.3 describes the necessary instructions for additional installations. Thus, whenever a sentence like 'requires module A' appears in this text – one look at page 377 tells you how to proceed.

1.3 Starting successfully

To begin with, as a quickie, probably the most well-known Perl program:

_____*hello.pl*

```
#!/usr/bin/perl

print("Howdy, world!\n");        # comment
```
_____*hello.pl*

Perl is an interpreted language. Just like in a shell script under UNIX, the first line of a Perl script defines the interpreter – in this case the Perl interpreter `perl`, which usually resides in the `/usr/bin` directory. Details on how to start Perl scripts can be found in Appendix B. Page 378 tells Windows users how to start their scripts.

As opposed to a shell interpreter, the `perl` interpreter does not read each single instruction for immediate execution, but analyzes the entire script with regard to syntax errors, translates it into byte code, and then executes this code with approximately the same speed as a compiled C program. The interpreter of the very popular Java language, instead, follows a different approach: it processes scripts that are already compiled in byte code. Perl scripts, in contrast, are present in source code; their byte code representation is only of a temporary nature, and is not accessible. At the time of writing this book, a Perl (native) compiler was under development as an alternative for interpreted processing.

1.4 Try and retry

A craft cannot be learned without exercise. If you immediately try out the examples with an installed Perl interpreter, you will quickly get a feeling for how things work. In order to save you a lot of annoying typing, the enclosed CD contains all longer examples ready to be used, so you only need to copy them – *and there you go*! If you have not yet installed Perl, you should consult Appendix A *now*. After that, you can either copy the file `hello.pl` from the `scripts` directory of the enclosed CD, or simply type the two lines from Listing `hello.pl` into a file `hello.pl`. Then you call

```
hello.pl
```

followed by a line feed. Appendix B will help if something does not work.

A word on the exercises scattered here and there across the book. Trying to actually do the exercises may be rather tedious – it is so much easier to look the solution up! But if you only *try* to solve the exercises, you will get things moving that you never even thought of! So invest some time and try in any case to get as far as possible before consulting the solution.

1.4.1 Help is near

Given the wealth of available Perl functions, it is difficult to memorize the calling conditions of each individual one. What was the order of parameters? And the return value? And what happens in this or that special case? Here, every installed Perl system provides you with the help you need:

```
perldoc perl
```

displays an overview of a large number of manual pages, each of which deals with a separate subject (Table 1.1).

For example, to obtain more information on the `print` function used above, you can now call

Table 1.1   Overview of Perl manual pages.

`perl`	This overview
`perldelta`	Changes against the previous version
`perlfaq`	Frequently asked questions
`perldata`	Data structures
`perlsyn`	Syntax
`perlop`	Operators and precedence
`perlre`	Regular expressions
`perlrun`	Perl execution and options
`perlfunc`	Perl built-in functions
`perlvar`	Predefined variables
`perlsub`	Subroutines
`perlmod`	How modules work
`perlmodlib`	How to use and write modules
`perlform`	Output format instructions
`perllocale`	Localization
`perlref`	References
`perldsc`	Introduction to Perl data structures
`perllol`	Data structures: lists of lists
`perltoot`	Introduction to object-oriented programming
`perlobj`	Objects in Perl

```
perldoc perlfunc
```

and work your way through the huge manual page that contains all Perl functions in alphabetical order, until you reach p for `print` – which takes forever. Therefore, the `-f` option of the `perldoc` program shows selected functions straight away:

```
perldoc -f print
```

displays only the information concerning the `print` function from the `perlfunc` manual page.

FAQs

During the past decade that Perl has been on the market, many people have grappled with the same beginners' problems. To flatten the learning curve for future Perl rookies, the so-called FAQs (*Frequently Asked Questions*) – that is, questions typically asked by beginners (and their answers) – are included with every Perl distribution, and are an inexhaustible source also for already advanced programmers.

```
perldoc perlfaq
```

displays an overview page showing the contents of the subsequent manual pages called `perlfaq1`, `perlfaq2`, and so on. Following the principle of 'How do I do this, how do I do that' the pages go from one subject to the next.

1.5 Data types and control structures

By definition, Perl supports a series of data types, including not only 'simple' types such as strings or numeric variables, but also ordered collections of the above, such as arrays or hash tables (associative arrays).

This kind of vocabulary makes many things in Perl so easy. Without thinking twice about implementation, limits, or performance, these extended data types allow compact processing of large amounts of data.

1.5.1 Scalars

Simple data types in Perl are also called scalars. They can either assume alphanumeric values or function as purely numerical variables. The line

```
$num = 42;
```

assigns the scalar `$num` the value 42. The 'dollar sign' `$` in front of the name `num` identifies the variable as a scalar, independently from whether it appears on the right-hand or left-hand side of an assignment. `$string`, a further scalar, receives its value by means of

```
$string = "abc";
```

The fact that a scalar can be interpreted either as a string or as a numerical variable makes a language purist's hair stand on end, but the main goal of Perl is to juggle elegantly with extracted text data. As an interesting side effect,

```perl
print("halfnum=", $num/2, "\n");
```

behaves as expected and displays half of the value of $num, whereas

```perl
print("halfstring=", $string/2, "\n");
```

will cause Perl in warning mode (call of the interpreter with the option -w, for example via an entry such as #!/usr/bin/perl -w (see Appendix B)) to display the message

```
Argument "abc" isn't numeric in divide at ./script.pl line 4.
```

An arithmetical operation on a text would also make little sense. The next example, instead, is completely legal:

```perl
$numstr = "5";
print("halfnumstr=", $numstr/2, "\n");
```

because, where necessary, Perl converts strings dynamically into numeric types – and back.

Scalar values may also be specified as floating point numbers (for example 3.1415 or 9.0E-4 for 9×10^{-4}), or in hexadecimal (for example 0xbeef) or octal notation (for example 010).

Strings can be enclosed either in single quotes (for example 'string') or in double quotes (for example "Value: $val"). While in the first case no variable expansion takes place, in the second case the interpreter substitutes variables with their values (Perl expands scalars and arrays enclosed in double quotes, as discussed in the next section), and resolves escape sequences (for example "\n" for a line feed). If you really want a backslash ('\') to appear in a string enclosed in double quotes, the sequence must read "\\", one quote being written as "\"".

For strings that do not contain any variables or escape sequences, the notations "..." and '...' are equivalent, although the author prefers "..." for strings even where no variable expansion takes place, because it corresponds to the notation of the C programming language.

If the variable $way has the value 42, "Distance: $waykm" does not yield the desired result 'Distance: 42km', because in this case, Perl tries to substitute the value of a non-existent variable $waykm and fails. To make Perl recognize the end of a variable in the string, its name needs to be enclosed in curly brackets (braces): "Distance ${way}km" will work.

If, on the other hand, the dollar sign does not denote a variable, but is really meant as '$', it must be preceded by a backslash: print "\$ 100.00" displays '$ 100.00'.

A non-initialized scalar has the value `undef`. Interrogation or output of scalars that do not yet contain a value is potentially dangerous. In warning mode, such unsafe actions cause the Perl interpreter to display corresponding messages. Whether a scalar is initialized or not can be determined by means of the `defined` operator:

```perl
if(defined $a) {
    print "Scalar \$a is defined!\n";
} else {
    print "Scalar \$a is 'undef'!\n";
}
```

Operations with strings

Two strings `$string1` and `$string2` are concatenated by the '.' operator into one string consisting of both strings in sequence one after the other.

```perl
$string = $string1 . $string2;    # string concatenation
```

Another legal notation is

```perl
$string = "$string1$string2";    # string concatenation
```

The `.=` operator appends a string to an existing one:

```perl
$string  = $string1;
$string .= $string2;              # append a string
```

The last character of a string is cut off by the function

```perl
chop($string);
```

It should be noted that `chop` does *not* return the reduced string, but merely works on the original string and yields the cut-off character as its return value.

If only trailing newline characters are to be removed,

```perl
chomp($string);
```

is the means to the end. `chomp` too does not return the resulting string, but the number of removed characters. If they are called without arguments, `chop` and `chomp` work on the variable '`$_`', as do many other Perl functions too.

A substring that begins at `$offset` characters from the start of the original string and is `$length` characters long, is accessed by

```perl
$partstr = substr($string, $offset, $length);
```

The length of a string can be determined by means of

```perl
$length = length($string);
```

Here documents

The construct of the *here document* known from shell programming can be used for easy writing of multi-line strings in a script.

The << operator specifies the termination string that ends a text of potentially several lines beginning in the subsequent line:

```
$text = <<LetterEnd;
Dear user!

Due to urgent maintenance work, the server
$server can currently not be accessed.

Enjoy a day of mental arithmetic!

    Your system administration
LetterEnd
```

The termination string (LetterEnd in the example) must stand alone at the beginning of the last line of the document to cause termination of the text.

Variables ($server in the example) are substituted by Perl with their values. An initial definition of the termination string by means of single quotes would, instead, cause Perl not to expand variables contained in the text, and therefore no escape sequences would be needed for special characters:

———*here.pl*

```
print <<'TheEnd';
The cost amounts to $100.
TheEnd
```

———*here.pl*

1.5.2 Lists and arrays

In Perl, scalars can be combined into ordered groups and associated to variables:

```
@array = ("First element", "", 42);
```

Subsequently, the array @array contains three scalars: two strings and one numeric variable. Please note that the terms 'list' and 'array' denote two *different* Perl constructs. Lists are ordered collections of scalars, whereas arrays are data types that can accommodate a list.

In a similar way as the dollar sign '$' identifies scalars, a prefixed at sign '@' identifies a variable as an array.

An empty array is created (or an existing array is emptied) by assigning an array variable an empty list:

```
@array = ();
```

In the definition of long lists of strings, the `qw` operator saves some typing effort. The array initialization

```
@array = ("string1", "string2", "string3", "string4");
```

can also be written as

```
@array = qw(string1 string2 string3 string4);
```

where the `qw` operator defines the limits between the elements by means of the spaces.

The elements of an array can now be accessed either via a series of manipulation functions, such as

```
push(@array, $scalar);        # inserts $scalar at the
                              # end of the array

$element = pop(@array);       # removes the last element of the
                              # array and assigns it to $element

unshift(@array, $scalar);     # inserts $scalar at the
                              # beginning of the array

$element = shift(@array);     # removes the first element of the
                              # array and assigns it to $element
```

or with the array syntax

```
$element = $array[2];         # copies the third element to $element
```

Careful: a common beginner's error would be to write `@array[2]`. This does not even cause Perl to signal a syntax error, because `@array[2]` returns – syntactically completely correctly – a sublist with one element instead of a scalar, as originally intended.

As in the C programming language, index numbering starts with 0 for the first element. The constructs

```
@part = @array[3,4,5,6,7];   # copies elements 4 to 8
@part = @array[3..7];        # ditto
```

return the elements on the specified index positions as a list that initializes the array `@part`. On the left-hand side of the list assignment it is also possible to have a list of named scalars that then receive the list values of the right-hand side of the equation:

```
($one, $two) = (1, 2, 3, 4); # list assignment
```

stores the values 1 and 2 in the scalars `$one` and `$two`. Superfluous elements on the right-hand side are eliminated. If the left-hand list contains more elements than those generated by the assignment, Perl assigns the superfluous elements the value `undef`.

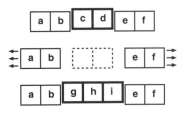

Figure 1.1 Illustration of the function `splice(@array, $offset, $length, ('g'..'i'))`; with `@array=('a'..'f')`, `$offset=2` and `$length=2`.

For each array `@array`, a scalar named `$#array` is always defined, which indicates the index of the last element. Since indexing of arrays begins with 0, the length of an array – that is, the number of its elements – is given by the value of '`$#array + 1`':

```
print "array: @array\n";            # display array elements
                                    # separated by blank spaces
print "Last index: $#array\n";      # index of the last element
print "Length: ", $#array + 1, "\n"; # number of elements
                                    # in the array
```

Thus the last element of an array is brought to light by `$array[$#array]`. An easier way to write this is by using negative indices, which roll the array up from the end: `$array[-1]` yields the last element, `$array[-2]` the last but one.

For more complex array operations, Perl also has the manipulation function `splice`. This can be used for easy removal of parts of an array and serial insertion of new elements in arbitrary positions.

The call

```
splice(@array, $offset, $length, insertlist);
```

can be translated into 'Substitute the row of elements of `@array` that begins at the index `$offset`, and is `$length` elements long, with the list *insertlist* and return the substituted sublist.'

Figure 1.1 shows what happens to the array `@array` when executing the following Perl code:

```
@array  = ('a', 'b', 'c', 'd', 'e', 'f');
$offset = 2;
$length = 2;

splice(@array, $offset, $length, ('g', 'h', 'i'));
```

The `splice` function removes two elements from the original array and squeezes in a three-element list instead.

The following examples show some special cases of splice, namely the simulation of the above-mentioned functions shift, unshift, pop and push.

```
$first = splice(@array, 0, 1);
                          # remove the first array element,
                          # return it, and assign it to $first

splice(@array, 0, 0, $element);
                          # insert $element at the beginning
                          # of the array

$last = splice(@array, $#array, 1);
                          # remove the last array element,
                          # return it, and assign it to $last

splice(@array, $#array + 1, 0, $element);
                          # insert $element at the end
                          # of the array
```

Thus, if the splice function contains a non-zero $length parameter without a matching list for insertion, it simply deletes the specified number of elements from position $offset onward.

If, on the other hand, the $length parameter is zero and a list to be inserted exists, splice inserts the specified list (in the above case, only a single element) at position $offset into the array, shifting the existing elements aside accordingly.

EXERCISE 1.1

Extract elements 2 to 4 from the array

```
@array = (1,2,3,4,5);
```

and assign them to the scalars $a, $b and $c, making use of

(a) index access to arrays (for example $array[2]),
(b) sublist access with @array[...] and
(c) the splice function.

Write one small Perl script each, which initializes the array, solves the required task, and outputs the result in the form "a=2 b=3 c=4" (*solution on page 96*).

Parameter lists

The fact that the `splice` function is called once with three and once with four parameters shows an important principle of Perl: each function determines how many parameters are ready to be passed and only fetches values that are really present.

Thus the `splice` function determines case by case whether there is a list to be inserted or not. If not, it just deletes the specified sublist without inserting new elements.

Therefore, as *insertlist* parameter, `splice` can handle either nothing, or an element, a list (for example `(1..10)`) or an expression (for example `@array`) that converts into a list (details of the so-called list context can be found in Section 1.5.5).

Perl does not require a fixed signature of functions (although Perl 5 has recently acquired a prototyping syntax, see Section 1.14.6); the called subroutines are, however, free to perform their own checks on the passed parameters. Strong *typing* is normally not an issue for Perl; however, the `splice` function does insist on a named array as its first parameter. 'Internal' Perl functions and user-defined subroutines with prototype definitions sometimes show this uncommon behavior.

In Perl function calls, the parentheses enclosing the parameter list may also be omitted:

```
print("Howdy, World!", "\n");
```

is equivalent to

```
print "Howdy, World!", "\n";
```

The enclosing parentheses are only occasionally needed to solve precedence conflicts or to show that the specified expression is indeed a function.

Lists of scalars are often not sufficient for processing complex structures. Therefore Perl 5 also allows modelling of arbitrary embeddings, such as lists of lists. Section 1.5.5 discusses the relevant details.

Map and `grep`

For quick manipulation of lists, Perl provides the functions `grep` and `map`, which are very useful for tasks such as extracting elements on the basis of specified conditions or processing all elements of a list in a particular way.

```
grep { Perl code } @array; # evaluates the code block for
                           # each array element and inserts it
                           # into the resulting list if
                           # the return value is true

map { Perl code } @array;  # evaluates the code block for each
                           # array element and inserts the
                           # return value into the resulting list
```

The grep function executes the specified code block for each element of the specified list (which need not necessarily be an array, but can be anything that yields a list). In each cycle, the variable '$_' assumes the value of the currently processed list element. $_ is practically the 'maid-of-all-work' among Perl's variables. Many operations refer to it by default in the absence of explicit input data.

The grep function returns the list of elements for which the code block during processing returned a true value (that is, anything except undef, 0, "0", or the empty string ""). The code block may include an arbitrary number of Perl instructions; the return value of the block is determined by the return value of the *last* one.

The map function works in a similar way, except that it returns a list whose elements correspond to the return values of the code block on all original list elements. Thus, in the normal case, map 'transforms' a list into another list of the same size, with the specified block describing the transition function. Note that, since the instructions executed on each element may also return lists, the size of the resulting list may exceed that of the original list – or be smaller if some empty lists () are returned.

Thus, while the instructions

```
@array = (1, 2, 4, 5);

@part = grep { $_ < 5; } @array;     # yields all array elements
                                     # that are less than 5
```

store the list

```
(1,2,4)
```

in @part, the instructions

```
@array = (1, 2, 4, 5);

$max = 3;               # limit maximum element value
                        # of result list to $max
@new = map { $_ > $max ? $max : $_ } @array;
```

generate the result

```
(1,2,3,3)
```

The construct condition ? a : b is taken from the C programming language, and yields a if the specified condition is satisfied, and b otherwise.

The return value of the code block is usually determined by a condition (for example $_ < 5), but function calls are possible as well. In

```
@part = map { int($_); } (1.23, 4.56, 7.89);
```

Perl's built-in int function rounds the floating point numbers in the list down to the next integer number, so the resulting array is (1,4,7). The following snippet prefixes each string element of `@array` with some numbering, so (`'Design'`, `'Implementa-tion'`, `'Test'`) becomes, for example, (`'1. Design'`, `'2. Implementation'`, `'3. Test'`) in the resulting list:

```
$i = 1;
@new = map { $string = "$i. $_"; # generate new string
            $i++;                # index for next cycle
            $string;             # return string (!)
          } @array;
```

If the code block contains several instructions, it is important to make sure that the correct value is returned. If the `$string;` instruction had been missing at the end of the code block, the result of each cycle would have been the return value of `$i++`, which would have stored (`1, 2, 3`) in the result array.

But so-called 'regular expressions' are also allowed in the code block. This Perl speciality, which is extensively discussed in Section 1.10, consists of pattern-matching operators that compare the current list element with a pattern and return a true value if the pattern is recognized. Thus

```
@array = ("tic", "tac", "toe");

@part = grep { /c/ } @array;  # yields all array elements
                              # containing the character "c"
```

returns the list (`"tic"`, `"tac"`), because `/c/` returns the empty string for elements that do not contain a 'c', which in turn causes the `grep` function to filter the corresponding elements out.

Loops over lists

Iteration over all elements of a list is carried out by means of `for` or `foreach` loops. A `foreach` loop is either accompanied by a loop parameter, as in

```
foreach $element (@array) {
    print $element, "\n" ;    # current element: $element
}
```

or, if it is omitted, as in

```
foreach (@array) {
    print $_, "\n" ;    # current element: $_
}
```

the crackerjack variable `$_` holds the current element value.

Alternatively, you can also use a 'conventional' `for` loop to iterate over the indices of the list elements:

```
for($i=0; $i<=$#array; $i++) { # loop over array indices
    print $array[$i], "\n";
}
```

The loop starts with $i equal 0, and increments $i (via $i++) untils the last index ($#array) has been reached.

Loop control

To intervene in the normal course of a loop, Perl provides the instructions next, redo, and last. The next command aborts the current loop cycle and continues with the next value of the loop variable, whereas redo executes another cycle with the same loop variable. last aborts the loop completely.

According to the above, the script

```
$first_time = 1;

foreach $i (1..3) {
    if($i == 1) {        # if i equals 1 start a new cycle
        next;            # with the new counter value
    }
    if($i == 3) {        # immediate termination if i equals 3
        last;
    }

    print "$i\n";

                         # if $i==2 repeat, but only the
                         # first time ($first_time equals 1)
    if($i == 2 && $first_time) {
        $first_time = 0;
        redo;            # repeat with the same $i
    }
}
```

generates the output

```
2
2
```

The first cycle through the loop is prematurely terminated by the next instruction, $i is incremented to 2. In the next cycle, the two if conditions above are not met; the subsequent print function outputs 2. The two expressions for the next if condition turn out to be true, and the logic AND (&&) joins them to form a true value: thus the body of the if construct is executed. There, $first_time receives the value 0, and the redo instruction triggers a repetition of the loop with $i equal to 2. Again, the print instruction outputs 2, but the subsequent if condition turns out this time to be false ($first_time is 0, thus false), and the loop begins the next cycle with $i equal to 3. This is, however, aborted by the last command before any further output takes place.

next, redo, and last usually refer to the current loop. For control of nested loops, loop labels may be defined:

```
outside:foreach $i (1..5) {
    for($j=1; $j<=5; $j++) {
        print "$i $j\n";
        if($i == 1 && $j == 4) {
            last outside;
        }
    }
}
```

In the example, the outer loop is tagged with the label outside. The instruction 'last outside' in the body of the inner loop thus aborts all cycles together at the same time.

The easiest way to iterate over all elements of an array is undoubtedly

```
foreach $element (@array) {
    print "$element\n";
}
```

The following construct, instead, makes the array shrink simultaneously with every processed element:

```
while($#array >= 0) {
    $element = shift(@array);
    print "CURRENT: $element, REMAINING ARRAY: @array\n";
}
```

The while construct executes the body of the loop until the array size shrinks to zero and the specified condition yields a false value.

If a loop is supposed to execute one action in any case and then, depending on a condition, either repeat or exit the loop, a do-while construct will help. Thus,

```
@array = (1,2,3);

do {
    print "\@array = (@array)\n";
    shift(@array);

} while($#array >= 0);
```

yields the sequence

```
@array = (1 2 3)
@array = (2 3)
@array = (3)
```

and would, even for an empty @array, at least output @array = () once before terminating the loop. An alternative could also be:

```
@array = (1,2,3);

{ print "\@array = (@array)\n";

    shift(@array);                    # remove first element

    if($#array >= 0) {
        redo;                         # repeat loop
    }
}
```

Thus loops do not presume for or while constructs; even a code block enclosed in {...} can implement a loop's behavior with the aid of the keywords redo and last.

Multi-dimensional arrays

Perl arrays are also suited for multi-dimensional applications. Just as in the C programming language,

```
$field[4][7] = 13;         # two-dimensional array
```

sets the value of a matrix point, while

```
$space[2][3][1] = "value";   # three-dimensional array
```

sets a points in a three-dimensional array. Perl allows creation of arrays with arbitrary dimensions without previous declaration – the necessary memory structures are simply created on demand. Note that, internally, no true three-dimensional array is created, but a structure that uses much less memory space than its array counterpart in C, if only a few elements are actually occupied.

EXERCISE 1.2

Create a two-dimensional array of 3 × 3 elements, whose entries are the following strings:

```
"0:0"   "0:1"   "0:2"
"1:0"   "1:1"   "1:2"
"2:0"   "2:1"   "2:2"
```

Make use of two nested `for` loops, in which you increment two indices $i and $j (*solution on page 96*).

Lists and strings

The elements of a list can be assembled into one string by means of the `join` command. As its first parameter, it expects a string that delimits the individual list entries in the resulting string from one another. With the newline character as a separator,

```
@array = ("One", "Two", "Three");   # create array
$string = join("\n", @array);       # concatenate entries
print $string, "\n";                # ... and output the result
```

yields the output

```
One
Two
Three
```

Conversely, strings can also be easily converted into lists. As a separator, the `split` function accepts a regular expression: that is, a search pattern as defined in Section 1.10. The construct

```
@array = split(/\n/, $string);     # lines -> array elements
```

converts the previously generated multi-line string back into a list and assigns it to the array `@array`.

Since Perl expands the values of an array enclosed in double quotes by itself,

```
print "@array\n";    # array elements with separating spaces
```

outputs all array elements including separating spaces. Since the `print` function normally processes its arguments without spaces,

```
print @array, "\n";  # array elements without separating spaces
```

provokes output of the array elements *without* separating spaces.

EXERCISE 1.3

Output the values of the array `@array = (1,2,3)` as a string in the format `"(1-2-3)"`. Assemble the string step by step using a `for` loop, making sure that no hyphen appears after the last value. Subsequently, solve the problem by means of a `join` instruction (*solution on page 96*).

1.5.3 Associative arrays

An associative array, in short *hash*, is a memory structure that efficiently manages key-value data pairs. In such arrays, elements are addressed not via index numbers, but via arbitrary strings.

%hash	
key1	value1
key2	value2
...	...

Figure 1.2   Key/value pairs in a hash.

The header of an *email message*, for example, consists of a number of lines that after an initial keyword (for example `Date:`) contain a corresponding item of information:

```
Date: Fri, 10 Jul 98 16:25:18 +0200
From: scx@softlab.de
To: gates@microsoft.com
Subject: Re: Newbie Unix Question
Status: RO
```

Now it would be rather useful to read the lines and store them in such a way that a (sample) function `hashme` with the keyword as an argument returned the associated value. Thus,

```
$value = hashme('Date:');
```

would return the string `"Fri, 10 Jul 98 16:25:18 +0200"`. Perl provides the functionality of *hashme* via a separate data type, the hash. The assignment

```
$mailheader{'Date:'} = 'Fri, 10 Jul 98 16:25:18 +0200';
```

creates a hash with the name `mailheader` (if this does not yet exist) and stores the specified date string under the key `'Date:'`. A call of

```
$value = $mailheader{'Date:'};
```

extracts the stored value from the hash and assigns it to the scalar `$value`. The hash itself is identified by `%mailheader`.

To iterate over all entries of the hash, you can use the following construct to extract all keys from the hash and then access the corresponding values:

```
foreach $key (keys %mailheader) {     # iterate over keys
    $value = $mailheader{$key};        # determine value
    print "Key: $key  value: $value\n";
}
```

The `keys` function returns all keys of the hash as a list. The loop variable `$key` contains the current hash key.

Conversely, the function `values` returns all *values* of a hash. However, since there is no way of getting from a hash value to its key, and the content of a hash is usually of interest only in the key-value form, `values` is of only minor importance. More frequently, instead, one encounters the iterator `each`, which step by step walks its way through a specified hash, supplying at each call the next key-value pair. Once arrived at the end of the hash, `each` returns the value 0, so that

```
while (($key, $value) = each %mailheader) {
    print "Key: $key  value: $value\n";
}
```

also outputs the hash data in the apparently random order so typical for hash iterators.

Whether a matching value exists in the hash for a given key can be determined using the `exists` function. A defined key-value pair in the hash is deleted by means of the `delete` instruction:

```
if(exists($mailheader{'Date:'})) {       # interrogate
    delete($mailheader{'Date:'});         # delete
}
```

Note that it is not sufficient to set the value of a hash entry to `undef`; in this case, the entry continues to exist.

Although arrays and hashes support completely different access methods, the data they contain can be easily converted from one structure into the other. A list with an even number of elements initializes a hash without problems. However, care must be taken to avoid the persistent beginner's error of writing `%hash = { ... }`; for reasons that are explained in Section 1.5.7, this is totally wrong, but it only triggers an error message in warning mode (`-w`).

```
%hash = ("key1" => "val1", "key2" => "val2");
```

The operator => merely replaces a comma, and provides a better visual structuring of the key-value pairs. Accordingly,

```
%hash = ();
```

assigns the hash %hash an empty list, thus removing all key-value pairs. The expression

```
print "Hash contents: @{[%hash]} \n";
```

outputs the data of the hash in the same way as that of a list, namely separated by spaces. The above construct evaluates the hash in the list context (Section 1.5.6), inserting the elements into the string separated by spaces. The constructs [...] or @{...} are discussed in Sections 1.5.5 and 1.5.7.

In Perl, variable names for scalars, arrays, and hashes are treated separately. Thus, for example, a scalar $name, an array @name, and a hash %name can coexist without problems, and do not cause any conflicts.

Hash or array?

Sometimes, data modeled as arrays can be more efficiently represented by a hash. If you frequently encounter tasks such as 'check whether an element is already present in the array,' or if you want to efficiently exclude elements from occurring in the data structure more than once, a hash is better suited than an array for modeling such data. For this purpose, the array elements are simply put as keys into the hash, and their associated values are for example set to 1, or that space is used for additional information:

```
@dups = ("apples", "pears", "plums", "apples");

foreach $element (@dups) {
    $uniq{$element} = 1;
}

foreach $element (keys %uniq) {
    print "$element\n";
}
```

This piece of code extracts the partly duplicate values from the array @dups, turns them into hash keys, and subsequently outputs a list freed from all duplicates:

```
plums
apples
pears
```

If, on the other hand, the order of the stored elements is significant, a hash is not suitable because (as you can see above) internally it mixes up the elements in a completely random order.

1.5.4 Functions, packages, and modules

As already mentioned in the previous section, Perl insists on a very idiosyncratic way of passing parameters to subroutines.

The following code fragment shows examples of how the user-defined function func can be called at any arbitrary place of the script with or without parameters:

```
func();              # call without parameters
&func();             # ditto

func($par1, $par2);  # call with parameters
&func($par1, $par2); # ditto
```

After the function definition or a prototype declaration (see Section 1.14.6) the following constructs are also possible:

```
sub func {           # definition
    # ...
}
                     # the following calls only _after_
                     # definition or prototype!
func;                # call without parameters
func $par1, $par2;   # call with parameters
```

The typical definition of a subroutine is shown by the following code:

```
sub func {
    my ($var1, $var2) = @_;

    # ...

    return 1;
}
```

In subroutines, the values of the passed parameters are always kept ready for use in an array with the reserved name '@_'. Perl usually works with the *call-by-value* principle (details of its counterpart, the *call-by-reference* principle, can be found in Section 1.5.5).

The first line of the above listing assigns the two scalars $var1 and $var2 the first two elements of the list @_. The prefixed operator my ensures that the variables are valid only inside the current function; otherwise, they would be present everywhere in the script.

The Perl default setting that causes all defined variables to be valid globally, contradicts the general understanding of structured programming. A loop variable $i, carelessly left global, can easily affect the course of a loop in another subroutine that also uses $i for loop control. Therefore the scope of variables that are only needed locally should be manually limited with the my operator to 'local scope'. (Section 1.14.3 shows a way to force Perl to stop if variables are left global without further specification.)

If the above defined function func is called with more than two parameters, for example with

```
func(1, 2, "three", "four");
```

the superfluous parameters are simply dropped – they do exist in @_, but they are never fetched. If, instead, the function is called with only one parameter, its value is assigned to $var1, whereas $var2 remains uninitialized and thus contains the value undef.

Functions that provide interfaces for other programmers (APIs) should themselves carry out a check on number and type of passed variables. This can be done in the following way:

```
sub func {
    my $var1 = shift;          # accept parameters

    if(! defined $var1) {      # called with zero parameters?
        return 0;
    }

    if($#_ >= 0) {             # more than one parameter?
        print "What am I supposed to do with so many parameters?\n";
    }

    # ...
    return 1;                  # return value
}
```

The above listing shows a second, very popular way of fetching Perl subroutine parameters from the transfer array @_: inside subroutines, and if no other parameter is specified, the shift function, which removes and returns the first element of an array, accesses the array @_.

The subsequent lines check whether fewer or more parameters than the requested *one* were passed. More sophisticated methods of parameter checking are provided by Perl's prototyping syntax, which is discussed in Section 1.14.6.

The return value of a function is determined by the return instruction. A successfully terminated Perl subroutine conventionally returns a non-zero value, whereas a return value of zero indicates an error. Frequently, Perl functions return entire lists –

a very elegant way of proceeding with several return values. If no `return` instruction is present, the last instruction of the subroutine determines the return value.

```
sub logic_and {
    $_[0] && $_[1];      # logical 'AND' over
}                        # both input parameters
```

The function `logic_and` thus returns the value of its input parameters joined with the logical AND operator (and, as you can see, index number access to the parameter array `@_` is legal too!). Thus `logic_and(1,0)` returns the value 0, whereas `logic_and(1,1)` returns 1.

   Passing of lists or hashes *by value* leads to long parameter lists containing scalars. Thus the instructions

```
@myarray = (1, 2);        # initialize array
$myhash{'key'} = 'value'; # initialize hash

func(@myarray, %myhash);  # pass array and hash to func()
```

result in the `func` subroutine in a parameter array `@_` of the following contents:

```
(1, 2, 'key', 'value')     # contents of @_
```

Thus the subroutine can no longer determine where the passed array ends and the hash begins. For passing arrays and hashes it is therefore preferable to use the *call-by-reference* method, which is discussed in Section 1.5.5.

EXERCISE 1.4

There *is*, however, a possibility to pass scalars and an array to a function *by value*: for this, the array must be the last parameter. Write a Perl function `func` that upon the call

```
$a = 1;
$b = 2;
@c = (3, 4, 5);

func($a, $b, @c);
```

copies the passed parameters into local variables and (verbatim) outputs

```
$a=1 $b=2 @c=(3 4 5)
```

(*solution on page 97*).

Packages

A package is a closed namespace for variables and functions. While two functions of the same name usually lead to collisions, they will not do any harm if they are encapsulated in different spaces by means of the `package` construct.

Listing `package.pl` shows the definition of two packages `Sample1` and `Sample2` and the call of the function `func` from package `Sample2`. The first call, which goes without a prefixed package name, specifies the function in the current package `Sample2`, while the subsequent *fully qualified* calls ('`package::function`' syntax) give explicit specifications.

————————————————————————————————————*package.pl*

```perl
#!/usr/bin/perl -w

package Sample1;            # 1st package

sub func {                          # function Sample1::func
    print "sample1\n";
}

package Sample2;            # 2nd package

sub func {                          # function Sample2::func
    print "sample2\n";
}

                # we are now in "Sample2"
func();         # implicitly calls Sample2::func();

Sample1::func();  # fully qualified notation
Sample2::func();  # fully qualified notation
```

————————————————————————————————————*package.pl*

The `package` constructs affect not only names of functions, but also names of variables. A global variable `$var` in the package `Sample1` would be invisible from package `Sample2` – unless it were specified via

`$Sample1::var`

This mechanism also holds without a package definition: the default package answers to the name of `main`. Thus a '*Howdy, world!*' could also be formulated like this (in a rather long-winded way):

```
package main;                        # main program: package main

CORE::print("Howdy, world!\n");      # print function from the
                                     # CORE package
```

Since the Perl main program is always (implicitly) located in the main package, a variable $i defined there is accessible from everywhere via $main::i – even if no 'package main;' construct explicitly marks the beginning.

In the normal case, the calls print and CORE::print cause the same action to be performed: the print function of the standard CORE package is executed.

Modules

Larger development projects sometimes require code to be stored in different files. Perl supports this approach with its module mechanism. A Perl module is a file with the extension .pm (for example Example.pm) whose contents can be accessed from the main program after the call of

```
use Example;
```

This instruction causes the Perl interpreter to search all known include paths for a file named Example.pm, which must contain the corresponding package definition (package Example in the above example). Paths are stored as strings in a predefined, extensible array named @INC.

Even hierarchical nesting of modules is allowed: thus the instruction

```
use Net::FTP;
```

searches for a module file named FTP.pm in a directory of the name Net that is located in one of the include paths. Figure 1.3 illustrates this procedure. The typical structure of a module is shown in Listing Example.pm.

Not only does the instruction use Example read all package and subroutine definitions contained in the Example.pm module, it also executes commands present outside the subroutine definitions. The use command expects the module to return a 'true' value: therefore you can usually find the instruction '1;' at the end of a module.

1.5.5 References

With respect to previous versions, Perl 5 introduces a completely new concept: references to data types.

Thus a variable can be addressed not only by its name, but also by any number of 'intelligent' pointers referring to it. References differ from normal pointers, such as those supplied by C, in the sense that the program counts internally how many references exist for a variable at any time. If the variable runs *out of scope* – that is, if it leaves its validity range – it nevertheless continues to exists as long as valid references point to it.

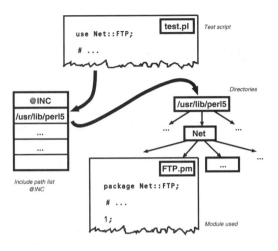

Figure 1.3 The instruction `use Net::FTP` triggers a search for the module `FTP.pm` in the directory `Net` which is in turn located in one of the directories stored in the `@INC` array.

Example.pm

```
package Example;

sub func {
    # ...
}

# ...

1;
```

Example.pm

If the number of references to a variable reaches zero, it is evidently no longer needed by anyone, and the memory area occupied by it can be released. Not only does this procedure clean up memory, it also prevents so-called *dangling pointers*, which point to invalid addresses because the object once located there no longer exists. Figure 1.4 illustrates the procedure.

Perl 5 offers this reference mechanism for all its data types: references can be used to point to scalars, arrays, hashs, and even functions.

Thus the assignment

```
$scalarref = \$scalar;
```

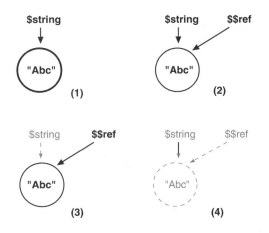

Figure 1.4   (1) The variable `$string` contains the string `"Abc"`. (2) The reference `$ref` additionally points to the contents of the variable. (3) `$string` becomes invalid. However, since there still is a reference to it, the variable is kept alive. (4) `$ref` becomes invalid – the variable disappears.

stores a reference to the scalar `$scalar` in the variable `$scalarref`. From the outside, `$scalarref` looks like a scalar, but in reality it is a reference. Access to `$scalar` can now be obtained either via the original with

```
$value = $scalar;           # assignment via original
```

or via the dereferenced reference with

```
$value = $$scalarref;       # or
$value = ${$scalarref};
```

Moreover, it is important to keep in mind that Perl never infers 'magically' from the reference to the referenced data type, but relies on the fact that this will result from the dereferenced code. Thus a reference to a hash type variable is set with

```
$hashref = \%myhash;
```

Access to the hash `%myhash` is now made either via the original with

```
$myhash{'KEY'} = 'VALUE';    # hash assignment
```

or, equivalently, via dereferencing the previously defined reference by means of

```
$$hashref{'KEY'} = 'VALUE';  # hash assignment via hash reference
```

or

Table 1.2 Working with references.

`$scalarref`	`=`	`\$scalar;`	scalar → scalar reference
`$scalar`	`=`	`$$scalarref;`	scalar reference → scalar
`$scalar`	`=`	`${$scalarref};`	ditto
`$arrayref`	`=`	`\@array;`	array → array reference
`@array`	`=`	`@$arrayref;`	array reference → array
`@array`	`=`	`@{$arrayref}`	ditto
`$element`	`=`	`${$arrayref}[2];`	array reference → element
`$element`	`=`	`$arrayref->[2];`	ditto
`$hashref`	`=`	`\%hash;`	hash → hash reference
`%hash`	`=`	`%$hashref;`	hash reference → hash
`%hash`	`=`	`%{$hashref};`	ditto
`$value`	`=`	`${$hashref}{'key'};`	hash reference → value
`$value`	`=`	`$hashref->{'key'};`	ditto
`$funcref`	`=`	`\&func;`	function → function reference
`&$funcref();`			function reference → call
`$funcref->();`			ditto

```
${$hashref}{'KEY'} = 'VALUE';   # hash assignment via hash reference
```

or even – entirely new in Perl 5 and, as the *perlref* manual page says – 'as a form of syntactic sugar' with

```
$hashref->{'KEY'} = 'VALUE';   # hash assignment via hash reference
```

Table 1.2 summarizes the complete reference notation for all possible data types.

Call by reference

With arrays or hashes, parameter passing to subroutines is carried out most efficiently *by reference*. Also, subroutines can be passed with this method.

The sample function `func`, which accepts an array reference, a hash reference, and a subroutine reference as parameters, is called as follows:

```
func(\@array, \%hash, \&subroutine);
```

The implementation of the function `func` could look like this:

```perl
sub func {
    my ($arrayref, $hashref, $subref) = @_;

    my @array = @$arrayref;    # copy list
    my %hash  = %$hashref;     # copy hash

    # ...

    &$subref();                # call subroutine
}
```

Scalar or reference?

Whether a variable $var contains a scalar value or a reference can be determined by means of the `ref` function: this yields an empty string for scalars, while it returns `"HASH"` for hash references, `"ARRAY"` for array references, `"CODE"` for function references, `"SCALAR"` for scalar references, and `"REF"` for references to references. Thus the true identity of $var is brought to light by the following lines:

```perl
if(!ref($var)) {
    print "var is a common scalar\n";
} else {
    print "var is a reference of type ", ref($var), "\n";
}
```

Listing `ref.pl` overleaf shows another sample script that initializes data of all standard types and defines references to them. Subsequently, it uses the `ref` operator for analyzing the data types hidden behind the references, dereferencing them, and displaying their values.

Finally, the output of `ref.pl` is

```
Data types:  SCALAR ARRAY HASH CODE REF
Values:      SCALAR_VALUE ARRAY_VALUE KEYHASH_VALUE
             RETCODE SCALAR_VALUE
```

1.5.6 Context

Perl functions can distinguish which kind of return value is expected from them. The instructions

```perl
$a = func();    # scalar context
@a = func();    # list context
```

ref.pl

```perl
#!/usr/bin/perl -w

                                             # definition of ...
$scalar        = "SCALAR_VALUE";             #    scalar
$hash{"KEY"}   = "HASH_VALUE";               #    hash
@array         = ("ARRAY_VALUE");            #    array


                                             # reference to ...
$scalar_ref      = \$scalar;                 #    scalar
$array_ref       = \@array;                  #    array
$hash_ref        = \%hash;                   #    hash
$code_ref        = sub { "RETCODE" };        #    code
$scalar_ref_ref  = \$scalar_ref;             #    reference

print "Data types: ",                        # determine types
      ref($scalar_ref), " ",
      ref($array_ref),  " ",
      ref($hash_ref),   " ",
      ref($code_ref),   " ",
      ref($scalar_ref_ref), "\n";

print "Values:      ",                       # dereferenced ...
      $$scalar_ref,       " ",               #    scalar reference
      @$array_ref,        " ",               #    array reference
      %$hash_ref,         " ",               #    hash reference
      &$code_ref,         " ",               #    code reference
      $$$scalar_ref_ref, "\n";               #    reference to
                                             #    scalar reference
```

ref.pl

differ in that the function func is expected to return a scalar and a list alternatively. The subroutine func recognizes the 'context' in which it is called: thus it has the capability of reacting differently in the two cases.

This information on scalar and list context is also used by some internal Perl functions – causing some confusion at first sight.

Thus, for example,

```perl
$line = <FILE>;        # scalar context
```

reads one single line via the file descriptor FILE, whereas

```perl
@file = <FILE>;        # list context
```

continues to read until it has reached the end of the data stream. (Reading files is discussed in detail in Section 1.8.) Now, how does a subroutine 'know' in which context is was called?

For this purpose, Perl provides the function `wantarray`, which returns a true value if a list context has been diagnosed.

_____*testcontext.pl*

```
sub testcontext {
    if(wantarray) {
        print "List context\n";      # list context diagnosed
    } else {
        print "Scalar context\n";    # scalar context diagnosed
    }
}
```

_____*testcontext.pl*

Confusion arises above all when the context in which a function is called is not completely evident. The function `localtime` (see Section 1.4.1), for example, which in a scalar context returns the current date and time in the normal UNIX format, while in a list context it returns a list of individual values, behaves somewhat strangely in the instruction

```
print "Date: ", localtime(), "\n";
```

because the output is

```
Date: 4737111689612591
```

What has happened? Perl interprets the call to `localtime` in the list context! `localtime` supplies the list (`$sec, $min, $hour ...`), and the `print` function subsequently outputs the individual values one after the other, without separating spaces (47 seconds, 37 minutes, 11 hours ...). The `scalar` operator, instead, enforces the scalar context. Thus,

```
print "Date: ", scalar localtime(), "\n";
```

yields the correct output

```
Date: Mon Sep 16 11:37:47 1996
```

EXERCISE 1.5

Determine in which context the following constructs call the function `testcontext()`:

```
@array  = testcontext();
$scalar = testcontext();
$scalar = somefunc(testcontext());
@array = (1, 2, testcontext());
testcontext();
if(testcontext()) { }
foreach $i (testcontext()) { }
@array = map { testcontext(); } ("element");
@array = grep { testcontext(); } ("element");
```

Verify your suppositions by copying the above function `testcontext` together with the constructs into a file, executing the Perl script, and analyzing the output (*solution on page 97*).

The opposite case, namely that the call is located in a scalar context while a list context would be needed, sometimes occurs in here documents (see Section 1.5.1), and can be resolved by means of the construct

```
@{[func()]}        # enforces list context for function func()
```

The function of this construct, which has already been used on page 20 for interpolation of lists into strings, is explained at the end of the next subsection.

1.5.7 Anonymous variables

A common procedure in Perl is to generate a 'mortal' variable of a specific type in a function ('my' variables lose their validity after termination of the function), and to return a reference to it. In particular, this method is used by Perl's object-oriented programming (see Chapter 2). The following function `ret_arrayref` creates a *local* array `@myarray` with contents, and returns an array reference:

```
sub ret_arrayref {
    my @myarray = (1, "two", 3);  # create array as
                                  # 'mortal' variable

    return \@myarray;             # return array reference
}
```

Even though the name `myarray` is no longer valid after termination of the function `ret_arrayref()`, the contents of the array continues to be accessible via the returned reference. Indeed, the array continues to be valid as long as the received array reference `$arrayref` exists in the main program:

```
$arrayref = ret_arrayref();        # create array

foreach $i (@$arrayref) {          # output array elements
    print "element: $i\n";
}
```

The name `@myarray`, under which the array was created, plays no role in this context; you might as well have used an 'anonymous' array.

The construct

```
[ 1, "two", 3 ]
```

creates an array with the specified elements; however, it does not assign it a name, but merely returns a reference to it. Thus, from a point of view of elegance,

```
sub ret_arrayref {                 # create anonymous array
    [ 1, "two", 3 ];               # and return reference
}
```

would be preferable to the earlier implementation of `ret_arrayref()`. By analogy to the anonymous array, the anonymous hash is created with the instruction

```
{ "key1" => "val1", "key2" => "val2" }
```

The operator `=>` is equivalent to a comma, and structures the key-value pairs that the hash will contain more clearly. The `{}` construct also returns a reference: thus a function `ret_hashref()`, which creates a hash and returns a reference to it, can be written as follows:

```
sub ret_hashref {
                                   # create anonymous hash
    return { "key1" => "val1", "key2" => "val2" };
}
```

Table 1.3 summarizes the notation for anonymous variables.

With this journey into the world of references, the construct `@{[func()]}`, presented earlier on pages 20 and 32, should also be clear. It calls the function `func()` (even inside a string) in list context and returns the resulting list: `[...]` creates an anonymous array, interpreting each of the specified elements (in this case, only one) in the list context. The array reference, dereferenced by means of the construct `@{...}`, finally supplies the required result, because Perl expands array variables inside strings, inserting their elements separated by spaces. This procedure is very inef-

Table 1.3 Anonymous variables.

`$scalarref`	`=`	`\42;`	anonymous scalar
`$scalarref`	`=`	`\"a";`	
`$arrayref`	`=`	`["a", 3, $element];`	anonymous array
`$hashref`	`=`	`{"key1" => "val1", ... };`	anonymous hash
`$funcref`	`=`	`sub {... };`	anonymous subroutine

ficient, but unfortunately sometimes (for example in a here document) the only means of enforcing execution of a function in the list context (see Section 1.5.1).

EXERCISE 1.6

Parameter hash

Write a function `paramhash`, which uses a parameter sequence like `('-name' => 'Kohl', '-first_name' => ...)` to initialize a hash with the key-value pairs `'name' => 'Kohl', 'first_name' => ...`, and return a reference to it, so that

```
testme(-name => "Kohl", -first_name => "Helmut", -weight => 200);

#----------------------------------------------------------------
sub testme {
#----------------------------------------------------------------

    my $p = paramhash(@_);      # to be written !!!

    print "$p->{first_name} $p->{name} weighs $p->{weight} kg\n";
}
```

generates the output `Helmut Kohl weighs 200 kg` (*solution on page 98*).

1.6 Conditions and error handling

Besides the C-style `if` condition (note, however, the idiosyncratic `elsif` instead of the 'else if' commonly used in C),

```
if($a == 42) {                   # if long form
    print "a equals 42\n";       # (braces are mandatory)
} elsif ($a < 42) {
    print "a is less than 42\n";
} else {
    print "a is greater than 42\n";
}
```

Perl also allows the short form

```
print "a less than 42\n" if $a < 42;   # if short form
```

It is used relatively often, because the 'long form' – as opposed to C – mandatorily requires the braces. Alternatively, the abbreviation via the logical AND operator can be used:

```
                                 # if replacement with && operator
exists($hash{'key'}) && print "\$hash{key} exists\n";
```

If the hash %hash contains a value for the key key, the left-hand side of the logical AND expression yields a true value, and the print instruction on the right-hand side is executed. Otherwise, Perl aborts on the left-hand side, because the result of the right-hand side plays no further role for the final result of the AND condition.

If several instructions are to be included on the right-hand side of a logical AND condition, they need to be encapsulated in a **do** construct:

```
                                 # message and return
$a > 42 &&                       # when condition is satisfied
    do { print "\$a < 42: function aborted!\n"; return 0; };
```

If $a is greater than 42, this construct displays a message and exits the current subroutine.

Like C, Perl too has the conditional operator. It can be used to abbreviate if-then-else conditions:

```
$max = $a > $b ? $a : $b;        # $max = maximum($a, $b);
```

This corresponds to if($a > $b) { $max = $a } else { $max = $b } and assigns $max the greater of the two scalars $a or $b.

The unless construct is responsible for unsatisfied conditions. It is used as the antipole of the if construct and is of particular importance in its short form:

```
                                 # unless short form
print "\$a is NOT greater than \$b + 1\n" unless $a > $b + 1;
```

Generally, if a subroutine returns an error value, immediate error handling is needed. In Perl, this process is usually controlled by the logical OR:

```
                                          # unless replacement
                                          # with || operator
open(FILE, ">$file") || die("Cannot open $file!");
```

The open function explained in Section 1.8 tries to open a file. If this fails, the script executes the built-in Perl abortion function die, which immediately terminates the program with an error message including an indication of the line number:

```
Cannot open myfile! at ./opentest.pl line 3.
```

If, instead of a brutal abortion, only a message is required to appear and the program should continue to run, the warn function can be employed instead of die. According to the Perl conventions, failed functions return either the value 0, an empty string, or the value undef. Successful processing of a function is signalled by a 'true' return value, in most cases '1'.

1.7 Operators

Perl comes up with the whole arsenal of C operators. Because of the special features of Perl scalars, which can simultaneously contain strings and numeric values, some additional syntax is required.

Comparison of two scalars $a and $b is performed at the numeric level by means of the operators

```
== < <= > >=
```

whereas

```
eq lt le gt ge
```

checks the alphanumeric properties. Since "a" stands before "b" in the alphabet, "a" lt "b" yields a *true* expression, in exactly the same way as 5 < 7 is *true* numerically. In addition, there is an operator that simulates the C function strcmp, namely cmp. The expression

```
$a cmp $b
```

yields −1, if $a lies alphabetically *before* $b; 0, if $a and $b are equal; and 1, if $a is alphanumerically greater than $b. If, instead, $a and $b contain numeric values, the comparison must be carried out with

```
$a <=> $b
```

The so-called 'spaceship' operator yields the correct result −1 in "5" <=> "10", whereas cmp is right with 1 at string level ("1" stands before "5" in the ASCII table, and thus the second character is of no further interest), but is completely wrong numerically.

Table 1.4 Perl operators.

`+ - * /`	Addition, subtraction, multiplication, division
`** % ++ --`	Exponentiation, modulo, increment/decrement
`& | ^ << >>`	Bitwise AND/OR/EXOR, shift left/right
`~`	Bit complement
`.`	Concatenation of two strings
`&& ||`	Logical AND/OR
`!`	Logical negation
`? :`	Conditional operator
`..`	Range operator (1..3) corresponds to (1,2,3)
`, =>`	Comma, list separator (both are equivalent)
`== eq != ne`	Equality/inequality numerical/string
`< lt > gt`	Less than/greater than numerical/string
`<= le >= ge`	Less equal/greater equal numerical/string
`<=> cmp`	Comparison numerical/string

The `sort` function sorts a list by definable criteria. Optionally, it also accepts a code block that compares the individual elements with each other. In the code block, the two values to be compared are available in some weird and wonderful way in the scalars `$a` and `$b`. Without specification of a routine, as in

```
sort @array
```

`sort` employs the default function `{$a cmp $b}`, which compares two elements `$a` and `$b` alphanumerically. For a numeric comparison, instead, the following call is required:

```
sort {$a <=> $b} @array
```

Sorting in descending order can be achieved either analogously with

```
sort {$b <=> $a} @array
```

or via the function `reverse`, which reverses a list:

```
reverse sort {$a <=> $b} @array
```

Table 1.4 summarizes the most important Perl operators.

1.8 Input and output

Similarly to the file descriptors in C, access to files in Perl is achieved via file handles. The `open` command opens the file access and returns a file handle for future identification of the data source or sink:

```
open(INFH, "<file.dat");   # read access

open(OUTFH, ">file.dat");  # write access (create or overwrite)

open(OUTFH, ">>file.dat"); # write access (create or append)

open(OUTFH, "+<file.dat"); # read/write access
```

In Perl, file handles are not marked by any special characters; they are not scalars, but separate data types.

Some file handles are available prior to the start of a program:

- STDIN, the standard input
- STDOUT, the standard output
- STDERR, the standard error output

A file is closed and its file handle returned by means of the command

```
close(FH);       # close file handle
```

But caution: file handles are second-class variables: thus, for example, they cannot be passed on to subroutines without some fancy tricks. Deeper insight into this subject is given in Section 3.1.

1.8.1 Read access

Depending on whether a scalar or a list is required, the <> operator fetches either one line or all lines from the file whose file handle it encloses.

```
$one_line   = <FH>;            # fetches one line from FH

@all_lines  = <FH>;            # fetches _all_ lines from FH
```

Line-by-line processing of all lines of a file is usually carried out by means of a `while` construct. The following code fragment outputs the read file on `STDOUT`:

```
open(MYFILE, "<data.dat") || die "Unable to read file 'data.dat'";

while(<MYFILE>) {
    print $_;        # $_ contains the current line
                     # (including the newline character)
}

close(MYFILE);
```

In the loop body, the content of the current line is accessed via the predefined variable $_.

1.8.2 Write access

Without indication of a specific file handle, `print` instructions simply use `STDOUT`. If, instead, the keyword `print` is followed by the file handle of a data sink opened for writing (without the subsequent comma!), the output is redirected to the corresponding file or pipe (see next subsection):

```
print MYOUTFILE "text\n";
```

The `print` function buffers its input data until a reasonable quantity has been reached, and then causes the output. This leads, for example, to the effect that a `print` command on the standard output does not let the specified text appear on screen immediately; usually, only the next newline character triggers a *flush*.

The throughput can, however, be controlled by means of the variable `$|`, which, if set to a value not equal to zero, activates the *autoflush*: that is, outputs every character immediately:

```
$| = 1;
...
print LOGFILE "Start func() ...";
func();
print LOGFILE " terminated.\n";
```

Owing to the true value of `$|`, the above code fragment writes the message `"Start func ..."` to the opened log file immediately; and even if `func()` did not return because of an error, this message would still be written.

Instead of writing data each time with `print FILEHANDLE`, you can also permanently redirect the output by means of the `select` function. After a

```
select(FILEHANDLE);
```

command, the `print` function writes to the output stream associated to `FILEHANDLE` even without specification of a file handle.

1.8.3 System-related file access

Similarly to the C function `write`, system programmers sometimes prefer to write a data block of known length using

```
$bytes_written = syswrite(FILEHANDLE, $buffer, $length, $offset);
```

`syswrite` writes a `$length` number of bytes from the scalar `$buffer` to the output channel specified via the file handle `FILEHANDLE`. The optional parameter `$offset` can be used to specify an offset in `$buffer`. `syswrite` returns the number of effectively written bytes – or `undef`, if something went wrong. Similarly, in

```
$bytes_read = sysread(FILEHANDLE, $buffer, $length);
```

sysread reads a $length number of bytes from the input channel associated to FILE-HANDLE and stores them in $buffer. sysread returns the number of effectively read bytes – or undef in case of error.

MS-DOS and all Windows variations write "\r\n" to the disk when they mean a newline ("\n"), and reverse this absurd transformation when reading files. If under these systems you really need to read or write raw data, you must first switch into *binary* mode with binmode(FILEHANDLE) to prevent destruction of binary data.

1.8.4 The printf function

The printf function outputs variables in a formatted fashion. Like the C function of the same name, it is passed a format string as its first parameter, which specifies how the subsequent parameters are to be arranged in the output. Thus

```
$n = 42;
printf("The number is %d\n", $n);    # => "The number is 42"
```

outputs the string shown in the comment. The format string %d tells printf to interpret the first following parameter as an integer value, and to insert it into the string. Please remember that, because of the special meaning of the percent sign in the format string, a percent sign to be literally printed in the string must be followed by another one: thus printf("%d%%", 100) outputs "100%". All this is nothing terribly new, because the already discussed print function supplies the same result, for example in

```
$n = 42;
print("The number is $n\n");          # => "The number is 42"
```

However, printf can do more, such as fitting numbers and strings right- or left-aligned into container strings, cutting decimal positions from floating point numbers, and so on. printf – like print – can also work with a file descriptor. Its useful sister function sprintf does not output the formatted string, but returns it as a value, so it can be used to manipulate strings.

To fit an integer value right- or left-aligned into a string, you can use the %d format prefixed with the maximum width of the required string:

```
printf("%5d", 42);              # => "   42"
printf("%-5d", 42);             # => "42   "
```

If an integer value is always to be represented with a constant length and potentially a leading zero, the length value must be preceded by a 0:

```
printf("%02d/%02d/%d", 11, 1, 1998);   # => "11/01/1998"
```

Numbers in the decimal systems can be converted into hexadecimal numbers by means of the format strings %x and %X:

```
printf("%x", 42);                # => "2a"
printf("%X", 42);                # => "2A"
```

The format string %f outputs floating point numbers with a specified number of decimal digits – the default value is six:

```
printf("%f", 1.23);              # => "1.230000"
```

The number of decimal digits is specified by a numerical value preceded by a dot '.':

```
printf("%.1f", 1.23);            # => "1.2"
```

The following formatting instructions (see above) are also allowed in the context of decimal digit processing:

```
printf("%5.1f", 1.23);           # => "  1.2"
printf("%-5.1f", 1.23);          # => "1.2  "
```

The format strings %e and %E are used to represent floating point numbers in exponential notation

```
printf("%e", 0.001);             # => "1.000000e-03"
printf("%E", 1000000);           # => "1.000000E+06"
```

whereas %g (and %G respectively) toggle between normal and exponential notation according to the size of the numerical value to be represented. If a value is less than 0.0001, or if it has at least as many zeros as the predefined precision, exponential notation is chosen (default is 6 decimal digits: thus %g changes to exponential notation from 1,000,000 onward). Otherwise, the value is output in floating point format.

```
printf("%g", 0.0001);            # => "0.0001"
printf("%g", 0.00009);           # => "9e-05"

printf("%g", 999999);            # => "999999"
printf("%g", 1000000);           # => "1e+06"

printf("%.2g", 99);              # => "99"
printf("%.2g", 100);             # => "1e+02"
```

Strings are handled by the %s format in a similar way as integer values by %d. A '-' preceding the minimum length of the resulting string, however, causes printf to left-align the string, while a '+' right-aligns it.

```
printf("%-10s", "string");       # => "string    "
printf("%+10s", "string");       # => "    string"
```

EXERCISE 1.7

Columnwise output of a hash

Let us assume a hash %hash with the following values:

```
%hash = ('Key'     => 'Value',
         'LongKey' => 'LongValue',
         'K'       => 'V');
```

Output the key-value pairs in two columns formatted in the following way:

```
K       V
Key     Value
LongKey LongValue
```

In a first loop, determine the length of the longest key in the hash and use this length to output the hash columnwise in a second loop. The key column shall be of constant length, with the current key fitted left-aligned (*solution on page 99*).

EXERCISE 1.8

Formatting date and time

Write a function get_formatted_date, which returns the current date and time in the format "03/01/1998 14:02:01". All fields are of constant length. Use the localtime function to fetch the parameters of the current time and format them with sprintf. To find out more about the parameters of the localtime function, simply call perldoc -f localtime or consult page 84 (*solution on page 99*).

1.8.5 Pipes

If required, instead of a file, open also taps the input or output of an external program. This mechanism, known from the UNIX shell, helps in reading and processing dynamically generated data or forwarding it to other programs. Of the two functions used in the following example, /bin/ls lists the contents of a directory, while /bin/lp forwards its input to the printer; both are standard UNIX programs. Under Windows, read access can be similarly implemented via open(PIPE, "dir |"), while write access might require a Perl script to be created for the purpose.

```
open(LS, "/bin/ls |");          # open pipe for reading
open(PRINTOUT, "| /bin/lp");    # open pipe for writing
```

When reading from a pipe, you should keep in mind that data arrives line by line, including the newline character. An intermediate `chop` command cuts the last character off each line. In the following code fragment, all file names of the current directory are read by the UNIX shell command `ls` and stored in the array `@allfiles`. Usually, efficient scanning of directories in Perl would be carried out by means of the commands `opendir`, `readdir` and `closedir` (see Section 1.9). This is only an illustrating example.

```
#!/usr/bin/perl -w

open(LS, "/bin/ls |");          # tap output of the ls command

while(<LS>) {                   # analyze line by line
    chop;                       # cut off newline
    push(@allfiles, $_);        # store line
}

close(LS);                      # close pipe
```

Specification of parameters for `chop` can be omitted, because `chop` without parameters automatically works with the variable `$_`, which contains the current line in the loop.

An alternative solution would be reading the pipe in the list context. This would get all of the lines, including the newlines, into the `@allfiles` array 'in one go.' A subsequent `chomp` command shortens each element by the last (the newline) character.

```
@allfiles = <LS>;               # read all lines
chomp(@allfiles);               # remove all newlines
```

Another peculiarity should be noted in the handling of pipes: even if the command triggered via the pipe causes an error in the shell, this does not lead to a corresponding return value of the `open` command. Only if you are in warning mode (-w), and Perl cannot execute the specified command at all, will a corresponding message be issued. Thus, the `die` instruction in

```
open(LS, "/bin/ls winword.exe |") || die "Error!";
```

will not be executed, even if the `ls` command aborts with an error because the specified file does not exist. A possibility of error detection is given by the `close` instruction:

```
close(LS) || die "Error!";
```

In the case of failure of execution of the pipe, it yields a 'false' return value, which in the above code fragment again activates the die routine.

EXERCISE 1.9

Pipes

Quickly implement a script `pwrite.pl` that outputs the elements of an array (for example ("abc", "def", "ghi")) line by line with line breaks. A second script `pread.pl` should call `pwrite.pl`, tap it for reading, receive the lines one by one, and output for each line `"pwrite.pl said: 'line contents'"` (*solution on page 99*).

1.8.6 Reading user input

Perl reads user input via the STDIN file handle, which is always open. Listing `stdin.pl` wrests from the user an answer to the 'Input>' prompt.

stdin.pl

```perl
#!/usr/bin/perl -w

print "Input> ";           # display input prompt

$word = <STDIN>;           # receive input

chop($word);               # cut off terminating newline

print "Input was: $word\n"; # display input for checking
```

stdin.pl

In a scalar context, `<STDIN>` reads exactly one line, while in a list context it reads several lines, until the user presses the key combination [Ctrl]-[D].

If the entered text is not to appear on screen, because it is secret data (for example a password), the easiest thing to do under UNIX is to switch the terminal to 'no-echo' mode by means of the command `stty -echo`. Once the input is terminated, however, an `stty echo` is needed to switch the terminal back to its normal state. Listing `pass.pl` shows an implementation using the `system` command, which executes a shell-command (see Section 1.11).

pass.pl

```perl
#!/usr/bin/perl -w

print "Hidden input> ";        # display input prompt

system("stty -echo");          # set terminal to no-echo
$word = <STDIN>;               # receive input
system("stty echo");           # reset terminal

chop($word);                   # cut off last newline

print "\nInput was: $word\n";  # display input for checking
```

pass.pl

1.8.7 Further possibilities of data input

Usually, either data to be processed gets into a script via

```
mysite> cat data.dat | script.pl
```

(in Windows, the equivalent of the `cat` command is `type`: thus the command line
would be written as `type data.dat | perl script.pl`), or data is present in files
whose names are passed to the script on the command line

```
mysite> script.pl data1.dat data2.dat
```

The already mentioned `<>` operator deals with both cases in a transparent fashion if no file handle is specified.

```perl
#!/usr/bin/perl -w

while(<>) {          # process STDIN or files on the
                     # command line
    chop;

                     # display input data for checking
    print "File: $ARGV Line: $_\n";
}
```

If file names are present as command line parameters, the script opens the data files
one after the other and processes one line of the data set per loop cycle. The variable
`$ARGV` contains the name of the currently processed file.

If data is, instead, coming in via the standard input, then in good UNIX tradition $ARGV is assigned the string "-", and the `while` loop processes the incoming lines piece by piece.

In any case, the command line parameters lie in the array @ARGV, whose length is (as usual in Perl) given by $#ARGV + 1. Differently from C, however, $ARGV[0] does not correspond to the name of the currently running script (which, instead, is stored in $0), but effectively to the first command line parameter.

A completely different functionality of the <> operator is the so-called *globbing*. This is capable of expanding shell wildcards that match files in a directory. Thus the instruction

```
@cfiles = <*.c>;
```

for example stores the names of all C files located in the current directory in the array @cfiles.

1.9 Access to the file system

Which files and subdirectories are located in a directory of the file system? This question is answered by the `readdir` function. It works with a *directory handle*, provided by the `opendir` function in analogy to the file handle of the `open` function:

```
opendir(DIR, "/usr/bin");
@entries = readdir(DIR);
closedir(DIR);
```

Similarly to the <> operator, in a scalar context `readdir` yields a single entry, and in the list context all entries at a time. Entry-by-entry processing can thus be implemented as follows:

```
$dir = "/tmp";                    # directory to be scanned
                                  # open /tmp for scanning
opendir(DIR, "$dir") || die("Cannot open $dir");

foreach $direntry (readdir(DIR)) {
    next if $direntry eq ".";     # ignore special directories
    next if $direntry eq "..";    # ditto

                                  # display other entries
    print "DIRECTORY: $direntry\n" if -d "$dir/$direntry";
    print "FILE: $direntry\n" if -f "$dir/$direntry";
}

closedir(DIR);                    # close scanner
```

Since `readdir` also returns the special directory entries '.' (link to the current directory) and '..' (link to the next higher directory), these must normally be eliminated before further processing. The next subsection deals with file operators such as -d and -f, which the above script uses to determine whether it is currently analyzing a file or a subdirectory.

1.9.1 File operators

Together with a file of a file system, most operating systems manage additional data, such as the time of last modification of a file, its size in bytes, and its owner.

Perl's file operators allow the properties of files to be checked in a very clear way. Whether a file whose name is stored in the scalar `$file` really exists, is brought to light by

```
if(-f $file) {
    print "File $file exists!\n";
}
```

However, the -f operator *also* yields a false value, if `$file` turns out to be no file, but a directory. The existence checker -e, instead, does not care about the nature of the entry; provided an entry exists, it returns a true value.

A script that expects a sequence of directories on the command line could check the validity of its input parameters with

```
#!/usr/bin/perl -w

while($#ARGV >= 0) {           # loop over all command line
    my $dir = shift(@ARGV);    # parameters
                               # check directory
    -d $dir || die "Invalid directory: $dir";
}
```

Whether the current script owns read, write, or execution rights for a file (or any other entry in the file system) `$file` is determined by the following code fragment:

```
(-r $file) && print "Read privilege for $file\n";
(-w $file) && print "Write privilege for $file\n";
(-x $file) && print "Execution privilege for $file\n";
```

Note that UNIX differentiates between privileges for the effective and the real user ID/group ID. The above example checks the rights by using the effective UID/GID, which is the common method.

Table 1.5 summarizes the most important file operators.

Table 1.5   File operators.

-r -R	Read privileges (UNIX: effective/real UID+GID)
-w -W	Write privileges (UNIX: effective/real UID+GID)
-x -X	Execution privileges (UNIX: effective/real UID+GID)
-o -O	UNIX: effective/real UID+GID is owner
-e -z	Exists/has size zero
-s	Greater than 0 bytes (returns size)
-f -d	Type: file/directory
-l	UNIX: symbolic link
-S -p	UNIX: socket/named pipe
-b -c	UNIX: block/char device
-u -g -k	UNIX: setuid/setgid/sticky bit set
-t	Is a tty/character device
-T -B	text/binary file
-M -C	Returns number of days between last modification/modification of privileges and the program start
-A	Number of days since last access

Under Windows, the file operators return 0 if the file system does not support the corresponding functionality.

1.9.2 The stat function

Similarly to the function of the same name of the C interface, the stat function determines all additional items of file information at once.

```
($dev, $ino,        # Device number in the file system
 $mode,             # File type and access rights
 $nlink,            # Number of hard links
 $uid, $gid,        # User ID, group ID
 $rdev,             # Device ID (special files only)
 $size,             # Size in bytes
 $atime,            # Time of last read access
 $mtime,            # Time of last modification
 $ctime,            # Time of last mode change
 $blksize,          # Preferred I/O block size
 $blocks)           # Number of blocks occupied
         = stat($filename);
```

Under Windows, $ino, $uid, $gid, $blksize, and $blocks are zero. The following script timestamp.pl displays the times of

- last modification,
- last read access, and

- last privilege change

of a file passed as a command line parameter in a readable format. For its own script file, it yields:

```
mysite> timestamp.pl timestamp.pl
timestamp.pl:
Read ........... Sun Oct 6 12:24:14 1998
Modified ....... Wed Sep 18 16:59:27 1998
Rights changed .. Tue Sep 24 19:45:50 1998
```

Since the script `timestamp.pl` 'reads' itself during the call, the time of last read access to the file `timestamp.pl` corresponds to the – *guessed it?* – current time of day.

_____*timestamp.pl*

```
#!/usr/bin/perl -w

while($#ARGV >= 0) {
    my $file = shift(@ARGV);

    (($atime, $mtime, $ctime) = (stat($file))[8..10]) ||
                    die "$file: stat error";

    print "$file:\n";
    print "Read ........... ", scalar localtime $atime, "\n";
    print "Modified ....... ", scalar localtime $mtime, "\n";
    print "Rights changed .. ", scalar localtime $ctime, "\n";
}
```

_____*timestamp.pl*

The three relevant timestamps are located on index positions 8, 9 and 10 in the array returned by `stat`. The usual 'seconds-since-1970' are converted by the `localtime` command in a scalar context into the more readable string format.

1.9.3 **Manipulating files in the file system**

The `rename` function renames a file. The call

```
rename("file", "/tmp/file.old") || die "rename error!";
```

assigns the file `file` the new name `/tmp/file.old`, which means that from now on, it is to be found in the `/tmp` directory under the name of `file.old`. Note that you can always write '/', even if your operating system uses other path separators, such as the backslash '\' – Perl deals with the necessary conversion. If /tmp is not located in the same file system as file, which is quite common in some operating systems, the rename function fails. Here, an additional module from the Perl standard library (included in the Perl distribution from version 5.004_04, otherwise available from CPAN) can help:

```
use File::Copy;
move("file", "/disk2/tmp/file.old");
```

The move function imported via File::Copy works on all operating systems in the same way as mv under UNIX, and therefore also supports a directory as the second parameter, in which it stores the specified file under the original name. File::Copy also exports the useful copy function which, with an instruction like

```
use File::Copy;
copy("file", "backups/file.bak");
```

copies files and can also work with a directory as the second parameter. Files can be permanently removed from the hard disk by means of the unlink function:

```
unlink("junk.doc") || die "Could not delete junk.doc ";
```

EXERCISE 1.10

Renaming files

Rename all files in the current directory that have the extension .pl into *.perl (*solution on page 100*).

EXERCISE 1.11

Creating backup copies

Rig up a script that saves all files passed to it on the command line in the directory /tmp/BACKUP. The copy of a file file should bear the current date in its name, in the format: file.YY-MM-DD.HH:MM:SS (*solution on page 101*).

1.9.4 Recursive directory search

Under UNIX, the find program systematically searches the file system for files of a specific name or contents.

With Perl's open command, a shell command can be issued, and its output intercepted and analyzed. The Perl script shown in Listing shellfind.pl searches all directories underneath the current one ('.') for files with the extension .pl, and outputs their names if they are greater than 1000 bytes and contain the string pattern.

_____*shellfind.pl*

```
#!/usr/bin/perl -w

open(FIND, "find . -name '*.pl' -print |");

while(<FIND>) {
    chop;
                        # analyze only files > 1000 bytes
    next if (stat($_))[7] <= 1000;
    next unless -f _; # economical stat()

                        # open and analyze file
    open(FILE, "<$_") || warn("Cannot open $_");
    print "$_\n" if grep(/pattern/, <FILE>);
    close(FILE);
}

close(FIND);
```

_____*shellfind.pl*

The call of stat() analyzes all parameters of the current directory entry. The parameter '_' for the subsequent test with -f ensures that -f does not interrogate the file system once again, but uses the intermediately stored values.

Independently of UNIX, such tasks can, however, be solved more elegantly with the module File::Find, which exports the function find that accepts as arguments the reference to a callback function and the starting directory for the search. For each entry found, File::Find::find jumps to the specified callback function, with the variable $_ containing the name of the found entry (file, directory, link), and $File::Find::dir the corresponding path. At the same time, File::Find::find changes to the currently searched directory, so found entries can be reached in the file system from within the callback function with $_. Please note, however, that File::Find gets confused if the callback function changes the value of $_.

Listing findgrep.pl implements a combination of the popular UNIX programs find and grep on other operating systems: beginning from a starting directory dir, the script works its way recursively through all subordinate text files and searches them for a specified pattern.

To search all text files in /tmp and the subordinate directories with findgrep.pl for the word main, the following call could be used

```
mysite> findgrep /tmp main
```

Please note, however, that (as of Spring 1998) findgrep.pl does not (yet) follow symbolic links on UNIX systems.

findgrep.pl

```perl
#!/usr/bin/perl -w

use File::Find;
use strict;
                                        # fetch command
my ($startdir, $pattern) = @ARGV;       # line parameters

# check command line parameters
(defined $startdir && defined $pattern) || usage();
(-d $startdir) || die "Cannot open directory $startdir";

# trigger traverse algorithm
File::Find::find(\&fc, $startdir);

################################################################
sub fc {                                # callback function
    my $file = $_;                      # save file name

    return unless -f $file;             # no directories
    return unless -T _;                 # text files only

                                        # text seach in file
    open(FILE, "<$file") || warn "Cannot open $file";
    while(<FILE>) {
        if(/$pattern/o) {               # match found?
                                        # output file and line
            print "$File::Find::dir/$file: $_";
        }
    }
    close(FILE);

    $_ = $file;                         # reset $_
}


################################################################
sub usage {                             # message in case of incorrect
                                        # command line parameters
    $0 =~ s#.*/##g;                     # basename() for script path

    print "usage: $0 startdir pattern\n";
```

```
        exit 0;                          # program termination
}
```
_____*findgrep.pl*

The regular expression searched for by `findgrep.pl` is present in the variable
`$pattern`. This causes the matcher to convert the expression every time from string
form into an internal format – the value of the variable might well have changed.
Since in the present case, however, `$pattern` remains constant over the whole running time of the script, the modifier `/.../o` instructs the matcher to carry out the
conversion only 'once.'

The next sample script, `latest.pl`, searches for the 10 most recently modified files underneath a directory branch. Absent-minded users in particular highly
appreciate this service, because when they no longer remember where they stored
that recently created file, `latest.pl` will eventually rummage through the whole hard
disk to find it.

In `latest.pl`, the `find` function penetrates into any depth of the directory
structure, stores found files and their modification dates in an internal memory structure, sorts it by date in descending order, and outputs the first 10 entries.

Since the time of modification of a file is usually stored only down to full
seconds, it may well happen that two or more files were modified at the 'same' time.

For this reason, a hash was chosen as memory structure, whose keys represent
the modification times, while the values represent references to arrays, which in turn
store a number of file names.

An interesting question would be, for example, which modules arrived last in
the library directory of the local Perl installation. `latest.pl` supplies the answer:

```
mysite> latest.pl /usr/lib/perl5
/usr/lib/perl5/site_perl/CGI.pm (Wed Jul 31 23:04:31 1998)
/usr/lib/perl5/site_perl/LWP/Protocol/ftp.pm (Tue Jul 30 22:06:47
1998)
/usr/lib/perl5/News/Newsrc.pm (Thu Jul 25 19:29:54 1998)
/usr/lib/perl5/i486-linux/5.004/perllocal.pod (Thu Jul 25 19:20:05
1998)
...
```
_____*latest.pl*

```
#!/usr/bin/perl -w

use File::Find;

foreach $arg (@ARGV) {          # cycle through all
    File::Find::find(\&fc, $arg); # specified directories
}                               # and build %Filesbydate
```

```perl
    $maxcount = 10;                        # output max. 10 files

                                           # evaluation: sort
                                           # by last date
hashloop:foreach $date (sort { $b <=> $a } keys %Filesbydate) {

                                           # lists of entries
    $timestr = localtime($date);  # of same date

    foreach $file (@{$Filesbydate{$date}}) {
        print "$file (", $timestr, ")\n";          # output with date
        last hashloop unless $maxcount--;          # terminate when enough
    }
}


################################################################
# Callback function of File::Find::find
################################################################
sub fc {
    my $filedate = (stat($_))[9]; # last modification date

    return unless -f _;           # no directories, economical
                                  # stat() call

                                  # date not yet occupied:
                                  # new array reference
    $Filesbydate{$filedate} = [] unless
                            exists $Filesbydate{$filedate};

                                  # include entry in array
    push(@{$Filesbydate{$filedate}}, "$File::Find::dir/$_");
}
```

_____*latest.pl*

EXERCISE 1.12

Deleting obsolete files

In the /tmp directory, file zombies lurch about that only eat up unnecessary memory space. Whatever is older than 10 days, has no place there. Write a script that makes use of File::Find, accepts a series of directories as parameters, and searches them recursively for files whose last modification date is older than 10 days. On your way down, delete all candidates found and write a status message for each of them, or an error message if problems occur (*solution on page 101*).

1.10 Regular expressions

Perl's regular expressions are ideally suited for extraction of information from texts. Whether a string contains a given text is analyzed by the condition

```
$string =~ /PATTERN/
```

It returns a true value if `$string` satisfies the conditions of PATTERN. In the easiest case, PATTERN represents a sequence of characters. The following construct determines whether the text in `$string` contains the name `Bill`:

```
if($string =~ /Bill/) {
    print "Bill in string!\n";
}
```

Several metacharacters allow defining of additional conditions. Thus /^Bill/ applies only if `Bill` stands at the beginning of the string to be analyzed, while /Bill$/ applies if the string ends with `Bill`.

Repetition of characters or sequences of characters is specified by the symbols `*` (zero or more times) and `+` (one or more times). Thus the expression /Billy*/ matches to `Bill`, `Billy`, `Billyy`, and so on, whereas /Billy+/ matches only `Billy`, `Billyy`, and so on.

Let us return once more to the mail header of Section 1.5.3:

———————————————————————————————————*mail*

```
Date: Fri, 12 Jul 96 16:25:18 +0200
From: schilli@remote.site.com
To: gates@microsoft.com
Subject: Re: Newbie Unix Question
Status: RO

Bill,

concerning your question, I can tell you that it isn't that easy.
```

———————————————————————————————————*mail*

In Section 1.5.3, the task was to store the contents of the header lines in a hash under the inital keyword. Now, the subject of this section is text analysis, aiming at a subdivision of the individual lines of text into *key* and *value*.

The code of Listing `mailheader.pl` reads the lines of the file `mail` one by one, analyzes their contents, and stores the gathered information in the hash `%mailheader`.

mailheader.pl

```perl
#!/usr/bin/perl -w

open(MAILFILE, "<mail") || die "Error opening 'mail'";

while(<MAILFILE>) {
    last if /^\s*$/;                # empty line: end of header

    next unless /^(\w+):\s+(.*)/;   # analyze header (key: value)

    $header{$1} = $2;               # store result in a hash
}

close(MAILFILE);
                                    # output
foreach $key (keys %header) {
    printf "KEY: $key VALUE: $header{$key}\n";
}
```

mailheader.pl

The first regular expression in the loop body searches for lines that contain nothing else but 'whitespace' (tabs or spaces), if any, and terminates processing as soon as a line satisfies this condition. The pattern

```
/^\s*$/
```

matches lines that show no or an arbitrary amount (*) of whitespace (\s) between the beginning of the line (^) and the end of the line ($).

Since the regular expression is not called with the construct

```
$var =~ /PATTERN/
```

it points to the default variable $_, which in `while(<...>)` loops always implicitly contains the current line. If the pattern matches, it returns a true value, so that the expression

```
last if /^\s*$/;        # empty line: end of header
```

Table 1.6   Sets of characters in regular expressions.

\s \S	Whitespace / no whitespace
\w \W	Word ([a-zA-Z_0-9]) / no word
\d \D	Digit/ no digit
\b \B	Word boundary / no word boundary

terminates the analysis of the mail file as soon as an empty line occurs which, by convention, separates the header from the message part of the mail. If the pattern is postfixed with the modifier x, Perl allows insertion of spaces, newlines, and comments to improve readability. Even the separation marks of the regular expression need not necessarily look like /.../: if they are prefixed with an m, they can be any pair of characters and brackets, such as m#...#, m{...}, m(...) – anything goes. It should, however, be noted that the separation marks ('/.../' in the example) must not appear in the comments.

Thus the condition formulated earlier can be written as follows, in a way that is more pleasing to the human eye:

```
last if m(
       ^        # beginning of line
       \s*      # whitespace: none or any amount
       $        # end of line
       )x;      # modifier x allows comments
```

The abbreviation \s represents a short notation for a range definition, which could also be written as [\t]: that is, a set of characters composed of spaces and tabs (in a multiline pattern match, \s also includes newlines, carriage returns, and vertical space). Alternatively, the condition could thus also be formulated as

```
last if /^[ \t]*$/;
```

In contrast to other tools that also support regular expressions (for example grep and awk), Perl provides a whole range of useful abbreviations for sets of characters, the most important of which are shown in Table 1.6.

The next instruction in Listing mailheader.pl

```
next unless /^(\w+):\s+(.*)/;
```

makes use of the grouping properties of regular expressions. It looks for a word (\w+) at the beginning of the line (^) followed by a colon (:) and one or more spaces (\s+). This is followed by a string of arbitrary characters up to the end of the line (.*). If the expression does not match the current line, the next loop cycle follows immediately with the next line.

The grouping brackets in the expression make sure that Perl stores the found strings in intermediate buffers whose contents are still available, even after execution of the pattern matching, in the special variables `$1`, `$2`, `$3`, and so on. In Listing `mailheader.pl`, `$1` contains the found keyword, and `$2` the following text, which

```
$header{$1} = $2;
```

finally stores in the hash `%header`.

Grouping brackets also influence the return value of a pattern-matching operation. While usually a true or false value is returned depending on whether the regular expression 'matched' or not, a grouped regular expression returns a list of the partial expressions found. The assignment

```
($keyword, $text) = /^(\w+):\s+(.*)/;
```

sets the scalars `$keyword` and `$text` to the corresponding values found in the text. Note that, since the regular expression yields the found text passage only in the list context, list parentheses must also be used if only *one* value is expected: `($val)` `= /(...)/` is correct, while `$val = /(...)/` would return a true value in case of success, and `undef` otherwise.

If the string to be analyzed is not present in `$_`, but in an arbitrary scalar `$string`, the construct is correspondingly written as

```
($keyword, $text) = ($string =~ /^(\w+):\s+(.*)/);
```

Numbering of found substrings is carried out from left to right. To determine the back reference number of a complex expression, you just count the number of *opening* brackets up to there. Grouped patterns with quantifiers create only *one* back reference, no matter how often they 'hit.' The content is determined by the *last* match. Thus

```
"One Two" =~ /((\w)+)/
```

stores two back references: `"One"` in `$1` (outer parenthesis) and `"e"` in `$2` (last match of the inner parenthesis at the end of `"One"`).

To avoid having to start longwinded counting actions in nested group structures, only those pattern groups should use back references whose contents are definitely needed at a later stage. If parentheses are used only for structuring purposes, it is often sensible to suppress back referencing by means of the construct `(?:...)`. The pattern-matching construct

```
"One Two" =~ /(?:(\w+)\s*)+/
```

searches for aggregations of letters separated from each other by spaces. Because of the '?:' operator, however, it creates only *one* back reference: `$1` is subsequently assigned the value `"Two"`.

Inside a regular expression, the contents of already found substrings are accessible via `\1`, `\2`, and so on. Thus

```
/\b(\w+)\s+\1\b/
```

finds a grouped number of alphanumeric characters after a word's beginning (\b), followed by an arbitrary amount of whitespace (\s+) and – a repetition of the already found substring (\1) with subsequent word boundary (\b). This means that the expression detects words that occur twice in a row.

1.10.1 How does the matcher work?

The way Perl's algorithm for pattern matching with regular expressions actually works is best shown with an example. When applied to the string

```
"Sriram Srinivasan"
```

the regular expression

```
/S\w+n/
```

will without doubt identify Srinivasan: an upper-case S, followed by a series of letters, and finally terminating with n, that is quite clear.

Unlike a human being, Perl's matcher, however, does not possess a billion-neuron system, and must reach this decision the hard way, working step by step through the regular expression, greedily gobbling up the string to be recognized.

The matcher starts with S in the regular expression and begins to trudge through the string. The first letter matches: *hurrah*! On we go in the regular expression: \w+ finds an r, an i, everything matches, up to the m in Sriram. Thus \w has done its service, because it does not match the following space. Only now it becomes clear to the matcher that the regular expression requires a subsequent n – and in the string, there is a space.

Has \w+ been too greedy? That's what the matcher is now asking itself. In the end, fewer letters would have been sufficient, even just one. Thus, go backward in the string: Srira? No n. Srir? No n. With Sr it is evident: this is not how it goes. What now?

Back to the beginning of the regular expression (S), and on we go in the string, beginning with the second character, until the expression matches again: r – i – r – a – m – space – S – *Aha*! Hope is here again. Subsequently, \w+ swallows the whole rinivasan character sequence, up to the string's end. But wait – according to the regular expression a single n is still missing. Thus, after the matcher has already gobbled its way to the string's end, it must go back once and – *lo and behold*! – here is the n. This makes the matcher happy – end of procedure.

The fact that it is the regular expression that determines the procedure is important for understanding the Perl matcher. In fact, this matcher is a Nondeterministic Finite Automaton (NFA), as opposed to other tools such as awk and sed, which also perform pattern matching, but implement a Deterministic Finite Automaton (DFA); see the extensive discussion in Friedl (1977). Thus the matcher navigates through the expression and tries to match the string.

Two rules play a major role:

- Once the expression matches, the matcher stops, and no alternative could be attactive enough to make it begin once again from the start.
- The more characters match, the better.

The second rule seems to contradict the first one, but in fact does not: the matcher indeed swallows as many characters as possible, but after it has found an expression, it would never go back to try and find another one that might be even better. This means that it prefers `Srinivasan` to the shorter `Srin` (which would also match), but that it would never get up again to search for new possibilities after `Srinivasan` (which, in the present case, would make no sense anyway).

EXERCISE 1.13

Including files

Write a script that takes one or more files as parameters, opens them, and outputs the lines that were read. Exception: lines that begin with the pattern `<include file="xxx">` should cause the script to open the specified file and insert it into the outgoing data stream.

Make use of a function `process_file`, which accepts a file as parameter, outputs lines that were read, and for lines that start with the pattern `<include file="xxx">` calls itself with the extracted file name.

Caution: file handles are global and, in recursive calls to a function, obviously lead to total confusion. To circumvent this difficulty, you should at the start of the function first read all lines into a local array `@lines`, and close the file, before you iterate over the array and thus over all of the lines of the file (*solution on page 102*).

1.10.2 Minimal matching

A bad surprise awaits the unexperienced regex programmer if he or she attempts to match a text such as

```
Subject: The colon : and its consequences
```

with a regular expression like

```
($key, $value) = /^(.+): (.+)/
```

and to search for an arbitrary number of characters before and after a colon. The result

```
$key:      Subject: The colon
$value:    and its consequences
```

shows that, in case of doubt, Perl tries to match a *maximal* number of characters with a subpattern, before it continues proceeding the whole pattern. In the present example, however, it 'swallows' more than actually intended. With the *non-greedy* operator instead – that is, with a question mark after the repeat operator – Perl is instructed only to attempt a *minimal* match. The instruction

```
($key, $value) = /^(.+?): (.+)/
```

then supplies the 'expected' result

```
$key:      Subject
$value:    The colon : and its consequences
```

1.10.3 Regular expressions over several lines

In its default mode, the Perl matcher also deals with multiline strings and, with the identifier \s, gobbles up not only whitespace in the form of spaces and tabs, but also newlines. This means that a condition such as

```
if($multiline_text =~ /\b(\w+)\s+\1\b/) {
    print "Repeated word: $1\n";
}
```

also responds to a text like

```
Regular expressions treat
treat newlines as whitespace
```

and detects repeated words across lines:

```
Repeated word: treat
```

The modifier /.../s in a regular expression, instead, causes Perl to handle a text to be processed as a one-liner, even if it consists of several lines, and with '.' to swallow newlines too.

If with '^' and '$' the matcher is required not only to recognize the beginning and end of a string, but also all beginnings and ends of the individual lines in a multiline string, the modifier /.../m is required.

Thus, in the above two-liner, /R.*e/s matches the entire expression, whereas /^t.*e$/m recognizes the second line.

Table 1.7   Regular expressions in Perl.

[1234] [1-4]	Set as collection/range
[^567] [^5-7]	Excluded sets
.	Arbitrary character (except newline)
	Quantifiers for preceding pattern:
*	Zero or more times
?	Zero or one times
+	One or more times
{m}	Exactly *m* times
{m,}	At least *m* times
{m,n}	At least *m* but not more than *n* times
\1, \2, ...	Backreference
(...)	Grouping
(?:...)	Grouping without backreference
^	Beginning of line
$	End of line
a|b|c	Alternatives
*? +? ?? {...}?	*Non-greedy* operator (minimal match)
(?=...) (?!...)	Lookahead positive/negative

1.10.4 Zero patterns

Some patterns define conditions without 'swallowing' parts of the input text. The pattern \b, which responds to word boundaries, is an example. Lookahead patterns work after the same principle: they define text that should (or should not) follow, without absorbing it.

Positive lookahead conditions are defined by the pattern (?=...); negative ones are described by the expression (?!...).

They are employed above all in search-and-replace patterns (Section 1.10.8). The pattern must nose around in potentially following text, but is not allowed to take it in, because otherwise it would also be replaced with the replace string.

Table 1.7 summarizes the most important regular expression constructs in Perl.

1.10.5 Searching for several expressions in a string

If the task is to scour all found patterns in a text, the g modifier helps by making the matcher remember the position of a hit, so that it will continue after this position at the next call. Typically, such a task is handled by a while loop, as shown in the following example, which counts all 'e's in a string:

```
$string = "How many times does the letter \"e\" occur?";

while($string =~ /e/g) {
    $count++;
}


print "Exactly $count times.\n";
```

Example: multiline pattern matching

Assume you downloaded the following HTML snippet from the Net and want to filter out determined parts (the HTML parser presented on page 284 analyzes HTML tags much more elegantly – this example is intended only to delve deeper into the possibilities of multiline matches):

_____*currency.html*

```
<TR>
<TD ALIGN="LEFT">Swiss Francs</TD>
<TD> 124.0300<BR>  123.8500 </TD>

<TR>
<TD ALIGN="LEFT">US Dollar</TD>
<TD> 1.8300 <BR> 1.8092 </TD>

<TR>
<TD ALIGN="LEFT">Spanish Pesetas</TD>
<TD> 1.1811<BR> 1.1782</TD>
```

_____*currency.html*

All lines are stored, separated by newlines, in the scalar `$data`. To output all HTML tags present in the string in the format

```
Tag: <TR>
Tag: <TD ALIGN="LEFT">
Tag: </TD>
Tag: <TD>
...
```

you could proceed more or less as follows:

```
while($data =~ /(<.*?>)/g) {
    print "Tag: $1\n";
}
```

With /.*?/, the regular expression /(<.*?>)/ defines a *minimal* coverage – otherwise, the matcher would be too greedy and combine charácters across tag boundaries. Together with the `while` loop, the modifier `/g` makes sure that all tags are worked through.

All currency names in the format

```
Name: Swiss Francs
Name: US Dollar
Name: Spanish Pesetas
```

are fetched by the Perl snippet

```
while($data =~ m{
                 ">         # tag end of "LEFT">
                 (.*?)      # minimal number of chars
                 </TD>      # ... up to </TD> tag end
               }gx) {
    print "Name: $1\n";
}
```

from `$data`. The whole paragraph that contains the character sequence `US Dollar` is extracted by

```
$data =~ /^$              # empty line
            (.*?US Dollar.*?)  # something with "US Dollar"
            ^$            # empty line
         /smx;
print "Paragraph: $1";
```

To make the Perl matcher swallow characters from `$data` across several lines with `.*`, the `s` modifier must step in. At the same time, however, it is supposed to interpret `^` as the beginning and `$` as the end of a line – this requires the `m` modifier.

All currency names, together with the first exchange rate specified in the format

```
Swiss Francs     124.0300
US Dollars         1.8300
Spanish Pesetas    1.1811
```

are finally obtained by

```
while($data =~ /
                 ">         # tag end of "LEFT">
                 (.*?)      # currency name
                 < .*? TD>  # forget tags up to TD>
                 \s*        # swallow spaces
                 ([\d.]+)   # value (numbers with decimal points)
```

```
        /sxg) {
    printf "%-18s %8s\n", $1, $2;
}
```

This example shows how, with minimal matches, it is possible to work your way from clue to clue, collecting data on the way.

EXERCISE 1.14

Regular expressions

The following text section is taken from the Perl manual page `perlre`, which can be called by means of `perldoc perlre` and summarizes all that needs to be known about regular expressions:

```
The /x modifier itself
needs a little more explanation.
```

Now to the exercise:
Assume that the above text is stored in a string `$string`. The left-hand side of the table below shows a regular expression. The associated middle column contains the text section to which the regular expression responds when carrying out the instruction

```
$string = ~ /regular expression/;
```

(caution: it does *not* contain the return value of this expression, but the piece of text found). Cover the middle column of the table with a piece of paper, and play *non-deterministic automaton* by applying the pattern to the above text line by line (of the table), finding out what the middle column should look like, and push the paper down one more line!

"The /x modifier itself needs a little more explanation." =~ EXPR;		
EXPR	Recognized pattern	Explanation
/T.*e/	"The /x modifier itse"	.* swallows as much as possible in a line
/T.*?e/	"The"	.*? swallows minimal amount
/\d+/	*Pattern does not match*	No digits occur in the text
/\w+/	"The"	The first word
/\W+/	" /"	Matches the space after "The" and the following "/"
/\bm.*r\b/	"modifier"	Begin of word m, end of word r
/\w?/	"T"	One letter or none – in *greedy* mode one

"The /x modifier itself needs a little more explanation." =~ EXPR;		
EXPR	Recognized pattern	Explanation
/\w??/	*empty string*	One letter or none – in *non-greedy* mode none
/\w*/	"The"	Zero hits would be enough, but *greedy* mode
/\w*?/	*empty string*	Zero hits are enough in *non-greedy* mode
/Tz*he/	"The"	"z" can be omitted, "The" matches
/Tz+he/	*Pattern does not match*	"z" must not be omitted, does not match
/^\w+/	"The"	Word at beginning of line
/\w+$/	*Pattern does not match*	End of string (second line!) is ".", \w does not match
/[A-Z0-9]*/	"T"	The first letter is a hit; the second one is not
/[A-Za-z0-9]*/	"The"	First word
/[^A-Za-z]+/	" /"	Anything except upper- and lower-case letters
/.{2}/	"Th"	The first two chars of the string
/.{2,5}/	"The /"	Two to five chars – five in *greedy* mode
/[a-z]{5}/	"modif"	At least five consecutive letters
/(.)\1/	"ee"	Double chars in a row - the two "e"s of "needs"
/\bn.*\b/	"needs a little more explanation"	Too greedy for a word with "n": matches up to the last word
/\bn.*?\b/	"needs"	A word with "n" – minimal
/\S+/	"The"	A sequence of non-spaces
/\S*/	"The"	Zero hits would be allowed – but we are in *greedy* mode
/T.*e/m	"The /x modifier itse"	Does not match newline in multiline mode
/T.*e/s	"The /x modifier itself needs a little more e"	... but in single-line mode!
/^n.*e/	*Pattern does not match*	^ in normal mode does not match beginning of second line
/^n.*e/m	"needs a little more e"	... but does in multiline mode!
/^n.*e/s	*Pattern does not match*	The single-line mode does not recognize ^ in follow-up lines
/da|xy|it/	"it"	Alternatives; the it in itself wins
/(T|Th)/	"T"	First alternative wins
/it(?=tle)/	"it"	Matches "little", but swallows only "it" (positive lookahead)

```
"The /x modifier itself
   needs a little more explanation." =~ EXPR;
```

EXPR	Recognized pattern	Explanation
`/it(?!s)\w*/`	`"ittle"`	Does not match `"itself"` because of negative lookahead
`/Th(?:e)/`	`"The"`	Grouping parentheses without backreference (no lookahead)

On the other hand, matching with a regular expression containing backreference creating parentheses returns the found substrings if the pattern did match. The construct

```
@match = ($string =~ /(__)__(__)/);
```

stores found matches that are also present in the variables `$1`, `$2`, and so on in `@match`. Thus the question for the next table is: which values will be found in the returned list, if the pattern in the left-hand column is matched with `$string` according to the above construct?

```
@found=("The /x modifier itself
   needs a little more explanation." =~ EXPR);
```

EXPR	Returned list @found	Explanation
`/^(\w+)/`	`("The")`	Word at beginning
`/(\w+)$/`	`()` – *expression does not match*	Word at end (full stop does not match)
`/(\w+)\W*$/`	`("explanation")`	Word and special char at end
`/T(.*)e/`	`("he /x modifier its")`	*Greedy*
`/T(.*?)e/`	`("h")`	*Non-greedy*
`/(\b\w*o\w*\b)/`	`("modifier")`	A word containing 'o'
`/(\w)\1/`	`("e")`	Word with double letter (first **e** of **needs**)
`/((\w)\2)/`	`("ee", "e")`	As above, except for different bracketing
`/(\b\w*(\w)\2\w*)/`	`("needs", "e")`	As above, but yields the word and the double char
`/(\w+)\s+(\w+)/`	`("x", "modifier")`	Two consecutive words
`/(?:modifier)\s*(\w+)/`	`("itself")`	Only one backreference
`/(m\w+)\s+(?!i)(\w+)/`	`("more", "explanation")`	First word with **m**; second word must not begin with **i**, negative lookahead
`/(m\w+)\s+(?=it)(\w+)/`	`("modifier", "itself")`	First word with **m**; second word must begin with **it**, positive lookahead

1.10.6 Masking of metacharacters

If metacharacters in regular expressions are to be deprived of their special properties, they must be prefixed with a backslash (\). Thus the regular expression /2\^16/ corresponds to the string "2^16" in a text, because '^' is in this case *not* intended to denote the beginning of the line.

The function `quotemeta` carries out this masking for a given string. Thus

```
$string = 'Dollar($) Backslash(\)';

print quotemeta($string), "\n";
```

yields the output

```
Dollar\(\$\)\ Backslash\(\\\)
```

`quotemeta` masks not only metacharacters known from regular expressions, but generally all non-alphanumeric characters.

1.10.7 Sample application

How elegantly regular expressions can be employed in Perl is shown by the following example. If the distribution files of the `mysoft` program are stored in a directory under the names

```
mysoft-1.01.tar.gz
mysoft-1.02.tar.gz
```

and if the question arises as to how the name of the next release can be determined, the answer is:

```
                              # determine old version number
($oldversion) = reverse sort map { /(\d\.\d+)/ } <mysoft-*.tar.gz>;

                              # construct new file name
printf "mysoft-%3.2f.tar.gz\n", $oldversion + 0.01;
```

The first line of this script consists of a long sequence of commands. To analyze it, you best proceed from right to left. One by one, functions are executed that return lists, which in turn serve as input parameters for further functions.

The globbing construct `<mysoft-*.tar.gz>` returns a list of all files in the current directory whose names match the specified pattern. Together with a regular expression that 'swallows' version indications such as `1.01`, the function `map` yields a list of version numbers found. This is because the regular expression contains back-referencing parentheses and thus returns for each file found a single-element list with the extracted version number.

A subsequent `sort` arranges the list of version numbers (for example `1.01`, `1.02`, and so on) in ascending order; the preceding `reverse` function reverses the list, and `$oldversion` on the left-hand side of the assignment is set to the first element – the highest version number.

Another important factor are the parentheses on the left-hand side: they force `reverse` to operate in a list context: that is, to return a list and not (as usual with `reverse` in a scalar context) the list in form of a string. On the left-hand side, we have a list of one element, which is assigned the list generated on the right-hand side – and as we know, superfluous elements are omitted.

To prevent a version `2.00` from being output simply as `2`, the format specification `%3.2f` in the format string of the `printf` instruction represents the version number in any case with two digits after the decimal point.

EXERCISE 1.15

Counting file types

Use a script to determine how many files and of which type exist in the current directory. If, for example, `test.pl`, `test2.pl`, and `word.doc` were present, the output could be something like: `"pl: 2, doc: 1"`. Rummage through the current directory with `readdir`, find the extension of each file by means of a regular expression, and make use of a hash with the extension as a key to count the number of files per file type (*solution on page 103*).

EXERCISE 1.16

Pattern matching with status information

Files where the mail system of Netscape Navigator stores its data have the following format:

```
>From - Sat Nov 15 09:54:52 1997
X-Mozilla-Status: 0001
...
To: Larry Wall <larry@wall.org>
...
Content-Type: text/plain; charset=us-ascii
Content-Transfer-Encoding: 7bit

Here, the mail message text includes two addresses: a@b.com and
c@d.com; both are to be found by the script.
```

```
>From - Sat Nov 15 10:10:51 1997
X-Mozilla-Status: 0001
...
To: Christian Kirsch <ck@held.mind.de>
...
Content-Type: text/plain; charset=iso-8859-1
Content-Transfer-Encoding: 8bit

In this text, twenger@t-online.de is buried.

>From - Sat Nov 15 10:11:39 1997
...
```

Obviously, a new mail header initiates with From - ..., which is in turn separated by an empty line from the mail body itself: that is, from the actual text of the message.

Write a script that finds and outputs all email addresses that occur anywhere in the mail texts (but not in the mail headers!).

For this purpose, you should work your way line by line through the file and, by means of regular expressions and a status variable $status, determine (and protocol) whether you are passing though a mail header or a mail body. When you are sure that you are inside a mail body, you should look for potential email addresses.

Recognizing an email address in a text by means of a regular expression is generally not easy at all. Friedl (1997) presents a rather long-winded general solution to the problem, but for this exercise a simple pattern such as

```
/[\w.-]+@[\w.-]+/
```

should be sufficient, which requires two elements, one before and one after an 'at' sign (@), each of which may be composed of alphanumeric characters, dots, underscores, and hyphens.

Please do not forget that a line might well contain several addresses (*solution on page 103*).

1.10.8 Search and replace

Perl does not only find patterns but, if required, immediately replaces them with given strings. By analogy with the syntax of the UNIX tool sed,

```
$text =~ s/search/replace/g;              # text replacement in $text
```

replaces all search patterns found in $text with replace. The *substitution* construct works *globally* if, as in the example, the modifier g is specified. In this case, not only is the first matching expression substituted, but also all occurrences that are found.

As an additional feature with respect to sed, the Perl substitution mechanism can also handle line breaks. Lines that are marked for being continued by a backslash (\) at the line end are joined with the next line by the instruction

```
$text =~ s/\\\n//g;        # \ before newline: replace with empty string
```

Thus

```
This line \
is being \
continued.
```

finally becomes

```
This line is being continued.
```

in $string. Instead of the separation character '/' you may also use any other character (for example '#') that does not occur in the pattern definition. Thus permanent masking of the '/' character can be prevented if it happens to occur in a pattern.

If the text is not to be replaced in the original variable, but the modified text is to be assigned to a different variable, leaving the original variable untouched, the following construct is required:

```
($base = $path) =~ s#.*/##;        # $base = `basename $path`
```

In the same way as the UNIX function basename, the example converts the path $path (for example /usr/bin/perl) into its last component (for example perl) and stores the result in $base, substituting any character sequence .* followed by a '/' with the empty string. Since in case of doubt Perl always matches the maximum number of available characters, in the example this refers to the character sequence from the beginning of the line up to the last '/' character.

Obviously, Perl's substitution operation also allows you to employ the s and x modifiers. The following example removes the C language comments from a program text. It works across lines with .* (modifier s) and replaces /* ... */ with the empty string.

```
$program =~ s@            # substitute (at sign as separator)
             /\*         # '/*' beginning of comment
             .*?         # minimum number of arbitrary characters
             \*/         # '*/' end of comment
@@gsx;                   # global, single-line, extended
```

Note that for precise detection of all comments in C programs you will in the end need the complete parsing properties of a C compiler. In fact, not only may the string "/*" appear in C strings, but also pre-compiler instructions such as #define CB /* would neatly defeat the above regular expression.

In contrast to the search expression, where found partial expressions are referred to by \1, \2, \3, and so on (see page 58), the substitution expression accesses partial hits of the search expression via $1, $2, $3, and so on. Thus, for example,

```
s#Subject: (.*)#Subject: Re: $1#g;
```

replaces "Subject: What's the Subject?" with "Subject: Re: What's the Subject?".

Problems of the kind 'mask special characters in a string by means of a prefixed backslash' can be resolved either by means of individual search and replace instructions or, more elegantly, by specification of a character class and backreference to the found character from the replacement string. Thus

```
s#([\$\\])#\\$1#g;
```

protects the potentially occurring characters $ and \ in a string by means of a backslash: thus '\$' becomes '\\\$'.

The e modifier for a substitution instruction even evaluates the replacement string before it actually gets into the text to be processed. Thus

```
s/([^a-zA-Z0-9])/"%" . sprintf("%02x", ord($1))/ge;
```

replaces all non-alphanumeric characters of a string with the representation %xx, where xx is the hexadecimal value of the character in the ASCII table. The replacement string consists of a Perl instruction that uses the '.' operator to concatenate two strings, the second of which dynamically generates the replacement string from the search result by means of the formatting function sprintf (see Section 1.8.4) and the conversion function ord (see Section 1.14.8). Thus, for example, a space in the original string becomes %20, because the space occupies position 32 in the ASCII table, and 32 corresponds to the hexadecimal value 20H.

EXERCISE 1.17

Synchronizing two directories

The files in a directory in are continuously edited under Windows and therefore contain the usual DOS \r\n (\015\012) as line separators – instead of \n (\012), which is the good and proper way for this to be. This clutters the vi editor under UNIX with ugly ^M characters. A periodically called script sync.pl has the task of running modified files from in through a filter that removes the \015 characters, and subsequently copying the filtered files to out. sync.pl must become active only for files that either exist only in in and not in out (file-operator -e), or which are present in in in a more recent version than in out (hint: determine the relative modification date with the aid of the -M operator).

Search the `in` directory for files with `opendir/readdir/closedir`, check whether copying is required and, if so, call a function `copy_and_filter()`, which takes the names of source and target file as arguments. This function should read the source file line by line, filter the lines with a substitution command, and copy them to the target file (*solution on page 104*).

EXERCISE 1.18

Splitting numbers

Insert separating commas in a large integer number, so that "1000000" becomes 1,000,000 and 10000 becomes 10,000. Forget trying to tackle this problem with a single call of a regular expression. Instead, search and replace several times by means of a `while` loop, making use of the fact that a substitution instruction returns a true value if a substitution actually took place.

Another hint, because this one is really a beast: search for the pattern "four consecutive digits at the back end of a word" (\b), and substitute it with the first digit found, a separating comma, and the remaining three digits.

Thus with "1000000" the first substitution gives "1000,000". In the second pass, the regular expression finds the separating comma as word boundary (!) and generates "1,000,000" (*solution on page 105*).

1.10.9 Haute école of masking

A somewhat more complicated search and replace problem is constituted by configuration files of the following kind:

```
###############################################################
###  Configuration file                                      #
###############################################################
#  Keyword                  1st parameter        2nd  3rd  #
###############################################################
     CUSTOMER_NUMBER         12345                 0    J
     NAME                    "Michael Schilli"     1    "a b"
     ORDER                   "A \"good\" lager"     2
     FAVORITE_WINDOWS        ""                     4
     FAVORITE_SPECIAL_CHAR   "The backslash (\\)"   3    N
```

Comments following '`#`' are ignored, and so are empty lines. Data lines contain a keyword and any number of parameters separated by spaces. If a parameter itself contains spaces, it must be enclosed in double quotes. If, instead, a parameter contains the '"' character, it must be masked out by means of a backslash (\). A backslash in the parameter must itself also be masked out ("\\"). This closes the masking spiral; the procedure is uniquely defined.

The script `readcfg.pl` on page 75 shows one possibility of pulling the data apart by means of a Perl script and (testwise) outputting the result more or less like this:

```
CUSTOMER_NUMBER
    12345
    0
    J
NAME
    Michael Schilli
    1
    a b
ORDER
    A "good" lager
    2
FAVORITE_WINDOWS

    4
FAVORITE_SPECIAL_CHARS
    The backslash (\)
    3
    N
```

About the implementation: After opening the file, `readcfg.pl` jumps into a `while` loop and line by line discards comments and empty lines.

The inner `while` loop searches a line for keywords and parameters. Two alternatives are available in the regular expression, which is split into several lines to improve readability. The first one,

```
"(?:\\\\|\\"|.)*?"
```

matches a string that begins with '"' and which, up to a closing '"', may contain any number of masked backslashes (\\), masked quotes (\"), or simply arbitrary characters ('.'). But caution: since the backslash has its own special meaning in regular expressions, \\ immediately becomes \\\\. Too many backslashes can trigger the dreadful 'Leaning Chopstick Syndrome' (LCS) – have a break and relax before you go on programming :-)

Since the expression contains parentheses with the aim of grouping alternatives, and not of storing backreferences, after the opening parenthesis `?:` switches off the reference mechanism for the parenthesis, thus facilitating future evaluation of the true backreferences.

Because of the *non-greedy* operator, the construct "(?:__|__|__)*?" allows only minimal coverage; otherwise the expression might swallow several parameters at once by combining the quotes of several expressions.

The second alternative in the second line of the regular expression

```
(\S+)
```

is simple: a string without spaces, a normal parameter of the analyzed file without enclosing quotes. The fact that this alternative comes *after* the first one is decisive: since the matcher always selects the first matching alternative, with (\S+) as its first alternative, it would never try the second alternative, and all the pretty logic would be in vain.

But which of the two alternatives in the entire expression did match? An expression such as /(a)|(b)/ returns a in $1 if a is the case, or b in $2 if b is the case. The non-matching alternative generates a backreference that is set to undef. For easy evaluation of such constructs, the last backreference set is available in the special variable $+.

With the construct while(/__/g) in readcfg.pl, the matcher works its way from parameter to parameter and replaces the masked characters \ and " with their originals in the found strings. After having removed the enclosing quotes, read-cfg.pl pushes the extracted parameters into the array @columns.

readcfg.pl

```perl
#!/usr/bin/perl -w

open(FILE, "mquote.dat") || die "Cannot open mquote.dat";

while(<FILE>) {

    s/#.*//;            # remove comments
    next if /^\s*$/;    # ignore blank lines

    @columns = ();      # delete buffer

    while(/("(?:\\\\|\\"|.)*?")|  # "parameter"
           (\S+)                  # or: parameter
          /gx) {
        my $match = $+;           # matching alternative
        if(defined $1) {          # parameter in quotes?
            $match =~ s/^"//;     # remove opening "
            $match =~ s/"$//;     # remove closing "
        }
        $match =~ s#\\\\#\\#g;    # \\ -> \
        $match =~ s#\\"#"#g;      # \" -> "
        push(@columns, $match);   # store
```

```
    }

    # output result:

    print shift(@columns), "\n";  # first keyword
    foreach (@columns) {          # remaining entries in the line
        print "    $_\n";
    }
}
close(FILE);
```

readcfg.pl

1.11 Perl and the shell

Perl also provides an interface with the UNIX shell. It delegates commands enclosed by *backquotes* to the shell (more precisely, to a subshell), and returns its output. Thus, for example, the current directory can be determined with

```
$dir = `pwd`;
```

In principle, with the corresponding DOS commands, these constructs will also work under the Windows command interpreter, but at the time of this book's going into print this interface was still very much afflicted with errors.

The `system` function also executes commands passed to it as a string in a subshell. The return value corresponds to the exit code of the called program.

```
system("cp file1 file2") && die "Copy failed";
```

uses the UNIX command `cp` to copy file `file1` to `file2`. In case of success, UNIX commands by convention return 0, while in case of failure a positive value is returned. For this reason, error checking (see above) must be carried out in a slightly different way from the usual Perl procedure: instead of the *command-or-error* logic, a logical AND is employed.

1.12 Extended data structures

'Simple' arrays and hashes are often not sufficient for representing complex data structures. The following subsections show solutions for more demanding modeling problems.

1.12.1 Arrays of arrays

The elements of an array can point to other arrays. If the necessity arises to store a number of different arrays coherently, the most suitable data structure is an array of array references:

```
@array1 = ("apples", "pears");
@array2 = ("ZZ-Top", "ACDC", "Pet Shop Boys");
@array_of_arrayrefs = (\@array1, \@array2);
```

Now, the array `@array_of_arrayrefs` contains references to the arrays `@array1` and `@array2`. Since, however, the names of the subarrays are not necessarily needed, the whole structure can also be formulated with anonymous arrays:

```
@array_of_arrayrefs = (["apples", "pears"],
                       ["ZZ-Top", "ACDC", "Pet Shop Boys"]);
```

Access to the subarrays and their entries is shown by the following code fragment:

```
foreach $arrayref (@array_of_arrayrefs) {
    print "ARRAY: ";
                           # dereference array reference and
                           # cycle through list of scalars
    foreach $element (@$arrayref) {
        print "$element ";
    }
    print "\n";
}
```

Since the structure of `@array_of_arrayrefs` corresponds exactly to the implementation of two-dimensional arrays in Perl, `$array_of_arrayrefs[0][1]` accesses the second element of the first array – that is, `"pears"`.

1.12.2 Arrays of hashes

By analogy with arrays of array references, it is also possible to create arrays of hash references:

```
$hash1{'key11'} = 'val11';
$hash1{'key12'} = 'val12';

$hash2{'key21'} = 'val21';
$hash2{'key22'} = 'val22';

@array_of_hashrefs = (\%hash1, \%hash2);
```

With references to anonymous hashes, the assignment is written as

```
@array_of_hashrefs = ({'key11' => 'val11', 'key12' => 'val12'},
                      {'key21' => 'val21', 'key22' => 'val22'}
                     );
```

The next piece of code cycles through the array of hash references and outputs the key-value pairs of each stored hash:

```
                            # cycle through list of
                            # hash references
foreach $hashref (@array_of_hashrefs) {
    print "HASH: ";
                            # dereference hash reference
                            # and cycle through all keys
    foreach $key (keys %$hashref) {
                            # output key and value
        print "$key => $hashref->{$key}  ";
    }
    print "\n";
}
```

Starting from `$array_of_hashrefs`, the construct `$array_of_hashrefs->[1]->{'key21'}` leads to the value matching the key `key21` in the second hash of the array.

1.12.3 Summary of extended data constructs

The following summary lists all extended array and hash constructs. The code samples define references to anonymous arrays or hashes that in turn contain anonymous arrays or hashes. In addition, the code fragments show how individual elements can be extracted from the complex structures.

Arrays of arrays

```
# reference to arrays of array references

$arrayrefref = [[1, 2], [3, 4, 5]];

foreach $arrayref (@$arrayrefref) {
    foreach $element (@$arrayref) {
        print $element;
    }
}
```

Arrays of hashes

```
# reference to arrays of hash references

$hashrefarrayref = [{'k11' => 'v11', 'k12' => 'v12'},
                    {'k21' => 'v21'}
                   ];

foreach $hashref (@$hashrefarrayref) {
    foreach $key (keys %$hashref) {
        print $key, $hashref->{$key};
    }
}
```

Hashes of array entries

```
# reference to hashes of array references

$hashref = {'key1' => [1, 2], 'key2' => [3, 4, 5]};

foreach $key (keys %$hashref) {
    foreach $element (@{$hashref->{$key}}) {
        print $element;
    }
}
```

Hashes of hash entries

```
# reference to hashes of hash references

$hashrefref = {'k1' => {'k11' => 'v11', 'k12' => 'v12'},
               'k2' => {'k21' => 'v21'}
              };

foreach $key_outer (keys %$hashrefref) {
    foreach $key_inner (keys %{$hashrefref->{$key_outer}}) {
        print $key_inner, $hashrefref->{$key_outer}->{$key_inner};
    }
}
```

EXERCISE 1.19

Sorting nested structures

Assume the following data structure:

```
%dealers = (
  "Beverly Hills Cadillac" => ["Cadillac", "Wiltshire Blvd"],
  "Hollywood Ford       " => ["Ford",     "Hollywood Blvd"],
  "Walker-Buerge Ford   " => ["Ford",   "Santa Monica Blvd"],
  "Felix Cadillac       " => ["Cadillac",   "S Figueroa St"]);
```

The hash %dealers contains the names of local (guess from which town) car dealerships as keys, and as values has a reference to an array that in the first two elements contains the make of car represented by the dealership and the business address. Sort the dealerships alphabetically by the specified street as only criterion and output the result in the form

```
Hollywood Ford        : Hollywood Blvd (Ford)
Felix Cadillac        : S Figueroa St (Cadillac)
Walker-Buerge Ford    : Santa Monica Blvd (Ford)
Beverly Hills Cadillac: Wiltshire Blvd (Cadillac)
```

Make use of a sorting function sort_by_street, which contains two dealership names as arguments, picks the corresponding addresses from the hash %dealers, compares them, and, according to the conventions for sorting functions, returns −1, 0 or 1.

Second part:
Write a subroutine sort_by_name_and_street, which sorts the data structure by make of car, and, within one make, by address. Thus the result should look as follows:

```
Felix Cadillac        : S Figueroa St (Cadillac)
Beverly Hills Cadillac: Wiltshire Blvd (Cadillac)
Hollywood Ford        : Hollywood Blvd (Ford)
Walker-Buerge Ford    : Santa Monica Blvd (Ford)
```

(Solution on page 106.)

EXERCISE 1.20

Analysis of a Web server log file

In the file logs/access_log, the Apache Web server protocols each request for a URL in the following format:

```
194.97.137.28 - - [21/Jan/1998:10:51:01 -0800]
    "GET /test/index.html HTTP/1.0" 200 465
```

Now, you can do all sort of statistics with this log file – how about this one: since each entry includes the path of the requested file (or the CGI script called), it might be interesting to find out which areas of the file system are most popular with the Web surfers. Write a script that reads the log file, extracts the access path information line by line, and on the basis of a data record like

```
/index.html
/test/index.html
/test/
/test/index.html
/test/home.html
```

churns out the result

```
index.html (1)
test (4)
    index.html (2)
    home.html (1)
```

Proceed as follows: extract the path information line by line with the aid of a regular expression. Split the path into its individual entries by means of a split operation.

Now it becomes really exciting: build up step by step a data structure that represents a directory tree. Suggestion: the entries of a directory level are held by a hash with the entry names as keys and an array reference as value. At its first element, the array contains a reference to a hash that accommodates subentries if the entry is a directory. The second element is a scalar, a counter that protocols how many times the path has been traversed. Thus a hash looks as follows:

```
Entry1 => [reference to next-level hash, counter],
Entry2 => [...
```

Output of the data structure is then carried out by a function printstats, which is passed as parameters a hash reference and enough spaces for indenting the current level. For a call of printstats, cycle through the keys of the hash and output them correctly indented, together with the corresponding counter.

Do this on a free evening and make sure your fridge is stocked with enough booze – this one is really tricky (*solution on page 106*).

The Schwartz transformation

Since the comparison routines of sorting algorithms are called very frequently (super-proportional with respect to the number of elements to be sorted), no expensive operations should take place there. To sort, for example, a number of files by their date of last modification, something like

```
@files = <*.pl>;

@sorted = sort sort_by_modtime @files;

print join("\n", @sorted);

sub sort_by_modtime {
    -M $a <=> -M $b;
}
```

would be required. A weird and wonderful Perl trick, the Schwartz transformation, invented by Randal L. Schwartz and presented in Hall and Schwartz (1998), helps the algorithm to gain speed: the list containing the files it transformed into a second list that, instead of file names, contains sublists, which in turn contain the file name and the date of last modification. This temporary list of lists can quickly be sorted and transformed back into a list of file names. Advantage: the expensive '-M' operator needs to define the modification date of each file only *once*.

```
@files = <*.pl>;

@sorted = map { $_->[0] }              # 3. back transformation
          sort { $a->[1] <=> $b->[1] } # 2. sorting
          map { [$_, -M] } @files;     # 1. transform: file/date

print join("\n", @sorted);
```

1.13 Persistent storage of hashes in DBM files

Persistent implementation of variables ensures their values even beyond the execution of a script. In case of restart, it guarantees their reinitialization.

With the `tie` function, Perl provides a possibility for all operating systems to bind variables to `dbm` files – the common UNIX fashion of persistently storing data in the *key-value* format. For this purpose – depending on the implementation of the underlying library – `tie` creates one or two files on the hard disk, in which it lets volatile variables 'hibernate.'

Listing `sdbm.pl` shows a hash `%myhash`, whose content is present, even after termination of the script, in the files `myhash.dir` and `myhash.pag`, which are typical for the SDBM implementation.

sdbm.pl

```perl
#!/usr/bin/perl -w

use SDBM_File;
use Fcntl;                          # definition of O_RDWR, O_CREAT etc.

$filename = "myhash";

                                    # open persistent hash
tie(%myhash, SDBM_File, $filename, O_RDWR|O_CREAT, 0644) ||
    die "Cannot open $filename";

                                    # initialization, if yet
                                    # undefined
$myhash{"key"} = 0 unless defined($myhash{"key"});

                                    # output value
print "myhash{key} = $myhash{key}\n";


$myhash{"key"}++;                   # set new value

untie %myhash;                      # release hash
```

sdbm.pl

At the first call, `sdbm.pl` creates the persistency files (O_CREAT flag of the `tie` function) and allows read and write access (O_RDWR flag). Both flags are imported by the `Fcntl` module. Then, unless it is already defined, `sdbm.pl` initializes the hash entry under the key `"key"` with 0 and increments this value to 1. (Whether a hash entry already exists should preferably be checked with `exists()` instead of `defined()`, but this does not (yet) function with the SDBM implementation.) The function `untie` closes the persistency files. Subsequent calls of `sdbm.pl` read the hash entry from the SDBM files and increment it, so that at each call `sdbm.pl` outputs a value higher by 1.

Alternatively to the SDBM method, there also exist NDBM, ODBM, and GDBM. These packages merely represent different implementations with the same interface.

Persistency methods for more complex data types are presented in Section 2.5 in the framework of a discussion of object-oriented programming.

1.14 Hints and tricks

1.14.1 Time and date

The time() function returns as current time the number of seconds passed since 1/1/1970, 00:00:00 GMT. A handier version is provided by the function local-time(), which in list context returns the list

```
($sec, $min, $hour,     # time of day
 $mday, $mon, $year,    # date (month 0-11)
 $wday,                 # day of the week (0-6: Sun-Sat)
 $yday,                 # Julian day
 $isdst)                # daylight saving time yes/no
```

for the current time and date. In the scalar context (see Section 1.5.6), it is a string such as, for example,

```
"Thu Sep 17 02:52:23 1998"
```

localtime() works either without parameters or with a scalar that contains the number of seconds passed, such as the one returned by the time() function. For more sophisticated calendar calculations, refer to Section 3.8.

1.14.2 Getting the most out of here documents

The definition of the terminations string of a here document may also be surrounded by Perl syntax, as shown by the following script, which trivially outputs all of the lines of the here document:

```
foreach $i (split(/\n/, <<TextEnd)) {
Line1
Line2
TextEnd
    print "$i\n";        # output line
}
```

It is also possible to insert dynamically generated values into texts of here documents. Return values of functions find their way into the text via the @{[...]} construct (see Section 1.5.7):

```
print <<EOT;
This line is generated @{[&getdata]}.
EOT

sub getdata {
    return ("dynamically");
}
```

Since the function `getdata` returns the string `"dynamically"`, the output of the above script is

```
This line is created dynamically.
```

1.14.3 Stricter variable conventions

A cleanly programmed script will show only very few global variables. The *Default-Global* setting of Perl is compensated by the `strict` module. When using

```
use strict;
```

before running the script, the interpreter checks whether all globally used variables are present in the *fully qualified* form `$Package::var`. Careless *globals*, in which only the `my` operator was forgotten, are thus detected immediately.

1.14.4 Error messages with the `Carp` package

Most applications react to serious errors with a call to the function `die`, which outputs a message and subsequently aborts the script. Similarly, the function `warn` is used to issue a specified warning.

For easier localization of an error, both of these standard functions output module name and line number in addition to the message. Thus, if an error occurs in an application module `Obscure.pm`, the output is something like

```
obscure error at Obscure.pm line 678
```

Often, however, this is not the required behavior. The error message should come from the employed module, but the error localization should instead specify the point where the application script branched into that module. This give users a hint as to where they have called a module function under potentially erroneous assumptions. The implementation of embedded modules is in any case required to be completely transparent to the user.

The module `Carp.pm` offers a contribution in this direction. It provides the following functions:

```perl
#!/usr/bin/perl -w

use Carp;

carp("Warningtext");  # output warning end line number

croak("Errortext");   # output error end line number
                      # and abort script

confess("Errortext"); # output error end line number and
                      # stack trace and abort script
```

If the sample module Obscure.pm uses the functionality provided by the Carp.pm package instead of the normal die emergency exits, a script obscuretest.pl, which includes the module Obscure.pm, outputs the following message if the module code runs into a carp instruction:

```
obscure warning at ./obscure.pl line 5
```

Thus line 5 of the script obscure.pl (empty lines count too) marks the entry point into the module, in which subsequently the error occurs.

—————————————————————————————————————*Obscure.pm*

```perl
package Obscure;

use Carp;                      # include Carp

sub obscure {
    carp "obscure warning";   # trigger warning
}

1;
```

—————————————————————————————————————*Obscure.pm*

—————————————————————————————————————*obscuretest.pl*

```perl
#!/usr/bin/perl -w

use Obscure;

Obscure::obscure();    # this is where the error will be triggered
```

—————————————————————————————————————*obscuretest.pl*

1.14.5 Exception handling

Perl does not provide an equally sophisticated exception handling as for example C++ does with its throw-catch mechanism, but a fatal error that in a code block or a subroutine triggers a `die` command can at least be captured in such a way that the running script does not immediately cease operation.

For this purpose, as shown in Listing `exception.pl`, the critical code block is enclosed by an `eval` construct. If an error occurs in the block, which causes execution of a `die` instruction or the corresponding command of the `Carp` package (Section 1.14.4), the interpreter aborts execution of the block, assigns the (otherwise output) error message text to the variable $@, and continues execution of the script with the first instruction *after* the offending block. In case of error-free execution of the block, $@ remains empty.

---
exception.pl

```
#!/usr/bin/perl -w

eval {            # critical block

    for($i=1; $i<10; $i++) {
        if($i == 9) {
            die "i is 9!";     # die() does _not_ abort the
                               # script, but only processing
                               # of the eval block
        }
    }
};                # end of the critical block

if($@) {          # has an error occurred?
    print "An error has occurred: $@";
}
```

---
exception.pl

1.14.6 Protoypes

For improved type security, since version 5.002 Perl has offered the concept of *prototyping*. Each function can thus decide which kinds of parameter it accepts.

If in a function call the data types of the supplied parameters do not match those of the prototype definition, or if the number of parameters is incorrect, Perl aborts the script with an error message.

The prototype declaration of a function that, for example, expects two scalars as parameters can be either explicitly specified in the code with

```
sub f($$);
```

or incorporated directly into the subroutine definition:

```
sub f($$) {
    my ($v1, $v2) = @_;


    # ...
}
```

Here, you find a number of possible declarations:

```
# Declaration # Call:
            #
sub f();     # f();         // no parameters expected
sub f($);    # f($a);       // one scalar expected
sub f($;$$); # f($a); or f($a,$b); or f($a,$b,$c);
            #              // ';' separates mandatory
            #              // from optional parameters
sub f(@);    # f(@l); or f($a, $b);
            #              // array or series of scalars
sub f(\@);   # f(@l);       // explicit array
sub f(\%);   # f(%h);       // hash
sub f(\&);   # f({ $a <=> $b});
            #              // code block (no reference!)
```

If the declaration shows an explicit array or a hash, passing of this extended data type is carried out *by reference* and not *by value*, as would be the case without prototyping. In this way (or also by reference), the subroutine can fetch arrays and hashes separately from the parameter passing list.

The function `hash_and_array` defined below accepts in its call

```
hash_and_array(%myhash, @myarray);
```

one hash and one array (no references!), but processes them internally as references:

```
sub hash_and_array (\%\@) {
    my ($hashref, $arrayref) = @_;

    print "The array contains: @$arrayref\n";

    foreach $key (keys %$hashref) {
        print "hash($key) = $hashref->{$key}\n";
    }
}
```

Table 1.10   Important formatting parameters for `pack/unpack`.

a	A	ASCII string, padded with zeros/spaces
b	B	Bit string, ascending/descending bit order
c	C	Signed/unsigned character
s	S	Signed/unsigned short
i	I	Signed/unsigned integer
l	L	Signed/unsigned long
n	N	Short/long in network format
h	H	Hex string, low/high half-byte first
f	d	Float/double in native format
u		String, uuencoded
p		Pointer to a null-terminated string
P		Pointer to a fixed-length string

1.14.7   Structures with `pack` and `unpack`

Perl does not support structures such as the ones provided by C; data structuring is carried out via the predefined extended data types such as arrays and hashes.

However, some operating system interfaces expect packed structures as parameters in *binary format*. Thus the `semop` function (see Section F.2 in Appendix F) expects as its second parameter a structure containing a series of *signed short* values. The function `pack` is dedicated to this kind of task, and 'packs' individual data into data buffers according to given formatting instructions. The function `unpack`, instead, 'unpacks' such buffers and extracts the individual values contained in them.

Thus the instruction

```
$buffer = pack('sss', 1, 2, 3);
```

creates a buffer `$buffer`, which contains the *signed short* values 1, 2 and 3 in packed form. The formatting instruction (`'sss'`) can also be marked with a repetition factor (`'s3'`). Thus

```
($v1, $v2, $v3) = unpack('s3', $buffer);
```

unpacks the values and stores them in `$v1`, `$v2`, and `$v3`.

Table 1.10 summarizes the most important formatting instructions of the `pack` and `unpack` functions.

An easy-to-handle way of carrying out `uuencode` coding or decoding is the use of the `pack` parameter `'u'`. The uuencode program allows you to convert binary files into text files with fixed line length that no longer contain any unreadable special characters. These files can then be sent as email via the Internet without problems.

After the addressee has executed a `uudecode`, the files are present again in their original form. Thus the result of

uuencode.pl

```perl
#!/usr/bin/perl -w

print pack('u', <<EndOfText);
This text consists of many, many
lines, which may or may not become very, very long, so long ... and
contains special characters such as \n, \r, and \f.
EndOfText
```

uuencode.pl

is the string

M5&AI<R!T97AT(&-O;G-I<W1S(&]F(&UA;GDL(&UA;GD-;&EN97,L('=H:6-H
M(&UA>2!O<B!M87D@;;
M(&UA>2!O<B!M87D@;;F]T(&)E8V]M92!V97)Y+""!V97)T(&QO;F<L('-O(&QO
M;F<@+BXN(&%N9"!C;VYT86EN<R!S<&5C:6%L(&-H87)A8W1E<G,@<W5C:"!A
2<R!<;;BP@7'(L(&%N9"!<9BX-`

The decoding program is shown in Listing `uudecode.pl`. For testing purposes, it attaches itself to the output of `uuencode.pl`, reads all lines into the array `@lines`, transforms it with a `join` instruction into a multiline string, and forwards this string to the `unpack` function for final decoding.

uudecode.pl

```perl
#!/usr/bin/perl -w

open(UUENCODE, "uuencode.pl |");
@lines = <UUENCODE>;
close(UUENCODE) || die "Error in uuencode.pl";

print unpack('u', join('', @lines));
```

uudecode.pl

Currently, `pack` does not (yet) support Base64 coding, which is becoming a standard above all with Microsoft products. For the sake of completeness, however, we present a script that uses the module `MIME::Base64` by Gisle Aas (see Appendix A on how to obtain freely available modules):

base64.pl

```perl
#!/usr/bin/perl -w

use MIME::Base64;
```

```
                              # Base64 encoding
$encoded = MIME::Base64::encode($data);

                              # Base64 decoding
$text = MIME::Base64::decode($encoded);
```

base64.pl

1.14.8 **Number and encoding systems**

A number entered as a hex string can be converted into a decimal number by means of the hex() function:

```
print "0xffff hex is ", hex("0xffff"), " decimal.\n";
print "ffff hex is ",   hex("ffff"),    " decimal.\n";
print "0xffff hex is ", 0xffff,         " decimal.\n";
```

The last line shows how in Perl you can simply 'jot down' hexadecimal numbers outside strings to have them interpreted as such. The output is

```
0xffff hex is 65535 decimal.
ffff hex is 65535 decimal.
0xffff hex is 65535 decimal.
```

Strings composed of numbers of the octal number system are transformed by oct(), as shown in

```
print "0644 octal is ", oct("0644"), " decimal.\n";
print "644 octal is ",  oct("644"),   " decimal.\n";
print "0644 octal is ", 0644,         " decimal.\n";
```

which yields the output

```
0644 octal is 420 decimal.
644 octal is 420 decimal.
0644 octal is 420 decimal.
```

A scalar is turned into a hex or octal number by means of the sprintf function with the formatting parameters %x and %o. Thus

```
print "65535 decimal is ", sprintf("%x", 65535), " hex.\n";
print "420 decimal is ",   sprintf("%o", 420),    " octal.\n";
```

outputs the following results:

```
65535 decimal is ffff hex.
420 decimal is 644 octal.
```

The `ord()` function takes you from a character to its ordinal number in the ASCII table, whereas `chr()` converts an ordinal number into the corresponding ASCII character.

```
print "The 100th ASCII character is '", chr(100), "'\n";
print "'d' is the ", ord('d'), "th ASCII character.\n";
```

produces the result (without considering special cases such as '1st,' '2nd,' or '3rd')

```
The 100th ASCII character is 'd'
'd' is the 100th ASCII character.
```

1.14.9 Dynamic code generation with `eval`

The `eval` command executes code passed to it as a string parameter (please note the difference between the string form of `eval` and the block form discussed on page 87):

```
$string = 'print "Howdy, world!\n";';
eval $string;
```

does indeed output

```
Howdy, world!
```

With this construct you can do all sorts of things: for example, you could ask the user of a program to enter code which is then executed. Another application is passing regular expressions to functions: since there are no variable types for regular expressions, you can pack them into strings, pass them to a function, and then find yourself having to face the probem of persuading the interpreter to execute a string as code – an ideal exercise for `eval`:

```
$regex = '(\w+)$';      # regular expression for the last word

print matchit("The last word", $regex), "\n";

###################################################################
sub matchit {
###################################################################
    my ($expr, $regex) = @_;
    my $ret;

    eval "(\$ret) = (\$expr =~ /$regex/)";

    $ret;
}
```

The `matchit` function receives a text string and a string with a regular expression as parameters. After evaluation,

```
eval "(\$ret) = (\$expr =~ /$regex/)";
```

becomes

```
($ret) = ($expr =~ /(\w+)$/);
```

which is executed by the interpreter. The last word found is stored in `$ret`, which is then returned by `matchit` to the main program.

1.15 Operating system interfaces

1.15.1 Processes

Under UNIX, the Perl function `fork()` creates a new process. Both the old process (*parent*) and the new process (*child*) begin to execute the code following the `fork` command. To be able to differentiate between them and if necessary send them along different ways, `fork` provides them with different return values:

- 0 to the freshly created child process,
- the number of the child process to the running (parent) process,
- `undef` in the case of an error.

The following Perl snippet shows the application:

```
if(!defined($pid = fork())) {
    die "Fork error!";        # error during creation
} elsif($pid == 0) {
                              # child process
    print "I am the child!\n";
    sleep(1);
    exit(0);                  # ... terminated
} else {
                              # parent process
    print "I am the parent!\n";
}

# only the parent ever gets here
wait();                       # parent waits until child terminates
```

A more user-friendly process handling is offered by the class `Process.pm`, which is introduced in Section 2.3.

Under Windows, the module `Win32::Process` provides at least an interface for starting of foreign programs in the background:

```
use Win32::Process;
                                        # start process
Win32::Process::Create($process,        # process handle
    "D:\\winnt35\\system32\\notepad.exe",   # program path
    "notepad temp.txt",                 # command line
    0,                                  # do not inherit handles
    DETACHED_PROCESS,                   # background process
    "."                                 # home path
    ) || die "Error!";

$process->Suspend();                    # suspend
$process->Resume();                     # resume
$process->Kill(0);                      # terminate
$process->Wait(INFINITE);               # wait for termination
```

1.15.2 Signals

UNIX processes can send and receive signals. They are usually used for inter-process communication, but are also sent to processes by the operating system for notification purposes. The most important signals are:

```
SIGHUP    # Process detached from tty (hangup)
SIGINT    # Abort, mostly by CTRL-C from keyboard
SIGQUIT   # Abort, mostly by CTRL-\ from keyboard
SIGUSR1   # User defined
SIGUSR2   # User defined
SIGALRM   # Alarm timer expired
SIGTERM   # Default signal of the kill command
SIGCHLD   # Child process terminated
SIGSTOP   # Interruption, mostly CTRL-Z
SIGCONT   # Continuation, mostly fg or bg
```

Windows 95 and NT do not support signals, but the ported Perl interpreter transforms the functionality wherever it makes sense. Thus, under Windows, you can define a handler for the INT signal to intercept the ⌈Ctrl⌉-⌈C⌉ of a user for program termination.

Received signals are processed via the definition of signal handlers: each potentially incoming signal is assigned a function that Perl enters in the corresponding case. Perl has a predefined hash named %SIG, which accepts the truncated signal names (without 'SIG') as *keys* and function references as *values*. The assignment

```
$SIG{'TERM'} = \&func;
```

determines the script to enter the function func if the running process receives the SIGTERM signal. Note that, traditionally, signal handlers have neither input parameters nor return values. Depending on the operating system, circumventing this standard may lead to undefined behavior.

IGNORE is a dummy that does *nothing* – it just ignores the incoming signal. Thus the assignment

```
$SIG{'INT'} = IGNORE;
```

makes a process insensitive to the key combination Ctrl-C, because from that moment on it simply does not process the corresponding signal.

1.15.3 Environment

In Perl, the environment variables that in C can be reached via the functions getenv and putenv are stored in the predefined hash %ENV.

Thus the path environment variable can be imported into Perl by means of

```
$path = $ENV{'PATH'};
```

A set environment variable devolves upon all subprocesses of the current process. Thus

```
$ENV{'NEWVAR'} = "newvarvalue";
system('echo $NEWVAR');
```

first sets a new value for the environment variable NEWVAR, and then calls a subshell that, by means of the echo command, outputs the value of NEWVAR (a shell variable!).

Solutions to the exercises

EXERCISE 1.1

Extracting elements from an array (page 10)

```
@array = (1,2,3,4,5);
$a      = $array[1];
$b      = $array[2];
$c      = $array[3];
print "a=$a b=$b c=$c\n";
```

```
@array = (1,2,3,4,5);
($a, $b, $c) = @array[1..3];
print "a=$a b=$b c=$c\n";
```

```
@array = (1,2,3,4,5);
($a, $b, $c) = splice(@array, 1, 3);  # offset 1, length 3
print "a=$a b=$b c=$c\n";
```

EXERCISE 1.2

Building a two-dimensional array (page 16)

```
for($i=0; $i<3; $i++) {
    for($j=0; $j<3; $j++) {
        $array[$i][$j] = "$i:$j";
    }
}
```

EXERCISE 1.3

Outputting an array as a string (page 18)

With a for loop:

```
@array  = (1, 2, 3);
$string = '(';
```

```
for($i=0; $i<=$#array; $i++) {
    $string .= $array[$i];      # append element
    if($i != $#array) {         # append separator - but not
        $string .= "-";         # to last element
    }
}

$string .= ')';

print "$string\n";
```

With a `join` instruction:

```
@array  = (1, 2, 3);

$string = join('-', @array);

print "($string)\n";
```

EXERCISE 1.4

Passing scalars and arrays to subroutines (page 23)

```
$a = 1;
$b = 2;
@c = (3, 4, 5);

func($a, $b, @c);

sub func {
    my ($a, $b, @c) = @_;

    print "\$a=$a \$b=$b \@c=(@c)\n";
}
```

EXERCISE 1.5

Scalar and list context (page 32)

```
sub testcontext {
    if(wantarray) {
        print "Array context\n";    # array context diagnosed
```

```
    } else {
        print "Scalar context\n";    # scalar context diagnosed
    }
}

sub somefunc {
}

@array  = testcontext();
$scalar = testcontext();
$scalar = somefunc(testcontext());
@array = (1, 2, testcontext());
testcontext();
if(testcontext()) { }
foreach $i (testcontext()) { }
@array = map { testcontext(); } ("element");
@array = grep { testcontext(); } ("element");
```

outputs

```
Array context
Scalar context
Array context
Array context
Scalar context
Scalar context
Array context
Array context
Scalar context
```

The function is in a scalar context

- if if its return value is not assigned or used at all;
- if its return value is explicitly assigned to a scalar;
- if its return value is interpreted as true or false (if, while or grep condition.

    The last instruction in a code block of the map command is in list context.

EXERCISE 1.6

Parameter hash (page 34)

```
###############################################################
sub paramhash {
###############################################################
    my @params = @_;            # copy all parameters into @params
    my %params = ();            # initialize hash
```

```
                              # remove key/value pairs from @params
    while(($key, $val) = splice(@params, 0, 2)) {
        $key =~ s/^-//g;       # option hyphens are omitted
        $params{$key} = $val;  # store key/value pair
    }


    return \%params;           # return reference to the hash
}
```

EXERCISE 1.7

Columnwise output of a hash (page 42)

```
$maxvlen = 0;                    # determine max. key length

foreach $key (keys %hash) {
    $maxvlen = length($key) if length($key) > $maxvlen;
}

foreach $key (sort keys %hash) {
                                 # dynamically generate format string:
                                 # "%-ns %s" with n = maxvlen
    printf "%-${maxvlen}s %s\n", $key, $hash{$key}, "\n";
}
```

EXERCISE 1.8

Format current date (page 42)

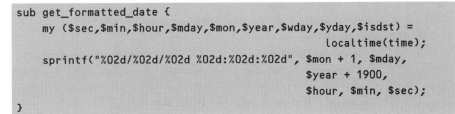

```
sub get_formatted_date {
    my ($sec,$min,$hour,$mday,$mon,$year,$wday,$yday,$isdst) =
                                              localtime(time);
    sprintf("%02d/%02d/%02d %02d:%02d:%02d", $mon + 1, $mday,
                                             $year + 1900,
                                             $hour, $min, $sec);
}
```

EXERCISE 1.9

Pipes (page 44)

First the writing `pwrite.pl`:

```
@array = qw(abc def ghi);      # three-element list

foreach $i (@array) {          # output elementwise
    print "$i\n";
}
```

... and here the `pread.pl` reading from the pipe:

```
open(PIPE, "perl pwrite.pl |") || die "Error!";
while(<PIPE>) {            # read output line by line
    chop;                 # remove linebreaks
    print "pwrite.pl said: '$_'\n";
}
close(PIPE) || die "Error!";
```

EXERCISE 1.10

Renaming files (page 50)

move.pl

```
#!/usr/bin/perl -w
###################################################################
# Call:        move.pl
# Description: renames all *.pl files in the current directory
#                into *.perl
###################################################################

use File::Copy;

opendir(DIR, ".") || die "Cannot open . ($!)";
while(defined ($file = readdir(DIR))) {
    next unless $file =~ /(.*).pl$/;   # only files with this extension
    $newname = "$1.perl";

    print "Moving $file to $newname\n";
    move($file, $newname) || die "Cannot move $file to $newname ($!)";
}
closedir(DIR);
```

move.pl

EXERCISE 1.11

Creating backup copies (page 50)

backup.pl

```perl
#!/usr/bin/perl -w
################################################################
# Call:        backup.pl file ...
# Description: copies the specified files with date extension to
#              the backup directory
################################################################

use File::Copy;
use File::Basename;

$backupdir = "/tmp/BACKUP";

for (@ARGV) {
    my ($sec,$min,$hour,$mday,$mon,$year,$wday,$yday,$isdst) =
                                              localtime(time);
    $newname = "$backupdir/" . basename($_) .
                  sprintf(".%02d-%02d-%02d.%02d:%02d:%02d",
                          $year, $mon+1, $mday, $hour, $min, $sec);
    print "Copying $_ to $newname\n";
    copy($_, $newname) || die "Cannot copy $_ to $newname ($!)";
}
```

backup.pl

EXERCISE 1.12

Delete obsolete files (page 54)

```perl
#!/usr/bin/perl -w
################################################################
# cleanup.pl
# Deletes (recursively!) all files in the specified directories
# and their subdirectories that are older than 10 days
################################################################

use File::Find;

for (@ARGV) {
    die "$_ not a directory" unless -d $_;
```

```
        find(\&process_dir, $_);
}

sub process_dir {
    return unless -f;          # only files

    my $nof_days = -M;         # age of the file in days since
                               # script start

    if($nof_days > 10) {
        print "Deleting $_ - not modified for $nof_days days\n";
        unlink($_) || warn ("Cannot delete $_: $!");
    }
}
```

EXERCISE 1.13

Including files (page 60)

```
#!/usr/bin/perl -w

foreach $file (@ARGV) {
    process_file($file);
}

sub process_file {
    my $file = shift;
    my $line;

    open(FILE, "<$file") || die "Cannot open $file";
    my @lines = <FILE>;
    close(FILE);

    for (@lines) {
        if(/^<include\s+file="([^"]+)/) {
            process_file($1);
        } else {
            print $_;
        }
    }
}
```

EXERCISE 1.14

Regular expressions (page 65)

Solution given on page 65 in the text.

EXERCISE 1.15

Counting file types (page 69)

—————————————————————————————————————*bysuff.pl*

```perl
#!/usr/bin/perl -w

opendir(DIR, ".") || die "Cannot open .";
foreach $file (readdir(DIR)) {
    if(-f $file &&                  # file?
       $file =~ /\.([^.]*)$/) {   # determine suffix
         $suffixes{$1}++;
    }
}
closedir(DIR);

foreach $suffix (sort keys %suffixes) {
    print ".$suffix: $suffixes{$suffix}\n";
}
```

—————————————————————————————————————*bysuff.pl*

EXERCISE 1.16

Pattern recognition with status information (page 69)

—————————————————————————————————————*parse.pl*

```perl
#!/usr/bin/perl -w
################################################################
# Call:        nsmail.pl
# Description: searches a Netscape mail file and outputs
#              the email addresses found in the message texts
################################################################

open(FILE, "< /home/mschilli/nsmail/Sent") || die "Cannot open
    mailfile";

$status    = "UNDEF";    # state of the parser
$emailchar = '\w-.';     # valid characters in an email address
```

```perl
while(<FILE>) {
    if(/^From - /) {        # start of a Netscape mail header
        $status = "HEADER";
        next;               # set state and go to next line
    }

    if($status eq "HEADER" && /^$/) {
                            # empty line after header -> body begins
        $status = "BODY";
        next;               # set state and go to next line
    }

    if($status eq "BODY") {
                            # find all email addresses in a line
        while(/([$emailchar]+@[$emailchar]+)/og) {
            print "$1\n";   # output found email
        }
    }
}
close(FILE);
```

parse.pl

EXERCISE 1.17

Synchronizing two directories (page 72)

sync.pl

```perl
#!/usr/bin/perl -w

$org_dir    = "in";
$mirror_dir = "out";

opendir(DIR, "$org_dir") || die "Cannot open $org_dir";

while(defined ($file = readdir(DIR))) {

    next if $file eq ".";       # ignore directory entries
    next if $file eq "..";

    if(! -e "$mirror_dir/$file" ||
       -M "$org_dir/$file" < -M "$mirror_dir/$file") {
```

```
            # mirrored file does not exist or is older
            # than the original -> copy
            cp_and_filter("$org_dir/$file", "$mirror_dir/$file");
        }
    }
    closedir(DIR);


    ################################################################
    sub cp_and_filter {
    ################################################################
        my ($file1, $file2) = @_;

        print "update: $file1 -> $file2\n";

        open(INFILE,  "<$file1")  || die "Cannot open $file1";
        open(OUTFILE, ">$file2")  || die "Cannot open $file2";

        while(<INFILE>) {
            s/\015//g;
            print OUTFILE $_;
        }

        close(INFILE);
        close(OUTFILE);
    }
```

sync.pl

EXERCISE 1.18

Splitting numbers (page 73)

```
$number = 1000000;

while($number =~ s/(\d)(\d\d\d)\b/$1,$2/) {
    ;       # no instructions needed in loop body
}

print "$number\n";
```

EXERCISE 1.19

Sorting nested structures (page 80)

First part:

```
foreach $dealer (sort sort_by_street keys %dealers) {
        print "$dealer: $dealers{$dealer}->[1] ($dealers{$dealer}-
>[0])\n";
}

sub sort_by_street {
    $dealers{$a}->[1] cmp $dealers{$b}->[1];
}
```

Sorting function for the second part:

```
sub sort_by_car_and_street {
    ($dealers{$a}->[0] cmp $dealers{$b}->[0]) ||
    ($dealers{$a}->[1] cmp $dealers{$b}->[1]);
}
```

This fancy solution builds on the fact that the logical OR in Perl does not return 0 or 1, but the value of the first expression that turns out to be *true*. In the case that the first cmp comparison (car makes) yields a value not equal to 0, the logical OR returns it to the main program. Otherwise, the second comparison comes into play and determines the return value of the function sort_by_car_and_street.

EXERCISE 1.20

Analysis of a Web server log file (page 81)

logstat.pl

```
#!/usr/local/bin/perl -w

$logfile = "/services/http/logs/access_log";

%stats = ();

open(FILE, "<$logfile") || die "Cannot open $logfile";
while(<FILE>) {
                            # extract individual elements
    my ($ip, $date, $url, $status, $bytes) =
        /(\S+) \S+ \S+ \[(.*?)\] "\w+ (\S+) .*?" (\S+) (\S+)/;
```

```perl
    $url =~ s#^/##g;            # strip leading '/'
    $url =~ s#\?.*$##g;         # strip query string

    $treeloc = \%stats;         # root of the structure

    foreach $entry (split(m#/#, $url)) {
                                # create new path if needed
        $treeloc->{$entry} = [{}, 0] unless exists $treeloc->{$entry};
                                # increment entry counter
        $treeloc->{$entry}->[1]++;
                                # go down
        $treeloc = $treeloc->{$entry}->[0];
    }
}
close(FILE);

printstats(\%stats, "");

###################################################################
sub printstats {
###################################################################
# Output data structure (hash of list entries)
###################################################################
    my ($treeloc, $indent) = @_;

    foreach $dir (sort keys %$treeloc) {
                                # output entry and counter
        print "${indent}$dir ($treeloc->{$dir}->[1])\n";
                                # does subdirectory exist?
        if($treeloc->{$dir}->[0]) {
                                # recursion
            printstats($treeloc->{$dir}->[0], "    $indent");
        }
    }
}
```

logstat.pl

Object-oriented programming

The release of version 5 has brought object orientation to Perl. What were the reasons? Object-oriented thinking stimulates software design on a more abstract level. It encourages clear, modular program logic, and thus facilitates maintenance and reusability. This structuring is very good for the Perl script language, because it already has a bad reputation as a 'write-only' language: you can do your programming with it very nicely, but afterwards you can no longer read the code. Another popular joke is that Perl is the only language that you can uuencode without subsequently noticing any difference in contents.

Perl has without doubt grown big through its 'throw-away' scripts. But for the development of more comprehensive systems, which will be modified maybe only after weeks and by complete strangers, stricter requirements apply. The new object-oriented features establish Perl as a language for more demanding applications.

2.1 Introduction

Object-oriented design and implementation are each a separate chapter and cannot be discussed in sufficient depth in this text. Recommended literature on this subject (although not related to Perl) includes Rumbaugh *et al*. (1991), Booch (1994), and Eriksson and Penker (1998); a catalog of well-proven modelings is provided in Gamma *et al*. (1995). Nevertheless, this short introduction may awaken the interest of readers who are not yet familiar with object-oriented methods.

2.1.1 Objects, data, and methods

'Everything is an object!' – nobody wants to hear this phrase any more. It is sufficient to state what an object *has*: a state and an interface for methods that modify or interrogate this state, which is a collection of probably the most disparate data.

For a practical explanation of the object-oriented methods discussed below, we will use a data structure suited for accommodating lists, which exists on the one hand as a 'normal' Perl array @parray and on the other hand as an object-oriented blackbox *myVector*. The implementation of this object will never play a role; it exists only as a ficticious entity for the explanation of object-oriented principles. The name *myVector* is a placeholder for the actual object representation, which will only be discussed later.

Both the Perl array @parray and the object *myVector* contain a number of values. In object-oriented terms, these values reflect the internal state of *myVector*.

For @parray, functions such as push, shift, and so on exist, which manipulate and interrogate the array contents. Thus the call

```
push(@parray, "item1");
```

adds the scalar "item1" to the end of the array.

The object *myVector*, instead, does not only keep its elements available, but also provides a fixed set of functions that allows access to its internals. The object 'knows' the operations allowed on its data. The method call equivalent to the above function call is

```
myVector->push("item1");
```

Starting from an object representation (*myVector*), the programmer accesses the object contents via a method (push) – and this is how the object-oriented music plays (the -> operator is discussed in Section 2.2.2).

2.1.2 Classes

The creation of an object, its instantiation, takes place according to the building plan of the corresponding class. The class defines the implementation of its objects. It specifies the internal data representation and the external interface for each object built after its model.

An object is created as an *instance* of a class, as an individual of a specific kind of make. Potentially, many instances of a class exist at a given moment, all of which have the same properties, but lead their own lives.

@parray is of Perl's 'array' data type. Similarly, the object *myVector* will derive from the fictitious class VectorClass, which defines the internal structure of *myVector*, together with the methods that are allowed to access it. Internally, *myVector* probably consists of a doubly linked list with dynamically allocated entries. But these internal structures are invisible from outside; methods such as push, shift, and so on neatly separate us from the actual, sometimes abominable, implementation.

This encapsulation principle, the 'hiding' of internal structures, is a central theme in object orientation. An object provides a method interface toward the outside; direct access to its data is taboo. This forces the developer to neatly separate implementation and interface in the software design. However, these efforts pay off at a later stage, when an older implementation can be exchanged or used elsewhere without problems, because the interface remains the same or at least upward compatible.

2.1.3 Class relationships

Object-oriented design, however, offers many more ways to save development time through reuse: class relationships allow us to establish connections between existing concepts.

Inheritance

Inheritance is probably the best-known class relationship. It is also known as generalization/specialization. General classes devolve their properties to specialized classes, which may employ or overload the inherited properties and also define additional functionalities.

A special type of the class `VectorClass` is the class `NumVectorClass`, whose objects can accommodate only numerical values. In its interface it provides all typical array functions, plus an additional method `sum`, which adds the stored numerical values. As an additional feature in the sense of type security, `NumVectorClass` modifies the inherited method `push` to allow only numerical values as parameters. This process is commonly also known as *overloading* of inherited functions.

Inheritance presumes support by constructs of the programming language. In this sense, the Perl interpreter automatically searches the implementation of the base class for methods and data structures not defined in the derived class. This process is not at all triggered by a special instruction. Search for methods in the class hierarchy is, on the contrary, an impressed behavior, implicitly determined by the class definition alone.

Inherited classes are related via the 'is a' relationship. But one concept is not always a special case of another one. Often, one class includes another one (aggregation, 'has a'), knows it flightily (association), or uses its services (using).

Aggregation

An aggregated class is factually part of the aggregating class, which is expressed by the 'is a part of' relationship. Aggregations are successful if the affected objects of both classes exist together and the object of the aggregating class assumes the responsibility for the aggregated object.

For a rapid search of elements, the implementation of the sample class `VectorClass` also keeps a hash, which via keywords assigns an index to all stored elements. Thus an object of the class `HashClass` is not only assigned to each instance of the class `VectorClass`, but 'enclosed' with it. Both objects only exist together, and the object of the `VectorClass` class is responsible for the hash object.

Association

Association, on the other hand, models a relationship in which the associating class only 'knows' the associated class, but does not include it. Aggregation and association can easily be confused, in particular because they are represented completely identically in the Perl code. [1]

In the end, only the intended usage decides whether classes are in an aggregating or associating relationship. The kind of selected relationship, however, entails additional side-effects: while in aggregation, for example, frequently only the common existence of objects of the aggregated class is sensible, associated objects are related so loosely that they can also exist individually. This effect finally influences the implementation, which must realize the 'responsibility' of aggregated objects for each other.

To be able to iterate elegantly over all entries of `VectorClass` objects, a class `VectorIterator` will be used. An object of this iterator class does nothing but initially position a pointer to the first element of the vector, which it then shifts from element to element when requested to do so. Thus there is an association relationship between the iterator class and the vector class `VectorClass` – it 'knows' `Vector-Class`, communicates with it, but does not include it.

Using

The using relationship implements a client/server architecture with the classes involved, with the client class using the services of the server class.

An example for a using relationship is the relationship between a vector class and an error class that is specialized in outputting error messages. Thus, in the case of an error, an object of the class `VectorClass` 'knows' that a matching error object exists; however, it does not contain it, but simply uses its services.

In contrast to inheritance, aggregation, association, and using can be simply implemented by class references at programming level and merely presume class support of the programming language.

This information from the world of classes and objects should initially suffice as a basis for applied object orientation in Perl. The following section introduces some details of programming.

2.2 Object-oriented Perl

Since version 5, Perl has supported constructs that allow the following modelings:

- classes,
- class relationships,
- instantiation of objects,

---

[1] In a similar fashion to the way this is often realized in C++, both aggregating and associating classes include references to objects of the target class.

- instance data access via methods.

Perl 4 also had a method of modularization – code packages could be stored in external files and included in the main program by means of the `require` command. The package construct made sure that each program package received its own name-space for variables, without, for example, intersecting with that of the main program.

With a sophisticated combination of references to hashes and module abstraction, Perl 5 managed to integrate object-oriented functionality without too many changes to the syntax of the language. The following discussion makes extensive use of the fundamentals of references explained in Section 1.5.5 and presumes their understanding.

2.2.1 Classes and modules

As disillusioning advance information, let us state straight away that in Perl 5 a class is nothing but a package whose subroutines manipulate objects and are therefore methods in the sense of object-oriented programming. Each of these methods expects an object reference as its first argument, and subsequently operates on the instance variables.

The typical class definition is written as

```
package Myclass;

sub new {              # constructor
    ...
}

sub method1 {          # method
    ...
}

sub method2 {          # method
    ...
}

1;
```

This merely creates a Perl package that usually resides in a module of its own. According to Perl conventions, the package yields 1 as its return value and signals proper initialization to the script that includes it (for basic information on module inclusion, see Section 1.5.4).

The defined subroutines implement the methods `method1` and `method2`, to-gether with the constructor `new`, which is responsible for object instantiation.

2.2.2 Objects

In contrast to object-oriented languages such as Java, C++, and Smalltalk, Perl 5 does not provide a mechanism for automatic instantiation of objects, but requires some manual work from the programmer.

The following considerations are intended to help in identifying what an object needs for itself to exist. An object

- realizes an imprinted behavior using its methods;
- is in a defined state at any given point in time, a state that is reflected by the values of the object's instance variables;
- has an identity: that is, it differs uniquely from other objects of the same class or from objects of other classes.

Thus the task of a constructor is to create an object that

- has a relationship with its class (that is, the object 'knows' which type it is), and thus knows its internal variables and methods;
- stores a set of values for its instance variables.

The class relationship of a new object is created by the function `bless`, which in some 'magical' way associates a data type with a package. But what is the Perl data type of an object?

For an answer to this question, we will look at the second requirement: realization of a separate namespace for instance variables of the object. This guarantees that the variable `membervar` of object A can assume a different value than the homonymous variable of object B of the same class.

This namespace is usually implemented by means of a hash, whose *keys* are the variable names and whose *values* are their values. The rest is simple: the `bless` command binds the hash to the corresponding class, and a reference to the hash is then used as an object reference.

For the `Myclass` package outlined above, the constructor is simply written as

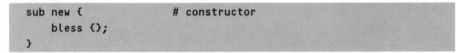

```
sub new {                    # constructor
    bless {};
}
```

Typically for Perl, this short notation defines a lot of functionality. First, {} creates an anonymous hash for the namespace of the new object and returns a reference. The hash does not need a name, because it will be later uniquely identifiable via the object reference. At the time of initialization, it is empty – that is, it does not contain any *key-kalue* pairs: no instance variables have as yet been defined for the object. Via the *keys* of this hash, the instance variables will later be accessed and supplied with values.

The anonymous hash realizes everything that makes the object: a namespace for instance variables and the class relationship. The latter is created by the `bless` function, which marks the hash as belonging to the class `Myclass`. Since `bless` at the same time returns the reference of the 'blessed' hash and furthermore is the last function of the constructor, new returns the hash reference to the calling main program – which subsequently interprets it as the 'object reference.'

In the main program,

```
use Myclass;

$objref = Myclass->new();
```

triggers the constructor call. After use Myclass has found and initialized the Myclass package, Myclass->new() activates the subroutine new, which, as specified above, returns the 'blessed' reference of the anonymous hash (the object reference).

2.2.3 Methods

The object reference not only has access to instance variables, but also has the class relationship, which allows calling of methods. Thus a subsequent call of

```
$objref->method1();
```

activates the method method1 in the Myclass package.

What does the implementation of a typical method of the Myclass class look like? This will be illustrated by an example, which defines a method check that checks the state of a (not yet defined) instance variable named running. For an undefined value and in the case of running == 0, check should return the value 0, in all other cases 1. The call

```
$ret = $objref->check();
```

in the main program activates the method check from the Myclass package and at the same time ensures that check receives the reference $objref as its first function parameter.

The method check itself fetches the object reference from the parameter list and can thus operate on instance data:

```
sub check {
    my $self = shift;

    exists($self->{'running'}) &&      # existence
        $self->{'running'};            # != 0
}
```

Thus the local variable $self is assigned the reference of the anonymous hash, which makes the hash data accessible via

```
$value = ${$self}{'key'}
```

or alternatively

```
$value = $self->{'key'}
```

(see Section 1.5.5). With this, $self corresponds more or less to the this keyword in Java, which is available in methods as a reference to the current object. In Perl, however, the $self initialization is not carried out by a compiler; instead, at the beginning of each method, the programmer explicitly assigns the variable $self the object reference passed via the parameter list.

Thus $self->{'running'} accesses the anonymous hash and fetches the value belonging to the *key* running. At the object level, this means interrogating the instance variable running of the current object.

2.3 A first example

Now is the time to tackle the first object-oriented sample application. The Process class defined below models UNIX processes.[2] Instantiated process objects behave in the same way as their real counterparts: they have methods for starting a process, interrogate its state, and terminate it. This abstraction can even be used to check processes that have already terminated their activity – their encapsulation objects outlive them.

Process objects model either shell processes or Perl subroutines. A shell process is started by a scalar, which contains the corresponding shell command line as a string, whereas a reference to a subroutine causes this subroutine to be started as a background process.

Listing process.pl shows a test sample of a sleep process. The constructor call creates a new process object, which subsequently calls the method start with the string "sleep 10" as parameter. At intervals of 1 second, the loop checks the process status; after the third cycle, the kill method prematurely terminates the process.

_____*process.pl*

```
#!/usr/bin/perl -w

use Process;

$myproc = Process->new();        # create new process object
$myproc->start("sleep 10") ||    # start sleep process
    die "Start: Error";          # error?
```

---

[2] Windows users should understand the following pages more as an introduction to object-oriented programming than as a practical example. To start external programs under Windows, the Win32::Process module is available (see page 93).

```
for($i=1; $i<=5; $i++) {          # periodically interrogate process
    if($myproc->poll()) {         # status
        print "Running\n";        # process active
    } else {
        print "Not running\n";    # process terminated
    }

    if($i==3) {                   # in the third cycle ...
        $myproc->kill() ||        # terminate process
            die "Kill: Error";
    }

    sleep(1);                     # sleep until next round
}
```

————————————————————————————————process.pl

Accordingly, the output of process.pl is

```
Running
Running
Running
Not running
Not running
```

The module Process.pm, included by process.pl at the beginning by means of the use Process; construct, represents a typical class implementation that, besides the new constructor, defines the methods start, poll, and kill.

————————————————————————————————Process.pm

```
package Process;

###################################################################
# $proc_obj=Process->new();          constructor
###################################################################
sub new {
  bless {};
}

###################################################################
# $ret = $proc_obj->start("prg");    start shell process in background
# $ret = $proc_obj->start(\&func);   start function in background
###################################################################
```

```perl
sub start {
  my ($self, $func) = @_;

  $SIG{'CHLD'} = sub { wait };          # prevent zombies

  $self->{'pid'} = fork();             # create subprocess
                                       # with fork
  if(!defined $self->{'pid'}) {
     return 0;                          # fork error
  } elsif($self->{'pid'} == 0) {        # child process:
     if(ref($func) eq "CODE") {
        &$func; exit 0;                 #   start subroutine
     } else {
        exec "$func";                   # start shell process
     }
  } else {                              # parent process:
     return 1;                          #   return OK
  }
}


#####################################################################
# $ret = $proc_obj->poll();          interrogate process status:
#                                     1="running" 0="not running"
#####################################################################
sub poll {
  my $self = shift;

  exists $self->{'pid'} &&             # pid initialized and
    kill(0, $self->{'pid'});           # ... process reacts
}


#####################################################################
# $ret = $proc_obj->kill([SIGXXX]);  send signal to process,
#                                     default parameter: SIGTERM
#####################################################################
sub kill {
  my ($self, $sig) = @_;

  $sig = 'SIGTERM' unless defined $sig; # if no parameter spec-
                                        # ified => SIGTERM signal

  return 0 if !exists $self->{'pid'};   # process initialized?

  kill($sig, $self->{'pid'}) || return 0; # send signal
```

HGT: WGT: BSA: 0:00

ALLERGIES/ADR'S: — *Toradol, Amoxicillin, PCN, Zithromax, PCN, Cephalosporins*

DIAGNOSIS : Abscess   - ABCESS

HOME MEDICATIONS:	DOSE	ROUTE	FREQUENCY	Continue on Admission	
TRILEPTIL	300MG	PO	TID (three times a d	Y	N
ZYPREXA	7.5 mg.	PO	hs	Y	N
VALIUM	10MG	PO	BID (two times a day	Y	N
~~CELEXA~~ *Lexapro* 10 ~~20~~ mg.		PO	~~AM~~ *B.I.D*	Y	N
TRAMADOL	100 MG	PO	TID (three times a d	Y	N
PRILOSEC	40MG	PO	BID (two times a day	Y	N
DEPAKOTE ER	500 MG.	PO	AM	Y	N
DEPAKOTE ER	1000MG	P.O.	Bedtime	Y	N

FOR NEW MEDICATIONS - PLEASE USE ADMISSION ORDER SHEET

Additional Comments:

Medication List Source: Pt/family recall   Medications verified by: ER.BAR.

```
    delete $self->{'pid'};              # delete process variable

     1;                                 # OK
}

1;
```

The implementation of the process class uses only one instance variable: the `start` method stores the number of the started process in the instance variable `pid`, so it is subsequently available to the methods `poll` and `kill`. Since the constructor does not carry out any initialization of instance variables, `pid` remains undefined until the start of the first process, which is in turn used by the methods `kill` and `poll` as information on whether a process has been active. The function

`exists($hashname{'key'})`

notoriously yields 1 if for a given *key* a *value* exists in the hash, whereas

`delete($hashname{'key'})`

breaks up the *key-value* relation, but lets the hash itself continue to exist.

The rest is UNIX: the `start` method uses the `fork` system call to create a child process. Depending on whether `start` finds a subroutine reference or a scalar as its first parameter, it starts a Perl function or a shell process whose command line is contained in the scalar.

While `exec` starts a shell that executes the given command, but never returns again into the flow of the calling program and terminates instead, the call of a specified Perl subroutine must be followed by an explicit `exit 0` command, because otherwise the child process follows the footsteps of the parent process and eventually gets into its way.

Another feature worth mentioning is the signal handler, which prevents the creation of zombies. *Zombies* are terminated child processes that have not yet been redeemed by their parent processes with a `wait` command, and are therefore condemned to roam around in the system in eternity.

In the example, the `SIGCHLD` signal that, as a parent process, receives news of the death of a terminating child process triggers a `wait` command in the signal handler which 'reaps a zombie.'

The `poll` mechanism is based on the fact that it is possible to send a running process the signal bearing the number 0 without error. If this action fails, the process no longer exists. The `kill` method, instead, sends the child process a specified signal or, if no parameter has been set, the `SIGTERM` signal (the default signal that is usually sent to a process by the `kill` command).

2.4 Object-oriented programming in detail

The first object-oriented steps with Perl 5 will now be followed by a more detailed discussion of its object-oriented features.

2.4.1 Package definition

To instantiate an object, the definition of the corresponding class must be known. The use Myclass construct causes the Perl interpreter to search all include paths for a file named Myclass.pm and to load the specified package definition from the module (see also Section 1.5.4).

It is important that the included file returns a 'true' value; otherwise the use Myclass instruction fails.

In addition, there is the possibility to store class definition and script in the same file:

```
package Myclass;

sub new {                    # constructor
    bless{};
}

...                          # further methods

package main;

$obj = Myclass->new();  # object instantiation

...
```

In contrast to the inclusion with use Myclass (which requires that the included file returns a value not equal to undef, 0, or the empty string), the concluding 1; may be omitted in the above construct.

2.4.2 Static and virtual methods

Perl differentiates between so-called static and virtual methods. Constructors are static by nature: since at their call no object reference is known, because they have to generate it first, they are specified by the package name. The instructions

```
$objref = Mypackage->new();
```

and

```
$objref = new Mypackage;
```

are equivalent, and call the subroutine `new` in the package `Mypackage`, passing it the name `"Mypackage"` as the first parameter. This information is used by several kinds of constructors (see below).

Subsequently, the object reference returned by the constructor can be used, by means of

```
$objref->method();
```

to access the so-called virtual methods. In contrast to static methods, these virtual methods do not expect a package name, but an object reference – which is what they are implicitly being supplied with by the above call.

2.4.3 Constructors

The short form

```
sub new {
    bless {};
}
```

used up to now does not in all cases provide the required functionality, because the `bless` instruction in the example binds the anonymous hash to the package that defines the constructor. The long form

```
sub new {
    my $class = shift;        # receive package name
    my $self = {};            # creat anonymous name hash
    bless($self, $class);     # bless
}
```

instead uses the extended signature of the `bless` instruction to bind the hash to the package whose name is by default available to the constructor, as a static method, as a first parameter. The long form is, in particular, used in class inheritance – and since you never know whether some day someone will want to inherit something from the class, experienced Perl programmers recommend using the long form in any case (see Section 2.4.6).

The constructor is the right point for initialization of instance variables too. After definition of the name hash,[3] assignments can be carried out. The important thing is that in the end, the constructor really returns the reference of the 'blessed' hash:

---

[3] Just to avoid creating the wrong impression: the hash as a storage medium for the instance variables of an object is not mandatory at all. It is merely *one* of several possible implementations.

```
sub new {
    my $class = shift;
    my $self = {};

    $self->{'varname'} = 42;       # initialization
                                   # of an instance variable

    bless($self, $class);          # bless and return
}
```

2.4.4 Destructors

The reference mechanism in Perl 5 automatically destroys instances that are no longer needed: that is, whose reference counter has reached zero. An object reference $objref provided by the constructor (and together with it, the object itself or the name hash) disappears only after an explicit

```
undef $objref;
```

or at the end of the validity range of $objref, provided no further references to the object exist.

If, however, additional cleaning-up operations for a class are needed, nothing can be said against implementing a destructor that should seemly be named

```
sub delete {
    ...
}
```

and be called explicitly with

```
$objref->delete();
```

before the object loses its validity. Shortly before the automatic destruction, which commences as soon as the last reference to an object disappears, the interpreter searches the package for a method named DESTROY and, if found, executes it. It is passed the last remaining object reference as its sole argument: that is, in the same way as all other methods, it can accept the reference to the name hash via the stack. Thus necessary last-minute actions before the *automatic* garbage collection find their appropriate place in the DESTROY method of a class defined for this purpose.

2.4.5 Instance variables

Access to instance variables is carried out via the object reference that each method is automatically passed as its first parameter. The instruction

```
$self->{'varname'}
```

returns the scalar value of the instance variable `varname` via the hash entry with the *key* `varname`. However, objects often consist of more complex data types and define in turn further arrays, hashes, or references to additional objects.

Since a hash value can accommodate either a scalar or a reference, the name hash may also contain references to further Perl types. If the instance variable `myarray` is to hold a Perl array,

```
$self->{'myarray'}
```

denotes an array reference that, by means of the dereferencing operator `@{...}`, changes into an array. This notation allows all possible array operations:

```
@{$self->{'myarray'}} = ("item1", "item2");   # assignment

push(@{$self->{'myarray'}}, "item3");          # push
pop(@{$self->{'myarray'}});                    # pop

$self->{'myarray'}->[1];                        # 2nd element
$self->{'myarray'}[1];                          # 2nd element
```

Similarly, instance variables can accommodate references to hashes or subroutines.

References to other objects are hash references and can be treated as such. In case of difficulties with the somewhat unusual dereferencing notation, please consult Section 1.5.5.

2.4.6 Inheritance

Inheritance is one way of creating relationships between concepts. Classes represent concepts: if it can be asserted that a class `Derivedclass` is 'a kind' of a class `Baseclass`, much can be said for having `Derivedclass` inherit the properties of `Baseclass`.

A car is 'a kind' of vehicle. Thus the derived class car can inherit a range of properties from its base class vehicle. For example, a car has the property, as do other vehicles, of being able to move. In addition, a car provides functionalities that clearly differentiate it from other vehicles: thus it can transport several seated persons, which is usually not possible with a bicycle, another class derived from the vehicle class.

The advantages of this procedure are obvious: not all classes must be implemented from scratch; instead, it is sufficient to take over a known concept and define additionally required functionalities. To activate this mechanism in Perl – as usual – some manual work is needed.

A package obtains the license to execute foreign methods via an entry in the package's own `@ISA` array.

The name of this array is intended to symbolize the inheritance-typical 'is a' relationship between classes, in the sense of 'is a' or 'is a kind of.' If an object does not find a method in its own package, it begins to search all packages contained in `@ISA`. This corresponds to a *depth-first* search in the class hierarchy: each checked

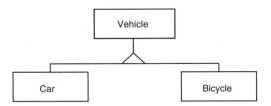

Figure 2.1   Inheritance.

package may in turn define an @ISA array and in this way utilize methods of other packages.

Thus an object can access not only its own methods, but also those of all packages from which its own class is directly or indirectly derived. This is carried out in a completely transparent fashion, without an indication in which package the sought method is finally located. Thus

```
package Deripac;
@ISA = ("Basepac1", "Basepac2");
```

specifies that the current package inherits the functionalities of Basepac1 and Basepac2.

In Java or C++, the compiler secretly inserts code into the constructors to make a generated object of a derived class call the constructor of its base class. In Perl, instead, the constructor is a method like any other. If the constructor of the base class needs to be called for the creation of a derived object, the implementation must explicitly guarantee this.

Usually, the constructor of a derived class simply calls the constructor of the base class. If the derived class does not need to initialize additional data, there is, however, a more elegant solution: the base class simply makes the derived class inherit its constructor.

Listing inhCon.pl shows inheritance of a constructor: the base class Basepac contains the constructor new; the derived class Deripac defines only one additional method derimethod.

inhCon.pl

```
#!/usr/bin/perl -w

#####################################################################
# Base class
#####################################################################
package Basepac;

sub new {                       # base class constructor
```

```perl
    my $type = shift;
    my $self = {};
    bless $self, $type;
}

sub basemethod {           # base class method
    print "method: basemethod\n";
}


#####################################################################
# Derived class
#####################################################################
package Deripac;

@ISA = qw ( Basepac );     # inherits from Basepac

sub derimethod {           # method of the derived class
    print "method: derimethod\n";
}


#####################################################################
# Main program
#####################################################################
package main;

$derobj = Deripac->new();  # initiate object of
                           # the derived class

$derobj->derimethod();     # own method
$derobj->basemethod();     # inherited method
```

inhCon.pl

If `main` now uses `Deripac->new()` to call the constructor of the class `Deripac`, Perl simply resorts to the `new` function of the base class, because this method does not exist in `Deripac`.

To make the resulting object belong to the class `Deripac`, and not to `Basepac`, the constructor must satisfy the requirements of inheritability. The short form

```perl
sub new {
    bless {};
}
```

used in Section 2.4.1 is no longer sufficient, because a `bless` of the anonymous hash on the current package `Basepac` would generate an object of class `Basepac` instead of a `Deripac` object. In contrast, the long form introduced in Section 2.4.3.

```perl
sub new {
    my $class = shift;
    my $self = {};
    bless $self, $class;
}
```

simply evaluates the class name passed by default, and binds the anonymous name hash to the correct class. What finally counts is which package has originally initiated the constructor call, and *not* in which package the constructor *is located*.

If, instead, both the derived and the base class must initialize their own variables, the derived class has no other choice than to explicitly call the contructor of the base class in its own constructor.

This is precisely what is realized by Listing inherit.pl. The constructor new of the class Deripac contains the instruction Basepac->new(), which creates the name hash of Basepac. Then, Deripac assigns the returned value to its own $self variable and uses it as if it were the reference to its own name hash.

This procedure automates overloading of variables of the base class from the part of the derived class, because both share one namespace.

inherit.pl

```perl
#!/usr/bin/perl -w

#####################################################################
package Basepac;                # base class

sub new {                       # constructor
  my $class = shift;
  my $self = {};

  $self->{'basevar'} = 'BASE';  # initialize base class variable
  bless $self, $class;
}

#####################################################################
package Deripac;                # derived class

@ISA = qw ( Basepac );          # inheritance

sub new {                       # constructor
  my $class = shift;
  my $self = Basepac->new();

  $self->{'derivar'} = 'DERI';  # initialize variable of the
                                # derived class
```

```
    bless $self, $class;
}

sub derimethod {              # output local variables and variables
my $self = shift;             # inherited in the derived class

    print "basevar=", $self->{'basevar'}, " ",
          "derivar=", $self->{'derivar'}, "\n";
}


###################################################################
package main;                 # main program

$derobj = Deripac->new();      # create object
$derobj->derimethod();         # output variables
```

_____*inherit.pl*

Back once more to inheritance of methods: in Listing inhCon.pl on page 124, the instruction $derobj->basemethod() triggers a search for methods. Beginning with the class $derobj belongs to, Perl attempts to find, *depth-first*, the next reachable method in the class hierarchy bearing the name basemethod.

Overloading of functions in a derived class, a typical feature of object-oriented programming, is thus possible at any time – provided a method of the same name is defined at a location where the search algorithm finds it first in the class hierarchy. Thus the method defined in the current class has precedence over all others.

The question of inheriting is solved – that of 'letting inherit' remains. While in C++ and Java there are rules about which part of a class is visible and to whom (via entries in the sections public and protected), Perl gives the programmer carte blanche: it is just not a 'totalitarian' language, as the manual pages so nicely state. All you need is a bit of common sense.

Theoretically, nothing is to be said against having a class inherit from several base classes. At least for the methods, this is not a problem, because it is sufficient to include the names of the involved packages in the @ISA array.

However, this is only one side of the coin: if the constructors of the base classes initialize data, the namespaces of all inherited classes must be merged. In the trivial case, where the packages use only a number of scalars as instance variables, multiple inheritance as shown in Listing inhMult.pl can be implemented. Here, the constructor of the derived class calls the constructors of the base classes one after the other and copies their scalar instance variables to the own name hash.

```perl
#!/usr/bin/perl -w

########################################################################
package Basepac1;                      # first base class

sub new {                              # constructor
  my $type = shift;
  my $self = {};
                                       # initialize base
  $self->{'b1'} = "b1";                # class 1 variable

  bless $self, $type;
}


########################################################################
package Basepac2;                      # second base class

sub new {                              # constructor
  my $type = shift;
  my $self = {};

  $self->{'b2'} = "b2";                # initialize base
                                       # class 2 variable
  bless $self, $type;
}


########################################################################
package Deripac;                       # derived class

@ISA = qw ( Basepac1 Basepac2 );       # multiple inheritance

sub new {                              # constructor
  my $type = shift;
  my $self = {};

  my ($pac, $key);

  foreach $pac (@ISA) {                # for all base classes ...
    my $hashref = $pac->new();         # call constructor

    foreach $key (keys %$hashref) {    # merge inherited
        $self->{$key} = $hashref->{$key}; # variables into the
    }                                  # local namespace
  }
```

```
    bless $self, $type;
}

sub derimethod {                              # output variables
  my $self = shift;

  my $key;

  foreach $key (keys %{$self}) {
      print "\$self->{'$key'}=", "$self->{$key}\n";
  }
}


##################################################################
package main;                                 # main program

$derobj = Deripac->new();                     # call constructor
$derobj->derimethod();                        # output inherited variables
```

inhMult.pl

However, since a class can not only define scalar variables, but also use its name hash to store references to new hashes and arrays or even foreign objects, this example is suited only for simple cases. In fact, in the case of more deeply nested structures, the script does not create a 'deep' copy of the data structure, but copies only the references of the highest level. An additional problem is constituted by double and circular references. A complete solution of the problem requires a recursive analysis of the name hash. A routine must follow the references down to an arbitrary depth of nesting and roam through all arrays and hashes found. Section 2.5 shows an application that implements this procedure.

The method of multiple inheritance must, however, be handled with great care: lack of attention in the class design very quickly leads to chaos, and inheritance conflicts require manual correction. Frequently, models that require multiple inheritance are only a tardy consequence of a wrong design.

Inheritance is, without doubt, the most popular class relationship. Frequently, however, designers caught up in their specialization euphoria overlook the fact that a relationship between two classes does not meet any inheritance-specific requirements. Just because a car and a wheel belong together in some way or the other, one must not crank up the inheritance machinery. A wheel is definitely not 'a kind of' car.

But even if arguments can be found in favor of inheritance, its use must not necessarily be the last resort. Frequently, a modeling problem can be more suitably solved by means of one of the following class relationships.

2.4.7 **Aggregation**

The 'has a' or 'whole-part' relation specifies that one class is a part of another class. Thus the date is a part of a letter, a scroll bar is a part of a window, and the address is a 'part' of a company. 1-to-1, 1-to-N, or M-to-N relations are all possible.

Figure 2.2   Aggregation.

Listing `aggregation.pl` shows an example. A car has four wheels. Therefore the instantiation of a new car is accompanied by the creation of four wheel objects in the car constructor.

aggregation.pl

```perl
#!/usr/bin/perl -w

####################################################################
package Wheel;                    # wheel class

sub new {                        # new wheel
    my $class = shift;
    my $self = {};
                                 # production number 1 ... n
    $self->{'serial'} = defined $serial ?
                        ++$serial : ($serial=1);

    bless $self, $class;
}

sub movewheel {                  # move wheel
    my $self = shift;

    print "Wheel $self->{'serial'}: is moving!\n";
}


####################################################################
package Car;                      # car class

sub new {                        # new car
    my $class = shift;
    my $self = {};
```

```
    foreach $i (1..4) {          # 4 wheels per car
        push(@{$self->{"Wheels"}}, Wheel->new());
    }

    bless $self, $class;
}

sub movecar {                    # move car
    my $self = shift;

                                 # move wheels
    foreach $i (@{$self->{"Wheels"}}) {
        $i->movewheel();
    }
}


###################################################################
package main;                     # main program

$car = Car->new();
$car->movecar();
```

_____*aggregation.pl*

The constructor of the car class stores in the instance variable Wheels a reference to an array that in turn contains references to the individual wheels. For each of the four required wheels, the car constructor calls the wheel constructor. The instantiated wheel objects carry nothing but a running serial number in the instance variable $self->{'serial'}.

The method movecar of the car class forwards the given driving task to the movewheel methods of the wheels aggregated in the car object. After dereferencing, the instance variable Wheels results in a list of references to wheel objects that is cycled through with a foreach instruction. The call of the movewheel method makes the wheels move one after the other. Thus the output of aggregation.pl is

```
Wheel 1: is moving!
Wheel 2: is moving!
Wheel 3: is moving!
Wheel 4: is moving!
```

Typically for an aggregation, the aggregating class Car takes the responsibility for objects of the aggregated class Wheel. The car constructor has four wheels made and stores the references in the name hash of the object. If the car object loses its validity, the wheel references are lost as well, and Perl lets the wheel objects vanish surreptitiously.

2.4.8 **Association**

The association describes a loose relationship between two classes. One class 'knows' the other, without aggregating it into itself.

A car is parked in a garage. Here, each car object is accompanied by the information on which garage it is currently parked in.

Figure 2.3   Association.

The association car → garage implements an instance variable `garage`, which is available for each car object and stores a reference to the associated garage object. Thus the car object 'knows' in which garage it is parked. Since in the sense of data encapsulation the instance variable `garage` is not accessible outside the car object, it is updated by the `setgarage` method with a garage reference as parameter. The implementation of the `setgarage` method fetches the reference to the `garage` object from the stack by means of a second `shift` instruction after the setting of `$self` and updates the instance variable `garage`.

garage.pl

```perl
#!/usr/bin/perl -w

####################################################################
package Garage;                    # garage class

sub new {
    bless {};
}

####################################################################
package Car;                       # Car class

sub new {
    bless {};
}

sub setgarage {                    # associate garage
    my $self = shift;

    $self->{'garage'} = shift;
}
```

```
####################################################################
package main;                    # main program

$garage = Garage->new();
$car    = Car->new();

$car->setgarage($garage);
```

garage.pl

The loose associative linkage of two classes also expresses the fact that there is next to no responsibility involved between the two counterparts. Thus a garage object exists completely independently from the cars that are parked in it. In the same way, a car can live without a garage. This is taken into account in the implementation by the fact that it is not the car constructor that creates the garage, but that both objects come to light in the main program independently from each other. If, as with aggregation, the reference to a garage object could be accessed only via the car object, the garage would be victim of the garbage collector in the event of the destruction of the car. But in this way both partner objects live a united and nevertheless independent life.

2.4.9 Using relationship

If there is a using relationship between two classes, one class uses the services offered by the other class for its own purposes.

A driver uses the services of a car to drive around.

Figure 2.4 Using.

A driver object supports the method `drive`, which moves a selected car. Typical for a using relationship, the reference of the used object (the car) appears in the method call parameter list of the using object (the driver):

```
$driverref->drive($carref);
```

In this simple example, the `drive` method merely implements the call of the `movecar` method of the car object used:

```
sub drive {
    my $self   = shift;
    my $carref = shift;

    $carref->movecar();
}
```

2.5 Persistence by inheritance

Inheritance of persistence methods is common in software development involving object-oriented databases to provide an interface between the object-oriented programming languages and the database.

Classes that not only need their data during a running program, but also require to have this data available after program termination and after a successful restart, employ persistence methods. Thus objects are stored not only in a transient medium such as RAM, but also on demand on persistent media such as hard disks.

Classes with persistent data inherit the methods `store` and `load` from a persistence class. `store` roams through the data of an object and stores the items one after the other in a database or a file. Similarly, a call of `load` causes initialization of an object with persistently stored data.

2.5.1 Implementation

Listing `Persistent.pm` on page 137 shows a persistence class whose methods are inherited by derived classes and used for their object data. This simple implementation does not address a database, but merely stores the instance variables in a 'flat' file.

An object of application class `Myclass`, which inherits from the class `Persistent`, can store its data in `filename` via the inheritance mechanism by calling

```
$objref->store("filename");
```

or restore the data with

```
$objref->load("filename");
```

Listing `persistent.pl` shows the corresponding test sample. The inherited routines `store` and `load` make use of the object's name hash to store or load the data. For this purpose, they must delve into arbitrary nesting depths of the data structure if the instance variables of the object are in turn references to further hashes, arrays, or other objects.

persistent.pl

```
#!/usr/bin/perl
```

```perl
######################################################################
  package PersTest;            # sample class that inherits
                               # persistent properties
######################################################################
use Persistent;

@ISA = qw ( Persistent );      # inherits from "Persistent.pm"

sub new {                      # constructor
    my $type = shift;
    my $self = {};
    bless $self, $type;
}

sub initdata {                 # initialize data
    my $self = shift;

    $self->{'the_hash'}   = \%the_hash;
    $self->{'the_array'}  = \@the_array;
    $self->{'the_scalar'} =
      "This scalar contains a very " .
      "long value with some special chars: " .
      " @,\$,\\,\",'.";
    $the_hash{'hash_key'} = 'hash_value';
    $the_array[1]         = 'array_value';

                                 # create new object as part
                                 # of the persistent object
    my $objref = PersTest->new();
    $objref->{'myobjvar'} = 'myobjvarval';
    $self->{'the_object'} = $objref;
}


######################################################################
  package main;                # main program
######################################################################

$obj1 = PersTest->new();       # create,
$obj1->initdata();             # initialize, and
$obj1->store("myobj.sav") ||   # store
    print "Cannot save\n";     # persistent object


$obj2 = PersTest->new();       # create new persistent
```

```
                              # object ... and
$obj2->load("myobj.sav") ||  # initialize it with the
    print "Cannot load\n";    # stored data of obj1

                              # ouput object data
print
  "\$obj2->{'the_object'}->{'myobjvar'} = ",
  "$obj2->{'the_object'}->{'myobjvar'}\n";
print
  "\$obj2->{'the_array'}->[1]             = ",
  "$obj2->{'the_array'}->[1]\n";
print
  "\$obj2->{'the_hash'}->{'hash_key'}   = ",
  "$obj2->{'the_hash'}->{'hash_key'}\n";
print
  "\$obj2->{'the_scalar'}               = ",
  "$obj2->{'the_scalar'}\n";
```

_____*persistent.pl*

First, `persistent.pl` creates an object of class `PersTest` and carries out the initializations contained in the function `init_data`, which gives rise to several instance variables, a hash, an array, a scalar containing special characters, and finally, for test purposes, another object of class `PersTest`. All of these values are stored in the file `myobj.sav` by `store()`, the persistency method inherited from `Persistent.pm`. The subsequently created, still uninitialized object `$obj2` loads the multiply nested values from disk with a simple `load()` call, and shows with the following `print` calls that it is in no way inferior to `$obj1`.

Listing `Persistent.pm` shows the implementation of the class `Persistent`, which through the methods `store()` and `load()` breathes eternal life into arbitrary objects in such an elegant manner. The `store` method analyzes the object data and stores

```
$self->{the_hash} = { 'hash_key' => 'hash_value' };

$self->{the_scalar} = 'This scalar contains a very long value \
with some special chars:  @,$,\\,",\'.';

$self->{the_object} = bless( { 'myobjvar' => 'myobjvarval'
                          }, 'PersTest' );

$self->{the_array} = [ undef, 'array_value' ];
```

in the file `myobj.sav`. Conversely, the method `load()` reads this Perl code, evaluates it with `eval`, and thus fills all of the instance variables with life.

Thanks to the `Data::Dumper` module by Gurusamy Sarathy (for installation of this module, see Appendix A.4), the difficult part, namely the analysis of the potentially deeply nested instance data of an object, becomes child's play. The constructor `new` accepts two array references: the first one points to an array of variables to be analyzed, the second one to an array of names under which `Data::Dumper` will finally create them. The call of the `Purify` method with a true value makes `Data::Dumper` handle circular references correctly. The `Dump` method of a `Dumper` object finally returns a string that contains Perl code to recreate the analyzed variable again.

One after the other, the `store` method fetches all keys from the instance variable hash of the current object and lets the `Data::Dumper` store the unrolled values in the format

```
$self->{key} = code for creation;
```

in the safeguarding file.

A problem is constituted by references to subroutines: they can be neither reasonably analyzed nor stored. If the `Data::Dumper` detects one of these, it outputs a warning and creates a dummy reference.

Persistent.pm

```
####################################################################
   package Persistent;
####################################################################

use Data::Dumper;                        # utility for data analysis

####################################################################
# $objref->store("filename")     # store object persistently in file
####################################################################
sub store {
    my ($self, $filename) = @_;

    open(FILE, ">$filename") || return 0;  # open file

    while (($key, $val) = each %$self) {   # entries in instance hash

        $d = Data::Dumper->new([$val], ["self->{$key}"]);
        $d->Purity(1);                     # circular references
        print FILE $d->Dump();             # output
    }

    close(FILE);                           # close file
    1;
}
```

```
#####################################################################
# $objref->load("filename")                  # load object
#####################################################################
sub load {
    my ($self, $filename) = @_;

    %$self = ();                             # empty out object
    open(FILE, "<$filename") || return 0;    # open file
    $data = join('', <FILE>);                # read all lines
    eval $data;                              # ... and evaluate them
    close(FILE);                             # close file
    1;
}

1;
```

Persistent.pm

2.5.2 Example

A practical application of the Persistent class is shown in Listing fortune.pl. This script contains a list of proverbs, one of which is at random displayed at each call. The list reduces itself persistently with each call of fortune.pl, so that each proverb appears exactly once, until all available proverbs have been processed. After the last proverb, the script reinitializes itself, and the cycle begins again from the start.

The information on which proverbs are still present in the list is stored by an object of the persistent class Fortune. Fortune inherits from the base class Persistent, and thus disposes of the methods store and load.

With each call, fortune.pl initializes an object of the Fortune class, uses the persistence method load to load its data from the file fortune.data, and selects an arbitrary proverb with the method getany. At the same time, getany removes the proverb from the list to be processed, which is internally managed by the fortune object.

In the event that no persistence data have actually been stored, or the list of proverbs has been completely processed, fortune.pl reinitializes the persistent object. The add method appends a number of proverbs to the object-internal list, which can be accessed via the instance variable aphorisms, which is a list reference.

Shortly before termination of the script, the transient object data is transferred by means of the store method into the persistence file fortune.data, to be available again at a new start of the script.

fortune.pl

```
#!/usr/bin/perl
```

```perl
######################################################################
   package Fortune;                 # persistent class
######################################################################

use Persistent;
@ISA = qw(Persistent);             # inheritance

######################################################################
sub new {                          # constructor
######################################################################
    my $class = shift;
    my $self = {};
    bless($self, $class);

    $self->{'aphorisms'} = [];  # reference to empty
                                # fortune list
    return $self;
}


######################################################################
sub getany {                       # fetch fortune
######################################################################
    my $self = shift;
                                        # random list index
    my $index = rand() * ($#{$self->{'aphorisms'}} + 1);
                                        # extract element
    splice(@{$self->{'aphorisms'}}, $index, 1);
}


######################################################################
sub add {                          # add fortune
######################################################################
    my $self = shift;
                                        # append list to list
    push(@{$self->{'aphorisms'}}, @_);
}


######################################################################
   package main;                   # main program
######################################################################

srand(time);                       # initialize random generator
                                   # (no longer needed since perl 5.004)
my $datafile = "fortune.data"; # file for
```

```
                                    # persistent data
my $text;

my $fortune = Fortune->new();   # create persistent object

if(! $fortune->load($datafile) ||    # load data from file
   ! ($text = $fortune->getany())) { # all fortunes used ?

   $fortune->add(                 # reinitialization
    "The trouble with troubleshooting is that the trouble shoots back",
    "If something can go wrong, it will go wrong",
    "Long live Fortran!",
    "True programmers do not fear GOTOs");

   $text = $fortune->getany();  # fetch fortune
}

print "$text\n";                 # output fortune

$fortune->store("$datafile");   # store modified object
```
_____*fortune.pl*

2.6 Hints and tricks

The following subsections explain some strategies that may be helpful for the use of extended object-oriented functionalities.

2.6.1 The SUPER class

Frequently, it happens that an existing class library only partially provides a required functionality. Modifying its freely available source code is in the main possible, but seldom advisable, because possible updates for bug fixes can no longer be integrated in the application.

A better way is to create a separate class that inherits methods from the library, but redefines them under the same name. These will then implement the required functionality but, where necessary, branch to the functions of the class library (for a different procedure, see Section 2.6.2).

Here we have the problem of persuading the interpreter to call the method `method` of the class library from a method `method` of the new class. Thus `method()` would result in a call of the `method` method of the current class, while *LibClass-Name*`::method()` would completely specify the name of the class library routine. However, if at some point an additional software layer were introduced between library and application, all method calls of the application would need to be amended.

This dilemma is resolved by the pseudo class SUPER.

```
$objref->SUPER::method();   # method() of the base class of $objref
```

calls the method method that appears in the first reachable base class above the class to which $objref belongs. The constructor of the first reachable base class above MyClass is instead reached by

```
MyClass->SUPER::new();      # new() of the base class of Classname
```

Large software packages such as the Perl/Tk package make frequent use of this feature.

Listing super.pl shows an example in which a derived class redefines a method of the base class, but nevertheless uses its functionality. The SUPER construct guarantees the derived class Derived independence from the base class: through its use, the name Base no longer appears – with the exception of the inheritance definition – anywhere in the code of Derived.

super.pl

```
#!/usr/bin/perl -w

####################################################################
package Base;             # base class

sub basemethod { print "Method of the base class\n"; }

####################################################################
package Derived;          # derived class

@ISA = qw(Base);         # inherits from 'Base'

sub new {                # constructor
    my $class = shift;
    bless {}, $class;
}

sub basemethod {         # redefines 'basemethod' of 'Base',
    my $self = shift;    # but uses its functionality

                         # method call in 'Base'
    $self->SUPER::basemethod();

                         # ... additional functionality ...
    print "Method of the derived class\n";
}
```

```
###################################################################
package main;              # main program

$dobj = Derived->new();    # create object

$dobj->basemethod();       # ...uses derived and base class
```

super.pl

2.6.2 Delegation with AUTOLOAD

A class that partly wants to use a functionality already present in a foreign class and partly wants to override it may also employ the feature of *autoloading* instead of the procedure decribed above.

However, without the inheritance propagated there, only explicitly programmed methods are available. The call of other methods inevitably leads to a runtime error – unless the class provides a method with the special name AUTOLOAD.

The AUTOLOAD method represents a central class function whose task is to intercept and forward all non-satisfiable method requests. If the interpreter finds a requested method neither in the class of an object nor in the base classes of any hierarchy level, it activates the AUTOLOAD method and sets the global variable $AUTOLOAD to the name of the required method. AUTOLOAD starts with the same arguments that were originally supplied to the nonfound method. The definition

```
sub AUTOLOAD {
    print "Method $AUTOLOAD not yet implemented\n";
    print "Arguments were: @_\n";
}
```

in a class intercepts a runtime error for calls of not yet implemented methods.

The AUTOLOAD mechanism can also be used to delegate functions to other modules. Provided it is known that the method exists in another class (and if not, the foreign class can in turn implement an AUTOLOAD deviation), AUTOLOAD simply deviates the call including all parameters to that method.

```
sub AUTOLOAD {

    $AUTOLOAD =~ s/.*:://;     # remove original
                               # package name

                               # assemble new function
                               # name and call it
    &{"Otherclass::" . $AUTOLOAD}(@_);
}
```

The sample code first removes the old package name from the contents of the variable $AUTOLOAD, and subsequently assembles the new, 'fully qualified' name via a simple string operation. The &{...} operator then turns the string into a callable function.

If the branched method was originally called with the syntax

```
$objref->method()
```

the parameter list contains the reference to the object that initiated the call as its first argument. If this is not the desired behavior, AUTOLOAD must remove the erroneous object reference from the argument list and conjure the correct one out of an instance variable:

```perl
sub AUTOLOAD {
    my $self = shift;         # remove incorrect object reference

    $AUTOLOAD =~ s/.*:://;    # remove original
                              # package name

                              # call method in foreign module
                              # with $self->{'delegate'}
                              # as object reference
    $self->{'delegate'}->$AUTOLOAD(@_);
}
```

With a call of the foreign class constructor, $self->{'delegate'} was set to a valid object reference in the constructor of the delegating class. The sample shown in Listing autoload.pl illustrates this procedure.

_____*autoload.pl*

```perl
#!/usr/bin/perl -w

###################################################################
package Otherclass;          # class to which the Delegate
                             # class delegates methods

sub new {                    # constructor
    my $class = shift;
    bless({}, $class);
}

sub method_delegated {       # method defined here, which
    my $self = shift;        # is used by the Delegate class

    print "Delegated method. Parameters: (@_)\n";
```

```perl
}

################################################################
package Delegate;               # delegating class

sub new {                       # constructor
    my $class = shift;

    my $self = bless({}, $class);

                                # call constructor of class
                                # to which method is delegated
    $self->{'delegate'} = Otherclass->new();

    return $self;
}

sub method_defined {            # self-defined method
    my $self = shift;
    print "Own method. Parameters: (@_)\n";
}

sub AUTOLOAD {
    my $self = shift;           # remove erroneous object reference

    $AUTOLOAD =~ s/.*:://;      # remove original
                                # package name

                                # call method in foreign module
                                # with $self->{'delegate'}
                                # as object reference
    $self->{'delegate'}->$AUTOLOAD(@_);
}

################################################################
package main;                   # main program

$dlgref = Delegate->new();      # create new object of
                                # delegating class

                                # method not defined by
                                # Delegate itself, but
                                # delegated to Otherclass
$dlgref->method_delegated("param1", "param2");
```

```
                              # method defined by
                              # Delegate itself
$dlgref->method_defined("param1", "param2");
```

_____*autoload.pl*

The `Delegate` class implements the method `method_defined` itself, but delegates calls of the method `method_delegated` to the `Otherclass` class.

Accordingly, the output of `autoload.pl` is

```
Delegated method. Parameters: (param1 param2)
Own method. Parameters: (param1 param2)
```

Prêt-à-porter modules

Perl lives with its developers, who recognize problems, solve them, pack the solutions into modules, and make these available to the public – not for money, but for the glory and a tiny piece of eternal life in the Perl universe. Well done!

This chapter shows how to use ready-made modules to extend the functionality of Perl and quickly solve everyday tasks. The examples we present intend to awaken the appetite for *more* – the complete documentation of installed modules is available via `perldoc module_name`.

The modules used in this chapter are all included on the enclosed CD-ROM; however, they are also freely available from the CPAN or – partly – included in the Perl distribution. How to obtain and install modules is described in Appendix A.4.

3.1 `IO::File` – the new file handle generation

Traditional file handles in Perl are second-class variables. Neither can their scope be limited with `my`, nor can they be passed to subroutines without some fancy tricks. Then, `IO::File` introduced an improvement: file handle objects.

The constructor call of the `IO::File` class returns an object reference if the specified file can be opened. If problems occur, `undef` is returned. The object references `$out` and `$in` acquired in the example `iofile.pl` behave like traditional file handles: `print $out` redirects the output, `while<$in>` reads line by line – exactly as usual.

iofile.pl

```perl
use IO::File;

$out = IO::File->new(">test.dat");     # write access

if(defined $out) {                     # opened successfully?
    print $out "Test!\n";              # output
    $out->close();
} else {
    die "Cannot open test.dat!";       # error
}


####################################################################

$in = IO::File->new("<test.dat");      # write access

if(defined $in) {                      # opened successfully?
    while(<$in>) {                     # read file
        print "$_";
    }
} else {
    die "Cannot open test.dat!";       # error
}
```

iofile.pl

Moreover, however, object references are first-class variables, which allow constructs such as

```perl
print_it_out($out, $text);

sub print_it_out {
    my ($fh, $text) = @_;                      # pass file handle

    print $fh $text;                           # output
}
```

The constructor new supports all variations of the open function:

```perl
IO::File->new("input_pipe |");         # open pipe for reading
IO::File->new("| output_pipe");        # open pipe for writing
```

and even some more that come from the world of C:

```
IO::File->new(">test.dat", 0644);        # open with 'rw-r--r--'

IO::File->new("test.dat", "w");          # open for writing
IO::File->new("test.dat", "r");          # open for reading

                            # read and write; create if necessary
IO::File->new("test.dat", O_RDONLY|O_WRONLY|O_CREAT);
```

If a file handle loses its validity, it automatically closes the connection with the subordinate data stream. The `close` method in

```
{
    my $fh = IO::File->new(">test.dat");
    print $fh "Test!\n";

} # implicit close call due to loss of scope
```

may thus be omitted, because `$fh` closes itself when the garbage collector gets it between its claws.

Required module: `IO::File` (contained in Perl 5.004).

3.2 **Time measurements**

Frequently, different ways lead to the same goal when solving a problem with Perl. But which one actually gets the most out of the Perl interpreter, and which one unnecessarily dissipates computing time? In the lowlands of Perl implementation, obscure things tend to happen, and surprises are the order of the day when comparing the runtime behavior of two implementations.

The `Benchmark` module helps with such comparisons. It provides functions that repeat specific parts of the code and measure the consumed computing time, thus allowing an objective comparison.

`Benchmark` measures the time only in full seconds, so you should set the number of repetitions of a piece of code to such a value that the execution takes about 10 seconds.

The `timethese` function accepts the number of required repetitions as its first argument. As a second parameter, it expects a reference to an anonymous hash that maps test names to code actually to be executed:

```
timethese($iterations, {'Name1', sub { ... },
                        'Name2', sub { ... }
                       });
```

`timethese` performs the tests with the specified number of repetitions and outputs the computing time consumed by each of them.

The following example compares the execution times of two different functions that do both the same: they determine whether a predefined array contains a specific value or not. The first function, `grepit`, uses Perl's builtin `grep` command. The other function, `loopoverit`, instead chooses the traditional approach. A loop iterates over all array elements until it finds the required element or reaches the end.

_____*benchtest.pl*

```perl
#!/usr/bin/perl -w

use Benchmark;

foreach $i (1..1000) {          # generate test data
    $element = "Value$i";
    $first   = $element unless defined $first;
    $last    = $element;
    push(@array, $element);
}

$noftimes  = 100;

timethese($noftimes, {"grep first" => sub { grepit($first) },
                      "grep last"  => sub { grepit($last) },
                      "loop first" => sub { loopoverit($first) },
                      "loop last"  => sub { loopoverit($last) }
                     });

#####################################################################
sub grepit {
#####################################################################
    my $searchfor = shift;

    grep { $_ eq $searchfor } @array;
}


#####################################################################
sub loopoverit {
#####################################################################
    my $searchfor = shift;

    foreach $val (@array) {
        return 1 if $val eq $searchfor;
    }
    return 0;
}
```

_____*benchtest.pl*

First, `benchtest.pl` generates a test array with 1000 entries (`Value1` to `Value1000`) and stores the values of the first and the last element in the variables `$first` and `$last`. Subsequently, `timethese()` executes four test cases: it lets both `grepit` and `loopoverit` search for the value of the first and the last element. The output is somewhat surprising:

```
Benchmark: timing 100 iterations of grep first, grep last, \
                               loop first, loop last...
grep first:  1 secs ( 1.25 usr  0.00 sys =  1.25 cpu)
 grep last:  2 secs ( 1.26 usr  0.00 sys =  1.26 cpu)
loop first:  0 secs ( 0.01 usr  0.00 sys =  0.01 cpu)
            (warning: too few iterations for a reliable count)
 loop last:  1 secs ( 1.46 usr  0.00 sys =  1.46 cpu)
```

Thus the (longwinded) search for the last element by means of our hand-knit loop runs – as expected – somewhat more slowly than with the `grep` command (1.46 against 1.26 user CPU seconds for 100 iterations). In the search for the first element of the array, however, the loop solution defeats the `grep` implementation devastatingly! It is so fast that `Benchmark.pm` even warns that the number of iterations selected was too small for a reliable measurement. Why?

The reason behind this is obvious: while the `foreach` loop in `loopoverit` immediately terminates with a matching element, `grep` must in any case scour the array to the end to capture potential multiple occurrences of the value.

Required module: `Benchmark` (contained in Perl 5.004).

3.3 Graphics with the `Chart` package

The `Chart` package by David Bonner allows you to create bar, pie, and other charts as shown in Figure 3.1 with less than 10 lines of code. Internally, `Chart` uses the `GD` library by Lincoln Stein to create GIF images that can either be stored as files on disk or, in the World Wide Web, be generated *on-the-fly* by the server and sent to the browser (see Section 5.8.5).

3.3.1 Bars

Assume the following sales figures:

```
@days    = qw/Mon Tue Wed Thu Fri Sat Sun/;  # X value set
@sales_a = qw/ 3   4   3   6   8   10  15/;  # Y value set 1
@sales_b = qw/ 5   5   5   6   6   7    7/;  # Y value set 2
```

Product A was sold three times on Monday, four times on Tuesday, and so on, while product B went across the counter five times on Monday, five times on Tuesday, and

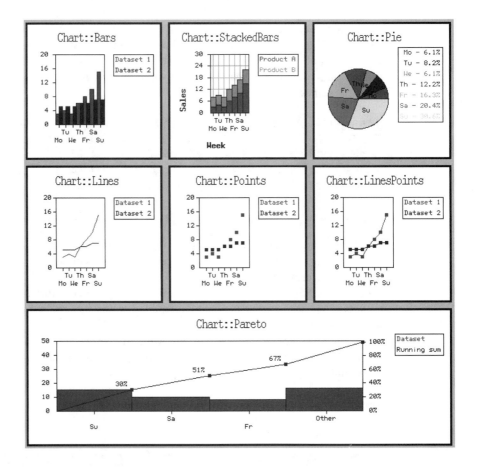

Figure 3.1 Graphics with the Chart package.

so on. These dry statistics are converted into the bar chart shown in the upper left part of Figure 3.1 by the following lines of Perl code:

```
use Chart::Bars;                          # include package
my $g = Chart::Bars->new(200,200);        # create object
$g->set('title' => 'Chart::Bars');        # set title
$g->add_dataset(@days);                   # X data set
$g->add_dataset(@sales_a);                # first Y data set
$g->add_dataset(@sales_b);                # second Y data set
$g->gif("chart.gif");                     # output gif file
```

First, the new constructor of the Char::Bars class creates a diagram object of 200 × 200 pixels. Subsequently, the method set sets the title parameter string "Chart::Bars" as diagram header. The following three calls of add_dataset supply the diagram with a value set for the X axis, followed by two data sets that specify the bar heights in the Y direction. The gif method writes the finished GIF file to disk – and that's it!

Since nothing was specified otherwise, the screen will show the sales figures of product A in red, the values for product B in blue. Chart::Bars standardizes the graph, and draws the axes and what else is needed. In the 'legend' on the right-hand side of the picture, the names of the two Y data sets appear as Dataset 1 and Dataset 2.

Chart::Bars can show one, two (as in the example) or more Y data sets next to each other. Appearance and legends can be freely configured, as the next example will show.

3.3.2 Stacked bars

The Chart::StackedBars diagram in Figure 3.1 top middle shows the two Y data sets of each X value not next to each other, but stacked on top of each other. Thus, besides the partial figures, the sum (total sales) appears too:

```
use Chart::StackedBars;                      # include package
my $g = Chart::StackedBars->new(200,200); # create object
$g->set ('title' => 'Chart::StackedBars');# set title
$g->set('x_label' => "Week");               # legend X axis
$g->set('y_label' => "Sales");              # legend Y axis
$g->set('grid_lines' => "true");            # draw grid
$g->set('max_val' => 30);                   # maximum Y value
                                            # colors: red and green
$g->set('colors' => [[255,0,0], [0,255,0]]);
$g->add_dataset(@days);                     # X data set
$g->add_dataset(@sales_a);                  # first Y data set
$g->add_dataset(@sales_b);                  # second Y data set
                                            # legends data sets
$g->set('legend_labels' => ["Product A", "Product B"]);
$g->gif("chart.gif");                       # output gif file
```

For embellishment, this Perl snippet sets some additional parameters, such as x_label/y_label (legend for the X and Y axes), legend_labels (a reference to an array with sensible names for the data sets instead of the automatically selected "Dataset *n*") and max_val (the maximum value represented in the Y direction). If grid_lines is set to "true", Chart draws a grid in the graph area that facilitates association of the Y values. The colors to be used for the data sets are specified by the colors parameter with a reference to an array of array references (now we will see who has done his/her homework) containing the RGB values of the corresponding colors. [255,0,0] is plain red, [0,255,0] pure green.

3.3.3 Pies

The pie diagram with the `Chart::Pie` object is particularly suitable for representing how the Y values of *one* data set are distributed across the X values. The pie chart in Figure 3.1 top right shows how much per day of the week was sold of product A. Sunday obviously yielded the best result. Creating this chart is as easy as this:

```
use Chart::Pie;                              # include package
my $g = Chart::Pie->new(200,200);           # create object
$g->set ('title' => 'Chart::Pie');          # set title
$g->add_dataset(@days);                      # part descriptions
$g->add_dataset(@sales_a);                   # part values
$g->gif("chart.gif");                        # output gif file
```

To the right of the pie, `Chart::Pie` automatically creates a small table that illustrates the percentages.

3.3.4 Lines and marking points

The middle row of Figure 3,1 shows the classes `Chart::Lines` and `Chart::Points`, which draw each Y data set over the X axis and either connect it with lines or leave it at points. `Chart::LinesPoints` finally combines both methods:

```
use Chart::LinesPoints;                          # include package
my $g = Chart::LinesPoints->new(200,200);        # create object
$g->set ('title' => 'Chart::LinesPoints');       # set title
$g->add_dataset(@days);                          # X data set
$g->add_dataset(@sales_a);                       # first Y data set
$g->add_dataset(@sales_b);                       # second Y data set
$g->gif("chart.gif");                            # output gif file
```

Thus the first data set (`@days`) passed with `add_dataset` is responsible for the discrete values on the X axis, the second one (`@sales_a`) for the height of the supporting points. The third data set (`@sales_b`) determines the course of the second curve.

3.3.5 Paretos

The pareto graph at the bottom of Figure 3.1 illustrates for a set of X-Y values which X values contributed most to the total sum of the Y values. It begins by lining up the largest Y values in a bar chart, showing at the same time which percentage of the total sum has already been reached. The diagram shows that the two strongest sales days, Saturday and Sunday, already achieve 50% of the turnover.

```
use Chart::Pareto;                       # include package
my $g = Chart::Pareto->new(630,200);     # create object
$g->set ('title' => 'Chart::Pareto');    # set title
$g->set ('cutoff' => 3);                 # terminate after 3 values
$g->add_dataset(@days);                  # X data set
$g->add_dataset(@sales_a);               # first Y data set
$g->gif("chart.gif");                    # output gif file
```

As shown in the sample code, the `cutoff` parameter specifies after how many values the pareto graph terminates, summarizing the remaining values under *Other*.

Required modules: `GD` and `Chart` (installation: see page 379).

3.4 **Controlling processes with** `Proc::Simple`

To optimize the throughput of a computer when a number of calculating jobs are consuming lots of CPU time, it is often sensible to start some jobs in parallel. Terminated jobs should be immediately replaced with new ones, so a constant number of jobs is constantly active on the computer. In this way, the computer is not overloaded, but no precious time is wasted either. In continuous 24-hour operation, manual 'feeding' of jobs is obviously out of the question – instead, the `Process.pm` module introduced in Section 2.3, available from the CPAN under `Proc::Simple`, is to take over this task for a UNIX system.

The script `parproc.pl` manages two queues: `@todo`, which contains jobs to be processed (stored as shell command strings), and `@running`, which contains the process objects of already started jobs.

As long as the `@running` queue contains fewer processes than the maximum number `$max_parallel_jobs` of allowed jobs, and jobs are still waiting in the `@todo` queue, `parproc.pl` goes on starting new processes. With a full `@running` queue, `parproc.pl` checks in one-second intervals whether capacities have been freed and, in the positive case, immediately enters new processes. If `@todo` is exhausted, `parproc.pl` waits until the last process has finished and terminates itself.

————————————————————————————————parproc.pl

```
#!/usr/local/bin/perl -w

use Proc::Simple;

$| = 1;                                  # debuffer output
$max_parallel_jobs = 5;                  # jobs processed in parallel
@running = ();                           # array of running jobs

foreach $job (1..9) {                    # create pseudo jobs
```

```
        push(@todo, "sleep 10");
}


###################################################################
                                        # while there are jobs to do
while($#todo >= 0 || $#running >= 0) {  # or started ones are running
    @running = grep { $_->poll() } @running;  # remove finished jobs

    if($#running + 1 < $max_parallel_jobs &&  # space free in running?
        defined($job = pop(@todo))) {          # ... and job available

        print "Starting job '$job' ... ";
        $proc = Proc::Simple->new();    # new process
        $proc->start($job) || die "Cannot start job $job";
        push(@running, $proc);          # include in running list

        print "STARTED. (Remaining: ", $#todo+1,
              " Running: ", $#running + 1, ")\n";
        next;                           # proceed without delay
    }
    sleep(1);                           # pause ... and proceed
}
```

_____*parproc.pl*

Required module: `Proc::Simple` (installation: page 379).

3.5 Command line options

In good old UNIX tradition, programs are passed parameters set in their call via *command line switches*. There are not only 'simple' switches such as the `-l` switch in

```
ls -l
```

which instructs the `ls` command to display its data in long form, but also options that convey values, as in

```
grep -f patternfile file      # pattern from "patternfile"
grep -fpatternfile file       # as above - "sticky argument"
```

Here, the option `-f` carries the argument `patternfile`, which once follows `-f` and once 'sticks' to `-f`. Options may also come in bulks, as in

```
ps -aux                       # equivalent to "ps -a -u -x"
```

To handle the above three cases transparently in a Perl script that accepts options, the `Getopt::Std` module is available. It exports the function `getopts`, which accepts as parameters a descriptive string of the supported options together with a reference to a hash that holds the data of the analyzed options ready for quick interrogation. In

```
use Getopt::Std;
getopts('abf:', \%opt);
```

`getopts` analyzes the command line, watching out for the options -a, -b, and -f. If other options are found, `getopts` signals an error and returns a false value. The colon after the f in the descriptive string instructs `getopts` to include a subsequent argument when an -f option occurs. If -a is set, a subsequent `$opt{'a'}` yields a true value; if an argument follows or sticks to -f, it will subsequently be located in `$opt{'f'}`.

In case of incorrect usage, a program that expects options should signal an error and output a *usage* message. A sample implementation is shown in `getopt.pl`.

---

getopt.pl

```perl
#!/usr/bin/perl -w

use Getopt::Std;

getopts('abf:', \%opt) || usage("usage:");

print "-a set!\n" if $opt{'a'};
print "-b set!\n" if $opt{'b'};
print "-f set to \"$opt{'f'}\"!\n" if $opt{'f'};

sub usage {
    $0 =~ s#.*/##g;
    print "usage: $0 [-a] [-b] [-f filename]\n";
    exit 1;
}
```

---

getopt.pl

The following calls of `getopt.pl` via the command line with the specified parameters generate the output shown:

```
$ getopt.pl -a
-a set!

$ getopt.pl -a -b
-a set!
-b set!

$ getopt.pl -ab
-a set!
-b set!

$ getopt.pl -g
Unknown option: g
usage: getopt.pl [-a] [-b] [-f filename]

$ getopt.pl -f filename
-f set to "filename"!

$ getopt.pl -ffilename
-f set to "filename"!

$ getopt.pl -abf filename
-a set!
-b set!
-f set to "filename"!
```

Required module: `Getopt::Std` (contained in Perl 5.004).

3.6 Terminal control

In addition to the procedure explained in Section 1.8.6, there are other methods (possibly also available soon under Windows) to change the terminal settings for a script: for example, to allow 'blind' password input. The `Term::ReadKey` module exports the function `ReadMode`, which uses the parameter string `'noecho'` to set the terminal to 'blind' password input and `'normal'` to set it back to normal mode. The `ReadLine` function reads the next typed-in character string with the parameter 0 and returns the captured value. A value greater than zero is interpreted as a timeout, after which `ReadLine` returns empty-handed if no input was made.

If an action is to be triggered immediately after each typed character, instead of waiting for the return key to terminate the entire string, the terminal must first be switched to 'raw' mode by means of `ReadMode('raw')`. Then, with 0 as argument, the `ReadKey` function, equally exported by `Term::ReadKey`, returns the corresponding character for each pressed key. An argument value greater than zero is interpreted as a timeout – if no input has been made after the specified number of seconds, `ReadKey` aborts and returns `undef`. −1 instead switches into *non-blocking* mode − the routine returns immediately, no matter whether an input has been made or not, and returns the value of the pressed key or `undef` if nothing happened.

If the terminal stays in 'raw' mode after termination of the script, the subsequently starting UNIX shell would get utterly confused − thus `ReadMode('normal')` switches the terminal back to normal mode before the program terminates.

Listing `readkey.pl` first shows a prompt for 'blind' input of a password. In the second part, `readkey.pl` waits 5 seconds for a key to be pressed. If a key is pressed, `readkey.pl` outputs the value of the pressed key; if the time span passes and nothing happens, *Hi there, wake up!* is displayed and the waiting loop is continued. Only the `'q'` character terminates the process.

_____*readkey.pl*

```perl
#!/usr/bin/perl -w

use Term::ReadKey;                       # include module
$| = 1;                                  # debuffer output


######################################################################
# 'Blind' input
######################################################################
ReadMode('noecho');                      # activate 'blind input'
print "Enter password: ";                # input prompt
$pass = ReadLine(0);                     # line input
chop($pass);                             # cut off newline
print "Password: '$pass'\n";             # output for testing
ReadMode('normal');                      # reset terminal


######################################################################
# Input of individual characters
######################################################################
$timeout = 5;                            # timeout after 5 seconds

print "Press any key, terminate with 'q': \n";
ReadMode('raw');                         # block control characters

while(1) {                               # endless loop
    while (!defined ($key = ReadKey($timeout))) {
        print "Hi there, wake up!\n";    # no input yet
    }
    print "Entered: '$key'\n";
    last if $key eq "q";                 # terminate or repeat
}
```

```
ReadMode('normal');                     # reset terminal mode
```

_____*readkey.pl*

Required module: `Term::ReadKey` (installation: page 379).

3.7 Text processing

If a text is present in columns that are too wide, or if it contains continuous sentences without newline characters, it must be broken (for example, before sending it via email) into narrower columns. The simple text wrapper `wrap` from the `Text::Wrap` module performs this task.

The first parameter of the `wrap` function specifies the indentation of the first line of a paragraph, while the second parameter defines the indentation of all following lines. The third parameter specifies the text to be formatted. Thus, a simple left-justified print is created by the combination `""` and `""`. The script

```perl
use Text::Wrap;

$text = "This line is very, very long; it is indeed so long that "
        "the text formatter must break it up several times.";

$Text::Wrap::columns = 40;
$first_indent = "      ";
$next_indent  = "";

print Text::Wrap::wrap($first_indent, $next_indent, $text), "\n";
```

generates the output

```
    This line is very, very long; it is
indeed so long that the text formatter
must break it up several times.
```

A word that is longer than a line is broken by the `wrap` function at the end of the line, without a hyphen or another separation symbol.

EXERCISE 3.1

Breaking lines
Write a script that formats the paragraphs of all files specified in the command line in a left-justified manner. The line length is to be max. 40 characters; indents are not required.

Read the entire input stream into a string, replace all newlines not followed by newlines (negative lookahead) with empty strings, and feed the result to `Text::Wrap::wrap` (*solution on page 166*).

Required module: `Text::Wrap` (contained in Perl 5.004). For more complex formatting problems you should resort to `Text::Format` by Gabor Egressy, which offers more options (available from the CPAN).

3.8 Date calculations

The `Date::Manip` module by Sullivan Beck deals with different calendar calculations in a user-friendly manner. 'How many days until 12/24?' 'Which date was last week's Monday?' 'How many working days remain until month end?' Whoever constructs scripts that need such dates for statistics or project plans need no longer battle with the peculiarities of our calendar system or be afraid of the year 2000 – `Date::Manip` performs this kind of counts in a jiffy.

To enable `Date::Manip` to calculate with a date, it must first convert it into its internal format. This is handled by the function `ParseDate`, which recognizes quite a lot of 'human' formats:

```
use Date::Manip;

$date = ParseDate("19980810");          # 10 aug 1998
$date = ParseDate("98-0810");           # 10 aug 1998
$date = ParseDate("19980810 12:00:00"); # 10 aug 1998 12:00:00
$date = ParseDate("last monday");
$date = ParseDate("next monday");
$date = ParseDate("first sunday in june 1998");
$date = ParseDate("today");
$date = ParseDate("yesterday");
$date = ParseDate("tomorrow");
```

These are only the most important ones; a complete list can be found with `perldoc Date::Manip`. Once `Date::Manip` has recognized a date, it allows calculations with `DateCalc`. The time between two (internal) data specifications in days, hours, minutes, and seconds is calculated by

```
$delta = DateCalc($date1, $date2, \$err);   # days between dates
```

The return value is a string of the format

```
0:0:days:hours:minutes:seconds
```

The strange format is due to the fact that `DateCalc` with 1 as fourth parameter also returns years and months. With the present signature, only days are counted. Thus

```
use Date::Manip;

$date1 = ParseDate("yesterday");
$date2 = ParseDate("tomorrow");

$delta = DateCalc($date1, $date2, \$err);

if(!defined $err) {              # successful
    my ($y, $m, $d, $h, $m, $s) = split(/:/, $delta);
    print "$d days of difference\n";
} else {                        # error
    print "Error!\n";
}
```

returns "`2 days of difference`" for the time difference between yesterday and to-morrow – *correct!* If `DateCalc` cannot perform the calculation because it was passed invalid date specifications, or another error occurs, it sets `$err` to a positive value; otherwise it remains `undef`.

Beginning with a start date and a time difference, `DateCalc` also calculates the resulting end date:

```
            # 2 days, 3 hours, 20 minutes later
$date2 = DateCalc($date1, "+ 2days 3hours 20minutes", \$err);

            # one month and three weeks earlier
$date2 = DateCalc($date1, "- 1months 3weeks", \$err);

            # one year and one second later
$date2 = DateCalc($date1, "+ 1years 1seconds", \$err);
```

As a third domain, `Date::Manip` displays internal date values in a flexibly con-figurable format.

```
$string = UnixDate($date, $format);
```

stores a date `$date`, formatted according to `$format`, in `$string`. Table 3.1 shows the allowed format specifications (by analogy with the `printf` function).
Thus, for example,

```
$date = ParseDate("20000101");

print UnixDate($date, "%d/%m/%Y %H:%M:%S"), "\n";
print UnixDate($date, "%d %b (%A)"), "\n";
```

Table 3.1 Formatting specifications for the `UnixDate` function.

%y	Year	00 ... 99
%Y	Year	0001 ... 9999
%m	Month	01 ... 12
%b	Month	Jan ... Dec
%B	Month	January ... December
%W	Calendar week	00 ... 53
%j	Day of the year	001 ... 366
%d	Day of the month	01 ... 31
%a	Weekday	Sun ... Sat
%A	Weekday	Sunday ... Saturday
%w	Day of the week	1 (Monday) ... 7
%H	Hour	00 ... 23
%M	Minute	00 ... 59
%S	Second	00 ... 59
%s	Seconds since 01.01.70	0 ... 4294967295
%z	Time zone	"PST", "GMT", ...

for the First of January 2000 yields

```
01/01/2000 00:00:00
01 Jan (Saturday)
```

Required module: `Date::Manip` (installation: page 379).

EXERCISE 3.2

Current calendar week

Output the days of the current calendar week in the format

```
Mon Tue Wed Thu Fri Sat Sun
17  18  19  20  21  22  23
```

Use `Date::Manip` to find the date of last Monday (if today is Monday, use today's date) and walk step by step seven days into the future (*solution on page 166*).

EXERCISE 3.3

Day planner

Between February 1st and March 15th, 1999 you want to read a 400-page strong book. Write a script `pages.pl` that, if called at an arbitrary day of this interval, shows how much time has elapsed and which page you should accordingly have reached in your reading. On February 1st, the output should read `0.0% of time - page 0`, while on March 15th it should read `100.0% of time - page 400`. Make use of `Date::Manip` to calculate the number of days between start date and current date and between start date and end date, trying to remember the rule of three from your school days ('If three workers need one day, how many ...') *(solution on page 167)*.

3.9 Packing data in `tar` format

If a script generates several files that are potentially located in arbitrarily nested directory structures (such as the `webgrab.pl` script presented on page 289), the `Tar` module by Calle Dybedahl comes in handy, because it generates file and directory structures in the `tar` format. This format, which originates from the UNIX world and is supported under Windows among others by the `WinZip` program, allows you to pack files and subdirectories, as they appear in the file system on disk, into one single file.

First, you use

```
use Archive::Tar;
$tar = Archive::Tar->new();          # create new Tar object
```

to create a new object of class `Tar`. Already existing files are included in the archive with

```
$tar->add_files("dir/file1", "dir/file2", ...);
```

A type of use that goes beyond the functionality of the `tar` or `WinZip` programs is provided by the `Tar` module with the `add_data` method, which allows storage of dynamically generated data in files of arbitrary directory nesting depth on the hard disk – without actually creating files or directories.

```
$tar->add_data("dir1/dir2/file", "text of file\n");
```

adds a file containing the line `text of file` in a directory named `dir1/dir2` to the Tar file managed by the object `$tar`.

```
$tar->write("result.tar");
```

writes the contents of the Tar file, kept in memory until this moment, in a real file that programs such as `tar` under UNIX and `WinZip` under Windows can open and decompose. If the method is given a true value as its second parameter, `write` compresses the data:

```
$tar->write("result.tgz", 1);
```

Conversely,

```
$tar->read("source.tar");
```

reads an existing Tar file from the hard disk; a true value as a second parameter again switches to compressed Tar files. The method

```
@files = $tar->list_files()
```

returns the file names of the Tar file in memory as a list.

Required modules: `Archive::Tar` and, if compression is used, `Compress::Zlib` (installation: page 379).

Solutions to the exercises

EXERCISE 3.1

Breaking lines (page 160)

```
use Text::Wrap;

$Text::Wrap::columns = 40;          # column width

$lines = join('', <>);              # read lines of all files
$lines =~ s/\n(?!\n)//g;            # remove single(!) newlines

print Text::Wrap::wrap("", "", $lines), "\n";
```

EXERCISE 3.2

Current calender week (page 163)

```
use Date::Manip;

    # determine date of last Monday
$date = ParseDate("last Monday");

    # add a week if today is Monday
if(UnixDate(ParseDate("today"), "%A") eq "Monday") {
    $date = DateCalc($date, "+7 days");
}

    # proceed day by day; save day of month
for (1..7) {
    push(@monthdays, UnixDate($date, "%d"));
    $date = DateCalc($date, "+1 days");
}

print "Mo Tu We Th Fr Sa Su\n", "@monthdays\n";
```

EXERCISE 3.3

Day planner (page 164)

```perl
#!/usr/bin/perl -w

use Date::Manip;

$start_date  = ParseDate("February 1, 1999");
$end_date    = ParseDate("March   15, 1999");
$today       = ParseDate("today");
$total_pages = 400;

$total_days  = (split(/:/, DateCalc($start_date, $end_date)))[2];
$days_passed = (split(/:/, DateCalc($start_date, $today)))[2];

$ratio = ($days_passed / $total_days);

printf "%3.1f%% of time -- page %d\n", ($ratio * 100),
       ($ratio * $total_pages);
```

Graphical interfaces with Tk

Anybody who has tried to use a toolkit such as *Motif* to build a graphical application, even a small one, knows that it can hardly take less than one page of code. Sophisticated interfaces sometimes require weeks of implementation. With the Perl/Tk package, a new age of GUI (*Graphical User Interface*) development begins. A quick prototype becomes just a matter of *minutes*.

4.1 Hello World

Before we begin the proper introduction to the Tk package, we would like to present one of the simplest Perl/Tk program possible: a window with a labeled button that, if pressed, terminates the program. The code will certainly arouse some questions; these will, however, only be clarified in Section 4.3, because some basic explanations of programming graphical interfaces still need to be given first.

Listing `hellotk.pl` shows how compact the formulation of this small task is in Perl/Tk.

Perl uses the Tk interface as a standard package. After including it by means of the instruction

```
use Tk;
```

the programmer can utilize the whole range of Tk functions for representation of dialog objects and processing of user input.

If the Tk package for Perl has been correctly installed, the script creates an interface like the one shown in Figure 4.1 (window layout and typeface may vary depending on the actual window manager used). The Tk installation procedure under UNIX is described in Appendix A.2; if you experience problems with the X Window system, please consult Appendix C.4. The Perl version for Windows, instead,

hellotk.pl

```perl
#!/usr/bin/perl -w

use Tk;                         # include Tk package

$top    = MainWindow->new();  # create application window

                                # create pushbutton,
                                # set text and callback

$button = $top->Button(-text =>
                    "Hello World! Push me to exit !",
                    -command => sub { exit 0 });

$button->pack();                # insert pushbutton in
                                # application window

MainLoop;                       # start main event loop
```

hellotk.pl

which you will find on the enclosed CD-ROM, contains the Tk package as a standard without requiring further settings.

Figure 4.1   The 'Hello World' of Perl/Tk programming.

The application provides full X Window or Windows functionality, because not only is the explicitly defined button in the middle of the window active, but so also is the frame made available by the window manager. With the mouse, the window can be moved and resized, and with the buttons included in the frame, it can be maximized, iconized, and closed.

4.2 Fundamentals of graphical user interfaces

Now, what is Tk? In a fairly non-descriptive way, the acronym simply stands for *Toolkit* – in reality, it is a graphical user interface that builds on the X Window system or on Windows. Even though in the following sections we will continuously talk

about X and UNIX, Perl/Tk applications run without problems under Win
NT with the Perl port by Gurusamy Sarathy. Windows and the X Window s
not have very much in common, but from a higher viewpoint such as Tk, eve
looks the same again.

4.2.1 The X Window system

The X Window system is *the* window system of the UNIX world. But it is extremely laborious to use it for development of graphical applications without using further tools, because the X Window API (the Xlib) provides only a rudimentary function-ality.

The first concept of the X Window system envisaged providing only a basic functionality. Thus the X Intrinsics, included in the distribution, offer an interface for higher-level toolkits, whose best-known representatives are probably OSF/Motif, Open Look, and the Athena widgets.

The X Window system provides only the management technology for graphical interfaces, whereas the toolkits bring *behavior* into play – a special *look and feel* of the user interface. The fact that a pulldown menu pops down at a click of the mouse or a pushbutton snaps in and then out again is a question of interface design of the toolkit. Thus the different systems also stand for fundamentally different philosophies of user guidance: everything is a question of ergonomy, habits – and even personal taste. It is, however, quite sensible to standardize the behavior of graphical interfaces; nobody really wants to learn new mouse and keyboard controls all over again for every application program – the user just *expects* standard given reactions.

4.2.2 Toolkits and their widgets

A common feature of all toolkits is that they define a range of so-called *widgets*, graphical units that function according to a specific pattern of behavior. The name *widget* itself is a contraction of *window* and *gadget*, and stands more or less for something like a 'dialog object.'

Well-known widgets are pushbutton, label, and listbox. All of these units have in common that they have a graphical layout, react according to a specific pattern to user input via mouse or keyboard (*user events*), and as a consequence change their status or process attached programs (*callbacks*).

Programming with the above-mentioned toolkits is, however, still relatively complex. The effort from design to the running program is still too much. An addi-tional flaw in larger applications is that, because of its epic length, the toolkit code quickly becomes too complicated to survey.

4.2.3 Tk and Tcl

The Tk toolkit, instead, allows substantially more compact formulation of graphical controls, even on the basis of the widget concept.

...usterhout, the inventor of Tk, introduced it together with the script lan-
...k itself is a mere toolkit, a library of functions for graphical applications,
...is a control language that now and then issues Tk instructions.

...oday, Tcl and Tk are practically indivisible – most Tk applications are
...cl. Syntactically, however, Tcl is most idiosyncratic, and with regard to
...e, it leaves very much to be desired. While Tcl scripts are executed with
...ately the same speed as comparable shell scripts, the equivalent Perl scripts
beat them by a factor of often more than 10.

Recently, an ingenious Perl developer, Nick Ing-Simmons, had the great idea
of including Tk code dynamically into object-oriented Perl, thus creating a combination of script language and GUI that has no equal. Perl's elegant language constructs
together with the powerful Tk commands amalgamate into a development environment that allows writing of graphical applications with an OSF/Motif-like *look and
feel* in breath-taking speed.

4.2.4 Event handling

How does a typical application provided with a graphical interface operate? Rather
differently, compared with conventional programs! This is because after the initializing 'paint process', which draws the external representation, i.e. the interface of the
application on the screen, the user can trigger a multitude of different processes by
opening this or that menu or pressing one button or another. Since no static sequence
can be determined, such programs are called *event-driven*.

Thus the implementation of graphical applications too differs from traditional
programs. The typical structure of a GUI application includes an initialization part,
which defines the layout of the interface, together with legal user reactions and their
potential handling.

The kernel of the program is then one single instruction, the main event loop,
in which a hidden mechanism accepts external events and initiates their processing.
Events in this sense are not only the mouse clicks of the user, but also, for example,
expired timers, or refresh events that signal to the application that a window that was
until now hiding a part of the interface has been pulled away and that the interface
graphics must now be redrawn.

This main loop is continuously active from the beginning of event control until
termination of the program, because the interface must at any time be able to react to
user input. Nothing is more disturbing than a seemingly 'dead' interface.

Actions triggered by the application as a reaction to specific user inputs are
called *callbacks*. In the initialization part of the implementation, the programmer
statically assigns the required actions to potentially occurring events. Once the main
event loop is active, everything takes its programmed course, and the course of the
program is exclusively controlled by the user, who navigates through the different
program parts by means of various kinds of input.

Let us look once more at the Perl/Tk program briefly presented at the beginning
of this chapter: apparently, the initialization part creates a button object whose callback routine consists of a subroutine that executes nothing but the `exit` command.

The `MainLoop` command at the end of the script causes the main loop to be entered: a loop out of which there is no escape except pressing the `Exit` button, thus triggering the mentioned callback, which in turn terminates the program.

4.2.5 Window hierarchy

A pushbutton always appears in an associated window. In reality, the button is hierachically subordinate to the window: a window contains a number of arranged widgets, some of which can in turn contain other widgets.

Thus, for example, a window can contain several frame widgets (simple frames as containers for other widgets), which in turn accommodate several pushbuttons. This

window $\rightarrow$ frame $\rightarrow$ pushbutton

hierarchy strongly determines the external representation of the application, because it specifies the order in which Tk draws the widgets and thus the way in which the widgets are arranged next to each other.

A properly programmed X Window application arranges the widgets in a container widget, such as the frame, without specification of any coordinates. Instead, vague location indications determine the scenery. Examples for positioning could be 'Place the frame top left in the window,' or 'These three text widgets stand in a row next to each other.'

Positioning individual widgets in Tk is cared for by the packer. Each widget object has its own `pack` method by means of which it packs itself – if not specified otherwise – into its parent widget. The hierarchical parent-child relationship is determined much earlier, because in Perl/Tk parent widgets really create their child widgets themselves: thus in the script `hellotk.pl` at the beginning of this chapter, we first create an object of the `MainWindow` type, which in turn uses its `Button` method to create a pushbutton object. The subsequent `$button->pack` makes the direct hierarchical subordination of the button to the top window also visible in the graphics: the button fits snugly into the window.

The window hierarchy then allows positioning instructions such as 'Position the two labels one underneath the other in the top left side of the window.' In this case, an auxiliary widget of frame type would enclose two labels arranged one underneath the other, and then pack itself away somewhere in the direction of the top left corner of the window. Figure 4.2 shows the visual representation. For the sake of clarity, the auxiliary frame widget has a frame that could, however, be omitted without consequences.

4.2.6 Clients and servers in the X Window system

The terms 'client' and 'server' assume a slightly confusing meaning when the X Window system comes into play. The program proper, the control code of the application, is the client that issues the graphical control commands to the display server. To draw the graphical representation, for example, the client passes the server the

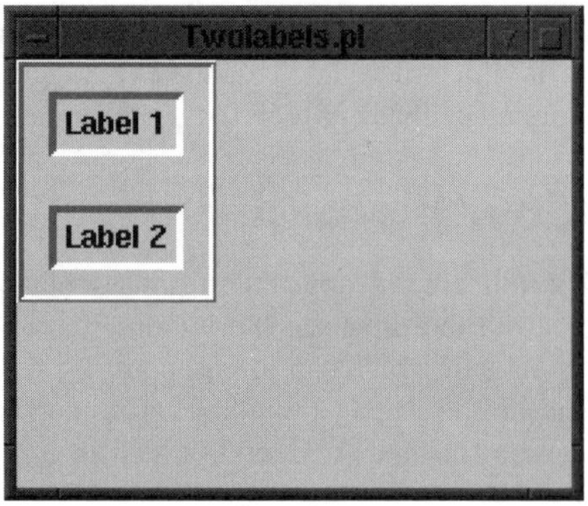

Figure 4.2   Two labels packed one underneath the other in the top left corner of the main window – realized by means of a frame widget.

data of lines and surfaces that are needed to represent the individual objects. The display server, instead, carries out the hardware-related tasks: it displays the objects on screen, captures the mouse and keyboard input of the user, and passes this back to the client.

Even more confusingly, the controlling client software frequently runs on larger hardware platforms for reasons of performance, whereas the display of the server is often delegated to a small PC, so that the intuitive rule of thumb server → large, client → small inevitably leads to the wrong result.

Obviously, server and client can also run on the same machine. However, in practice we often find so-called X terminals, screens with a built-in small computer, which only process the display server code, whereas the application itself runs on a powerful computer in the network.

4.2.7 The window manager

The central client application in the X Window system is the window manager. It is responsible for managing the different application windows. An important principle of the X Window system is that only the application is responsible for the contents of its window(s). Conversely, the windows manager cares about frames for these windows and provides the functionality for modifying the windows. If, however, a window needs to be redrawn, for example because it is no longer covered as a consequence of a moving action, the window manager merely sends a redraw message with coordinate specifications to the application, which itself carries out the redraw of the affected rectangles.

These brief notes on X Window technology should be sufficient for using the Tk applications presented in this book successfully. More detailed information on basic issues and programming can be found in Nye (1990). Useful hints for the end user of X applications are given in Quercia and O'Reilly (1990).

4.3 Classes and objects in the Tk package

Widget classes represent the available widget types, such as buttons, labels, and listboxes. The basis of every application, however, is always an object of the `MainWindow` class: that is, the main window of the application under whose hierarchy level all other widgets are created.

```
$top = MainWindow->new();
```

or alternatively

```
$top = new MainWindow;
```

creates a reference `$top` to a new object of the `MainWindow` class defined in the Tk package, which now in turn provides methods to create additional widget objects. Thus, a button, a frame, and a text field located in the main window are simply created by means of:

```
$button = $top->Button();  # create button widget object
$frame  = $top->Frame();   # create frame widget object
$text   = $top->Text();    # create text widget object
```

Also all of the other classes provide these methods – through inheritance. Thus an additional button can be created within the frame `$frame`:

```
$button_in_frame = $frame->Button();
```

A brief description of all widgets currently supported by Tk is given in the following list. Obviously, the number of widget types increases with further developments of the Perl/Tk package. Section 4.6 is dedicated to the technical details of the individual types of widget.

Button Pushbutton: for example, the OK button of a dialog.

Canvas Universal widget for arranging objects such as lines, polygons, bitmaps, or text strings.

Checkbutton Toggle switch that changes and displays its state (on/off).

Entry Editable one-line text field.

Frame Container widget with adjustable frame for spatial arrangement of other widgets.

Label Non-editable text field.

Listbox List of selectable strings, which together with a scroll bar gives a typical select box.

MainWindow The 'mother' of all widgets. This is the main window of the application whose frame is drawn by the window manager.

Menu Menu bar, the top bar from which the pulldown menus drop down.

MenuButton Entry of a pulldown menu.

Message Label consisting of several automatically broken lines, used for display of messages.

Radiobutton Check button, which together with other radio buttons forms a unit in which only one button is active at a time.

Scale Slide rule with numerical indication.

Scrollbar Widget at the border of Listbox, Canvas, or Text widgets that controls their scrolling when they exceed the size of their enclosing widget and thus can no longer be displayed all at once.

Text Editable text field of several lines.

Toplevel New window at the same hierarchy level as `MainWindow`. Used mainly for display of messages and errors.

To each of these widget types corresponds a construction method of the same name, which creates a new widget object of the required type, appends it as a new child hierarchically underneath the calling parent object, and returns an object reference.

4.4 Options

The typical call of a widget constructor also passes a number of *option-value* pairs that specify form and function of the new widget.

Name and current value of an option are separate parameters. For the sake of clarity, Tk programming uses the => operator as a replacement for the comma. Since Perl 5.001 this has yielded the additional advantage that *quoting* the option name can be omitted, because the => operator recognizes it as such even without the quotes:

```
$widgetref = $parentwidgetref->widgetmethod(-opt1 => "val1",
                                            -opt2 => "val2");
```

An existing widget can still change its status by means of the `configure` method:

```
$widgetref->configure(-opt1 => "val1", -opt2 => "val2");
```

Table 4.1 shows a range of options supported by default by many widgets.

Table 4.1 Widget options.

-background	=>	*colorname*	Background color
		"blue"	String format
		"#0000ff"	Numerical format
			#rrggbb
			(page 219)
-foreground	=>	*colorname*	Foreground color
		"red"	String format
		"#ff0000"	Numerical format
			#rrggbb
			(page 219)
-bitmap	=>	*bitmap*	Surface pattern
			(Section 4.6.14, page 211)
		'@bitmapfile'	Bitmap file
		"tk_bitmap_name"	Predefined Tk bitmaps
			(page 220)
-borderwidth	=>	*pixels*	Border width
			(Section 4.6.4, page 186)
		2	2 pixels
-command	=>	*funcref*	Action to be called
			(Section 4.6.1, page 182)
		sub { ... }	Anonymous subroutine
		\&*funcname*	Function reference
		[*command_list*]	Internal Tk commands
			(Section 4.6.11, page 204)
-font	=>	*fontname*	Font (page 219)
		"9x15"	9x15 font
		"*times-*-r-*12*"	Times Roman
			12pt font
-geometry	=>	*w*×*h*	Width and height
		"200x100"	
-width	=>	*width*	Width
		"200"	200 pixels
-height	=>	*height*	Height
		"100"	100 pixels
-orient	=>	*orientation*	Orientation
			(Section 4.6.14, page 211)
		"horizontal"	Horizontal
		"vertical"	Vertical

Table 4.1: Widget options (*continued*).

-relief	=>	*reliefstyle*	3D effects
		"flat"	No 3D effects (default)
		"groove"	Groove
		"raised"	Raised
		"ridge"	Ridge
		"sunken"	Sunken
-state	=>	*status*	Status
		"normal"	Can be activated
		"disabled"	Cannot be activated
		"active"	Selected status for buttons
-text	=>	*text*	Legend
		"text"	
-textvariable	=>	*variableref*	Reference to text variable
		\$scalar	

4.5 The packer

Initially, a created widget remains invisible. Thus, for example, a button may hierarchically be correctly subordinate to a window, but Tk needs additional information on the relative position of the button in the window before it can actually draw it. This geometrical positioning of widgets next to each other is the responsibility of the Tk packer. Each widget object supports the `pack` method, by means of which it can position itself at a specific location within a reference widget.

In the normal case, a widget is geometrically located inside the parent widget to which it is also hierarchically subordinate:

```
$widget->pack();
```

packs `$widget` into the widget by which it was created. With the option

```
$widget->pack(-in => $otherparent);
```

it is instead possible to place a widget `$widget` geometrically in another widget `$otherparent`. However, this happens only seldom, because the created widget hierarchy should reasonably also be reflected in the layout.

If several widgets are packed into a parent widget, the option `-side` specifies the placement strategy. At each call, the packer faces the problem of placing a widget in a given field that is usually larger than the widget itself. With the default setting `-side => "top"`, the packer places the widget at the top border of the free space and reduces the available space accordingly. If a second widget object of the same hierarchy level calls its `pack` method with `-side => top`, the same algorithm is started – with the result that widget number 2 now lies directly underneath widget number 1.

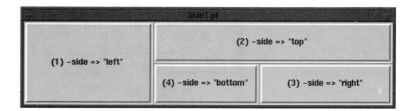

Figure 4.3 Labels packed with the -side options left, top, right, bottom.

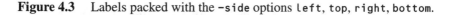

Figure 4.4 Labels packed with the -side options top, right, bottom, left.

Thus with -side => "top" the packer positions widgets of the same hierarchy level *underneath* each other. The same applies to pack without specification of a -side option.

According to the above logic, several pack processes with the option -side => "left" line up the widgets *side by side*. The same applies to "right", except that the widget packed first is located to the extreme right and all others are arranged side by side from right to left.

Figures 4.3 and 4.4 clarify this procedure. Both are a result of packing actions of four label widgets. The script that generated Figure 4.3 packed the first label widget with the option -side => "left". The left part of the window thus being filled; the second widget, packed with -side => "top", was allocated the upper part of the remaining space. The last two widgets were then placed with the -side options "right" and "bottom". Another sequence is shown in Figure 4.4: here, the packing processes were called with the -side options "top", "right", "bottom", and "left".

Frequently, several widgets of the same hierarchy differ in length, for example because of different-length labeling. With these arranged one below the other, the visual outcome is not very appealing. Thus it is better to tell the packer to fill the available space and stretch the shorter widgets to a standard length. This behavior is controlled by means of the -fill option. Parameters are none, the default value which causes no stretching at all, x and y, which stretch horizontally and vertically, and finally both, which stretches the affected widget in all directions.

The option -expand specifies how the interface behaves in the case of manual expansion of the application window by the user. With -expand => "yes", the affected widget claims potentially available additional space for itself, as soon as the user resizes the window with the mouse. With -fill => "none", the widget remains

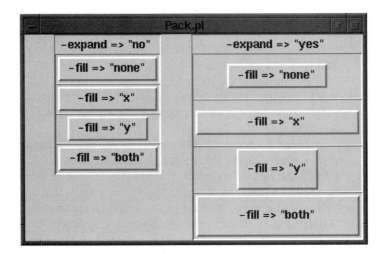

Figure 4.5 The effect of −fill and −expand options with the original window size ...

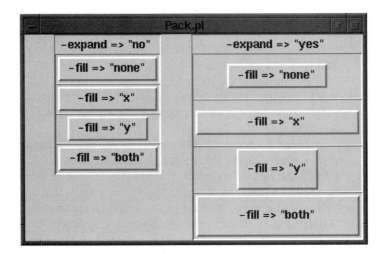

Figure 4.6 ... and with the expanded window.

of the same size, but positions itself centrally in the expanded space. With other values of −fill, the widget expands in the specified directions.

If several widgets of the same hierarchy level have the −expand option set, they use the newly available space in equal parts.

Figures 4.5 and 4.6 show the effects of possible value combinations for the −fill and −expand options, once with the original window size, and once with a manually resized window.

Figure 4.7 Expanded window with stretched button.

bigbutton.pl

```perl
#!/usr/bin/perl -w

use Tk;

$top=MainWindow->new();

$button=$top->Button(-text => "I will grow",
                    -command => \&exit);
$button->pack(-expand => "yes", -fill => "both");
MainLoop;
```

bigbutton.pl

Since the implementation of Figures 4.5 and 4.6 also entails the use of concepts of grouping with frame widgets, which are not discussed until Section 4.6.4, a simplified code sample will suffice at this point: in Listing `bigbutton.pl`, a button like the one shown in Figure 4.7 always assumes the size of the enclosing window.

If the individual widgets of one hierarchy level are not required to lie directly side by side or below each other, but to leave some space in between, the options `-padx` and `pady` provide the possibility of defining intermediate spacing. The corresponding parameter values can be specified in millimeters, centimeters, inches, or points. The length specifications `1i` and `72p` are identical, because one point is $\frac{1}{72}$ of an inch. An indication of `-padx => "15m"` specifies a horizontal distance of 15 millimeters, and `-pady => "1c"` a vertical distance of one centimeter.

A non-expanding widget in an oversized container usually floats in the middle. The `-anchor` option fixes it at one of the cardinal points `"n|ne|e|se|s|sw|w|nw"` (North, Northeast, and so on) at the border of the container. Figure 4.8 shows possible settings. It should however be noted that the `-anchor` option closely cooperates with the `-side` option: a widget packed with `-side => "left"` would not completely stick to the right-hand side even with `-anchor => "e"`.

The most important packer options are summarized in Table 4.2.

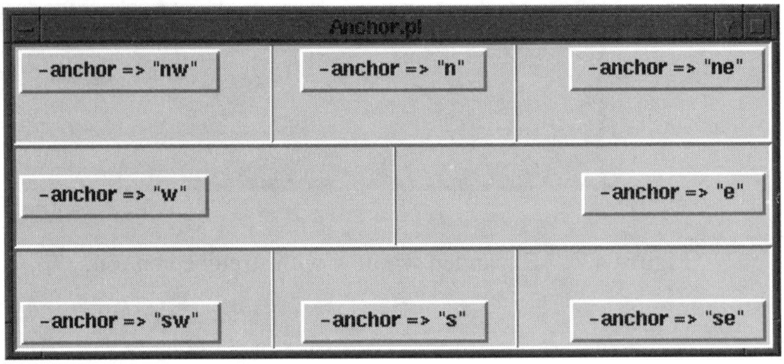

Figure 4.8   The -anchor option and its parameters.

Table 4.2   Options of the pack method.

`-in`	`=>`	`$widget`	Geometrical parent
`-side`	`=>`	`"top|left|right|bottom"`	Positioning
`-expand`	`=>`	`"yes|no"`	Expansion yes/no
`-fill`	`=>`	`"none|x|y|both"`	Expansion direction
`-padx`	`=>`	`"widthc|m|i|p"`	Distance to left/right neighbor
`-pady`	`=>`	`"widthc|m|i|p"`	Distance to upper/lower neighbor
`-anchor`	`=>`	`"n|ne|e|se|s|sw` `|w|nw|center"`	Anchor

4.6 Widgets in detail

Different widget types support different options: thus, for example, a button can specify its text or a frame its border width. The following subsections explain the functionality of the different widgets in more detail, and present sample applications.

However, the following selection is only a small part of the options provided by Tk. Thus we have omitted features that are seldom employed or are used only for visual embellishment. The emphasis of our collection lies on practical usability. A detailed list can be found in the standard book by John K. Ousterhout (1994) or in one of the practical reference guides on the Internet (see Appendix G).

4.6.1 Buttons

The first example of a button was presented at the beginning of this chapter as *Hello World*. There, the button had the sole purpose of terminating the program when pressed. The relevant lines were

```
                                # create pushbutton
$button = $top->Button(-text =>
                    "Hello World! Push me to exit !",
                    -command => sub { exit 0 });
$button->pack();                # insert pushbutton in
```

The option `-text` specifies the labeling of the button, while `-command` specifies the code to be executed in case of activation. The code reference can either be included directly in the function call as an anonymous subroutine, as above, or it can refer to a defined Perl function `func`, for example in the form of `\&func`. If this so-called callback function expects parameters, it is recommended that the alternative of the anonymous subroutine be used: in the same way as in the above example the `exit` function is passed the parameter `0`, other functions can be passed variables of any kind.

The labeling of the button can also be defined dynamically by means of a variable:

```
$buttontext = "Hello World! Push me to exit !";
$button = $top->Button("-textvariable" => \$buttontext,
                    "-command" => sub { exit 0 });
```

If the value of the variable is changed in the course of the script, the button text is immediately amended. In some contexts, the button also needs to be disabled. This is achieved by means of the `-state` option, which changes the status of the button to inactive with `disabled` and reenables it with `normal`. Table 4.3 shows common options for the button widget.

Table 4.3 Common button options.

`-command`	=>	`\&subname`	Activation callback
`-command`	=>	`sub { ... }`	
`-state`	=>	`"normal"`	Enabled
`-state`	=>	`"disabled"`	Locked
`-text`	=>	`$scalar`	Labeling
`-textvariable`	=>	`\$scalar`	Text variable

4.6.2 Check buttons

The check button ('checkbox' in Windows terminology) supports all the options of the common button – and some more: the `-variable` option, together with a reference to a scalar, specifies the variable that controls the state of the check button.

If this variable assumes a value of zero, the check button is switched 'off'; otherwise, if the value does not equal zero, the check button is switched 'on.' Conversely,

Figure 4.9 Check button.

the check button also controls the value of the variable: a switched-on check button sets the variable to 1; a switched-off button sets it to 0.

Listing checkbutton.pl shows a brief implementation that yields the result shown in Figure 4.9. The defined subroutine callback outputs the value of the variable $checkvalue, which, depending on the status of the check button, contains the string "ON" or "OFF", because it was explicitly assigned to the check button as a status variable.

_____*checkbutton.pl*

```perl
#!/usr/bin/perl -w

use Tk;

$top=MainWindow->new();

$top->Checkbutton(-text => "Check me",
                  -command => \&callback,
                  -variable => \$checkvalue,
                  -onvalue => "ON",
                  -offvalue => "OFF")->pack();
MainLoop;

sub callback {
    print "Check button is $checkvalue\n";
}
```

_____*checkbutton.pl*

Table 4.4 shows an overview of the most important check button options.

4.6.3 Radio buttons

Old-fashioned radios have a row of station selection buttons, of which only one can be pressed at any given time. If one key is pressed down, the one that was previously depressed pops up.

Table 4.4   Common check button options.

`-command`	`=>`	`\&subname`	Activation callback
`-command`	`=>`	`sub { ... }`	
`-state`	`=>`	`"active"`	Activated
`-state`	`=>`	`"normal"`	Not activated
`-state`	`=>`	`"disabled"`	Disabled
`-text`	`=>`	`$scalar`	Labeling
`-textvariable`	`=>`	`\$scalarref`	Text variable
`-variable`	`=>`	`\$scalaref`	Status variable
`-onvalue`	`=>`	`$scalar`	Variable value if activated
`-offvalue`	`=>`	`$scalar`	Variable value if not active

Radio buttons are check buttons that imitate precisely this behavior: only one radio button out of a defined group may be active at any one time. If the user selects another button, the first one is automatically deactivated.

Each radio button of a group assigns, if pressed, a characteristic value to a target variable defined for that group and, in addition, triggers a possibly defined callback.

Listing `radiobutton.pl` defines two radio buttons that share the variable `$radiovar`. Since the activation of callbacks happens in the same way as with all other buttons, `radiobutton.pl` does not provide an example of the `-command` option.

radiobutton.pl

```perl
#!/usr/bin/perl -w

use Tk;

$top=MainWindow->new();

$top->Radiobutton(-text => "Radio(1)",
                  -variable => \$radiovar,
                  -value => "R1" )->pack();

$top->Radiobutton(-text => "Radio(2)",
                  -variable => \$radiovar,
                  -value => "R2" )->pack();

MainLoop;
```

radiobutton.pl

After the start of the program, the value of the variable `$radiovar` is initially undefined, and none of the buttons is visually marked as active. If the user selects the bottom button, $radiovar is assigned the value "R2", and the application shows itself as viewed in Figure 4.10.

Radio buttons belonging to one group synchronize exclusively via the name of the target variable. Even if the actions to be carried out are defined via the -command option, a common variable -variable is needed to ensure the typical radio button behavior.

Figure 4.10   Radio buttons.

Table 4.5 shows the most important options supported by the radio button widget.

Table 4.5   Radio button options.

-command	=>	\&subname	Activation callback
-command	=>	sub { ... }	
-state	=>	"active"	Activated
-state	=>	"normal"	Not activated
-state	=>	"disabled"	Disabled
-text	=>	$scalar	Labeling
-textvariable	=>	\$scalarref	Text variable
-value	=>	$scalar	Value of -variable if active
-variable	=>	\$scalarref	Common target variable of all radio buttons of a group

4.6.4 Frames

Properly speaking, the container widget frame is good for nothing – except for drawing a frame and, as other wigdets, accommodating child widgets in its midst. If, for example, the problem is to place three label widgets in such a way that one stays on top and the other two side by side underneath, a frame widget provides indispensable services: the available space is shared by two invisible frame widgets, one below the other, which each accommodate one or two labels and arrange them accordingly:

frame.pl

```
#!/usr/bin/perl -w

use Tk;

$top = MainWindow->new();

                               # create the two frames
$upperframe = $top->Frame()->pack();
$lowerframe = $top->Frame()->pack();

                               # labels in the upper frame
$upperframe->Label(-text => "Label1")->pack();

                               # labels in the lower frame
$lowerframe->Label(-text => "Label2")->pack(-side => "left");
$lowerframe->Label(-text => "Label3")->pack(-side => "right");

MainLoop;
```

frame.pl

Figure 4.11   Arranging labels using hidden frame widgets.

Borders

Frames not only help with special positioning requirements, they are also helpful for adornment purposes. The border of a frame can assume various forms. In the simplest case, it is invisible; with the option -relief it can (as many other widgets too) give a three-dimensional impression. Legal parameters for this option are the values flat, groove, raised, ridge, and sunken. In addition, the option -borderwidth specifies the pixel width of the selected border. Figure 4.12 shows a window with framed labels of all possible types of relief.

In each of the loop iterations, the corresponding script creates a frame of the required type and places a label with the corresponding text into it.

Figure 4.12   Frame widgets with different relief values.

_____*framestyle.pl*

```perl
#!/usr/bin/perl -w

use Tk;

my $top = MainWindow->new();

foreach $reliefstyle ("flat", "raised", "sunken",
                      "ridge", "groove") {

                # create frame around the label
    $frame = $top->Frame(-relief => $reliefstyle,
                         -borderwidth => 5);

                # pack side by side and towards
                # top with 2mm distance
    $frame->pack(-side => "left", -padx => "2m",
                                  -pady => "2m");

                # create label
    $frame->Label(-text => $reliefstyle)->pack();
}

MainLoop;
```

_____*framestyle.pl*

Height and width

The height and width of a widget should really not be set manually – this is the task of
the packer, which dynamically adjusts it to the size of the parent window. However,
from time to time a widget may take on such a meager size that manual expansion
becomes necessary. A frame always takes on the size of the widgets it encloses. If
none are present, the frame shrinks to zero and remains invisible even if a border
has been defined. Thus an empty frame must always be configured with the options

-width and -height. On the other hand, these options have absolutely no effect on frames that house other widgets, because a frame always shrink-wraps the widgets it encloses in an air-tight envelope.

Frames and the packer

If a frame groups a number of child widgets that want to expand, the frame itself (and also its parents) must have the -expand property set; otherwise the desired effect will not be achieved.

Table 4.6 summarizes the most important options of the frame widget.

Table 4.6   Important options of the frame widget.

-width	=>	widthc|m|i|p	Width in cm, mm, inches or points
		"1c"	1 centimeter
		"10m"	10 millimeters
		"0.7i"	0.7 inches
		"30p"	30 points
-height	=>	heightc|m|i|p	Height in cm, mm, inches or points
-relief	=>	"flat"	No 3D effects (default)
-relief	=>	"groove"	Groove
-relief	=>	"raised"	Raised
-relief	=>	"ridge"	Ridge
-relief	=>	"sunken"	Sunken
-borderwidth	=>	$scalar	Border width in pixels

4.6.5 Entry widgets

This editable single-line text field provides full cursor control as known from X Window applications, without any intervention by the programmer. Not only do Backspace, Delete, or positioning via cursor keys function without fail, but they are also actioned with the mouse.

The option -textvariable, already used with other widgets, specifies the Perl variable that will finally contain the manipulated text. With -state => "disabled", the text can be overwrite protected; -state => "normal" switches back to editing mode.

Table 4.7   Entry options.

-textvariable	=>	\$scalar	Text variable
-state	=>	normal|disabled	Editing mode on/off

Figure 4.13 Entry widget.

Listing `entry.pl` implements the interface shown in Figure 4.13: one label and one entry widget that – for test purposes – use the same text variable. The outcome of this is that, during keyboard input in the entry widget, the text of the label widget is constantly refreshed.

entry.pl

```
#!/usr/bin/perl -w

use Tk;

$top = MainWindow->new();

$label = $top->Label(-textvariable => \$text);
$entry = $top->Entry(-textvariable => \$text);

$label->pack(-side => "left");
$entry->pack(-side => "left");

MainLoop;
```

entry.pl

4.6.6 Labels

A label widget contains non-editable text. It supports the options `-text` and `-textvariable`, which specify either a fixed text or a reference to a variable containing text. If the variable text changes, the widget is immediately redrawn with the adjusted text.

For adornment, the label widget has the same border layout options as the frame widget.

Table 4.8   Label options.

`-text`	`=>`	`"text"`	Text
`-textvariable`	`=>`	`\$scalar`	Text variable
`-borderwidth`			As frame widget (page 189)
`-relief`			As frame widget (page 189)

4.6.7 Listboxes

With `ScrlListbox`, Perl/Tk provides an easy-to-use listbox widget that also supports
a built-in scrollbar. Scrollbar and listbox constantly communicate with each other:
when the list of entries changes, the appearance of the scrollbar changes; when a
user moves the scrollbar, the listbox displays a different section of its contents. In
contrast to a scrollable text widget (page 208), a scrollable listbox requires only one
instruction:

```
$parent->ScrlListbox();
```

With the listbox, the `-height` option does not specify the absolute height of the
widget, as with the frame widget, but defines the number of listbox entries visible
together at any one time.

The `-selectmode` option defines the mode of selection. `-selectmode => "sin-
gle"` allows only a single selection, while with `"extended"`, contiguous zones can be
selected by simply clicking and dragging with the mouse. Furthermore, in the `"ex-
tended"` mode a simple mouse click while keeping the (Ctrl) key depressed allows
selection of several, even noncontiguous entries. A contiguous block can also be
marked with a simple click on the entry starting the block, followed by a (Shift)-click
on the entry closing the block. Figure 4.14 shows the different possibilities.

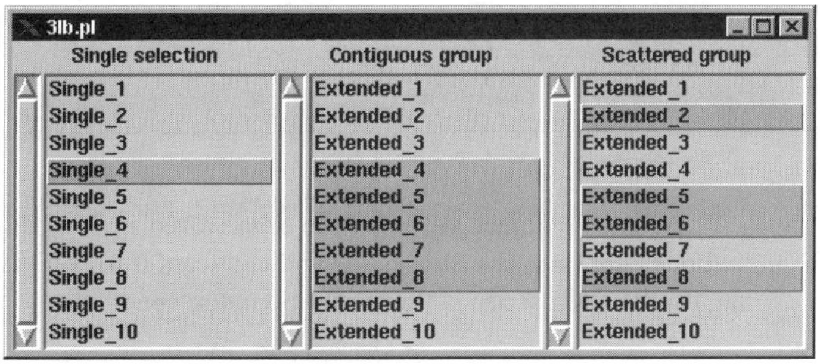

Figure 4.14   Sample selections in listboxes.

To make the three listboxes in Figure 4.14 support simultaneously active selections, the application must give up the X Window-specific selection control which
immediately cancels all selections in a listbox as soon as the user selects elements

from another listbox. The −exportselection option with the parameter 0 makes the desired behavior feasible, as Listing 3lb.pl shows.

```perl
#!/usr/bin/perl -w

use Tk;

my $top = MainWindow->new();

$listbox1 = $top->ScrlListbox(-label => "Single selection",
                             -selectmode => "single",
                             -exportselection => 0
                             )->pack(-side => "left");
$listbox2 = $top->ScrlListbox(-label => "Contiguous group",
                             -selectmode => "extended",
                             -exportselection => 0
                             )->pack(-side => "left");
$listbox3 = $top->ScrlListbox(-label => "Scattered group" ,
                             -selectmode => "extended",
                             -exportselection => 0
                             )->pack(-side => "left");

foreach $i (1..10) {
    $listbox1->insert("end", "Single_$i");
    $listbox2->insert("end", "Extended_$i");
    $listbox3->insert("end", "Extended_$i");
}

MainLoop;
```

A listbox object accesses the data stored in it via member functions. These methods address n list entries via indices from 0 to n−1. The last entry of a listbox can also be addressed via the symbolic index "end".

$listbox->insert($index, $item, ...) inserts one or more entries into the list *before* the specified index. For insertion at the end of the list, "end" is specified as index.

$listbox->delete($index1, $index2) deletes the list entries from index position $index1 to position $index2. $index2 is optional; if it is omitted, only the element on index position $index1 is deleted.

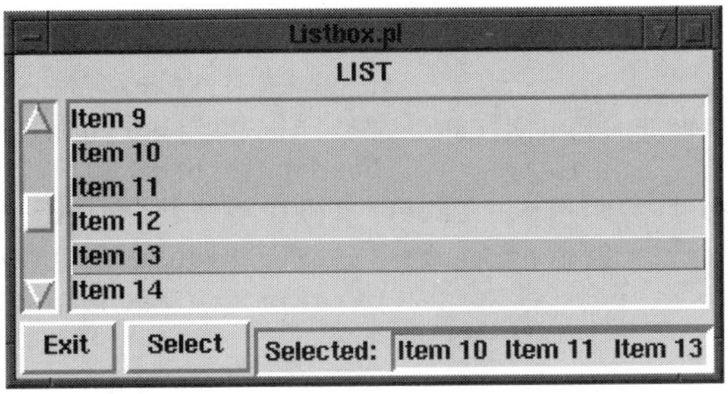

Figure 4.15 Sample listbox.

`$listbox->selection("set", $from, $to)` marks the entries from index position `$from` to position `$to` as selected. `$to` can be omitted if only one element is selected.

`$listbox->selection("clear", $from, $to)` deselects the entries from index position `$from` to position `$to`. `$to` can be omitted if only one element is deselected.

`$listbox->Getselected()` returns a list of selected listbox entries. In single-select mode, the result is always one individual entry.

The test sample of this section presents a scrolled listbox running in `"extended"` mode. Successful selection of one or more entries is indicated by a label. In Figure 4.15, two contiguous and one individual entries are selected.

_____*listbox.pl*

```perl
#!/usr/bin/perl -w

use Tk;

my $top = MainWindow->new();

                            # create listbox
$listbox = $top->ScrlListbox(-label => "LIST",
                             -height => 6,
                             -selectmode => "extended");

                            # buttons
$exitbutton   = $top->Button(-text => "Exit",
                             -command => \&exit);
$selectbutton = $top->Button(-text => "Select",
                             -command => \&proc_selection);
```

```perl
                                # display
$frame = $top->Frame(-relief => "sunken",
                     -borderwidth => 2);
$label = $frame->Label(-text => "Selected: ");
$entry = $frame->Label(-textvariable => \$seltext,
                       -relief => "sunken");

                                # pack all
$listbox->pack(-fill    => "both", "-expand" => "yes");
$exitbutton->pack(-side => "left");
$selectbutton->pack(-side => "left");
$frame->pack(-side => "right", "-anchor" => "se");
$label->pack(-side => "left");
$entry->pack(-side => "left");


                                # fill listbox
foreach $i (1..20) {
    $listbox->insert("end", "Item $i");
}
                                # set preselection
$listbox->selection("set", 0);
                                # simulate selection
$seltext = proc_selection();


                                # define action for double
                                # click on listbox entry
$listbox->bind("<Double-Button-1>" => \&proc_selection);

MainLoop;

###
### proc_selection() - process selection event
###
sub
proc_selection {
                                # fetch selected entries,
                                # concatenate them to a string,
                                # and store them in the text
                                # variable of the label widget
    $seltext = join(' ', $listbox->Getselected);
}
```

listbox.pl

Selection of entries is carried out either via a preselection (simple mouse click) and a subsequent click on the Select button, or via a double click on the listbox entry. The latter is activated by a call to the bind method, whose peculiarities are discussed in Section 4.7.5.

If one does not wish to show the listbox from the very beginning, but rather to make an entry selected in the depths of hidden values appear as if by magic,

```
$listbox->yview("moveto", 10);
```

for example, does not show the entries starting with the first one, but starts with entry number 10.

4.6.8 Menu widgets

The pulldown menu technique is the probably best-known example of graphical user interaction. Starting with the menu bar that sits directly underneath the title bar of a window and contains the top entries (menu buttons), a mouse click lets menus drop down showing selectable entries.

Figure 4.16 shows a sample and the most important denominations.

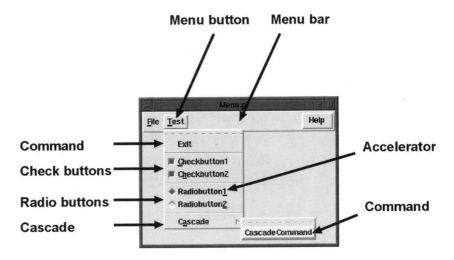

Figure 4.16   Pulldown menus and their elements.

Menu bars

The bar at the top of the window is nothing but a frame widget, defined with −relief option "raised" and −borderwidth => 2, and the top menu entries hierarchically subordinate as menu button widgets. Usually, top menu entries such as File are positioned on the left-hand side of the menu bar, whereas special entries such as Help or copyright information are to be found on the right-hand side. This positioning is controlled by the `-side` option of the `pack` method.

Menu buttons

The top menu entries that, when selected, make the pulldown menus appear, consist of so-called menu button widgets. The call of the method

```
$menubutton = $menubar->MenuButton(-text => "File");
```

creates a new top menu entry as a child of the menu bar. A subsequent `pack` puts it to the requested position in the menu bar. With the returned reference to a menu button object, the pulldown menu entries are created via method calls at a later stage.

The pulldown menu entries themselves are divided into five different types, of which the command widget is probably the best known one: an entry that upon activation triggers a command, such as the `Quit` entry in the `File` menu, which terminates the program.

Menu commands

All the menu button objects on the menu bar support the `command` method, which creates a pulldown menu entry. This is initially hidden, and is displayed only when the user activates the associated top entry, for example with a click of the mouse.

As options, the `command` method is passed a label text, such as `-label => "Exit"`, together with a reference to a subroutine, for example in the form `-command => sub { }`, which will be executed upon activation of the button.

```
$menubutton->command(-label => "Exit",
                     -command => sub { exit 0 });
```

Menu check button

Pulldown menu entries can, however, also show a check button behavior. The `checkbutton` method of the menu button object creates an object in the pulldown menu whose text is specified with `-label` and which otherwise supports all the options of the check button widget (see page 183):

```
$menubutton->checkbutton(-label => "Check1",
                        -variable => \$checkvar,
                        -command =>
                            sub { print "$checkvar\n" });
```

Menu radio buttons

In addition to the check button widget as a menu entry, Tk also provides the radio button variation. A radio button menu entry created with `$menubutton->radiobutton()` supports the entire functionality of its counterpart in dialog handling. The corresponding options are described in Section 4.6.3.

```
$menubutton->radiobutton(-label => "Radio1",
                         -variable => \$radiovar,
                         -value => "Radio1",
                         -command =>
                             sub { print "$radiovar\n" });
```

Menu separator

A separator divides contents-related groups of pulldown menu entries from each other and serves only for visual improvement, but cannot be activated. It merely draws a horizontal separation line in the pulldown menu. The call

```
$menubutton->separator();
```

appends a separator to the current end of the current pulldown menu.

Cascades

The call of `$menubutton->cascade()` inserts an entry into an existing pulldown menu that refers to a cascaded menu. First, however, a new menu must be created as a hierarchical child of the existing one. For this purpose, the method

```
$oldmenu = $menubutton->cget(-menu);
```

is used to find out the menu reference of the menu button object, and a subsequent

```
$newmenu = $oldmenu->Menu();
```

creates a new menu object into which entries can in turn be inserted by means of the above-mentioned methods `command`, `checkbutton`, `radiobutton`, `cascade`, and `separator`.

Thus the call of the `cascade` method of a menu button object is written as

```
$menubutton->cascade(-label => "Mycascade", -menu => $newmenu);
```

Locking and activating menu entries

To prevent users from selecting specific entries from a pulldown menu, the Menubutton object can lock those entries by means of the `entryconfigure` method. Thus

```
$menubutton->entryconfigure(1, -state => "disabled");
```

greys out the first menu item and instructs it not to accept mouse clicks.

```
$menubutton->entryconfigure(1, -state => "enabled");
```

reactivates the entry.

Accelerators

Users can control X Window interfaces not only with the mouse, but also via the keyboard. Thus the key combination (Alt)-(F) selects the menu entry bearing the accelerator 'F'. The accelerator is usually the first letter of an entry, but it may be any other letter if the first one leads to overlapping with another accelerator.

In Perl/Tk, the option -underline => $scalar specifies the accelerator during creation of a menu entry. $scalar indicates the offset of the marked letter in the menu entry, with 0 standing for the first letter. The Quit entry in the menu, which uses the Q as accelerator, is thus defined as

```
$menubutton->command(-label => "Quit", -underline => 0);
```

Deactivation

Depending on the context of an application, some menu entries are temporarily not to be activated. Similarly to the button widget, the -state option is available, which sets this behavior by means of the parameter values normal or disabled. The status of already existing widgets can be changed at any time by means of the configure method, as mentioned above.

Summary

Table 4.9 summarizes the menu-specific options of the command, checkbutton, radiobutton, and cascade widgets.

Listing menu.pl shows a sample application that uses all common menu functions. In Figure 4.17, this interface can be seen in full action.

Table 4.9   Options for the command, checkbutton, radiobutton, and cascade menu entries.

-label	=>	"text"	Menu entry
-command	=>	\& subname	Activation callback
-state	=>	"normal|disabled"	Activated/disabled
-underline	=>	$offset	Accelerator character as offset

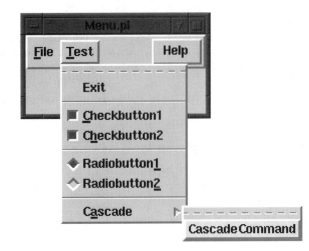

Figure 4.17 Sample menu.

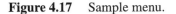*menu.pl*

```perl
#!/usr/bin/perl -w

use Tk;

$top = MainWindow->new;

                               # menu bar
$menu = $top->Frame(-relief => 'raised', -bd => 2);

                               # menu bar entries
$menu_pulldown1 = $menu->Menubutton(-text => "File",
                                    -underline => 0);
$menu_pulldown2 = $menu->Menubutton(-text => "Test",
                                    -underline => 0);

                        # popup menu as pushbutton
                        # in menu bar
$menu_popup = $menu->Button(-text => "Help",
                    -command =>
                        sub { print "Help\n" } );

                        # normal pulldown entry
$menu_pulldown2->command(-label => "Exit",
                    -command => sub { exit 0 });
```

```perl
$menu_pulldown2->separator(); # separator


                               # check button pulldown entry
$menu_pulldown2->checkbutton(-label => "Checkbutton1",
                             -underline => 0,
                             -variable => \$checkvar,
                             -command =>
                                  sub { print "Check1\n" });
$menu_pulldown2->checkbutton(-label => "Checkbutton2",
                             -underline => 1,
                             -variable => \$checkvar,
                             -command =>
                                  sub { print "Check2\n" });
$checkvar = 1;

$menu_pulldown2->separator(); # separator


                               # radio button pulldown entry
$menu_pulldown2->radiobutton(-label => "Radiobutton1",
                             -underline => 11,
                             -variable => \$radiovar,
                             -value => "Radio1",
                             -command =>
                             sub { print "$radiovar\n" });
$menu_pulldown2->radiobutton(-label => "Radiobutton2",
                             -underline => 11,
                             -variable => \$radiovar,
                             -value => "Radio2",
                             -command =>
                             sub { print "$radiovar\n" });


$radiovar="Radio1";               # default value: radio button 1

$menu_pulldown2->separator(); # separator


                               # cascade menu
$newmenu = $menu_pulldown2->cget(-menu)->Menu();

$menu_pulldown2->cascade(-label => "Cascade",
                         -underline => 1,
                         -menu => $newmenu);


                               # normal entry in
                               # cascaded menu
$newmenu->command(-label => "CascadeCommand",
```

```
                                   -command => sub { exit 0 });

                                   # pack all
$menu->pack(-side => 'top', -fill => 'x');
$menu_pulldown1->pack(-side, 'left');
$menu_pulldown2->pack(-side, 'left');
$menu_popup->pack(-side, 'right');

MainLoop;
```

_____*menu.pl*

The dotted separator that, as can be seen in Figure 4.17, is the first entry underneath the top menu entry, is a special feature of Tk. In contrast to the Motif standard, it can be activated, and it creates a new toplevel window that contains the menu item pushbuttons. Thus a permanently visible copy of the pulldown menu stays on screen.

4.6.9 Messages

The `Message` widget formats multiline texts such as those usually occurring in error messages. Lines are, if possible, broken at word boundaries; the option -justify => left|right|center aligns the text left or right, or centers it.

_____*message.pl*

```
#!/usr/bin/perl -w

use Tk;

$top = MainWindow->new();

$top->Message(-width => "3c", -justify => "left",
              -text => "This is a left-ranged message"
              )->pack(-side => "left");
$top->Message(-width => "3c", -justify => "right",
              -text => "This is a right-ranged message "
              )->pack(-side => "left");
$top->Message(-width => "3c", -justify => "center",
              -text => "This is a centered message"
              )->pack(-side => "left");

MainLoop;
```

_____*message.pl*

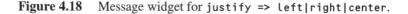

Figure 4.18   Message widget for `justify => left|right|center`.

4.6.10 Scales

Scales are labeled slide rules that can be adjusted with the mouse. They are frequently to be found in programs in which a visual or acoustic value such as brightness or volume is to be set. Every movement of the rule, as small as it may be, immediately triggers the callback specified by means of the `-command` option, which then accesses the set value via the `$scale->get()` method of the scale widget.

As a small application, Figure 4.19 shows an RGB editor that changes its own background color according to the scale settings of the base colors red, green, and blue.

The script exploits the fact that the color manipulation options `-foreground` and `-background` recognize not only colors expressed in clear text, such as `"blue"`, but also numerical values composed of RGB settings. More about this can be found in Section 4.7.6.

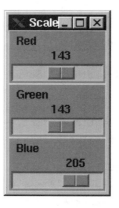

Figure 4.19   RGB control with three scale widgets.

The foreground color – that is, the color of the labeling – must always be in good contrast to the current background to keep the text readable. Therefore, from a specific brightness threshold onward, which is determined by the sum of the selected RGB parts, the script changes the foreground color from "white" to "black".

```perl
#!/usr/bin/perl -w

use Tk;

$top = MainWindow->new();

$red = $top->Scale(-from => 0, -to => 255,
                   -orient => "horizontal",
                   -label => "Red", -command => \&upd_color);
$green = $top->Scale(-from => 0, -to => 255,
                     -orient => "horizontal",
                     -label => "Green",
                     -command => \&upd_color);
$blue = $top->Scale(-from => 0, -to => 255,
                    -orient => "horizontal",
                    -label => "Blue",
                    -command => \&upd_color);

$red->pack();
$green->pack();
$blue->pack();

MainLoop;

# upd_color - update foreground and background color

sub upd_color {
    my $background = "#";
    my $total      = 0;

    # read values and build numerical color description
foreach $i ($red,$green,$blue) {
        my $value = $i->get();
        $background .= sprintf("%02x", $value);
        $total += $value;
    }

    # labeling color in function
    # of total brightness
    my $foreground = $total < 255 ? "white" : "black";
```

```
foreach $i ($red,$green,$blue) {
    $i->configure(-background => $background,
                  -foreground => $foreground);
}
}
```

scale.pl

4.6.11 Scrollbars

The scrollbar is already known from the ScrlListbox widget. But a listbox is not the only one that needs scrolling services: multiline text widgets or canvas objects too can assume sizes that make it impossible to view them in one piece.

Here, Tk must mediate between the scrollbar and the scrolled widget. A change of the scrollbar by a user's mouse click is signaled to the affected widget by means of a callback routine. The information on which of the widgets has to be notified is built into the scrollbar during its definition:

```
my $scrollbar = $top->Scrollbar(-command =>
                                [yview => $scrolledwidget]);
```

This slightly unconventional syntax has its origin in the obscure Tcl programming logic. The callback attached to the scrollbar requires information on the affected widget object and the name of the scroll method. By convention, the `-command` option is passed a reference to an anonymous list of parameters, if we are dealing with a Tk-internal callback. It is of no importance whether the widget object or the method comes first in the list, because Tk always analyzes the parameters by type. The notation chosen above has the advantage that the quotes can be omitted from the first argument, since an option standing in front of the `=>` operator is automatically interpreted as a string from Perl 5.001 onward. In the opposite case, we would need to write `[$scrolledwidget, 'yview']`.

It is of utmost importance that the specified widget object should exist at the time of the above construct. The `Scrollbar` method is passed the parameter `$scrolledwidget` *by value*; thus the value of the parameter is defined at callback definition and is not adjusted any further.

Conversely, the manipulated widget needs a connection with the scrollbar, because if it changes the scroll position on its own, the scrollbar must adapt its status. Since the scrollbar object already exists, the `configure` method simply changes the parameters of the `yscrollcommand` option:

```
$scrolledwidget->configure(-yscrollcommand =>
                           [set => $scrollbar]);
```

The parameter supply (with coordinates, and so on) of the callback calls is taken over in both communication directions by Tk in a completely transparent manner. The next section shows a text widget that modifies its visible section by means of a scrollbar.

4.6.12 Text

Editable text fields are small editors. They provide a comprehensive functionality, because Tk takes over the complete cursor management. Usually, they form a unit with the associated scrollbar widgets that scroll the text in the x and y directions.

Text widgets are also suited for simple representation of text without editing facilities. The `"disabled"` parameter of the `-state` option sets the text widget to read-only mode. `"normal"` allows further input to be made, and again displays the insertion point cursor. But attention: even for programmed changes in the text, the text widget must be in the `normal` state. Thus, to display a non-editable text, you must first insert the text and only then call

```
$text->configure(-state => "disabled");
```

Line breaking

Line breaking is controlled by the `-wrap` option. `"char"` is the default setting, which sends the cursor into the next line as soon as the current line is full. In contrast, `"-word"` considers word boundaries and simulates the behavior of common word processing programs, which allow fluent writing of long, coherent texts. `"-none"` disables line breaking and must be set if an appropriate scrollbar supports horizontal scrolling.

Table 4.10   Text widget options.

`-wrap`	`=>`	`"none|char|word"`	Line breaking
`-status`	`=>`	`"normal|disabled"`	Editing/read-only

Lines and columns

The methods of the text widget that insert or delete text are passed line and column specifications as information for a specific text position. Line numbers start with 1, for historical reasons, whereas the characters in a line are numbered from 0 to end. Line and column together form a string of the format `"line.char"`. Thus

    `"1.0"` addresses the first character of the first line,

    `"2.11"` addresses the tenth character of the second line,

"2.end" addresses the last character of the second line,

"end" addresses the last character of the document.

Text strings, including the newline characters that separate the lines, are inserted into the document by means of the $textwidget->insert method; similarly, $textwidget->delete deletes sections from the text, and $textwidget->get copies them to a string. In the method calls shown below, pos_from and pos_to mark the text positions as strings in the format "line.char". pos_from identifies the start position, pos_to the end. pos_from lies inside the selected area, whereas pos_to lies outside.

```
$textwidget->insert($pos_from, "text");              # insert text

$textwidget->delete($pos_from, $pos_to);             # delete text

$textstring = $textwidget->get($pos_from, $pos_to); # get text
```

The instruction

```
$textwidget->insert("3.0", "Text of the new third line\n");
```

inserts a text string (of potentially several lines) between the second and the third line of the document.

```
$textwidget->delete("3.0", "4.0");
```

deletes the third line from the text.

```
$textstring = $textwidget->get("3.0", "4.0");
```

allows access to the third line of the text, with the returned string $textstring including the newline character.

Position specifications refer to the original lines; line breaks inserted by means of the -wrap option do not exist in the document itself and therefore play no role in positioning.

Tags

Another mechanism for addressing text areas is *tagging*. A tag marks a contiguous text area with a unique name. The same area of text can even be marked by overlapping tags. According to the position specifications introduced above, the call

```
$textwidget->tag("add", "tagname", "3.0", "4.0");
```

marks the entire third line as belonging to the tag tagname.

Now, what are tags good for? Tag-marked text areas behave like small partial documents: thus background colors or the text font used can be specified individually for each tag. The configure command

```
$text->tag("configure", "tagname", -background => "black",
                                   -foreground => "white");
```

for example, shows marked text in the form of 'white letters on a black background.' The applications presented in Sections 4.9.4 and 4.9.6, two browsers for the colors and fonts provided by the X Window system, make use of the tag mechanism by assigning tags to the lines of a scrollable text widget and changing their settings.

As an example, Listing `text.pl` shows a text widget with a horizontal and a vertical scrollbar related to the text widget according to the specifications discussed in Section 4.6.11. To make horizontal scrolling work properly, line breaking must be set to `-wrap => "none"`.

`text.pl` modifies the contents of the lines of the text widget: it deletes the third line and replaces it with new text; subsequently it swaps the fourth and fifth line.

_____*text.pl*

```
#!/usr/bin/perl -w

use Tk;

my $top = MainWindow->new();

my $frame = $top->Frame();

my $text = $frame->Text(-wrap => 'none');

                              # define scrollbars
my $yscrollbar = $frame->Scrollbar(-command =>
                                   [yview => $text]);
my $xscrollbar = $top->Scrollbar(-orient => 'horizontal',
                                 -command => [xview => $text]);

                              # ... and set them
$text->configure(-yscrollcommand => [set => $yscrollbar]);
$text->configure(-xscrollcommand => [set => $xscrollbar]);

                              # pack all
$yscrollbar->pack(-side => 'right', -fill => 'y');
$xscrollbar->pack(-side => 'bottom', -fill => 'x');

$frame->pack(-expand => 'yes', -fill => 'both');
$text->pack(-expand => 'yes', -fill => 'both',
            -side => 'left');

foreach $row (1..30) {          # insert 30 lines
```

```
        $text->insert("end", "Line $row\n");
}


# delete third line
$text->delete("3.0", "4.0");

# insert new third line
$text->insert("3.0", "Text of the new third line\n");

# swap fourth and fifth line

$line4 = $text->get("4.0", "5.0");          # get line 4
$line5 = $text->get("5.0", "6.0");          # get line 5
$text->delete("4.0", "6.0");                # delete lines 4 and 5
$textstring = $text->insert("4.0", $line5); # insert new line 4
$textstring = $text->insert("5.0", $line4); # insert new line 5


MainLoop;
```

text.pl

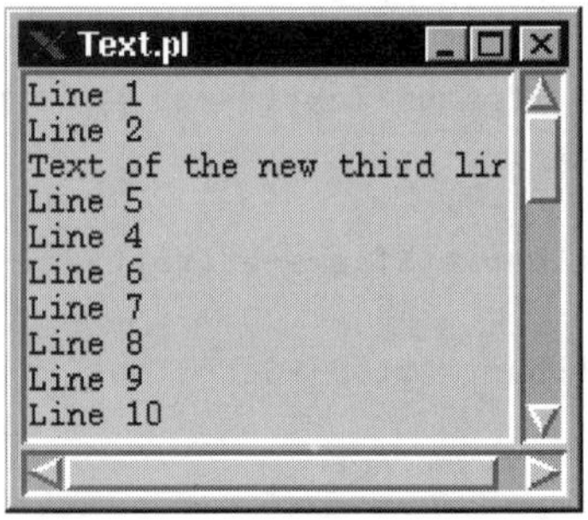

Figure 4.20   Text widget with two scrollbars.

Hyperlink browsers can also be easily implemented with tags. When the mouse pointer reaches the area of the embedded hyperlink, either the text color changes, or the address of the linked document appears at the bottom of the text window. A mouse click on the link then usually triggers a change to the referenced document. These actions are controlled by bind commands on tags. These commands branch into different functions upon occurrence of specific events. For example, as soon as the mouse pointer enters the area defined by the tag tagname, the instruction

```
$text->tag("bind", "tagname", '<Any-Enter>' => \&doit );
```

causes the interpreter to call the function `doit` with `$text` as the first parameter. Binding in full detail will be the subject of Section 4.7.5. A sample implementation with hyperlinks follows in the practice part in Section 4.9.3.

4.6.13 Toplevel

Frequently, graphical applications create new windows on the screen, for example a file selection dialog or the display of an error message in a box. The method

```
$newtop = $top->Toplevel();
```

initializes a new window and immediately displays it. Additional child widgets are inserted in the same way as in the main window of the application. The dialog window is finally removed from the screen by means of the method $newtop->destroy().

Figure 4.21   An object of the MessageDialog class.

The dialog widget implemented in Listing `md.pl` displays a message and waits for a mouse click on the OK button before it vanishes.

The `MessageDialog` class in the `MessageDialog.pm` module presented in the following paragraphs provides a constructor of the form

```
$md = MessageDialog->new($top);
```

which as a parameter receives a reference to the current main window of the application. The message box is opened by the call

```
$md->start($title, $messagetext);
```

and sets title and message text according to the parameters `$title` and `$message-text`. Listing `MessageDialog.pm` shows the class implementation. The `new` constructor merely creates the namespace common in object orientation (see Section 2.2.2) and stores the value of the parent window parameter for later use. The `start` method, instead, opens a new toplevel window and immediately assigns the Exit button located in it a callback function that makes the toplevel window disappear when the button is activated. Thus the main program, which issued the error message, is free of any obligation with regard to the new window – it closes practically by itself.

```
###
### Message dialog widget class
###
package MessageDialog;

use Tk;
use strict;

###
### $md = MessageDialog->new($topwindow) - new message dialog
###
sub new {
    my($type, $parentwin) = @_;

    my $self = {};

    $self->{'parentwin'}   = $parentwin;

    bless($self, $type);
}


###
### $md->start("Title", "MessageText") - display message dialog
###
sub start {
    my $self     = shift;
    my $title    = shift;
    my $message  = shift;

    $self->{'topwin'} = $self->{'parentwin'}->Toplevel();

    $self->{'topwin'}->configure(-title => "$title");

    $self->{'topwin'}->Message(-text => "$message",
                               -width => "10c")->pack();
    $self->{'topwin'}->Button(-text => "OK",
        -command => sub { $self->{'topwin'}->destroy() }
                              )->pack();
}

1;
```

```
#!/usr/bin/perl -w

###
### Application of the message dialog
###

use Tk;                              # include Tk package
use MessageDialog;                   # MessageDialog package
use strict;

my $message = "This is an error message. Close " .
              "this window with a click on the " .
              "OK button.";

my $top = MainWindow->new();

my $md=MessageDialog->new($top);

### define widgets
$top->Button(-text => "Start message dialog",
      -command => sub { $md->start("Error message", $message);
                      })->pack();
$top->Button(-text => "Exit",
              -command => sub { exit 0 } )->pack();

MainLoop;
```

Even while the error message is shown on screen, the main application can still be manipulated. In many cases, this is not the required behavior; instead, the user should be forced to acknowledge the error message first with a click on the OK button and only then continue working with the main application window. The required settings of the so-called *grab* are described in Section 4.7.1.

4.6.14 Canvas

The canvas widget is probably the most general and functionally most powerful of all Tk widgets. It displays geometrical objects and other widgets in a predefined area and can also scroll its contents in the x and y directions. To remain within the scope of this book, the present introduction to the Tk package must unfortunately limit itself to a tiny fraction of the available options. The best-known canvas feature is the display of bitmaps.

The sample program `canvas.pl` displays a bitmap in a scrollable canvas widget.

_____*canvas.pl*

```perl
#!/usr/bin/perl -w

use Tk;

my $top    = MainWindow->new();

my $canvas = $top->Canvas();

$canvas->create('bitmap', 0, 0, -bitmap=>'@bitmap.xbm',
                               -anchor => 'nw',
                               -foreground => 'black',
                               -background => 'white');

my $yscrollbar = $top->Scrollbar(-command => ['yview', $canvas],
                                 -orient => 'vertical');
my $xscrollbar = $top->Scrollbar(-command => ['xview', $canvas],
                                 -orient => 'horizontal');

$canvas->configure(-scrollregion => [0, 0, 330, 240]);

$canvas->configure(-xscrollcommand => ['set', $xscrollbar],
                   -yscrollcommand => ['set', $yscrollbar]);

$yscrollbar->pack(-side => 'right', -fill => 'y');
$xscrollbar->pack(-side => 'bottom', -fill => 'x');

$canvas->pack(-expand => 'yes', -fill => 'both');

MainLoop;
```

_____*canvas.pl*

The canvas widget is also capable of displaying images of other formats, provided these have previously been converted to the Tk-internal image format by means of the photo widget. The call

```perl
$canvas->create('image', $xpos, $ypos,
                -image => $photowidget,
                -anchor => 'nw');
```

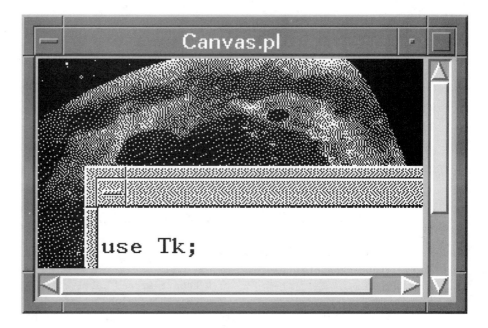

Figure 4.22 Bitmap in a canvas widget.

defines an image object, whose resources are sustained by the `photo` widget discussed in the next section. The two coordinates `$xpos` and `$ypos` define the reference point for the specified anchor. Caution: in the default setting `-anchor => "center"`, `$xpos` and `$ypos` define the point where the center of the image will be located; for a reference point of `0,0` this results in the required behavior only in very rare cases. An anchor set to `'nw'`, as shown above, will most probably be a better choice.

An application that uses the `image` interface of the canvas widget for this purpose is the image viewer presented in Section 4.9.5.

4.6.15 Photos

The photo widget is a relatively new construct in the Tk world. It supports the most disparate image formats in a completely transparent way: the file name of the current image is fed to the option `-file`, and Tk converts it in its own internal format for later display.

The button and label widgets have the `-image` option, whose parameter is the responsible photo widget object. The canvas widget includes the photo widget via the call shown at the end of the previous section.

The script `photo.pl` defines a label, whose graphical content is an image stored as a file in GIF format on the hard disk.

————————————————————————————————photo.pl

```perl
#!/usr/bin/perl -w

use Tk;

$top = MainWindow->new();

                              # create photo object and
                              # initialize with GIF image
$photo = $top->Photo();
$photo->configure("-file" => "earthris.gif");

                              # include photo in label
                              # and display
$label = $top->Label(-image => $photo, -text => "hallo");
$label->pack();
                              # create second label with
                              # "Width x Height" text
$top->Label(-text => $photo->width . "x" . $photo->height)->pack();

MainLoop;
```

————————————————————————————————photo.pl

Height and width of the read image are provided by the methods `width` and `height` of the photo object.

4.7 Widgets in interaction

4.7.1 The grab

If an application starts a second window, for example to display an error message, further manipulation of the main window should under certain conditions be made impossible. In Tk, such a behavior is called 'local grab.' In rarer cases, even all other applications must be 'frozen' ('global grab'), until the user has acknowledged the error message with a click on the OK button.

To enable a window to receive the grab, however, it must be visible. With the `"visibility"` parameter, the `tkwait` method (Section 4.7.2) provides the possibility of delaying the program until the window actually appears on screen.

```perl
$toplevelwidget->tkwait("visibility", $toplevelwidget);
```

Each toplevel window object possesses the `grab` method, which confers the grab to the window in question. Without parameters, `grab` initiates the local grab; with the `-global` option, it triggers the global one:

```
$toplevelwidget->grab();            # local grab
$toplevelwidget->grab("-global");   # global grab
```

4.7.2 Waiting for events

If the program flow stops because a script expects a reaction from the user, restart is usually defined by a callback to the expected event. At that moment, the program iterates through the event loop `MainLoop` and waits for expired timers, pressed buttons, or certain mouse movements.

This procedure, however, makes it difficult to define the program flow as such. A called callback in turn sets callbacks to expected events and immediately terminates itself.

As a variation of this programming style, Tk provides the possibility of explicitly waiting for events without leaving a callback function. The `tkwait` routine blocks the execution of the program until a specific event occurs, but in the meantime continues to manage the interface. If, instead, the program were blocked in a user-defined routine, the interface would be 'dead.'

`tkwait` recognizes three different types of event. With

- `tkwait("visibility", $toplevelwindow)` it waits for the toplevel window `$toplevelwindow` to appear on screen,
- `tkwait("window", $toplevelwindow)` it waits for the toplevel window `$toplevelwindow` to disappear from the screen,
- `tkwait("variable", \$scalar)` it waits for the variable `$scalar` to change its value.

4.7.3 Dialog control

For a user-friendly dialog control in message boxes that potentially contain several buttons to be chosen from, Tk provides the dialog widget.

After inclusion of

```
use Tk::Dialog;
```

the command

```
$dialog = $top->Dialog();
```

creates a new dialog widget that supports the options listed in Table 4.11.

For the purpose of illustrating the message to be displayed, the dialog widget also supports the `-bitmap` option, which visualizes either Tk built-in bitmaps (see page 220) or user-defined bitmaps next to the message text.

Table 4.11   Dialog widget options.

`-title`	`=>`	`"titletext"`	Title
`-text`	`=>`	`"messagetext"`	Text

`-bitmap`	`=>`	`"error|gray25|`
		`gray50|hourglass|`
		`info|questhead|`
		`question|warning"|`
		`'@filename'`
			Illustration icon

`-buttons`	`=>`	`\@buttons`	Button texts
`-default_button`	`=>`	`$button`	Default button text

The `Show` method of the dialog widget draws the dialog box in a new window on the screen and, as soon as one of the defined buttons is pressed, returns the label text.

Without parameter specifications in the `Show` call, the dialog widget receives the local grab, with the option `"-global"`, the global grab.

```
$dialog->Show();             # local grab
$dialog->Show("-global");    # global grab
```

Listing `dialog.pl` shows a small application, which upon demand opens a dialog box and, after one of the three buttons is pressed, returns the text of that button.

dialog.pl

```perl
#!/usr/bin/perl -w

use Tk;
use Tk::Dialog;

$top = MainWindow->new();

$top->Button(-text => "Start dialog",
             -command => sub { dialog($top); })->pack();
$top->Button(-text => "Exit", -command => sub { exit 0 } )->pack();

MainLoop;

sub dialog {
    my $top = shift;

    my $okButton     = 'OK';
    my $cancelButton = 'Cancel';
    my $helpButton   = 'Help';
```

```
my $dialog = $top->Dialog(
        -title => 'Title',
        -text  => 'Text of the error message, and so forth',
        -bitmap => 'info',
        -default_button => $okButton,
        -buttons => [$okButton, $cancelButton, $helpButton]);

if(($returnButton=$dialog->Show('-global')) eq $okButton) {
    print "OK\n";
} elsif ($returnButton eq $cancelButton) {
    print "Cancel\n";
} elsif ($returnButton eq $helpButton) {
    print "Help\n";
}
}
```

_____*dialog.pl*

4.7.4 Communication with the window manager

Position, size, and border of a window are the job of the window manager, as already explained in Section 4.2.7. The method wm, provided by every toplevel widget, causes the window manager to carry out the appropriate corrections.

Probably the most important option in Table 4.12 is geometry, which specifies the size of the application window as length times width in pixels.

Occasionally, the title option may be useful too, if the title bar of the window is required not to show the name of the executed script, but to show a specific text.

maxsize is often used to prevent scrolled widgets from exceeding a maximum size.

Table 4.12   Commands for the window manager.

`$widget->wm("geometry", "w×h");`	Set width and height
`$widget->wm("iconify");`	Window → icon
`$widget->wm("deiconify");`	Icon → window
`$widget->wm("iconbitmap", $bitmap);`	Iconized window bitmap
`$widget->wm("iconname", "name");`	Name of icon
`$widget->wm("maxsize", $width, $height);`	Maximum possible size
`$widget->wm("minsize", $width, $height);`	Minimum reduction
`$widget->wm("resizable", 1|0);`	Resizable window
`$widget->wm("title", "name");`	Title text

4.7.5 Bindings

Bindings define actions that are to take place following specific events. Each widget already has a predefined set of bindings: thus moving the mouse pointer over the surface of a button makes the button change color, or a simple mouse click triggers the execution of predefined actions.

For some widgets it is sensible to define application-specific bindings in addition to the standard ones: a double click with the mouse, for example, on a listbox element of a file selector usually selects the corresponding entry, while in an error message with acknowledgment button, pressing the ⏎ key usually triggers the OK button.

Each Tk widget supports the method in the form

```
$widget->bind("<event_name>", \&function)
```

which includes two parameters: an event description, and the associated action as a function reference. The detailed description of an event is derived from Table 4.13, whose column contents are simply placed one after the other with hyphens.

For example, `<Shift-Control-Button-1>` defines a click of the first mouse button while the key combination Shift-Ctrl is kept depressed. The name `<Control-Key-c>`, instead, stands for the key combination Ctrl-C. `<Any-ButtonRelease>` means any released mouse button.

The terms `Enter` and `Leave` refer to the mouse pointer that enters or leaves a defined field, each time triggering an action. For example,

```
$button->bind("<Any-Enter>", sub {exit 0});
```

causes program termination when the mouse pointer gets into the area of the button `$button`. Some more definitions:

- `<Button-1>` Left mouse button pressed
- `<Double-Button-1>` Left mouse button double clicked
- `<Key-Return>` Return key pressed
- `<Key-F1>` F1 key pressed

Table 4.13 Event descriptions.

Any	Control	Double	Key	Return
	Shift	Triple	KeyRelease	Escape
	Meta		Button	
				Key (a–z, A–Z, 0–9 ...)
	Lock		ButtonRelease	*Mouse button* (1–5)
	Alt		Enter	
			Leave	

- `<Any-Enter>`   Mouse pointer enters the area of the widget
- `<Any-Leave>`   Mouse pointer leaves the area of the widget

4.7.6 Fonts and colors

As any other X Window program, a Perl/Tk script too can freely choose the labeling font of its widgets. Thus each widget that contains text supports the `-font` option, which allows selection of the most varied X Window fonts.

The `xlsfont` program, a tool of the X Window system, displays all supported types and sizes. There are fonts with short identifiers that use standard types and set only the size, such as `9x15`, but there are also detailed descriptions such as, for example,

```
-adobe-times-bold-i-normal--17-120-100-100-p-86-iso8859-1
```

We will not discuss the meaning of the individual elements, but we would like to refer you to the font viewer presented in Section 4.9.4, which shows all available fonts in a scrollable listbox, thus allowing selection by visual criteria.

Wildcards too can be used in font specifications. In Tk, the above Adobe Times font could as well have been selected by means of

```
-adobe-times-bold-*--17*
```

Colors

The colors of a widget are defined by means of the options `-foreground` and `-background`, which determine the foreground and background colors. As parameters, you can use either the clear text names usually stored (under UNIX) in the file `/usr/lib/X11/rgb.txt`, or their hexadecimal representation.

The numerical format consists of a prefixed hash sign (#) followed by two digits each of red, green, and blue parts in the range from 0 to 255 in hexadecimal notation. Thus the numerical value for `"black"` is `"#000000"`, while the value for `"white"` is `"#FFFFFF"`.

4.7.7 Bitmaps

For illustrations, Tk offers a range of predefined bitmaps. Buttons and labels, as well as the dialog widget introduced in Section 4.7.3, support the option `-bitmap`, which expect as a parameter either a file in the form of

```
$top->Label(-bitmap => '@filename');
```

or the name of a Tk bitmap such as, for example,

```
$top->Label(-bitmap => 'hourglass');
```

Figure 4.23 shows the bitmaps predefined in Tk. They have been generated by means of Listing `bitmaps.pl`.

_____*bitmaps.pl*

```
#!/usr/bin/perl -w

use Tk;

my $top = MainWindow->new();

foreach $bitmapstyle (qw(error gray25 gray50 hourglass
                         info questhead question warning)) {
    $frame = $top->Frame();
    $frame->Label(-bitmap => $bitmapstyle)->pack();
    $frame->Label(-text => $bitmapstyle,
                  -font => "*helvetica-bold-r-*12*"
                )->pack(-anchor => "s");
    $frame->pack(-side => "left", -anchor => "s");
}

MainLoop;
```

_____*bitmaps.pl*

Figure 4.23   Predefined bitmaps in Tk.

4.8 Hints and tricks for Perl/Tk programming

At the beginning, programming of event-driven applications looks a bit difficult because of the unusual program structure. In this section, some practical examples will point out common problems and illustrate their solution.

4.8.1 Long-running functions

If a user triggers an event that activates a long-running callback, the main event loop cannot handle any more events – the interface is 'dead.' This excludes the user from any further manipulation of dialog objects, including the interruption of the callback. In fact, the user can do nothing but wait until the callback terminates itself and returns control to the main event loop. Even worse: if, in the meantime, another application covers and then releases the window of the dead GUI, the window manager sends the redraw signal, but even this cannot get through – the result is an ugly empty spot on the screen.

For this reason, no callback must block the main loop for a significant time. In the case of long-running callbacks, remedy is brought under UNIX by a child process that the callback creates to perform the processing as such. Thus the callback returns immediately and hands control back to the main event loop.

Subsequently, the main program can find out about successful or failed execution of the callback either by periodical polling in the background (see Section 4.8.2) or by intercepting the signal of the terminating child process. This is because, if in UNIX a child process terminates, the parent process receives the SIGCHLD signal.

Listing tkfork.pl creates a window with one button and, upon activation of this button, starts a long-running callback, namely the function sleep(5). To enable the interface to continue to react 'lively' to user input, the callback function takes_long employs the Process.pm package introduced on page 117. The process object $proc uses the start method to start the sleep command in the background so that, for the application, this matter is dealt with and it can immediately return to the main event loop. Before doing this, it sets the text of the label to "BUSY" to make the start of the process visible to the outside world.

In order to enable the main program to know that the child process has been successfully terminated, it redefines the signal handler for the SIGCHLD signal in such a way that, upon arrival of this signal, not only is the usual wait command for zombie control issued, but the text of the label is set back to "READY".

_____*tkfork.pl*

```
#!/usr/bin/perl -w

use Tk;
use Process;

my $topwindow = MainWindow->new();

                          # button with long-running callback
$button = $topwindow->Button(-text => "Press to Start",
                             -command => \&takes_long);

$labeltext = "READY";
```

```perl
$label = $topwindow->Label("-textvariable", \$labeltext);

$button->pack();
$label->pack();

$proc = Process->new(); # create process object

MainLoop;

# long-running subroutine
sub takes_long {

                # start background process
    $proc->start(sub { sleep 5; });

                # intercept returning child
    $SIG{CHLD} = sub { wait; $labeltext = "READY"; };

                # display status
    $labeltext = "BUSY";
}
```

_____*tkfork.pl*

4.8.2 Periodical execution of functions

Because of the special program structure of static callback definition and event handling, a special construct is needed for periodical interruptions of the main event loop: the function `after`, which, after a set time has elapsed, executes a specified function. A function that calls itself via the `after` command at fixed time intervals is known as a periodically running callback:

```perl
sub looper {

    # put periodically running code here
    # ...

    # time control
    after(1000, \&looper);          # keep on looping
}
```

Apparently, the `looper` function calls itself recursively – but this is not quite correct. Because of the time delay, the script runs completely through the function before a new run is started. Thus, even with eternal repetition, the stack does not overflow.

Functions such as looper can be either started before the main loop begins or triggered as callbacks. In any case, they reach all the global Perl variables and can thus control the dynamic texts of label or text widgets.

The Stopwatch class introduced below serves as a sample application. As with 'real' stopwatches, there are the methods start, stop, reset, and gettime.

A particular feature of the application is that the constructor of the class is given a reference to an update function to be cycled through periodically, together with a time interval. Thus, as soon as the stopwatch is running, the code jumps in regular intervals corresponding to the set time lap to a specified function, for example to increment the counter string of a label widget in the interface from 00:00:00 to 00:00:01.

Figure 4.24   The stopwatch interface.

The corresponding Perl script builds the graphical interface and defines the function update_func, which, while the stopwatch is running, periodically updates the display in the window. For this purpose, it merely modifies the global variable $stopwatch_display, which functions as a dynamic text variable of the corresponding label widget.

stopwatch.pl

```
#!/usr/bin/perl -w
######################################################################
# stopwatch.pl: stopwatch with start/stop/reset function and
# GUI display
######################################################################
use Tk;
use Stopwatch;                    # include 'Stopwatch' class

my $top = MainWindow->new();
                                  # create label with dynamically
                                  # modifiable text
$top->Label(-textvariable => \$stopwatch_display)->pack();

$top->Button(-text    => "Start", # Start button
          -command => sub { $sw->start() })->pack(-side => "left");
```

```
$top->Button(-text    => "Stop",   # Stop button
           -command => sub { $sw->stop() })->pack(-side => "left");

                                   # Reset button (reset with
$top->Button(-text    => "Reset",  # simultaneous stopwatch update)
           -command => sub { $sw->reset(); update_func($sw) }
           )->pack("-side" => "left");

$top->Button(-text    => "Exit",   # Exit button
           -command => sub { exit(0) })->pack("-side" => "left");

                                   # new stopwatch
$sw = Stopwatch->new(\&update_func, 1000);

update_func($sw);                  # display at 00:00:00

MainLoop;                          # main event loop

#########################################################################
sub update_func {
#########################################################################
# read seconds counter of the stopwatch, convert into HH:MM:SS-Format
# and set the variable $stopwatch_display
#########################################################################
    my $self = shift;

    $seconds = $self->gettime();   # stopwatch time check

                        # seconds -> HH:MM:SS
                        # gmtime(0) is 00:00:00, localtime() in GMT
    ($sec, $min, $hour) = gmtime($seconds);

                                   # set GUI display
    $stopwatch_display = sprintf("%02d:%02d:%02d", $hour, $min, $sec);
}
```

_____*stopwatch.pl*

_____*Stopwatch.pm*

```
#########################################################################
# Stopwatch
#########################################################################
```

```perl
package Stopwatch;

use Tk;                              # 'after()' - defined in Tk.pm
#####################################################################
# $sw=Stopwatch->new(\&update_func, $update_time); - constructor
#####################################################################
sub new {
    my $self = bless({}, shift);

    $self->{'usrproc'}     = shift;  # user-defined callback
    $self->{'interval'}    = shift;  # update interval in seconds

    $self->{'running'}     = 0;

    $self->{'starttime'}   =
    $self->{'stoptime'}    = time;

    # no update interval below 1 second
    if($self->{'interval'} < 1000) {
        print "Stopwatch: No update intervals < 1000 accepted." .
            " Not started.\n";
        return undef;
    }

    $self->looper();                 # start loop process

    $self;                           # object reference
}


#####################################################################
# $sw->looper(); - internal(!) loop function
#####################################################################
sub looper {
    my $self = shift;
                                     # call user function
    &{$self->{'usrproc'}}($self) if $self->{'running'};

                                     # loop (no recursion)
    after($self->{'interval'}, sub { $self->looper()});
}


#####################################################################
# $sw->start(); - start stopwatch
#####################################################################
```

```perl
sub start {
    my $self = shift;

    # set start time: eliminate time
    # between last stop and now
    unless($self->{'running'}) {
        $self->{'starttime'} += time - $self->{'stoptime'};
    }

    $self->{'running'}   = 1;
}


########################################################################
# $sw->stop(); - stop stopwatch
########################################################################
sub stop {
    my $self = shift;

    $self->{'stoptime'} = time if $self->{'running'};

    $self->{'running'} = 0;
}


########################################################################
# $seccount=$sw->gettime(); - interrogate time on stopwatch
########################################################################
sub gettime {
    my $self = shift;

    time - $self->{'starttime'};
}


########################################################################
# $sw->reset(); - reset stopwatch
########################################################################
sub reset {
    my $self = shift;

    $self->{'starttime'} =
    $self->{'stoptime'}  = time;
}

1;
```

4.9 Sample applications

4.9.1 File selector

As a first practical example, we would like to present a simple file selector. It consists of two listboxes, one entry widget, and three pushbuttons. For the special arrangement according to Figure 4.25, the packer needs another two frame widgets to accommodate the listboxes and the buttons.

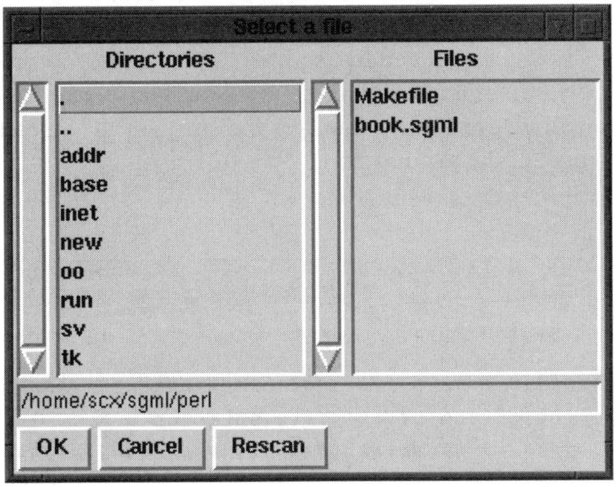

Figure 4.25 File selector.

The file selector is controlled via the mouse and the ⏎ key on the keyboard:

- A double click on a file selects the file and terminates the function.
- A double click on a directory (including '..') changes to that directory.
- A single click on a directory (including '..') and a subsequent click on the OK button changes to that directory.
- A single click on a file and a subsequent click on OK selects the file and terminates the function.
- A click on the Cancel button terminates the function without a selected file.
- A new path entered in the text field becomes active after a click on the OK button or the Rescan button.
- A click on the OK button returns a file entered in the text field even if this file does not (yet) exist.
- Pressing the ⏎ key is equivalent to a click on the OK button.

Thus activating the OK button or pressing the ⏎ key can trigger three different actions, depending on whether the text field was modified, or the directory listbox or the file listbox were selected.

First, however, a few words on the usage of the file selector package: after inclusion with `use Fs;` the constructor `$fs = Fs->new()` creates a new file selector object. As parameters, it expects a reference to the top window of the application, a reference to the function to which the program should jump when terminating the selector, and the title to be displayed in the title bar of the file selector window. The callback specified in the second parameter is called by the file selector either after a valid file selection is carried out or after the application is aborted with the Cancel button. In the first case, the callback is passed the selected file including the absolute path as a first parameter, whereas in the second case, it is passed the empty string that signals the abortion.

The associated test script `fs.pl` too shows a visually appealing interface (Figure 4.26): at a click on the button, the file selector opens, and after termination, the function `fscallback` transfers the string of the selected file to the appropriate entry widget of the test interface.

fs.pl

```perl
#!/usr/bin/perl -w

#######################################################################
# Application of the file selector
#######################################################################
use Tk;                                 # include Tk package
use Fs;                                 # file selector
use strict;

my $top = MainWindow->new();

                                        # initialize variables
chop(my $startpath = `pwd`);            # start: current path
my $fileSelected = "Nothing selected as yet";

my $uframe       = $top->Frame();       # define widgets

my $startbutton = $uframe->Button(-text => "Fileselector Startup",
                                   -command => \&fsStartup);

my $exitbutton  = $uframe->Button(-text => "Exit",
                          -command => sub { exit 0 } );

my $lframe       = $top->Frame(-relief, "sunken", -bd => 2);
my $fixtext      = $top->Label(-text, "Selected:");
my $label        = $lframe->Label(-textvariable, \$fileSelected);

$uframe->pack();                        # pack all
```

```
$startbutton->pack(-side => "left");
$exitbutton->pack(-side => "left");
$fixtext->pack(-side => "left");
$lframe->pack(-fill => "both", -expand => "yes", -side => "left");
$label->pack();

MainLoop;

############################################################
# Create and activate file selector: fsStartup();
############################################################
sub fsStartup {
    my $fs = Fs->new($top, \&fscallback, "Test selector");
    $fs->start($startpath);
}


############################################################
# Callback function for OK/Cancel button: fscallback($filename);
############################################################
sub fscallback {
    my $file = shift;

    $fileSelected = $file;
}
```

_____*fs.pl*

Figure 4.26   Control of the file selector.

A few words on the implementation of the `Fs.pm` module: the constructor merely defines the usual name hash and stores top window, title and callback reference for the current file selector object. The startup method `start` creates a dialog window separate from the top window and packs all required widgets into it. Furthermore, it defines the actions that are to follow the different events. For reasons of clarity, the callbacks are in turn subdivided into the functions `switch2dir`, `okAction`, `rescanAction`, and `fsexit`.

The `switch2dir` function causes the file selector to change to the specified directory and to update the listboxes and the entry widget accordingly. If the selected directory is not readable, or a manually entered directory makes no sense, it returns the value 0, whereas normally the return value is the newly set path.

The okAction method is the callback that belongs to the mouse click on the OK button. It recognizes whether a directory or a file was entered manually, or a directory or a file was selected, and initiates the corresponding measures.

The rescanAction method performs a directory change initiated by the Rescan button.

After termination of the selection with a double click on a file, activation of the OK button with a selected or manually entered file, or abortion with the Cancel button, fsexit reads possibly defined path and file specifications, stores them, and deletes the dialog window of the file selector from the screen. Subsequently, it calls the user callback defined in the constructor.

This procedure is typical for the programming of event-driven interfaces: there is no program flow as such, and there are no function calls with return code that would branch the program to follow different ways; there are only event-triggered actions which in turn initiate further callbacks.

All of the functions are implemented as methods: that is, as a first parameter they expect the object reference because they must access variables at object level. Thus, in subsequent calls, the file selector 'keeps in mind' in which directory the last selection was made or the procedure terminated. As long as the file selector object exists, any number of calls to the start routine are allowed.

_____*Fs.pm*

```
####################################################################
# Fs - file selector package
####################################################################
package Fs;

use Tk;
use Path;
use strict;

####################################################################
# Define new file selector:
# $fs = Fs->new($topwindow, \& callback, $title);
####################################################################
sub new {
    my($type, $parentwin, $callbackref, $title) = @_;

    my $self = {};


    $self->{'callbackref'} = $callbackref;  # store parameter
    $self->{'parentwin'}   = $parentwin;    # in instance
```

```perl
    $self->{'title'}         = $title;          # variable

    bless($self, $type);
}


####################################################################
# Display and start file selector: $fs->start($startdir);
####################################################################
sub start {
    my $self     = shift;
    my $startdir = shift;

    $self->{'topwin'} = $self->{'parentwin'}->Toplevel;

    $self->{'topwin'}->configure(-title => $self->{'title'});

    # directory and file listboxes
    my $listFrame = $self->{'topwin'}->Frame();

    $self->{'dirList'}  =
        $listFrame->ScrlListbox(-label => "Directories");
    $self->{'fileList'} =
        $listFrame->ScrlListbox(-label => "Files");

    # entry widget for selected path/file
    my $fileText =
            $self->{'topwin'}->Entry(-textvariable =>
                                    \${$self}{'pathtext'});


    # Buttons
    my $buttonFrame  = $self->{'topwin'}->Frame();
    my $okButton     = $self->{'topwin'}->Button(
                        -text => "OK",
                        -command => sub { $self->okAction });

    my $rescanButton = $self->{'topwin'}->Button(
                        -text => "Rescan",
                        -command =>
                            sub { $self->rescanAction });

    my $cancelButton = $self->{'topwin'}->Button(
                        -text => "Cancel",
                        -command =>
                            sub { $self->cancelAction });
```

```perl
    # pack all
    $listFrame->pack(-fill => "both", -expand => "yes",
                     -side => "top");

    $self->{'dirList'}->pack(-fill => "both",
                             -expand => "yes",
                             -side => "left");

    $self->{'fileList'}->pack(-fill => "both",
                              -expand => "yes",
                              -side => "left");

    $fileText->pack(-fill => "x", -expand => "yes",
                    -anchor => "s");

    $buttonFrame->pack(-fill => "x", -expand => "yes",
                       -anchor => "s");
    $okButton->pack(-side => "left");
    $cancelButton->pack(-side => "left");
    $rescanButton->pack(-side => "left");


    # define double-click actions on lists
    $self->{'dirList'}->bind("<Double-Button-1>" => sub {
        $self->switch2dir($self->{'dirList'}->Getselected());
        $self->{'pathtext'} = $self->{'path'} });

    $self->{'fileList'}->bind("<Double-Button-1>" =>
                              sub { $self->fsexit() });


    # define return key action
    $self->{'topwin'}->bind("<KeyPress-Return>" =>
                            sub {$self->okAction});


    # set initial path to current directory
    $self->{'path'} = $startdir unless defined $self->{'path'};
    $self->switch2dir(".");
    $self->{'pathtext'} = $self->{'path'};
}


#######################################################################
# Change to a new directory, update listboxes:
# $fs->switch2dir($directory);
```

```
######################################################################
sub switch2dir {
  my $self = shift;
  my $dir  = shift;
                                        # new path for test purpose
  my $newpath = Path::cd($self->{'path'}, $dir) || return 0;

  return 0 unless opendir(DIR, "$newpath");

  my @files = sort readdir(DIR);    # read directory
  closedir(DIR);
                                        # update directory listbox
  $self->{'dirList'}->delete(0, "end");
  $self->{'dirList'}->insert("end",
                            grep(-d "$newpath/$_" , @files));
  $self->{'dirList'}->selection("set", 0);
                                        # update file listbox
  $self->{'fileList'}->delete(0, "end");
  $self->{'fileList'}->insert("end",
                            grep(-f "$newpath/$_", @files));

  $self->{'path'} = $newpath;         # set new path
}


######################################################################
# Action upon activation of the OK button
######################################################################
sub okAction {
    my $self = shift;

    my $item;

    if($self->{'pathtext'} ne $self->{'path'}) {
        # enter path string manually
        if($item = $self->switch2dir($self->{'pathtext'})) {
            $self->{'pathtext'} =
                $self->{'path'} = Path::absolute($item);
        } else {                        # new file selected
                                        # close dialog window
            $self->{'topwin'}->destroy;
                                        # trigger callback
            &{$self->{'callbackref'}}($self->{'pathtext'});
        }
    } elsif(($item = $self->{'dirList'}->Getselected())) {
        # new directory selected
```

```perl
        $self->switch2dir($item);
        $self->{'pathtext'} = $self->{'path'};

    } elsif($self->{'fileList'}->Getselected()) {
        # file selected
        $self->fsexit();
    }
}


#######################################################################
# Action upon activation of the Rescan button
#######################################################################
sub rescanAction {
    my $self = shift;

    my $item;

    if($self->{'pathtext'} ne $self->{'path'}) {
        # enter path string manually
        (($item = $self->switch2dir($self->{'pathtext'})) &&
            ($self->{'pathtext'} =
              $self->{'path'} = Path::absolute($item))) ||
                ($self->{'pathtext'} = $self->{'path'});

    } elsif(($item = $self->{'dirList'}->Getselected())) {
        # new directory selected
        $self->switch2dir($item);
        $self->{'pathtext'} = $self->{'path'};
    }
}


#######################################################################
# Action upon activation of the Cancel button
#######################################################################
sub cancelAction {
    my $self = shift;

    $self->{'fileList'}->selection("clear", 0, "end");
    $self->fsexit();
}


#######################################################################
# Store selected file together with path and remove window
#######################################################################
sub fsexit {
```

```
    my $self = shift;

    # read selected path/file
    my $item = $self->{'fileList'}->Getselected();

    # append file to path
    $self->{'path'} =~ s,/$,,g;
    $self->{'selected'} = defined $item ?
                                    "$self->{path}/$item" : "";

    $self->{'topwin'}->destroy;      # close dialog window

                                     # call callback function
    &{$self->{'callbackref'}}($self->{'selected'});
}


#####################################################################
# Interrogate selected directory/file
#####################################################################
sub getselected {
    my $self = shift;

    $self->{'selected'};
}

1;
```

_____Fs.pm

Easy-to-handle path arithmetic is provided by the included module `Path.pm`, whose method `Path::cd($path, $dir)` determines the target directory where you would arrive, starting with the start directory `path`, if you issued the `cd dir` command of the UNIX shell. In the simplest case, `dir` can be an absolute path, but also relative indications are correctly handled by the function: for example, a `Path::cd` from '/usr/bin' to '..' results in the directory '/usr,' a change from '/' to '..' results again in '/,' provided, obviously, that the specified directories are no symbolic links.

`Path.pm` utilizes the `Cwd.pm` module of the Perl standard distribution and its `chdir` function, which performs a change of the current directory.

_____Path.pm

```
package Path;

use Cwd;
```

```perl
use strict;

#######################################################################
# Determine absolute path from relative path and current directory:
# $abspath = Path::absolute($relpath);
#######################################################################
sub absolute {
    my $relpath = shift;

    Path::cd(cwd(), $relpath);
}


#######################################################################
# Relative change to a new directory:
# $newpath = Path::cd($path, $chdir);
#######################################################################
sub cd {
    my($from, $to) = @_;

    my $current = cwd();    # store current directory

                            # change to start directory
    Cwd::chdir($from) || return undef;

                            # relative change of
                            # target directory
    Cwd::chdir($to) || (Cwd::chdir($current), return undef);

    my $retval = cwd();     # store target directory

    Cwd::chdir($current);   # reset current
                            # directory
    return $retval;
}

1;
```

_____*Path.pm*

4.9.2 A small editor

Together with the file selector presented in the previous section, we now construct
a simple text editor. The highly complex control of the editing process as such is
taken over by a ready-made text widget in cooperation with an additional scrollbar.

A menu-driven interface allows easy loading of text files and saving of edited texts under the original or a different name.

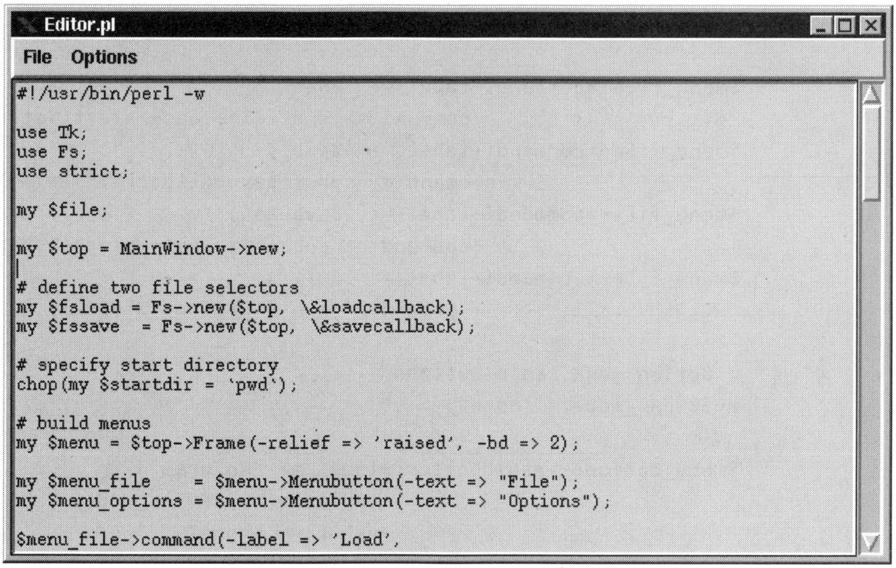

Figure 4.27 A small editor.

editor.pl

```perl
#!/usr/bin/perl -w

use Tk;
use Fs;
use strict;

my $file;

my $top = MainWindow->new;

# define two file selectors
my $fsload = Fs->new($top, \&loadcallback);
my $fssave  = Fs->new($top, \&savecallback);

# specify start directory
chop(my $startdir = `pwd`);

# build menus
```

```perl
my $menu = $top->Frame(-relief => 'raised', -bd => 2);


my $menu_file    = $menu->Menubutton(-text => "File");
my $menu_options = $menu->Menubutton(-text => "Options");


$menu_file->command(-label => 'Load',
                      -command => sub { $fsload->start($startdir)});
$menu_file->command(-label => 'Save',
                    -command => sub { savecallback($file) });
$menu_file->command(-label => 'Save As',
                    -command => sub { $fssave->start($startdir)});
$menu_file->command(-label => 'Quit',
                    -command => sub { destroy $top });


# Option menu radio buttons
my $wrap_mode = "none";


$menu_options->radiobutton(-label => "No wrap",
                             -variable => \$wrap_mode,
                             -value => "none",
    -command => \&set_wrap);


$menu_options->radiobutton(-label => "Char wrap",
                             -variable => \$wrap_mode,
                             -value => "char",
    -command => \&set_wrap);


$menu_options->radiobutton(-label => "Word wrap",
                             -variable => \$wrap_mode,
                             -value => "word",
    -command => \&set_wrap);


# editable text field with scrollbar
my $text = $top->Text(-borderwidth => 2, -setgrid => 1);
my $scrollbar = $top->Scrollbar(-command => [yview => $text]);
$text->configure(-yscrollcommand => [set => $scrollbar]);


# pack all
$menu->pack(-side => 'top', -fill => 'x');
$scrollbar->pack(-side => 'right', -fill => 'both');
$text->pack(-side => 'left', -fill => 'both', -expand => 'yes');
$menu_file->pack(-side, 'left');
$menu_options->pack(-side, 'left');


MainLoop;
```

```perl
#####################################################################
# Load file into the text widget: loadcallback($file);
#####################################################################
sub loadcallback {
  $file = shift;

  return unless defined $file;

  open(FILE, $file) || return 0;

  $text->delete("1.0", "end");

  while(<FILE>)
  {  $text->insert("end", $_);
  }
  close(FILE);
  set_wrap();
}


#####################################################################
# Save text of the text widgets: savecallback($file);
#####################################################################
sub savecallback {
  $file = shift;

  return unless defined $file;

  open(FILE, ">$file") || return 0;
  my @lines = $text->get("1.0", "end");
  print FILE @lines;
  close(FILE);
}


#####################################################################
# Set wrap mode (callback)
#####################################################################
sub set_wrap {
    $text->configure(-wrap, $wrap_mode);
}
```

4.9.3 Hyperlinks

One implementation of the hypertext issue addressed in Section 4.6.12 is shown in Listing `hypertext.pl`. In the text widget defined in this listing, the subroutine `hyperlink_insert` inserts color-highlighted text, which is also marked with a tag. Subsequently, `hyperlink_insert` assigns this tag the following event callbacks:

Entry of the mouse pointer in the hyperlink area Copies the name of the hyperlink into the text variable of the widget that displays the name in the bottom left corner.

Exit of the mouse pointer from the hyperlink area Sets the text variable of the label to the empty string, thus deleting the bottom left name display.

Single mouse click on the hyperlink Issues a message to STDOUT. In a real hypertext browser, this action would trigger loading of a new file.

Figures 4.28 and 4.29 show the reaction of the script to the entry of the mouse pointer into the defined hypertext field.

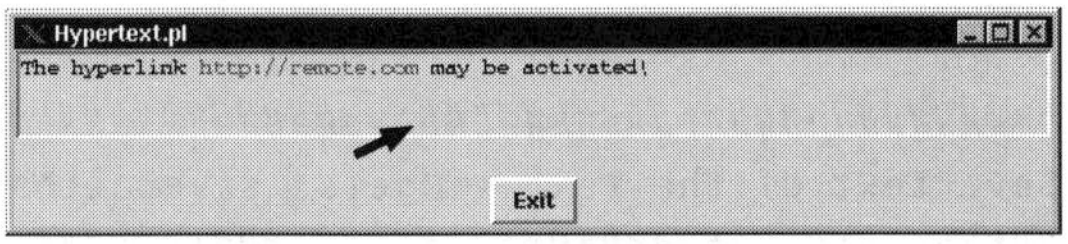

Figure 4.28   Mouse pointer outside ...

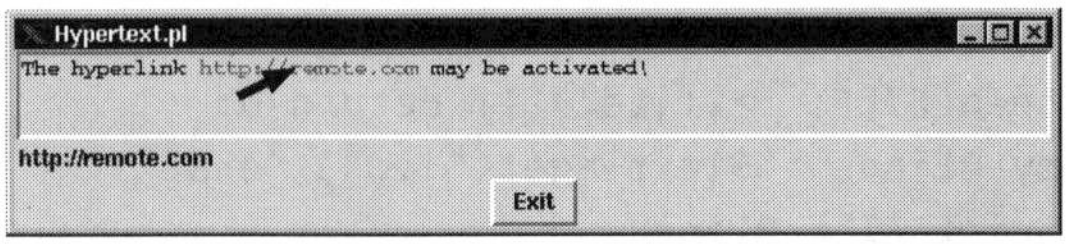

Figure 4.29   ... and inside the hyperlink field.

--*hypertext.pl*

```perl
#!/usr/bin/perl

use Tk;

my $ttag;
                             # create widgets
$top = MainWindow->new();
```

```
                               # text area
$text  = $top->Text(-wrap => 'word', -height => 3);


                               # bottom left hyperlink display
$urltext = "";
$label = $top->Label(-textvariable => \$urltext);


                               # Exit button
$exit  = $top->Button(-text => 'Exit', -command => \&exit);


                               # pack
$text->pack();
$label->pack(-anchor => "w");
$exit->pack();


                               # insert text
$text->insert('end', "The hyperlink ");
                               # insert hyperlink
hyperlink_insert($text, 'end', "http://remote.com", "tag1");
                               # insert text
$text->insert('end', " may be activated!\n");


                               # make text window read-only
$text->configure(-state => "disabled");

MainLoop;


####################################################################
# Integrate an activatable hyperlink into a text widget
####################################################################
sub hyperlink_insert {
    my($text, $where, $name, $tag) = @_;


                                   # insert text
    $text->insert($where, $name, $tag);


                                   # set highlighted text color
    $text->tag('configure', $tag, -foreground => "blue");


                                   # upon mouse pointer touch
                                   # display URL bottom left
    $text->tag('bind', $tag, '<Any-Enter>' =>
                          sub { $urltext = $name; } );


                                   # delete display when
```

```
                                             # mouse leaves area
              $text->tag('bind', $tag, '<Any-Leave>' =>
                                          sub { $urltext = ""; } );


                                             # action in case of
                                             # mouse click activation
              $text->tag('bind', $tag, '<1>' =>
                        sub { print "Activated:", $name, "\n"; });
       }
```

_____hypertext.pl

4.9.4 Font viewer

The X Window system offers hundreds of fonts in different sizes for its applications. Under UNIX, the `xlsfonts` command lists them all.

Listing `font.pl` implements a small browser that displays all of the available fonts in a scrollable window. For this purpose, it simply defines a different tag for each line of the text widget used, and sets the tag font to the corresponding value. The fonts that are available on the current system are read at the beginning by means of the `xlsfonts` command.

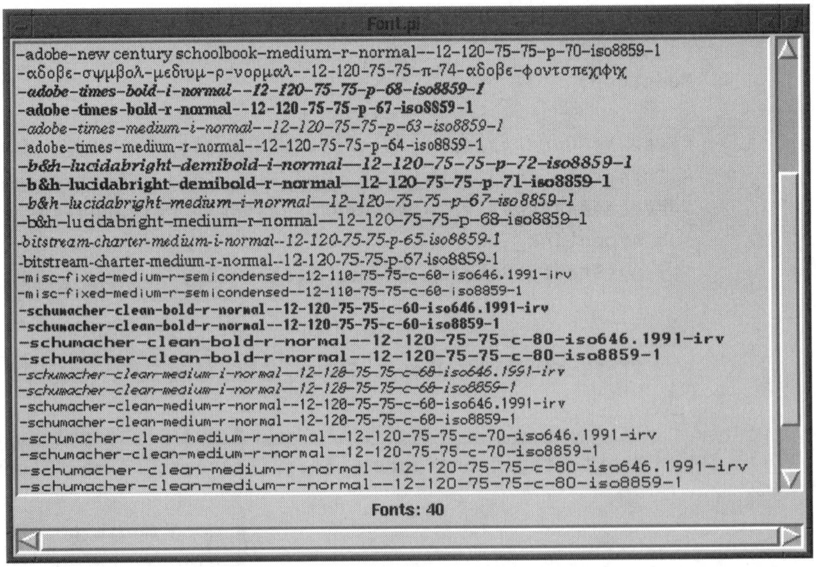

Figure 4.30   Font viewer.

```perl
#!/usr/bin/perl -w

use Tk;
use strict;

my $top = MainWindow->new();

my $frame = $top->Frame();
my $text  = $frame->Text(-wrap => 'none',
                          -font => '*helvetica-bold-r-*12*');

my $labelvar = "";
my $label = $top->Label(-textvariable => \$labelvar);

my $yscrollbar = $frame->Scrollbar(-command =>
                                     [yview => $text]);
my $xscrollbar = $top->Scrollbar(-orient => 'horizontal',
                                  -command => [xview => $text]);

$text->configure(-yscrollcommand => [set => $yscrollbar]);
$text->configure(-xscrollcommand => [set => $xscrollbar]);

### pack all
$yscrollbar->pack(-side => 'right', -fill => 'y');
$xscrollbar->pack(-side => 'bottom', -fill => 'x');
$label->pack(-expand => 'yes', -fill => 'x',
             -side => 'bottom');

$frame->pack(-expand => 'yes', -fill => 'both');
$text->pack(-expand => 'yes', -fill => 'both',
            -side => 'left');

open(FONTS, "xlsfonts |") || die "xlsfonts: not found";
my $i=1;
while(<FONTS>) {
    next unless /--12/;          # only fonts of size 12
    chop(my $font = $_);
    $text->insert("end", $_);   # insert text in text widget
                                # (including newline \n)

                                # define tag and
                                # set font there
    $text->tag("add", $i, "$i.0", sprintf("%d.0", $i+1));
    $text->tag("configure", $i, -font => $font);
```

```
        $text->update();
        $i++;
        $labelvar="Fonts: $i";
}
close(FONTS);

MainLoop;
```

_____*font.pl*

4.9.5   Image viewer

The following script for display of arbitrary images in a scrollable canvas widget makes use of the user-friendly interface of the photo widget (see Section 4.6.15) toward images of the most varied formats. The Fs class introduced on page 227 implements the file selector with which the user can browse through the directories and select the required images.

_____*img.pl*

```
#!/usr/bin/perl -w

use Tk;
use Fs;

my $top = MainWindow->new();
                                        # initialize file selector
my $fs = Fs->new($top, \&load_image, "Select an image");

                                        # menu bar and pulldowns
$menubar  = $top->Frame(-relief => 'raised', -bd => 2);
$menu_file = $menubar->Menubutton(-text => "File",
                                  -underline => 0);
$menu_file->command(-label => "Load",
    -command => sub { $fs->start("."); });
$menu_file->command(-label => "Exit",
                    -command => sub { exit 0 });

$canvas  = $top->Canvas();
$photo   = $top->Photo();
$canvas->create('image', 0, 0, -image => $photo,
                                -anchor => 'nw');

my $yscrollbar = $top->Scrollbar(-command =>
```

```
                                        ['yview', $canvas],
          -orient => 'vertical');
my $xscrollbar = $top->Scrollbar(-command =>
                                        ['xview', $canvas],
          -orient => 'horizontal');

$canvas->configure(-xscrollcommand => ['set', $xscrollbar],
    -yscrollcommand => ['set', $yscrollbar]);

$menubar->pack(-expand => 'yes', -fill => 'x', -anchor => 'n');
$menu_file->pack(-anchor => 'w');

$yscrollbar->pack(-side => 'right', -fill => 'y');
$xscrollbar->pack(-side => 'bottom', -fill => 'x');

$canvas->pack(-expand => 'yes', -fill => 'both',
                -anchor => 's');

MainLoop;

####################################################################
# load_image callback function
####################################################################
sub load_image {
    my $file = shift;

    $photo->configure(-file => $file);

    my $newwidth  = $photo->width;
    my $newheight = $photo->height;

    $canvas->configure(-scrollregion =>
                        [0, 0, $newwidth, $newheight],
        -width => $newwidth,
        -height => $newheight);
}
```

_____*img.pl*

4.9.6 **Color viewer**

Under UNIX, the code of the font viewer (page 242) can be easily changed into a color viewer that displays the whole color palette of the X Window system. Only the central piece, which in the font viewer collects the fonts and sets the tags of the text widget, is replaced. Instead of the fonts, the routine now reads the available colors from the file `rgb.txt` and sets the background color of the text tags accordingly.

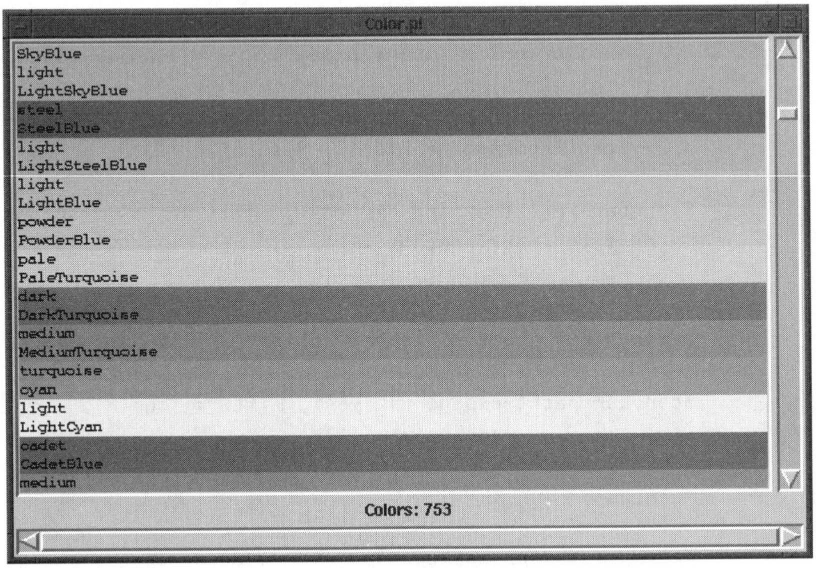

Figure 4.31   Color viewer.

color.pl

```
### Read colors and color text lines
open(COLORS, "< /usr/lib/X11/rgb.txt") ||
                        die "rgb.txt not found";
my $i=1;
while(<COLORS>) {

    s/!.*//;           # remove comments
    next if /^\s*$/;   # ignore empty lines

    my ($red, $green, $blue, $name) = split(' ', $_);
    my $col = sprintf("#%02x%02x%02x", $red, $green, $blue);

    ### labeling color white for dark background colors
    my $foreground =
            ($red + $green + $blue < 350) ? "white" : "black";

    $text->insert("end", "$name\n");  # insert text into text
                                      # widget (including newline \n)
```

```
### Define tag and set color
$text->tag("add", $i, "$i.0", sprintf("%d.0", $i+1));
$text->tag("configure", $i, -background => $col,
                              -foreground => $foreground);

### Immediately display each new color
$text->update();

### Refresh display
$i++;
$labelvar="Colors: $i";
}
close(COLORS);
```

_____*color.pl*

4.9.7 Viewer for SDBM files

Persistent hashes store their data in `dbm` files (see Section 1.13), which for reasons of efficiency are coded in a binary format and thus cannot be analyzed as clear text. For testing purposes, however, it is often desirable to be able to examine persistently stored data. With a short Perl/Tk script a persistent hash can be visualized in a listbox that can easily be scrolled. The following script reads the data from the `*.pag` or `*.dir` files of a `SDBM` hash and displays the key-value pairs graphically.

_____*sdbmview.pl*

```
#!/usr/bin/perl -w

use Tk;
use POSIX;
use SDBM_File;

usage() if $#ARGV < 0;
                                # open persistent hash
tie(%myhash, SDBM_File, $ARGV[0], O_RDONLY, 0644) ||
    do { print "Cannot open $ARGV[0]\n"; usage() };

my $top = MainWindow->new();


                                # create listbox
$listbox = $top->ScrlListbox(-label => "Hash: $ARGV[0]");
```

```
                                # buttons
$exitbutton   = $top->Button(-text => "Exit",
                             -command => \&exit);


                                # pack all
$listbox->pack(-fill   => "both", "-expand" => "yes");
$exitbutton->pack(-side => "left");


                                # fill listbox
foreach $i (keys %myhash) {
    $listbox->insert("end", "$i> $myhash{$i}");
}


MainLoop;

###################################################################
# usage
###################################################################
sub usage {
    ($func = $0) =~ s,^.*/,,g;
    print "usage: $func dbmfilename\n";
    exit 1;
}
```

sdbmview.pl

Perl programming on the Internet

The Internet offers an unbelievable amount of information for all kinds of use. Access is mostly interactive: whether a user surfs through the World Wide Web by means of a browser such as *Netscape Navigator*, sends electronic mail via a mail program such as `elm`, or downloads the latest release of a freely available program from a server by means of the `ftp` transfer tool – none of this is possible without some manual typing effort.

The majority of programming interfaces with protocols of the Internet that govern access modalities to foreign information are complex and unclear, so that the programming conquest of the Internet was until now reserved to UNIX experts of guru status.

Books like Stevens (1990) and Stevens (1994) show in a detailed and illustrative manner how communication between networked computers works at various levels of communication. However, if one builds on these C interfaces, any automatic application that offers similar services as its interactive counterparts quickly evolves into a code monstrosity.

Perl, in contrast – in addition to an operating system interface at C level that is a standard part of the Perl language (sockets) – provides an interface at user level. It cleanly cuts off the boring chores from the users so they can, with the same ease as in interactive operation, automatically extract their data from the network of all networks.

Because of its portability, Perl is very well suited for employment in the heterogeneous hardware and software structure of the Internet. A Perl script is really 100% portable, and the Perl interpreter is available on nearly all possible and impossible platforms, down to Windows NT.

Finally, the most popular application of Perl is as a script language for CGI applications. Section 5.8 guides you through all important application areas. Section 5.8.7 shows how Perl scripts in CGI applications unleash unthought-of powers.

5.1 Help from the CPAN

The modules included in the Perl distribution, together with the extensions available from the CPAN (Comprehensive Perl Archive Network) (see Appendix A[1]) allow the Perl programmer to download a document from a server or to fetch an HTML page from the WWW (World Wide Web) with less than 10 lines of code.

In particular, the following package collections

- `libnet` and
- `libwww`

which are both available from the CPAN, will frequently be used in this section.

Thus, for Perl scripts in general and Internet applications in particular, the golden rule applies once more: it is better to search twice in the CPAN to see whether a suitable module exists than to invest precious development time in an already solved problem for the nth time.

5.2 Netiquette

However, this drastic simplification of programmed Internet access also entails a number of problems. Programming of so-called *robots*, which automatically search the network for information, is a delicate subject, because the activity of these indefatigable servants encumbers the network and slows down the data flow on the information highway.

The vast Internet community therefore sticks to the so-called *netiquette*: that is, simple guidelines that ensure operation of this unique organization even for the future.

Perl-aware Internet programmers always operate in a small border area: there is nothing to be said against saving boring typing effort and carrying out simple transfers automatically, but searching dozen of servers for information must be reserved to central institutions that publish the results of their research and allow global search access.

One of the principles of Perl – quoted from the *perlmod* manual page – is:

> It would prefer that you stayed out of its living room because you weren't invited, not because it has a shotgun.

This maxim also applies to the private sphere of Internet servers. In order to preserve it, there are the so-called *robot rules*. These allow each server to ask aggressive search robots to keep out. Polite robots not only stick to these rules, but also avoid aggressive timeout/retry strategies in order not to disturb other network users.

Programming of robots is discussed in detail in Section 5.5.3. Until then, the author heartily asks all readers to refrain from using the presented scripts to start network-pilfering actions.

---

[1] All required modules are also included on the enclosed CD-ROM (see Appendix H).

The following sections deal with services provided by the Internet, the underlying protocols, and their control by means of Perl.

5.3 FTP

FTP, the *File Transport Protocol*, allows transfer of files via network connections. Its most popular application, the interactive program `ftp`, connects the user with an FTP server that provides the file transfer as a service. After an introductory login and password entry, `ftp` provides a minimal set of commands that allow navigation in directory structures and downloading and uploading of files.

The so-called *anonymous FTP servers* of the Internet also allow file transfer to users who specify *anonymous* as their login and their email address as a password, and thus are important institutions within the Internet community. New, freely available program versions thus find their way even to the most remote corner of the world: program authors upload their products (with the prior consent of the relevant system administrators) to anonymous FTP servers and publish this news in a newsgroup (a kind of pinboard; see Section 5.11). Subsequently, interested users can download the version via `ftp` to their home computers, compile it if necessary, and use it.

The following transcription of an interactive session with an anonymous FTP server shows some typical actions: the user identifies him/herself as `anonymous` and enters his/her email address `me@mysite.com` as a password. The example shows how the file `downfile.remote` is downloaded from the `pub` directory of the FTP server to the local computer, where it is stored as `downfile.local` in the current directory. Furthermore, it shows how the local file `upfile.local` is uploaded in the `incoming` directory of the FTP server under the name of `upfile.remote`. Finally, the `quit` command terminates the connection.

```
mysite> ftp remote.host.com
Connected to remote.host.com.
220 darkstar FTP server ready.
Name (remote.host.com:myname): anonymous
331 Guest login ok, send complete e-mail address as password.
Password: me@mysite.com
230-Welcome, archive user! If you have any unusual
230-problems, please report them via e-mail to
230-postmaster@darkstar
230-
230 Guest login ok, access restrictions apply.
Remote system type is UNIX.
Using binary mode to transfer files.
ftp> cd pub
250 CWD command successful.
ftp> get downfile.remote downfile.local
200 PORT command successful.
```

```
150 Opening BINARY mode data connection for downfile (17 bytes).
226 Transfer complete.
17 bytes received in 0.000858 secs (19 Kbytes/sec)
ftp> cd ../incoming
250 CWD command successful.
ftp> put upfile.local upfile.remote
200 PORT command successful.
150 Opening BINARY mode data connection for upfile.remote.
226 Transfer complete.
640 bytes sent in 0.00104 secs (6e+02 Kbytes/sec)
ftp> ls
200 PORT command successful.
150 Opening ASCII mode data connection for /bin/ls.
total 3
drwxrwxrwx 2 root wheel 1024 Jun 9 21:58 .
drwxrwxr-x 9 root wheel 1024 Jun 6 10:33 ..
-rw------- 1 root daemon 640 Jun 9 21:58 upfile.remote
226 Transfer complete.
ftp> quit
221 Goodbye.
mysite>
```

With the following routines, access to FTP servers is not only reseved to inter-active applications. The Perl interface allows easy-to-handle object-oriented control.

Non-interactive utilization of the FTP service usually requires a lot of know-how about the FTP protocol and network-specific details. Programmed access under Perl can also be carried out from system level, but there are easier ways to achieve this.

For user-friendly access to FTP servers, there is the readily available Perl package Net::FTP, which is part of the libnet module collection and can be obtained via the CPAN. (Another alternative is the Expect program [see Libes, 1995], which allows control of interactive programs following a send-expect scheme. However, it is based on the slightly antiquated script language Tcl.)

5.3.1 Net::FTP

The Net::FTP package by Graham Barr provides a programming interface that is nearly as easy to handle as the interactive ftp program.

An ftp connection to the sample server ftp.host.name is established by the instruction

```
$ftp = Net::FTP->new("ftp.host.name");
```

which, at the same time, returns a reference to an FTP object. Subsequent calls of methods of this object correspond to requests to the connected FTP server ftp.host.name. Thus

```
$ftp->login("anonymous", "me\@my.host.name");
```

logs the user in as anonymous at ftp.host.name and specifies, as usual with anonymous FTP access, the email address (in the example me@my.host.name) as the password. Please note that the @ sign in the string must be masked out to prevent it from being interpreted as a Perl array. The method

```
$ftp->cwd("/pub/comp");
```

changes to the /pub/comp directory on the FTP server, while a list of the files stored in the current directory is supplied by the methods dir and ls:

```
@filelist_dir = $ftp->dir();        # verbose listing
@filelist_ls  = $ftp->ls();         # short listing
```

The 'verbose' list @filelist_dir contains entries of the form

```
total 1984
-rw-rw-rw-   1 root      sys       1000448 May 15 13:52 file1
-rw-rw-rw-   1 root      sys       1000448 May 15 13:52 file2
```

as strings without newline characters, whereas @filelist_ls contains only the found file names as elements:

```
file1
file2
```

The file file1 of the server is transfered by the call

```
$ftp->get("file1", "file1.loc");
```

in the current directory of the home computer as file1.loc, because similarly to the get command of the interactive FTP program, $ftp->get allows a local name to be specified as a second parameter that is different from the original file name. In the same way,

```
$ftp->put("file1.loc", "file1");
```

transfers a local file to the server – provided it allows write access to the specified directory. Finally, the end of an FTP connection is signaled by

```
$ftp->quit();
```

For settings that deviate from the default values, it is possible to pass the new constructor introduced at the beginning of this section specifications regarding port number, timeout, and debug level. The call

```
$ftp = Net::FTP->new("ftp.host.name", Port => 21,
                     Timeout => 120, Debug => 0);
```

sets the default setting, which uses FTP port 21, switches the debug mode off, and terminates the connection after 120 seconds of silence.

Depending on the server, the default transfer mode is set either to `ascii` or to `binary`. In ASCII mode, FTP converts text documents in such a way that newline characters correspond to the currently used operating system. This is, however, not the required behavior for documents that contain binary data: compressed files get damaged and can thus no longer be decompressed at the client side after the transfer. To avoid this problem, it is recommended that you always set the required mode yourself. Binary transfer mode is activated by

```
$ftp->binary();        # binary transfer
```

whereas ASCII text transfer is activated by

```
$ftp->ascii();         # ASCII text transfer
```

All methods of the `Net::FTP` package return a 'true' value if their execution is successful, and a 'false' value if an error occurs. Methods that return a value, for example `dir()`, return `undef` in the case of an error.

File::Listing

As discussed in the previous section, the `dir` method displays the contents of an FTP server directory in the format:

```
-rw-rw-rw-   1 root     sys      1000448 May 15 13:52 file
dr-xr-xr-x   2 ftp      other       1024 Apr 21  1994 dir
```

Obviously, it would be child's play to extract information from this raw listing as to whether an entry represents a file or a subdirectory, and which size or which access rights it has. But as (nearly) always, before you start typing `vi script.pl`, it is worth checking the CPAN: the module `File::Listing`, which does precisely the required job, is there ready and waiting.

With the above output as the input parameter, the function `parse_dir` of `File::Listing` yields a list of elements that in turn refer to lists that contain the required information in the format

```
($name, $type, $size, $mtime, $mode)
```

where `$name` contains the name of a file or a subdirectory; `$type` evaluates to 'f' (file) or 'd' (directory); `$size` indicates the size of a file in bytes; `$mtime` indicates the time stamp of last modification (as usual in UNIX, in seconds since January 1st, 1970); and finally, `$mode` shows the access rights as a decimal number.[2]

---

[2] The access mode is shown in the same format as returned by the `stat` function of the UNIX C Library in the field `st_mode`. The value 0 corresponds to the access right ----------. Each set bit in the decimal number represents an entry in the privilege string. Thus a mode of 493 (better known as octal 0755) specifies access rights of the form: -rwxr-xr-x.

Together with the `dir` method of the `Net::FTP` package, the construct

```
foreach $entry (File::Listing::parse_dir($ftp->dir())) {
    my ($name, $type, $size, $mtime, $mode) = @$entry;


    # ...
}
```

permits deeper insight into the entries on an FTP server. This example shows reference handling at its finest. As a reminder: the call

```
$ftp->dir();
```

performs the network operation proper, whose result in a list context is a list (in a scalar context, `dir()` yields a list reference). This list is taken as an input parameter by `parse_dir`, which transforms it into a list of list references, which is then processed element by element by the `foreach` loop. For each cycle, the variable `$entry` holds a list reference, which the `@` operator in the loop body dereferences into a list and splits into its elements.

Listing `ftpfetch.pl` shows a small application that processes the contents of an FTP directory and, for test purposes, outputs the result in the format

```
file: README (2407 bytes)
directory: pub (privileges: 040755)
```

_____*ftpfetch.pl*

```perl
#!/usr/bin/perl -w

use Net::FTP;
use File::Listing;

$dir     = "/pub";
$host    = "remote.host.com";
$email   = "me\@mysite.com";

$ftp = Net::FTP->new($host, Timeout => 60) ||
    die "Cannot connect: $host";

$ftp->login("anonymous", $email) || die "Login failed";

$ftp->cwd($dir) || die "Directory $dir doesn't exist";
$ftp->binary();

foreach $entry (File::Listing::parse_dir($ftp->dir())) {
    my ($name, $type, $size, $mtime, $mode) = @$entry;
```

```
    if($type eq 'd') {
        printf "directory: $name (privileges: 0%o)\n", $mode;
    }
    elsif($type eq 'f') {
        print "file: $name ($size bytes)\n";
    }
}

$ftp->quit();
```

ftpfetch.pl

5.3.2 LWP::Simple

Yet another easy access to FTP servers is provided by the LWP::Simple interface discussed in Section 5.5.1. The examples presented there for WWW access via the HTTP protocol can be easily adapted to FTP.

5.4 Introduction to the World Wide Web (WWW)

To the outside world, the Web presents itself as a multitude of nicely formatted pages that are linked to one another via so-called *hyperlinks*. If the user clicks on a marked hyperlink in the document, the system switches to the page connected with this link.

The principle of this navigation is dead easy. Documents in the Word Wide Web are files written with the use of HTML (*Hypertext Markup Language*), a text formatting language. To load a page from a remote computer, the browser connects to it, sends the server a GET command for a specific file, receives this file, and displays it according to the formatting commands of its text. A user's click on a hyperlink causes the next Web document, specified by a URL[3] (*Uniform Resource Locator*), to be loaded and displayed.

A URL uniquely specifies a specific file on an arbitrary computer of the network. For HTTP, the protocol of the World Wide Web, URLs are of the form

```
http://remote.host.com/path/file.html
```

Here, the target computer of the request is indicated by remote.host.com; the required file is file.html in the directory path. The http protocol determines the rules for the communication between local computer and target computer. Thus, with this protocol, the local computer needs only to issue a GET request, whereas in FTP, for example, a login with name and password would be required.

---

[3] The acronym URI (*Uniform Resource Identifier*) is used with the same meaning.

5.4.1   HTML as a formatting language

The transferred document can be viewed with a standard ASCII text editor, but the HTML commands certainly do not improve readability. HTML is a text formatting language whose commands are scattered throughout the text, enclosed in angle brackets <>, and specify what the logical representation of the document should look like.

Formatting commands specify whether the affected text is meant, for example, as a header or the start of a new paragraph, or whether an image is supposed to be inserted at that point. HTML supports a strict separation between the contents of the text and its representation, by defining so-called *tags* that identify a text section as an independent unit and assign it a number of properties. HTML does not specify exactly how large and in which typeface a headline is to be set, but merely defines *that* a text fragment *is* a headline. The final layout is always determined by the interpreting browser.

Listing `example.html` shows a simple example of an HTML document, which the browser interprets as shown in Figure 5.1.

example.html

```
<HTML>

<HEAD>
<TITLE>This is a test page</TITLE>
</HEAD>

<BODY><H1>Headline</H1>

<p>
The list has the entries

<UL>
<LI>element one
<LI><I>element two is italic</I>
<LI><B>element three is bold</B>
</UL>

</BODY>
</HTML>
```

example.html

Listing `example.html` defines the page title, a headline, a paragraph of text, and a list, which contains three elements, two of which are visually highlighted.

Hyperlinks too are created by means of simple HTML commands. The entry

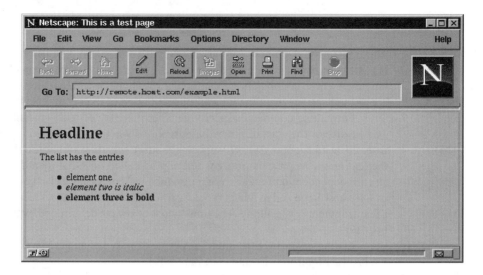

Figure 5.1 Document representation of the HTML file `example.html` in the browser.

```
<A HREF="http://faraway.host.com/jumphere.html">
   Click here! </A>
```

causes the browser to display the text 'Click here!' with some highlight attribute. If the user clicks the entry once with the mouse, the browser fetches the document `jumphere.html` from the computer `faraway.host.com` and displays it in lieu of the document shown up to now.

Within the framework of this book, it is unfortunately impossible to treat HTML exhaustively. However, the most important commands are illustrated in Appendix D. Detailed descriptions can be found in the literature (for example, Spainhour and Quercia, 1996) and as freely accessible documents on the Internet (see Appendix G).

The emphasis of this discussion will instead be put on the HTTP protocol via which the Perl programmer will in future access HTML documents available on the Internet.

5.4.2 Headers

To ensure that HTTP server and client understand each other, they exchange important information before and during the transfer of documents. Since the most disparate partners can communicate on the Internet, it is important to find the greatest common denominator in the communication.

Thus the server defines the format of a document via the standardized MIME (*Multipurpose Internet Mail Extensions*) header, which specifies, among others, the length of the transferred document, its contents type (video, audio, image data, text), and the format used (for text, for example, HTML or plain text). MIME headers come from the email world, where they are used to specify the contents of multimedia messages.

With this procedure, a server communicates the format of the required data prior to the actual data transfer, giving the client the possibility of choosing the appropriate means for further elaboration. Thus a browser displays a page sent as clear text without further ado, whereas an HTML page passes through the browser-internal formatter first.

However, not only the server that provides a document, but also the client that requests it uses this communication route to tell the server in advance in which form it should – if possible – transfer the information. Thus a client request not only specifies the requested document, but also communicates MIME-coded format requirements to the server.

Header fields are identified by names, and carry values. The most important header fields of a request are summarized in Table 5.1, and the corresponding fields of the response header are shown in Table 5.2.

Table 5.1   Important request header fields.

Header field	Sample entry	Description
Accept	text/html	Text formats
	text/plain	
	image/gif	Image formats
	image/jpeg	
User-Agent	Mozilla/3.04Gold (X11; I; Linux)	Client software
	AIR MOSAIC (16bit)/v1.00.198.07	
If-Modified-Since	Tue, 21 Jul 1998 10:45:55 GMT	Transmission if file modified

5.4.3 Hidden actions

The user of a browser obviously does not see the contents of the transmitted header fields. Thus more things go on behind the scenes than one might think at first sight. It may, for example, happen that a page no longer exists at the specified location, but has been relocated. In this case, the answer of the server contains an appropriate notice in the `Status` field of the header, together with the new location of the document in the `Location` field. The browser 'swallows' this redirection specification and tries immediately to load the document from the new location. If this succeeds, the user will at first not notice the deviations followed to process the request – only a look at the displayed URL reveals what really happened.

Table 5.2 Important response header fields.

Header field	Sample entry	Description
Date:	Sun, 07 Jun 1998 19:47:33 GMT	Sending date
Server:	Apache/1.2.5 mod perl/1.08 Netscape-Enterprise/2.01	Server software
Content-Length:	1024	Document length in bytes
Content-Type:	text/html	HTML text
	text/plain	Clear text
	octet (binary)	Binary data
Location:	http://other.host.com/redirect.html	Redirect (Section 5.4.3)
Last-Modified:	Fri, 22 May 1998 18:12:35 GMT	Last modification

5.4.4 Errors

An error status of a request is transmitted by the server before the header lines themselves. If something has gone wrong, the first line contains the error number and the
associated descriptive error text. Possible error situations in the communication with
HTTP servers on the World Wide Web are listed in Section 5.5.1.

5.5 Programming with the LWP

The LWP (Library for WWW access in Perl) by Gisle Aas and Martijn Koster provides a comprehensive collection of modules that allow access to WWW pages.

5.5.1 Simple access via `LWP::Simple`

A simple interface for accessing World Wide Web documents is provided by the
`LWP::Simple` package. Fetching an HTML page of the WWW requires next to no
effort. Listing `lwpsimple.pl` shows the palette of possible applications.

lwpsimple.pl

```perl
use LWP::Simple;

$url = "http://remote.host.com/dir/file.html";


                    # store page text in $doc
$doc = LWP::Simple::get($url);


                    # output page on STDOUT
$rc  = LWP::Simple::getprint($url);
```

```
                      # store page in file
$rc  = LWP::Simple::getstore($url, "localfile.html");

                      # load if modified
$rc  = LWP::Simple::mirror($url, "localfile.html");
```

_____*lwpsimple.pl*

The get function fetches a document and returns its contents as a character string. The string $doc contains all lines of the document, including the newline characters and the HTML commands. getprint outputs the page as HTML text on STDOUT, while getstore stores it in a file whose name the function expects as the second parameter. mirror works in a similar way, but it loads the document only if the local copy is no longer up to date.

A brief analysis of a document in the World Wide Web is carried out by the head function. The call

```
($content_type, $document_length,
 $modified_time, $expires, $server) = LWP::Simple::head($url);
```

yields a list of document-specific parameters: $content_type specifies the document format (text, image, audio, video), $document_length the document length in bytes, $modified_time the time stamp of the last modification, $expires, if defined, the expiry date, and finally $server the software version of the server. If the document does not exist, or another error occurs, the return value is undef.

All in all, the LWP::Simple interface provides only a limited functionality. Applications that actively communicate with servers or cooperate with password-protected Web servers need the LWP::UserAgent, the object-oriented interface of the libwww (see Section 5.5.2).

Error handling

Access to a WWW document can fail for a whole series of reasons. Whether no host exists with the specified name, a server is temporarily out of service, or the selected page does not or no longer exist – an application must react flexibly to all sorts of possible error situations.

The get function of the LWP::Simple package returns undef if an error occurs, whereas the functions getprint, getstore, and mirror return detailed indications about the cause of the error. These values can be checked for success or failure by means of the is_success() and is_error() functions equally provided by the LWP::Simple package.

As a mnemotechnical aid for the various return values, the HTTP::Status package, which is automatically included when loading LWP::Simple, supplies a range of functions that behave in the same ways as macros:

```
RC_CONTINUE
RC_SWITCHING_PROTOCOLS
RC_OK
RC_CREATED
RC_ACCEPTED
RC_NON_AUTHORITATIVE_INFORMATION
RC_NO_CONTENT
RC_RESET_CONTENT
RC_PARTIAL_CONTENT
RC_MULTIPLE_CHOICES
RC_MOVED_PERMANENTLY
RC_MOVED_TEMPORARILY
RC_SEE_OTHER
RC_NOT_MODIFIED
RC_USE_PROXY
RC_BAD_REQUEST
RC_UNAUTHORIZED
RC_PAYMENT_REQUIRED
RC_FORBIDDEN
RC_NOT_FOUND
RC_METHOD_NOT_ALLOWED
RC_NONE_ACCEPTABLE
RC_PROXY_AUTHENTICATION_REQUIRED
RC_REQUEST_TIMEOUT
RC_CONFLICT
RC_GONE
RC_LENGTH_REQUIRED
RC_UNLESS_TRUE
RC_INTERNAL_SERVER_ERROR
RC_NOT_IMPLEMENTED
RC_BAD_GATEWAY
RC_SERVICE_UNAVAILABLE
RC_GATEWAY_TIMEOUT
```

In this way, you can also find out which specific error actually occurred. The following code fragment issues an HTP request and subsequently checks its status. If an error has occurred, it also checks whether this error is RC_NOT_FOUND, which means that a document is not present on the specified server.

```perl
use LWP::Simple;

$url = "http://remote.host.com/dir/file.html";

$ret = LWP::Simple::getstore($url, "local.html");
```

```
if(LWP::Simple::is_success($ret)) {
    print "OK\n";

} else {
    if($ret == RC_NOT_FOUND) {
        print "Document not found on server\n";
    } else {
        print "General Error: $ret\n";
    }
}
```

5.5.2 General access via `LWP::UserAgent`

A *user agent* accepts requests for network searches, executes them upon demand, and if required stores the results until the mandator calls them. The `LWP` provides an object-oriented interface for controlling these useful helpers.

Request and response objects

A user agent makes use of objects of the classes `HTTP::Request` and `HTTP::Response`, which function as containers for request and result data. The user agent itself is responsible for the access as such.

Listing `uasimple.pl` shows a simple access to a document of the World Wide Web.[4] For its `request` method, which starts the network action itself, the user agent `$ua` created in `uasimple.pl` needs an object of type `HTTP::Request`, which stores the URL of the required document together with the access method (`'GET'`). The result of the request can subsequently be found in `$response`, a reference to an object of the `HTTP::Response` class.

In the case of an error, the `is_success` method of an `HTTP::Response` object returns 0. A more precise analysis of the error cause is provided by the methods `code` and `message`, which return error code and error text.

In the case of success, the `content` method returns the content of a found document in its original form: thus, for an HTLM page, the returned scalar contains the lines of the HTML text (HTML→text and HTML→PostScript conversion is shown in Section 5.7).

The document content is then stored in the file `file` by means of the call

```
open(FILE, ">file") || die "Cannot open file";
print FILE $response->content();
close(FILE);
```

---

[4] The UserAgent fetches not only simple Web documents, but also files from FTP servers, provided the corresponding URLs were specified with `ftp://....`. The installation described in Section 6 of Appendix A also opens access to documents of 'secure' Web servers that use the `https` protocol.

uasimple.pl

```perl
#!/usr/bin/perl -w

use LWP::UserAgent;

$ua = LWP::UserAgent->new();  # create user agent

                            # create request
$request = HTTP::Request->new('GET',
                         'http://remote.host.com/index.html');

$response = $ua->request($request);    # execute network access

if($response->is_success()) {          # check for error
    print $response->content(), "\n";  # output contents

} else {                               # error message
    print "ERROR code: ", $response->code(),
          " Message: ", $response->message(), "\n";
}
```

uasimple.pl

However, this can also be carried out by the `request` method of the user agent, because

```perl
$response = $ua->request($request);
$response = $ua->request($request, $localfilename);
$response = $ua->request($request, \&callback, $chunksize);
```

are all valid signatures of `request`. In the first case, `request` processes the request as discussed above. If, as in the second example, a scalar appears as the second parameter, `request` interprets it as a file name on the local system and uses it to store the content of the document. This form of call frees the response object from buffering the contents.

If the second and the third parameter correspond to a subroutine reference `\&callback` and a scalar `$chunksize`, the `request` method jumps to the specified `callback` function after each transmission 'morsel' of `$chunksize` bytes, passing it as parameters

- a scalar containing a data packet,
- a reference to the `HTTP::Response` object,
- a reference to an object (used only internally) of the `LWP::Protocol` class.

The callback function is then entirely responsible for the data processing. This procedure is particularly suitable for transmission of longer documents via a low-quality network connection, because processing of the data can begin while the transmission is still in course.

The uachunk.pl script presented below accepts as command line parameters a URL and the name of the file in which the transmitted data is to be stored. During the transfer process, uachunk.pl displays the number of received bytes in the standard output, thus providing continuous feedback about the status of the transmission.

For this purpose, uachunk.pl supplies the request method of the user agent with a reference to a callback function that accepts a data packet as its first parameter, updates the counter in the standard output, and accumulates the transmitted data in a file.

_____*uachunk.pl*

```perl
#!/usr/bin/perl -w
######################################################################
# uachunk.pl URL localfile - fetch file morsel by morsel
######################################################################
use LWP::UserAgent;                    # WWW access
$| = 1;                                # do not buffer STDOUT output

($url, $localfile) = @ARGV;            # analyze command line
$#ARGV == 1 || usage("Wrong argument count");

$ua  = new LWP::UserAgent;             # create user agent and request
$req = HTTP::Request->new('GET', $url);

open(FILE, ">$localfile") || usage("Cannot open '$localfile'");

$response = $ua->request($req,
                sub { $data = shift;          # morsel
                      $total += length($data); # bytes up to now
                      print FILE $data;        # -> file
                      print "\r$total";        # -> display
                    },
                    1000);            # proceed by 1000 at a time
close(FILE);

die $response->as_string() if $response->is_error();

######################################################################
sub usage {
######################################################################
    ($prog = $0) =~ s#.*/##;
```

```
print "$prog: @_\n";
print "usage: $prog URL localfile\n";
exit 0;
}
```

uachunk.pl

Headers

Prior to loading a large file over the network, it is often useful to check its size. If you specify 'HEAD' as the request method for the user agent, it fetches only the header information of a document, as already discussed in Section 5.5.1 in a similar fashion.

Listing uahead.pl shows how a HEAD request proceeds and how the response object method headers_as_string subsequently outputs the acquired information in the following format:

```
Date: Fri, 07 Jun 1996 19:47:33 GMT
Server: Apache/1.2.5 mod_perl/1.08
Content-Length: 18289
Content-Type: text/html
Last-Modified: Fri, 22 May 1998 18:12:35 GMT
Client-Date: Sun, 07 Jun 1998 20:53:39 GMT
```

In the command line, uahead.pl accepts one or more URLs, which it scours on the network one by one.

The content of individual header fields is accessed by the **header** method, which returns the value of a named field. The length of a document, for example, is extracted by the call

```
$size = $response->header("Content-Length");
```

Error handling

A response object does not only master the methods is_success, **code** and **message** presented on page for checking and displaying of errors, but with the error_as_HTML method, it is also capable of formatting error texts in HTML format. Even a comparison between the return value of the **code** method and the mnemonic error codes presented in Section 5.5.1 is possible, provided the HTTP::Status module is loaded:

uahead.pl

```perl
#!/usr/bin/perl -w

use LWP::UserAgent;

$ua = new LWP::UserAgent;

foreach $url (@ARGV) {
    $req = HTTP::Request->new('HEAD', $url);      # head request
    $response = $ua->request($req);

    if($response->is_success()) {                 # OK?
        print $response->headers_as_string(), "\n";
    } else {                                      # error?
        print $response->message(), "\n";         # error message
    }
}
```

uahead.pl

```perl
use HTTP::Status;

if($response->code() == RC_NOT_FOUND) {
    print "Document doesn't exist!\n";
}
```

Whether a protocol is already supported by the current implementation of the libwww can be found out by means of the method is_protocol_supported:

```perl
if($ua->is_protocol_supported("ftp")) {
    print "FTP is already implemented!\n";
}
```

Redirects

The request method processes so-called *redirects* by itself. If the server does not respond to a URL request with a document, but with a reference to a new location, the request method fetches the requested data from there without the user knowing anything about it. The simple_request method, in contrast, which has a signature compatible with request, does not follow a URL any further, but returns a redirection error (RC_MOVED_PERMANENTLY or RC_MOVED_TEMPORARILY). Neither does simple_request, as opposed to request, handle authentication by itself: it merely returns RC_UNAUTHORIZED.

Authentication

If, for reasons of security, the server requires a valid UserID/password combination to access specific documents, the `request` method automatically supplies this to the server on demand. It must, however, be known to the user agent beforehand.

Security zones to which the server allows access only to authenticated clients are called *realms*. To help the user remember which user/password combination belongs to which zone, each *realm* has a name. This can be easily determined by using a browser to access a protected zone of the server. In such a case, the browser displays a dialog box like the one shown in Figure 5.2, which contains the realm name together with a request to enter UID and password.

Figure 5.2   Authorization box of the server `remote.host.com` for the realm `Security_Hell`.

The necessary authentication parameters for the sample realm are set by the user agent method

```
$ua->credentials("remote.host.com", "Security_Hell",
             "USERNAME", "PASSWORD")
```

It requires server and realm names together with the user name and a valid password. The call of `credentials` must be executed before issuing the request itself. If the server cannot properly identify the client on the basis of the specified parameters, the `request` method returns with the error code `RC_UNAUTHORIZED`. Note that the user agent does not show the correct behavior if it is not the addressed server, but a proxy (page 269) functioning as a firewall, to request authentication. In this case, UID and password can be passed as parameters to the `authorization_basic` method of the created `Request` object, which then carries out the authentication process.

Mirroring instead of copying

A local copy of a network document should possibly be present in the latest available version. To ensure this, the client periodically issues requests to the server asking, however, to transmit the document only if it has changed in the meantime.

The user agent carries out the mirroring request by means of the `mirror` method. This issues a so-called 'conditional request' to the server. The `If-`

`Modified-Since` header, which is set to the last modification date of the local mirror file, instructs the server to transfer the file only if it has been modified since the specified date and time.

```
use LWP::UserAgent;
use HTTP::Status;

$ua = LWP::UserAgent->new();  # create user agent

$response = $ua->mirror("http://remote.host.com/index.html",
                        "localfile");

if(($ret=$response->code()) == RC_NOT_MODIFIED) {
    print "Document up to date - no transfer required.\n";

} elsif($ret == RC_OK) {
    print "Document has been updated.\n";
} else {
    print "Error: ", $ret->as_string();
}
```

Additional settings

The agent's waiting time for a request to be completed before it terminates it with the error code `RC_REQUEST_TIMEOUT` is set with the method

```
$ua->timeout(100);   # timeout of 100 seconds
```

Each agent, be it a browser or a home-made Perl script, usually identifies itself to the WWW server to which it issues a request with its own software version. The user agent of the `libwww` is no exception: its name is `libwww-perl/x.xx`, where `x.xx` stands for the version number of the `libwww` used. The `agent` method of the user agent assigns this entry a new value. Since many WWW providers carry out statistical evaluations of their server log files, an entry such as

```
$ua->agent("Nintendo Gameboy");
```

would cause some confusion.[5]

Proxy settings

Between the client requesting a document and the server providing it, a proxy server may be in action buffering passing documents in a cache.

---

[5] The idea for this gag comes from Randal L. Schwartz.

In this case, the client does not issue its requests directly to the target computer, but communicates exclusively with the proxy, which, if it does not have the document available itself, carries out the actual access to the requested document.

Because of this separation of client and Internet, proxies are also frequently used as firewalls. Thus a proxy can protocol which pages are requested or deny access to specific localities.

The proxy method of a user agent object sets the correct proxy settings for the access via the LWP library. Frequently, the port number of the proxy service must be additionally specified in the URL, because it is not standardized. The call

```
$ua->proxy(['http', 'ftp'], "http://proxy.com:8080");
```

instructs the user agent $ua to fetch documents according to the HTTP and FTP protocols via the proxy server proxy.com on port 8080. The proxy method expects as its first parameter an anonymous array containing the names of the protocols for which the user agent will in future consult the proxy server specified in the second parameter.

A subsequent call of the method no_proxy, instead, excludes utilization of proxy services for accessing a range of selected servers. Thus a document, whose URL refers to one of the specified hosts, is always fetched from the original server.

```
$ua->no_proxy('remote.host.com', 'near.host.com');
```

If the proxy settings are already stored in the environment variables

```
http_proxy='proxy.http.com'
ftp_proxy='proxy.ftp.com'
# ... more definitions
no_proxy='near.host.com,verynear.com,fastserver.uk'
```

the method

```
$ua->env_proxy();
```

of the user agent reads them and simply takes over the set values.

If the proxy requires authentication, the authorization_basic method of the created Request object should be used (see page 268).

Debug options

For the purpose of fault analysis, all LWP library functions can be set to debug mode from within an application to be tested by calling the LWP::Debug::level function. A range of parameters are available to set different debug levels according to the required level of detail of the output or the volume of output that can be handled.

```
LWP::Debug::level('+');          # all debug functions ON
LWP::Debug::level('-');          # all debug functions OFF


LWP::Debug::level('+trace');     # trace functions
LWP::Debug::level('-trace');     # do not trace functions


LWP::Debug::level('+debug');     # output debug info
LWP::Debug::level('-debug');     # do not output debug info


LWP::Debug::level('+conns');     # output transfer data
LWP::Debug::level('-conns');     # do not output transfer data
```

5.5.3 Robots

For search robots that rummage through directories of foreign computers, different rules apply than for scripts that put only a minimal load on servers and networks. The robot user agent RobotUA operates according to the rules set forth as a standard in http://info.webcrawler.com/mak/projects/robots/norobots.html, but otherwise behaves in exactly the same way as a common user agent, and issues its requests as described in Section 5.5.2.

Prior to entering foreign directories, the robot checks whether it is welcome, and it completely avoids computers that on principle do not appreciate visits at all. In addition, the delay method can be used to set the delay between two server accesses, configuring yet another degree of fairness.

Listing robot.pl shows a robot that searches the pub directory of an FTP server, working its way deeper and deeper into the directory structure. It outputs the name and size of each file found.

_____*robot.pl*

```
#!/usr/bin/perl -w

use LWP::RobotUA;
use File::Listing;
                   # create robot
$robot = LWP::RobotUA->new('my_fair_robot/1.0', "me\@mysite.com");

                   # scan directory recursively
deep_scan('ftp://remote.host.com/pub');

######################################################################
# Recursive directory scan: deep_scan($url_string);
######################################################################
sub deep_scan {
```

```perl
    my $url_string = shift;

                    # specify directory
    my $request = HTTP::Request->new('GET', $url_string);

                    # carry out network access
    my $response = $robot->request($request);

                    # error check
    $response->is_success() || die $response->message();

                    # process listing
    for (File::Listing::parse_dir($response->content())) {
        my ($name, $type, $size, $mtime, $mode) = @$_;

                    # files: output URL and size
        print "$url_string/$name ($size)\n" if $type eq "f";

                    # directories: continue scanning
        deep_scan("$url_string/$name") if $type eq "d";
    }
}
```

_____*robot.pl*

5.5.4 Practice: checking Web pages

You have two possibilities of finding out whether the contents of an interesting Web page have changed: either a friendly colleague tells you, or you periodically scour interesting URLs with your browser.

The script urlchk.pl shows how manual checking can be mechanized: it takes a URL as a parameter, fetches the corresponding page from the Internet, uses

```
unpack("%16C*", $dat);        # calculate 16-bit checksum from $dat
```

to calculate a 16-bit checksum out of the incoming HTML code, and compares this with previously calculated values.

For this purpose, urlchk.pl keeps a small persistent database in GDBM format (page 82), in which it stores a comparative value for every URL it has ever fetched from the Internet.

If the specified Web page has not changed, urlchk.pl silently returns; otherwise it says:

```
http://www.abc.de changed.
```

The -v option makes `urlchk.pl` a bit more talkative:

```
Checking http://www.abc.de ... unchanged.
```

is displayed if nothing has changed, and the delay between the first and the second part of the message gives a feeling for how long the network access actually takes.

The script unfolds its full usefulness when the user wishes to carry out a daily check as to whether a range of Web pages has changed. Thus, if once a day a series of commands such as

```
urlchk.pl -v http://website1/doc1.html
urlchk.pl -v http://website2/doc2.html
urlchk.pl -v http://website3/doc3.html
```

is issued, changes are signaled with a maximum delay of one day.

Since many Web pages change their contents dynamically at specific positions (for example, changing advertising banners), `urlchk.pl` can also be passed a regular expression that cuts out a section of the HTML code fetched and submits only *this* part to the modification check:

```
urlchk.pl -v http://www.abc.de '<TABLE.*?</TABLE>'
```

checks, for example, whether the contents of the first table found in the HTML code (minimal match between `<TABLE` and `</TABLE>`) have changed. In most cases, it is possible to find an anchor point to monitor only the interesting part of a page.

Highly specific changes in the page contents, for example, the sentence *Coming soon!* disappearing from the announcement page of a new book, are monitored with

```
urlchk.pl -v http://some.bookstore/goodbook.html 'Coming soon!'
```

If the page no longer contains this piece of text,

```
Checking http://some.bookstore/goodbook.html ... \
    NO MATCH (/Coming soon!/) changed.
```

is displayed – evidently, the book is finally on the market!

If `urlchk.pl` fails to fetch the required page, it shows the corresponding HTTP error message together with the associated error text. This is a good way of waiting for not yet existing Web pages to appear. Thus, prior to the appearance of an expected article,

```
http://some.magazine/1999/01/index.html
```

displays

```
http://some.magazine/1999/01/index.html FAILED (404: Not found)
```

which, as soon as the page becomes available, turns into `changed`.

```perl
#!/usr/bin/perl -w
###################################################################
# urlchk.pl - check URL for modifications
###################################################################
# urlchk.pl [-v] URL [snippet-regex]
#   -v:    verbose
###################################################################

$pfile = "$ENV{HOME}/data/urlchk.dat"; # path for persistency file

use LWP::UserAgent;                    # WWW accesses
use GDBM_File;                         # persistent hash
use Fcntl;                             # O_CREAT, O_RDWR, and so on

$| = 1;                                # do not buffer output

                                       # open persistent hash
tie(%MEM, GDBM_File, $pfile, O_CREAT|O_RDWR, 0644) ||
    die "Cannot open $pfile";

$verbose = 0;                          # output required?
@ARGV = grep { !(/^-v$/ && ($verbose = 1)) } @ARGV;
                                       # check number of parameters
usage("Wrong argument count") if $#ARGV < 0 || $#ARGV > 1;

($url, $regex) = @ARGV;                # fetch parameters

print "Checking $url ... " if $verbose;

$ua = LWP::UserAgent->new();           # create user agent

                                       # set URL
$request = HTTP::Request->new('GET', $url);

                                       # carry out network access
$response = $ua->request($request);

if($response->is_error()) {            # failed?
    print "$url " unless $verbose;
    print "FAILED (", $response->code(), ": ",
        $response->message(), ")\n";
    exit 0;
}
```

```perl
if(defined $regex) {                # snippet match if defined
    # multi-line, ignoring upper/lower case spelling
    $response->content() =~ /$regex/si;

    if(defined($&)) {
        $dat = $&;                  # search result
    } else {
        print "NO MATCH (/$regex/) " if $verbose;
        $dat = "";
    }

} else {
    # no pattern defined - entire content required
    $dat = $response->content();
}

$chksum = unpack("%16C*", $dat);    # 16-bit checksum

if(!exists $MEM{$url} || $chksum ne $MEM{$url}) {
  print "$url " unless $verbose;
  print "changed.\n";
} else {
  print "unchanged.\n" if $verbose;
}

$MEM{$url} = $chksum;               # store change persistently
untie(%MEM);                        # close persistent hash

######################################################################
sub usage {
######################################################################
    my $message = shift;
    ($prog = $0) =~ s#.*/##g;

    print "$prog: $message\n";
    print "usage: $prog [-v] URL [snippet]\n";
    exit 1;
}
```

urlchk.pl

The implementation: first, urlchk.pl uses tie to bind the hash %MEM to the GDBM file data/urlchk.dat in the home directory of the user. Here, the stored checksum values of all fetched Internet pages survive the running time of the program and are available for the next call.

The following `grep` command pulls a possible `-v` argument out of the command line and, if required, sets the variable `$verbose` which controls the amount of script output.

The user agent of the LWP library fetches documents from the network and displays appropriate error messages if something goes wrong.

For each URL, the value of the 16-bit checksum determined by means of the `unpack` function is stored in the hash `%MEM`, whose data is finally sealed in the preservation file by the `untie` function.

5.6 Analyzing URLs

Internally, each user agent uses the class `URI::URL`, which splits URLs into their elements, thus allowing easy further processing. It has been designed by the authors of the `libwww`, Gisle Aas and Martijn Koster.

`URI::URL` saves the developer the effort of parsing strings of the format

```
"http://host/path/file"
```

and also helps with decomposing and decoding of attached query information (see Section 5.8) in the format

```
?key1=value1&key2=value2
```

During its construction, an object of the `URI::URL` class is supplied the URL as a string. Via a set of methods, the following elements can be accessed:

- protocol,
- host name,
- path of the requested document,
- port number,
- query.

Listing `url.pl` shows initialization and access to elements of a URL object.

_____*url.pl*

```perl
#!/usr/bin/perl -w

use URI::URL;

$url = URI::URL->new(
        "http://remote.host.com/~user/dump.cgi?p1=d%201&p2=d%202"
        );

                              # output URI as a  string
```

```
print "as_string: ", $url->as_string(),  "\n";
                        # protocol
print "scheme:   ", $url->scheme(), "\n";
                        # target computer name
print "host:     ", $url->host(),   "\n";
                        # port number
print "port:     ", $url->port,     "\n";
                        # path
print "path:     ", $url->path(),   "\n";
                        # query with %xx characters
print "equery:   ", $url->equery(), "\n";
                        # query (processed)
print "query:    ", $url->query(),  "\n";

#--- break down query parameters
%form = $url->query_form();
foreach $i (keys %form) {
    print "QUERY($i): $form{$i}\n";
}
```

url.pl

The script of Listing url.pl creates the following output (reflecting the fact that URLs without port specifications refer to port 80):

```
as_string: http://remote.host.com/~user/dump.cgi?p1=d%201&p2=d%202
scheme:    http
host:      remote.host.com
port:      80
path:      /~user/dump.cgi
equery:    p1=d%201&p2=d%202
query:     p1=d 1&p2=d 2
QUERY(p1): d 1
QUERY(p2): d 2
```

URI::URL also supports easy conversion of relative URLs into absolute URLs. If, for example during the analysis of an HTML document, one bumps into an anchor that does not contain a complete URL but only a relative path specification, the abs method converts it into an absolute URL. For this purpose, besides the relative path specification, abs also accesses a 'base' – the URL of the reference document.

Listing uriabs.pl shows how, besides the (relative) URL ../dir, the constructor URI::URL->new() also receives the base specification http://www.com/path1/path2/file.html, in order to give the subsequently called abs method a base for the conversion into a fully qualified URL.

uriabs.pl

```perl
#!/usr/bin/perl -w

use URI::URL;
                                    # URL object with base specification
$url = URI::URL->new("../dir",    # create
                "http://www.com/path1/path2/file.html");


                                    # ouptput relative path
print "Relative: ", $url->as_string(), "\n";
                                    # output absolute URL
print "Absolute: ", $url->abs(), "\n";
```

uriabs.pl

The output of the `uriabs.pl` script is

```
Relative: ../dir
Absolute: http://www.com/path1/dir
```

Similarly, the `rel()` method converts absolute URLs into relative ones, as shown by the following construct, which outputs '`subdir/file.html`':

```perl
use URI::URL;

$url = new URI::URL("http://host.com/dir/subdir/file.html",
                "http://host.com/dir/");

print $url->rel(), "\n";
```

It should be generally noted when processing URLs that URLs denoting directories principally terminate with a slash – the fact that Web servers seemingly understand the notation without the concluding path separator is due to the fact that, in such a case, they first return a *Redirect* instruction, which causes the browser to repeat the request with a new name that now contains the final slash.

5.7 Processing of HTML documents

Web pages are usually present in HTML format. With a browser such as Netscape Navigator the commands woven into the text create wonderfully formatted pages, but in their raw state they appear quite jumbled. For the purposes of printing or clear text analysis, the HTML module provides the possibility of converting HTML into PostScript or into ASCII text.

5.7.1 ASCII and PostScript conversion

The `parse_file` method of an object of `HTML::TreeBuilder` type analyzes an HTML file and returns a reference to a newly created parse tree.

Objects of `HTML::FormatText` or `HTML::FormatPS` type in turn provide a `format` method that accepts a parse tree reference as a parameter and returns the analyzed content either in clear text or in PostScript format.

html2text.pl

```perl
#!/usr/bin/perl -w

use HTML::FormatText;
use HTML::TreeBuilder;

$tree = HTML::TreeBuilder->new();          # create TreeBuilder
$tree->parse_file("example.html");         # parse file

$formatter = HTML::FormatText->new();      # formatter object
print $formatter->format($tree);           # output
```

html2text.pl

Listing `html2text.pl` shows how to convert an HTML file to pure text. The HTML file is initially present in the format

```html
<HTML>

<HEAD>
<TITLE>This is a test page</TITLE>
</HEAD>

<BODY><H1>Headline</H1>

<p>
The list has the entries

<UL>
<LI>element one
<LI><I>element two is italic</I>
<LI><B>element three is bold</B>
</UL>

</BODY>
</HTML>
```

This is analyzed by the `parse_file` method, which, as a result, stores the reference to the parse tree (whose internal structure will be discussed further below) in the variable `$tree`. If the document to be analyzed were present in a scalar `$doc`,

```
$tree->parse($doc);
```

would be the means to the end.

The `format` method of the subsequently created formatter object of the `HTML::FormatText` class finally returns the parse tree formatted as 'junk-free' clear text (provided the document does not contain tables, which the formatter cannot (yet) handle). Thus the output of `html2text.pl` looks as follows:

```
Headline
===========

The list has the entries

   * element one

   * element two is italic

   * element three is bold
```

Listing `html2ps.pl` works in a similar way, except that instead of ASCII text it creates PostScript commands:

html2ps.pl

```perl
#!/usr/bin/perl -w

use HTML::FormatPS;
use HTML::TreeBuilder;

$tree = HTML::TreeBuilder->new();           # create TreeBuilder
$tree->parse_file("example.html");          # parse file

                                            # formatter object
$formatter = HTML::FormatPS->new(FontFamily => 'Helvetica',
                                 PaperSize  => 'Letter');

print $formatter->format($tree);            # output
```

html2ps.pl

Thus the HTML text can be output on the printer in a nicely formatted layout. Obviously, the `format` method of the `HTML::FormatPS` object used provides a more sophisticated interface for formatting options. Table 5.3 summarizes the different possibilities.

Table 5.3   Options for conversion from HTML to PostScript.

`-PaperSize`	`=>`	`"A3" "A4" "A5"` `"B4" "B5" "Letter"`	Paper size
			Or, instead of `-PaperSize`:
`-PaperWidth`	`=>`	`$nof_points`	Paper width
`-PaperHeight`	`=>`	`$nof_points`	Paper height
`-LeftMargin`	`=>`	`$nof_points`	Left margin
`-RightMargin`	`=>`	`$nof_points`	Right margin
`-TopMargin`	`=>`	`$nof_points`	Top margin
`-BottomMargin`	`=>`	`$nof_points`	Bottom margin
`-PageNo`	`=>`	`1 0`	Page numbering on/off
`-FontFamily`	`=>`	`"Courier"` `"Helvetica"` `"Times"`	Font
`-FontScale`	`=>`	`$factor`	Font size, as a factor, e.g. ”1.3”
`-Leading`	`=>`	`$factor`	Leading as a multiple of the font size. Default: ”0.1”

5.7.2 Analysis of HTML documents

Objects of the `HTML::TreeBuilder` class use `parse_file` to analyze an HTML document or `parse` to analyze a string containing HTML data. In each case, the result is a parse tree that can be further analyzed. It is composed of nodes of HTML elements of `HTML::Element` type, which are linked hierarchically with each other and represent the tags of the document. Typically an HTML document consists of one single tag of type `HTML`, which contains the head (`HEAD`) and the text (`BODY`) of the document. The `BODY` tag in turn contains the most varied HTML tags such as headlines, lists, hyperlinks, and so on.

The reference to a parse tree object, returned by the two methods `parse` and `parse_file`, provides the `traverse` method, which traverses the parse tree down to a selectable depth and calls a callback function for every node found, passing it the following parameters:

- a reference to the found object of type `HTML::Element`,
- a start flag, which is set if the tag is the start tag (and not the end tag),
- the depth of the tree currently reached by the parser.

The callback function analyzes the current node a step further. The most important methods of an object of type HTML::Element are:

```
$node->tag();        # <A HREF=url>text</A>  -> 'a'
$node->starttag();   #                       -> '<A HREF=url>'
$node->endtag();     #                       -> '</A>'
$node->content();    #                       -> ['text']
$node->attr('href'); # ·                     -> 'url'
```

The tag method specifies the tag name of the HTML element; starttag and endtag supply the character sequences of the instructions beginning and ending the tag. content returns a reference to a list that contains strings for text to be formatted and references to HTML::Element objects for possibly existing subtags.

The attr method fetches the values of attributes from an HTML command. Thus an anchor generally uses the HREF attribute to define the URL that points to the referenced document. Thus, if called with the parameter 'href', attr yields the URL as attribute value.

If the callback routine does not return a 'true' value, the traverse algorithm does not penetrate deeper into the parse tree. Thus it is possible to use the callback routine to 'brake' the parsing process.

Listing htmltitle.pl fetches the title of an HTML document. It traverses the parse tree until it finds the title tag, and then outputs its contents.

htmltitle.pl

```perl
#!/usr/bin/perl -w

use HTML::TreeBuilder;

$tree = HTML::TreeBuilder->new();           # create TreeBuilder
$tree->parse_file("document.html");         # parse file

$tree->traverse(\&callback);                # traverse parse tree

$tree->delete();                            # release memory

#################################################################
sub callback {
#################################################################
    my($node, $start, $depth) = @_;

        # if $node is no HTML::element object, it is a piece of text
        # - but we are only interested in HTML::element objects
    return 1 unless ref($node);
```

```perl
                    # no interest for closing tags
    return 1 unless $start;

    if($node->tag eq "title") {          # Aha! An opening TITLE tag!
        print "Title: @{$node->content()}", "\n";
        return 0;                        # terminate parsing process
    }

    1;                                   # continue
}
```

htmltitle.pl

The call $node->content() in htmltitle.pl returns a reference to a list that (since no further subtags are defined in the title of an HTML document) contains only one element: the string with the title text.

As a further example, Listing htmllinks.pl works its way through all anchor tags, which, as everybody knows, are marked with <a>. Subsequently, the attr method fetches the value of the 'href' attribute – the URL of the anchor.

htmllinks.pl

```perl
#!/usr/bin/perl -w

use HTML::TreeBuilder;

$tree = HTML::TreeBuilder->new();        # create TreeBuilder
$tree->parse_file("document.html");      # parse file

$tree->traverse(\&callback);             # traverse parse tree

$tree->delete();                         # release memory

###################################################################
sub callback {
###################################################################
    my($node, $start, $depth) = @_;

        # if $node is no HTML::Element object, it is a piece of text
        # - but we are only interested in HTML::Element objects
    return 1 unless ref($node);

    return 1 unless $start;

    if($node->tag() eq 'a') {
```

```perl
        print "TEXT: ", @{$node->content()}, " ";
        print "HREF: ", $node->attr('href'), "\n";
    }


    1;
}
```

htmllinks.pl

Extraction of the hyperlinks of a document is a frequently requested task. Therefore, with the `extract_links` method, the HTTP library provides an easy-to-handle procedure.

Starting with the node object, `extract_links` traverses all child nodes and returns a reference to a list that in turn contains a number of references to sublists. These contain as elements the hyperlink URL found and a reference to the corresponding `HTML::Element`. A practical application of this method is shown in Listing `exlinks.pl`. The script opens an HTML document and outputs the found hyperlinks via a `print` instruction.

exlinks.pl

```perl
#!/usr/bin/perl -w

use HTML::TreeBuilder;

$tree = HTML::TreeBuilder->new();          # create TreeBuilder
$tree->parse_file("document.html");        # parse file

for(@{$tree->extract_links()}) {           # extract hyperlinks
    my ($linkname, $reference) = @$_;
    print "$linkname\n";
}

$tree->delete();                           # delete parse tree
```

exlinks.pl

If the `extract_links` method is to analyze only hyperlinks of specific tags, these can be specified in the parameter list. Thus

```perl
$tree->extract_links("a", "img");
```

fetches only tags of the kinds `<A HREF=...>` and `<IMG SRC=...>`, leaving the others out of account.

5.7.3 Parsing HTML

If it is not sufficient to extract only the links of an HTML document, but the document is to be actively manipulated and turned inside out, heavy guns must be brought into action: with the `HTML::Parser` as a base class, you can quickly write a parser that hops from HTML element to HTML element, releasing tags and text for modification. A new `HTML::Parser` object is created by means of

```
$parser = HTML::Parser->new();                  # create object
```

and processes a file or a text string with

```
$parser->parse_file($filename);                 # parse file
$parser->parse($text);                          # parse text
```

The parser subdivides the HTML text into five groups: opening tags (for example `<HTML>`), closing tags (for example `</HTML>`), comments (`<!-- ... -->`), declarations (for example `<!DOCTYPE ... >`), and normal text.

For each HTML unit recognized, it jumps to an internal function to which it passes the parser object reference (these functions are *methods*, after all) and, in addition, a range of parameters that describe the contents of the HTML unit found: thus the `text`-method that the parser visits if it finds normal text is additionally passed a scalar with the contents of the found text. The following list specifies the names of the five groups and their parameters:

```
Function
    Parameter

start                   # start tags, such as "<A href=file.html>"
    $tag                # tag name: "A"
    $attr               # reference to hash of attribute names/values:
                        # {'href' => 'file.html', ...}
    $attrseq            # list of attribute names: ('href', ...)
    $origtex            # original text: "<A href=file.html>"

end                     # end tags, such as "</A>"
    $tag                # tag name: "A"

text                    # texts, such as "Click here!"
    $text               # text: "Click here!"

comment                 # comments, such as "<!--comment-->"
    $comment            # text: "comment"

declaration             # declarations, such as "<!DOCTYPE...>"
    $declaration        # declaration text: "DOCTYPE..."
```

The hitch is that this does not help too much in this form, because `HTML::Parser` leaves the bodies of the methods empty – in the end, nothing happens at all. However, if you derive a user-defined class from `HTML::Parser` and overwrite the base class methods with your own, things get going: step by step the HTML document is walked through, and the methods can manipulate text and tags to their hearts' content.

As a sample application, we will discuss a parser that converts the absolute hyperlinks of a document into relative ones wherever this is sensible. To keep things as general as possible, Listing `LinkTrans.pm` defines a class derived from `HTML::Parser` whose parser object calls a callback function for each hyperlink and inserts its return value into the document instead of the original URL. Moreover, objects of the `LinkTrans` class have an instance variable `linktrans_result` that, after termination of the parsing process, contains the result.

Before we start implementing `LinkTrans.pm`, some words need to be said about its utilization: `linktrans.pl` includes a callback routine `translate_url`, which determines whether the URL passed as a parameter specifies a document subordinate to `http://here.com/doc/` – in the positive case, `translate_url` returns a relative value in substitution of the absolute one.

Everything else happens in the last three lines: first, a parser object is created that is passed the reference to the callback function; then the parser starts analyzing the text string `$doc` by means of the `parse` method; and finally `get_result()` fetches the result:

```
<html> This link (<a href="http://nowhere">Click!</a>) should
remain.  This one instead (<a href="subdoc/doc.html">Link!</a>
should become relative. </html>
```

Thus the link `http://here.com/doc/subdoc/doc.html` was successfully made relative, while `http://nowhere` remained untouched.

linktrans.pl

```perl
#!/usr/bin/perl -w

use LinkTrans;                          # special module
use URI::URL;                           # manipulate URLs


######################################################################
sub translate_url {                     # callback for LinkTrans
######################################################################
    my $urlstring = shift;              # URL as argument

    my $towatchfor = "http://here.com/doc/";

    if($urlstring =~ /^$towatchfor/) { # make relative if required
        return URI::URL->new($urlstring)->rel($towatchfor);
```

```
        }

    return $urlstring;                      # return untouched
}


$doc = <<EOT;
<HTML> This link (<A HREF=http://nowhere>Click!</A>) should remain.
This one instead (<A HREF=http://here.com/doc/subdoc/doc.html>Link!</A>
should become relative. </HTML>
EOT


$parser = LinkTrans->new(\&translate_url);   # create object

$parser->parse($doc);                        # start parser

print $parser->get_result(), "\n";           # output result
```

linktrans.pl

Now to the implementation of `LinkTrans.pm`: the constructor `new` fetches the class name and the callback reference from the parameter list and subsequently uses the `SUPER` construct (see page 140) to call the constructor of the base class `HTML::Parser`. `LinkTrans` defines two instance variables of its own: `href_callback`, which contains the callback reference, and `linktrans_result`, the result string.

In four of five of the parser hooks, namely in `end`, `text`, `comment`, and `declaration`, `LinkTrans` copies the incoming contents merely correctly formatted into the result string. The `start` method is the place where the music plays: for `SRC` attributes from `IMG` tags and obviously `HREF` attributes from `A` tags, `start` calls the callback defined in the constructor, passes the current URL, and substitutes it in the result string with the return value of the callback.

The additionally defined `get_result` method returns the contents of the result string after termination of the parser run.

LinkTrans.pm

```
####################################################################
   package LinkTrans;
####################################################################
use HTML::Parser;                       # parser for HTML
use HTML::Entities;                     # codes special characters

@ISA = qw(HTML::Parser);                # base class: HTML::Parser
```

```perl
#####################################################################
# constructor: LinkTrans->new(\&callback);
#####################################################################
sub new {
  my ($class, $callback) = @_;

  my $self = $class->SUPER::new();       # call base class constructor
                                         # own instance variables:
  $self->{href_callback} = $callback;    # callback function for URLs
  $self->{linktrans_result} = "";        # result string
  $self;                                 # return object reference
}


#####################################################################
# ... is called for things like "<!DOCTYPE ...>"
#####################################################################
sub declaration {
  my ($self, $declaration) = @_;
  $self->{linktrans_result} .= "<!$declaration>"; # take over
}


#####################################################################
# ... is called for each start tag, such as "<A HREF=...>"
#####################################################################
sub start {
  my ($self, $tag, $attrhr, $attrseq, $origtext) = @_;

  $self->{linktrans_result} .= "<$tag";              # copy tag name

  foreach $key (keys %$attrhr) {         # iterate over attribute keys

    my $val = $attrhr->{$key};

    if($tag eq "a"   && $key eq "href" ||    # call callback for
       $tag eq "img" && $key eq "src") {     # '<A HREF' or '<IMG SRC'
                                             # and substitute value
$val = $self->{href_callback}->($val);
    }
                                              # mask special characters
    $val = HTML::Entities::encode($val, '<>&"');
    $self->{linktrans_result} .= " $key=\"$val\"";    # append
  }

  $self->{linktrans_result} .= ">";                # terminate
}
```

```
#####################################################################
# ... is called for each end tag, such as "</A>"
#####################################################################
sub end {
  my ($self, $tag) = @_;
  $self->{linktrans_result} .= "</$tag>";      # simply take over
}


#####################################################################
# ... is called for each piece of text (no tags)
#####################################################################
sub text {
  my ($self, $text) = @_;
  $self->{linktrans_result} .= "$text";        # simply take over
}


#####################################################################
# ... is called for each comment "<!-- ... -->"
#####################################################################
sub comment {
  my ($self, $comment) = @_;                    # simply take over
  $self->{linktrans_result} .= "<!-- $comment -->";
}


#####################################################################
# return result
#####################################################################
sub get_result {
  my ($self) = @_;
  $self->{linktrans_result};
}

1;
```

———————————————————————————————————LinkTrans.pm

5.7.4 Practice: the grabber

Listing `webgrab.pl` shows a script that fetches Web documents from the Internet and, if required, extracts URLs contained in them. Since it is called from the command line and therefore its output can be manipulated with shell tools and redirected into files, it allows collating of distributed WWW documents without even one click of the mouse. The call

```
webgrab.pl -g http://remote.com/doc.html
```

with the option –g for *grab* fetches the document `doc.html` of the fictitious Web site `http:://remote.com` from the network and outputs its contents. If the HTML text of the page branches to other documents via hyperlinks,

```
webgrab.pl -e http://remote.com/doc.html
```

with the option –e for *extract* not only grabs the the page `doc.html`, but also analyzes its contents and outputs the found hyperlinks of the tags `<A>`, `<IMG>`, and `<AREA>` as strings on the standard output:

```
http://hyperlink1
http://hyperlink2
...
```

Upon demand, `webgrab.pl` also fetches Web documents in batches. If, together with the option –f, it is passed a file, it interprets each line as a URL and fetches the corresponding documents one after the other:

```
webgrab.pl -g -f files.dat -t file.tar
```

While in the normal case `webgrab.pl` simply sends all of its output to STD-OUT, the option –t channels the HTML stream of fetched documents into a `tar` file, which subsequently contains the Web pages as files under the access path of the current Web server. Thus, in the specified tar file `file.tar`, the URL `http://remote.com/dir/doc.html` simply becomes `dir/doc.html`.

This procedure can also be used to copy a range of documents that contain images to the local computer. The tar file expanded by means of a tool such as `tar` or `WinZip` creates all required subdirectories and files. After opening the entry file with an "Open File" of the browser, you can rifle through manual pages or specifications to your heart's content. Via relative hyperlinks, you can even leaf through linked documents (for conversion of absolute into relative URLs see the previous section).

More detailed information on the course of operation can be obtained via the –v option. Loss of memory is prevented by the –h option, which helps out with a list of legal call parameters:

```
usage: webgrab.pl -g [-f URLfile] [-t tarfile] URL ...   # get URLs
       webgrab.pl -e [-f URLfile] URL ...                # extract links
options:
       -h: help
       -v: verbose
```

Another hint: if a specified URL does not address a file but a directory, `webgrab.pl` insists on an appended '/', otherwise the calculation of the absolute path cannot work. Thus: `http://path/` instead of `http://path`.

webgrab.pl uses the module Getopt::Std introduced in Section 3.5, which reflects the values of set command line options (for example '-x') in entries of a selected hash (for example $opt{x}).

The two functions info and err defined at the beginning are used for output of entertainment value messages (with the -v option set) and error messages.

The option -t activates the Archive::Tar module presented in Section 3.9 whose add_data method comes in really handy for insertion of data as files into tar archives.

For the -e option, webgrab.pl decomposes the HTML text by means of an HTML::TreeBuilder object into a syntax tree, extracts tags such as <A>, <IMG>, and <AREA>, and analyzes their HREF attributes.

The hash %links contains one entry for each URL found and ensures that the URL list output by webgrab.pl does not contain any duplicates.

Since an HTML tree may contain circular references, and Perl's garbage collector does not remove them automatically, the delete method deletes the TreeBuilder object on completion and releases the memory occupied by the syntax tree.

webgrab.pl

```perl
#!/usr/bin/perl

use Getopt::Std;             # command line parameter catcher
use LWP::UserAgent;          # WWW utility
use HTML::TreeBuilder;       # HTML parser
use Archive::Tar;            # tar archiver
use URI::URL;                # manipulate URLs


                             # define message functions
sub info { print STDERR @_ if $opt{v};}  # verbose mode output
sub err  { print STDERR @_; }            # error output

getopts("ef:ght:v", \%opt);  # get command line parameters
usage() if(defined $opt{h}); # help option set?
                             # without extract or get -> error
usage() unless grep {defined} ($opt{e}, $opt{g});

                             # create tar object
my $tar = Archive::Tar->new() if $opt{t};

if(defined $opt{f}) {        # fetch URLs from a  file ...
  push(@ARGV, $opt{f});      # simply append file
                             # to the command line
  while(<>) { chop; push(@urls, $_); }
} else {                     # ... or URLs from the command line
  push(@urls, @ARGV) || usage();
```

```perl
}

foreach $url (@urls) {            # all URLs are now in @urls
  info "# GET URL $url ... ";  # message

  $ua = LWP::UserAgent->new(); # create user agent

  $request = HTTP::Request->new('GET', $url); # create request
  $response = $ua->request($request);      # carry out network access

  if($response->is_error) {     # error check
      err "ERROR code: ", $response->code(),
          " Message: ", $response->message(), "\n";
  }

  $doc = $response->content(); # document OK
  info "OK\n";
                               # with -t option set:
  if($opt{t}) {                # do not output => tarfile
    my $path = URI::URL->new($url)->path;           # path from URL
    $path =~ s,/$,/index.html,g;      # without file name -> index.html
    $path =~ s,^/,,g;                 # strip leading '/'
    $tar->add_data($path, $doc);      # data into archive
    next;                             # process next URL
  }

  if($opt{g}) { print "$doc"; next; }  # without -t option
                                       # simply output document


                              # extract links
  my $tree = HTML::TreeBuilder->new->parse($doc);

                                    # <A>, <AREA> and <IMG>
  for (@{$tree->extract_links(qw/a area img/)}) {
    my $l = URI::URL->new($_->[0]);   # href attribute
    ($s = $l->abs($url)) =~ s/#.*//g; # URL absolute, #.. out
      print "$s\n" unless $links{$l}++; # output if new
  }

  $tree->delete();                        # delete parse tree
}

if($opt{t}) {
  $tar->write($opt{t});                   # ctreate tar file
  info "$opt{t} ready.\n";                # message in verbose mode
```

```
}

sub usage {
##################################################################
    $0 =~ s,.*/,,g;              # remove path

    print <<EOT;
usage: $0 -g [-f URLfile] [-t tarfile] URL ...   # get URLs
       $0 -e [-f URLfile] URL ...                # extract links
options:
       -h: help
       -v: verbose
EOT
    exit 1;
}
```

webgrab.pl

5.8 CGI programming

Often one encounters Web pages on the Internet that do not carry only static information. Some have a counter that displays the number of accesses to the document; others show highly topical information, such as the current score of an ongoing tennis match.

Obviously enough, such pages are not continuously updated by some restless programmer in some hidden basement, but by so-called CGI (*Common Gateway Interface*) programs, which are usually realized by means of script languages like Perl.

If an HTTP server receives a request, the specified URL can point not only to an HTML page, but also to an executable program of the server. In this case, the server does not simply send the contents of a document back to the client, but executes the specified program, whose task is to create some output that the server accepts and returns to the client – that is, to the browser – as if it were a normal Web page.

The CGI program itself can draw its information from all kinds of sources: databases, files available on the server, or even other computers. The HTTP server is interested only in the output of the CGI program, which is usually structured by using HTML.

Frequently, the CGI program carries out the construction of a dynamic Web page according to special client input data. The communication channel needed for this purpose is opened up by the forms technology.

Forms are Web pages that contain a number of fields that react to user input. Editable text fields, selection boxes, and various kinds of buttons invite users to start individual queries or to get actively in contact with service suppliers. Appendix D summarizes the most important form types and their HTML representation. The next section shows how forms are dynamically created from scripts.

5.8.1 The client side

When the Web surfer fills in the required fields and presses the submit button (with single fields, it is often sufficient to press the (←) key), the server reacts specifically to that input and sends a corresponding response. How does this work?

Interaction fields are also HTML elements. Thus

form.html
```
<HTML>
<BODY>
  <FORM METHOD=GET ACTION="http://remote.host.com/cgi-bin/dump.cgi">
    Name <INPUT TYPE=TEXT NAME=customer>

    Mastercard <INPUT TYPE=RADIO NAME=cc VALUE="mc" checked>
    Visa <INPUT TYPE=RADIO NAME=cc VALUE="visa">

    <INPUT TYPE=SUBMIT VALUE=Order>
  </FORM>
</BODY>
</HTML>
```
form.html

defines a single-line input field together with two radio buttons and an adjacent **submit** button with the legend 'Order'. If the user clicks on it with the mouse, the browser issues an HTTP request including the contents of the text field and an identification of the selected radio button. On the server side, the specified URL addresses a CGI program that analyzes these parameters, reacts accordingly, and produces an output made to measure, which the HTTP server in turn sends back to the client as an HTML document.

The data that the user enters into the form can reach the server via two different methods. Information concerning selected check buttons and radio buttons, as well as filled-in text fields, is coded by the browser in a *name-value* scheme and sent to the CGI program via either

- a GET request or
- a POST request

The choice of names of the methods GET and POST is somewhat unlucky because, in the end, both perform the same action: an HTTP request.

The difference between the two procedures lies only in the fact that the GET request appends the name-value pairs of the form information to the URL in a coded format, so that they are interpreted by the server and passed to the starting CGI program in an environment variable. The parameters of a `POST` request, in contrast, are not visible in the URL, but are sent separately to the server, which passes them to the appropriate CGI program via the standard input.

Thus, for larger forms, the `POST` method is preferable, because a URL with appended additional information quickly becomes difficult to handle and is furthermore subject to a length restriction of 1024 bytes (this varies from server to server, but 1024 bytes should be the greatest common divisor).

Encoding of parameters is required because form information may also contain spaces and special characters, which in a URL are prohibited or reserved for other purposes.

In the HTML file `form.html` on page 294 the `method` attribute of the `form` tag specifies the transfer method `GET`. Therefore – because the contents of the editable items on the page are transmitted too – upon activation of the submit button the browser requests the URL

```
http://remote.host.com/cgi-bin/dump.cgi?customer=Schr%F6der&cc=mc
```

The URL as such is followed, after an initial question mark, by the values of the form fields in the format `name1=value1&name2=value2`. The `name` parts correspond to the `NAME` attributes of the form fields, while the `value` parts contain the values entered or selected by the user. Special characters are converted by the browser into the `%xx` format, where `xx` stands for the hexadecimal number of the coded character in the ASCII table. Thus, 'Schröder' is converted into the string `Schr%F6der`.

The credit card selected by the user by means of the two radio buttons is determined by the CGI program via the `cc` parameter (value: `mc` or `visa`).

Figure 5.3 shows Netscape Navigator with the loaded and filled-in form of Listing `form.html`, shortly before the user clicks on the submit button with the legend 'Order'.

Figure 5.4 shows the situation shortly afterwards: the browser has issued a GET request to the CGI analysis program introduced on page 299 and now shows its output.

Thus, this is what happened: the browser used the `GET` method to send the form data to the server, where a CGI program interpreted and processed it and sent it back in HTML text format.

Following the `POST` method, instead of

```
http://remote.host.com/cgi-bin/dump.cgi?customer=Schr%F6der&cc=mc
```

the request would have simply asked for

```
http://remote.host.com/cgi-bin/dump.cgi
```

supplying the parameters in some hidden way. Figure 5.5 shows the result: as opposed to Figure 5.4, the URL text field of the browser does not show any query information.

The analysis program `dump.cgi` receives the transmitted parameters through some other ways, but hides this fact and outputs them as before in HTML format.

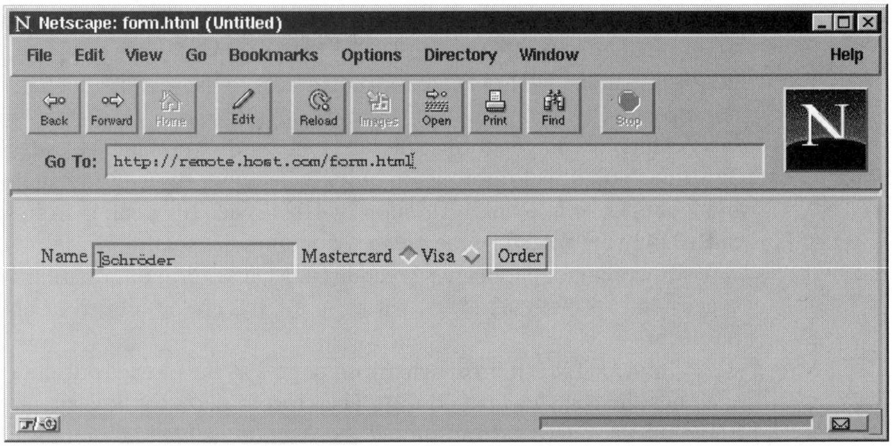

Figure 5.3 Form that upon pressing a button issues a GET request.

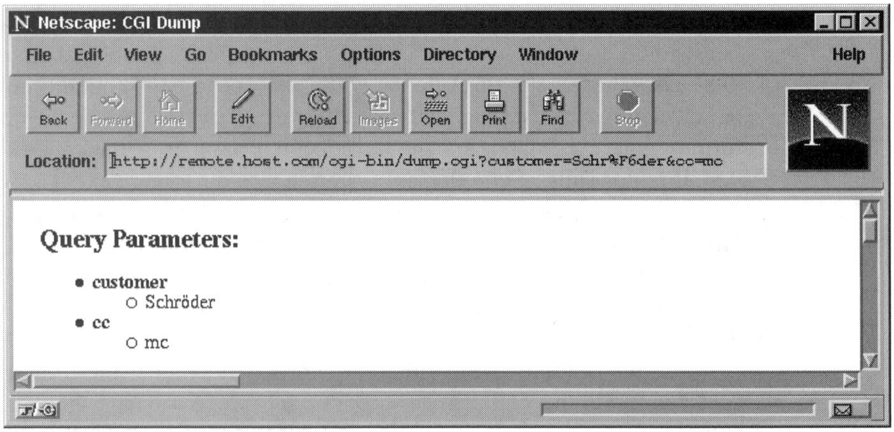

Figure 5.4 A GET request to the CGI program `dump.cgi`.

5.8.2 The server side

The relevant CGI program on the server is passed the parameters of the request automatically by the HTTP daemon.

To process the request correctly, the CGI program must first analyze its environment variables. The variable REQUEST_METHOD indicates whether the request is a GET or a POST request: in the first case, further form information can be found in the variable QUERY_STRING; in the second case, it is waiting in the standard input of the program.

However, Perl programmers need not bother about these details, because all parameters are accessible via a higher-level interface.

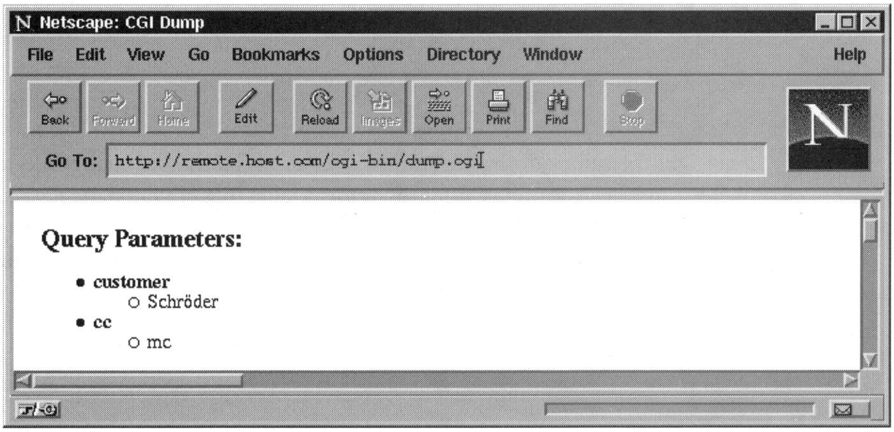

Figure 5.5   A POST request to the CGI program `dump.cgi`.

The CGI.pm package

It is the task of the CGI program to read the transferred information, evaluate it, and output a dynamically processed HTML page on the standard output.

The Perl package `CGI.pm` by Lincoln D. Stein supports programmers on the server side of the World Wide Web. It includes methods that

- analyze and process the parameters of incoming requests,
- help with sending back HTML documents.

Appendix A explains how to obtain `CGI.pm` via the CPAN or the enclosed CD-ROM.

As you already know, parameters passed to a CGI program are accessible as environment variables (GET method of the client) or via the standard input (POST method). `CGI.pm` usually abstracts the access to incoming parameters by means of a query object:

```
use CGI;
$query = CGI->new();                    # create query object
$value = $query->param('name');         # interrogate parameters
```

assigns the value of the CGI parameter `'name'` to the scalar `$value`. In hard day-to-day business, however, the `$query` object just complicates programming unnecessarily. With a list after the `use` command, which contains the `:standard` tag, `CGI.pm` stretches the point and imports the CGI methods as functions into the namespace of the script:

```
use CGI qw/:standard/;
$value = param('name');                 # interrogate parameters
```

If the specified parameter is not defined, `undef` is returned. Since the CGI protocol also envisages the transfer *several* of values with *one* parameter,

```
@values = param('name');                    # interrogate parameters
```

assigns all values of the parameter `'name'` to the list `@values`. Called without parameters, instead, the `param` function returns a list that contains the names of all incoming CGI parameters.

The script `dumptest.pl` scours all transferred parameters one after the other and outputs their names and values:

_____*dumptest.pl*

```
#!/usr/bin/perl -w

use CGI qw/:standard/;

foreach $name (param()) {           # iterate over all parameter names
    print "$name: ";                # output names
    @values = param($name);         # get values of a parameter
    print join(', ', @values), "\n";    # ... and output them
}
```

_____*dumptest.pl*

Before a CGI script creates confusion in the `cgi-bin` directory of the Web server, it should have at least one dry run without error. A Perl script that includes `CGI.pm` 'knows' whether it has been called from the command line or by the server. In the first case, if at some point it processes CGI input parameters, it takes value pairs of the form `key=value` from the command line. The call

```
dumptest.pl name1=value1 name2=Schr%F6der name1=value3
```

yields the following output:

```
name1: value1, value3
name2: Schröder
```

The parameter `name1` contains the two values `value1` and `value3`, which were passed to it one after the other. The `Schr%F6der` string was nicely decoded by the `param` function in `dumptest.pl` into 'Schröder'.

To turn the test script `dumptest.pl` into the CGI analysis program `dump.cgi`, which resides in the `cgi-bin` directory of a Web server and, for test purposes, nicely formats the passed parameters and returns them to a requesting browser, three things are needed:

- The output must be preceded by an HTTP header that tells the browser the type of the subsequent document. Even the server expects a CGI script to prefix its output with a header. If this is omitted, the server assumes that the script has crashed and sends the browser an *Internal Server Error*.

- `dump.cgi` should structure its output in HTML, which is then displayed formatted by the browser.

- Not only the transmitted query parameters play a role for CGI programs. The environment variables surrounding the script contain many important items of additional information and should also be output by `dump.cgi`.

The first point is satisfied by a call of

```
print header();    # outputs the string
                   # "Content-type: text/html\r\n\r\n"
```

If called without parameters, the function `header()` of the `CGI` module returns a minimal HTTP header including the necessary line feeds that separate the header from the following output. To ensure that no system misses out on the separation between header and document, the HTTP protocol prescribes – at least in the header – `\015\012` as line separators. The `Content-type` header set to `text/html` indicates to the receiving browser that an HTML document is going to follow. Other document types are preceded by the `-type` parameter set to the appropriate values:

```
print header(-type => 'text/plain');    # unformatted text
print header(-type => 'image/gif');     # GIF image
print header(-type => 'image/jpg');     # JPG image
```

Listing `dump.cgi` shows the implementation of the analysis script. The function `start_html` of the `CGI` module supplies the initial sequence of each and every HTML document. The title is set by the `-title` parameter[6] to 'CGI Dump', while `-bgcolor` sets the background color to a neutral white.

The function `as_string()` of the same module simply returns all received query parameters as an HTML list in a string.

Listing `dump.cgi` uses `as_string` to output all parameters HTML-formatted, but in addition creates a list containing the values of its environment variables so that the HTTP response of `dump.cgi` always contains all parameters that are available to the CGI script.

dump.cgi

```
#!/usr/bin/perl -w
```

---

[6] Since Perl 5.003, the first part of a *key/value* combination such as `-title => 'abc'` can also do without safety quotes, but given the fact that the `CGI` module exports a whole lot of functions, confusion may arise: the Perl interpreter could understand `-title` as the negative return value of the `title()` function exported by `CGI.pm`. With the `-w` option set, `perl` grumbles accordingly. `'-title'` (*with quotes!*) re-establishes calm and clarity.

```
use CGI qw/:standard/;

print header(),                            # CGI- header
      start_html('-title'   => "CGI Dump", # start sequence and title
                 '-bgcolor' => "white"),   # background color
      h2("Query Parameters:"),             # H2 headline
      CGI::as_string(),                    # CGI parameters formatted
      h2("Environment:"),                  # H2 headline
                                           # output environment
      (map { p("$_ => $ENV{$_}") } sort keys %ENV),
      end_html();                          # termination
```

_____*dump.cgi*

As Section 5.8.3 will show in detail, the `CGI` module provides functions for simple HTML output that bear the names of their corresponding HTML tags. Thus, for example, `h2("Environment:")` returns the HTML string "`<H2>Environment:</H2>`", allowing output of a second-level headline without using many special characters that would otherwise disturb the Perl code in a visually unpleasant way.

By means of a `map` construct, `dump.cgi` packs the output of the environment variables into one single line. For each key in the hash of the `%ENV` environment variable, `map` returns a string in the format "`<P>$key => $ENV{$key}`". The function `end_html()` closes HTML output with an HTML termination sequence.

`dump.cgi` is very useful where one has to analyze the flow of data that actually arrives at an HTTP server. If a local HTTP server is available, `dump.cgi` should be installed for the subsequent explanations. Appendix A shows how this is done on page 389.

5.8.3 HTML output with the CGI module

For the multitude of different HTML tags, `CGI.pm` provides one function each that frees the Perl code from the grove of '`<><><>`' brackets. Thus, a level one headline

```
print "<H1>Subject</H1>";                        # headline
```

becomes simply

```
print h1("Subject");                             # headline
```

while a bulleted list of the form

```
print "<UL><LI>Item 1</LI><LI>Item 2</LI></UL>"; # bulleted list
```

is simplified to

```
print ul( li("Item 1"), li("Item 2") );          # bulleted list
```

Thus, while HTML encloses an expression with one opening and one closing tag, the set of functions of `CGI.pm` requires nested function calls to create the required structure. Tags with attributes are simply written using an anonymous hash as a first parameter that contains attribute names and values as key/value pairs:

```
                                                           # hyperlink:
print "<A HREF="http://www.com">Click me!</A>";            # conventional
print a({href => "http://www.com"}, "Click me!");          # using CGI.pm
```

Listing `basehtml.pl` shows a CGI script that uses the most important tags of the HTML standard range: lists, various fonts, and hyperlinks.

Once stored in the `cgi-bin` directory of the Web server, a call of `http://server/cgi-bin/basehtml.pl` in the browser gives rise to the output shown in Figure 5.6.

_____*basehtml.pl*

```perl
#!/usr/bin/perl -w

use CGI qw/:standard/;

print header,
      start_html('-title'  => 'HTML-Tags', '-bgcolor' => 'white'),

      h2("Bulleted list"),
      ul( li( i("italic") ), li( b("bold") ), li( tt("typewriter") ) ),

      hr(),   # horizontal line
      p(),    # paragraph

      h2("Glossary list"),
      dl(
         dt("Hyperlink"),
         dd(
            a( {href => 'http://www.com'}, "Click here!")
          ),
         dt("Hyperlink as an image"),
         dd(
            a( {href => 'http://www.com'},
               img({src => "/pic.gif"}))
          )
       ),

      end_html();
```

_____*basehtml.pl*

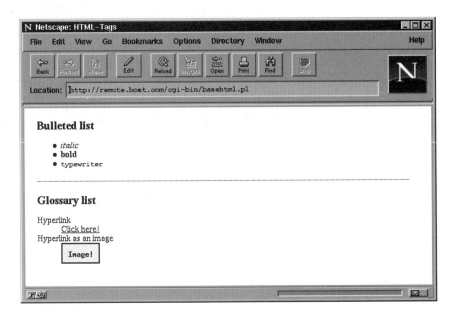

Figure 5.6   HTML tags from the standard range.

Tables

Tables are created by means of the functions `table`, `TR`, `th`, and `td`, which correspond to the HTML tags `TABLE`, `TR`, `TH`, and `TD` (the `TR` function is only written in upper case because there is already a Perl function named `tr`). To make the `CGI` module export them, the `:html3` tag must be used:

```
use CGI qw/:html3/;

print table(
        {-border => 1, -bgcolor => 'beige'},     "\n ",
        TR( th("Column1"), th("Column2") ),      "\n ",
        TR( td("Field 1/1"), td("Field 1/2") ), "\n ",
        TR( td("Field 2/1"), td("Field 2/2") ), "\n",
    );
```

From an HTML point of view, the newlines are not needed, but they facilitate reading the output:

```
<TABLE BORDER="1" BGCOLOR="beige">
 <TR><TH>Column1</TH> <TH>Column2</TH></TR>
 <TR><TD>Field 1/1</TD> <TD>Field 1/2</TD></TR>
 <TR><TD>Field 2/1</TD> <TD>Field 2/2</TD></TR>
</TABLE>
```

If the table content is dynamically constructed by Perl code, the problem often arises of collecting all table data within one table(...) call. This would be a sensible thing to do, but it cannot be done because their creation is too complicated. Splitting up the task makes it easier:

```
use CGI qw/:html3/;

foreach $row (1..2) {                          # create table contents
    $rowcontent = "";
    foreach $col (1..2) {
        $rowcontent .= td("Field $row/$col");
    }
    $tablecontent .= TR($rowcontent) . "\n";
}

print table(                                   # ouput table
        {-border => 1, -bgcolor => 'orange'}, "\n",
        TR( th("column1"), th("Column2") ),    "\n",
        $tablecontent
    );
```

Perl's map function handles loop-typical taks even without loops. Without much ado, the following snippet makes a table out of a list of column headings (@head) and an array that contains references to the rows of the table as sublists:

```
use CGI qw/:standard :html3/;

@head = ("1st column", "2nd column", "3rd column");
@lol  = ([1,2,3], [4,5,6], [7,8,9]);

print table(
        TR(map { th($_) } @head), "\n",
        map { TR(map { td($_) } @$_) . "\n" } @lol
    );
```

The first line of the table() call encloses each entry in @head with <TH>...</TH> and the whole lot with <TR>...</TR> – and there is your table header. As you will remember, the map command returns a new list in which each element of the list passed to it is substituted with the expression in curly brackets.

In the line directly below, which contains the two map commands, the outer map command scours @lol, lets the found sublists (@$_) be processed by the inner map command, writes its <TR>...</TR> around the result, and returns it. The inner map command encloses each sublist entry in <TD>...</TD>. Got it?

Additional tags

`CGI.pm` recognizes all HTML tags, even if they are not necessarily included in the accompanying documentation (appears via `perldoc CGI`). In most cases, the HTML tag written in lower case represents the corresponding function of `CGI.pm`. Attributes (such as the `SRC` attribute in the `IMG` tag) are set by an anonymous hash as the first argument. As these functions are normally not exported with the `:standard` tag, a prefixed module identifier such as `CGI::` helps. Thus

```
print CGI::font({size => '+1', color => 'red'}, "Caution, red!");
```

changes font size and color in HTML with

```
<FONT SIZE="+1" COLOR="red">Caution, red!</FONT>
```

Forms

Figure 5.7 shows which types of forms `CGI.pm` can create: popup menus which pop up at the click of a button and allow a selection; selectable radio buttons and check-buttons; single- or multiline text fields; scrollable lists; and finally buttons for sending and resetting the form information.

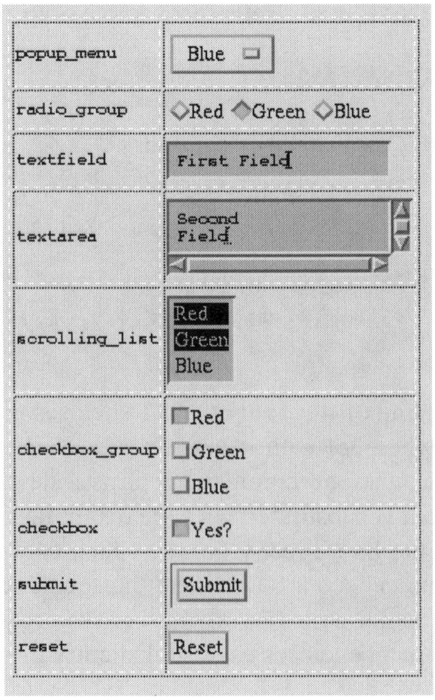

Figure 5.7   Output of `form.pl`.

The CGI script of Listing `form.pl` on page 306 is responsible for this output. The function `popup_menu` stores the HTML code for a popup menu in the variable `$popup_menu`. This form element bears the name `color1`. And this will also be the name of the variable that the browser, after having submitted the form, sends back to the server, set to the value chosen by the user. Internally, the choice is `'r'`, `'g'`, and `'b'`, but the user only gets to see the words Red, Green, and Blue, mapped via the `%labels` hash. The color preselected by the browser is `'r'`, thus `'Red'`.

A group of radio buttons, such as the one stored in the following listing in the variable `$radio_group`, is a number of on/off switches of which exactly one is selected ('on'), thus defining the value of the output variable.

The `textfield` and `textarea` elements accept texts entered by the user and supply them to the server under the name of the field. They differ only by the number of lines of the input window – *one* for `textfield`, *any number* for `textarea`.

The listbox element created by the `scrolling_list` function works in a similar way as the popup menu decribed above, except that it can immediately display several values and fetch the invisible ones via the scrollbar. The option `-size` specifies the number of visible entries, and when `-multiple` is set to `'true'`, several entries can be selected.

The group of switches created by `checkbox_group` is similar to the previously presented group of radio buttons, except that it allows several options to be selected ('on') at the same time. The subsequent `checkbox` function, in contrast, supplies the HTML code for one *single* switch.

The submit button is used to send the form. The `-value` option of the `submit` function defines its label. The browser transmits this value in the variable defined via the `-name` entry. Thus the server side can determine which submit button has been pressed out of a number of them.

The reset button can only set its label via the `-value` parameter; nothing more is required because it never gets in connection with the server, but merely resets the form parameters to their original values after the user has been playing around with them.

After the definition of the fields, `form.pl` starts to output the whole lot, beginning with the header and the `start_html` sequence. The `start_form` routine begins the HTML form defininition and sets the transfer method to GET (standard is POST) and the `-action`, that is the CGI script to be called, to `/cgi-bin/dump.cgi` – our CGI analysis script.

Then `form.pl` packs the form elements into a two-column table with border and puts `end_form` and `end_html` at the end, cleanly closing both the form and the HTML code.

Put into the `cgi-bin` directory of the Web server, `form.pl` supplies a browser pointing to it with `http://server/cgi-bin/form.pl` the image shown in Figure 5.7. If the user presses the submit button with the legend Submit, the browser contacts the script `cgi-bin/dump.cgi` specified in the `start_form` routine, using the GET method. Full of consternation, this script outputs the values as shown in Figure 5.8.

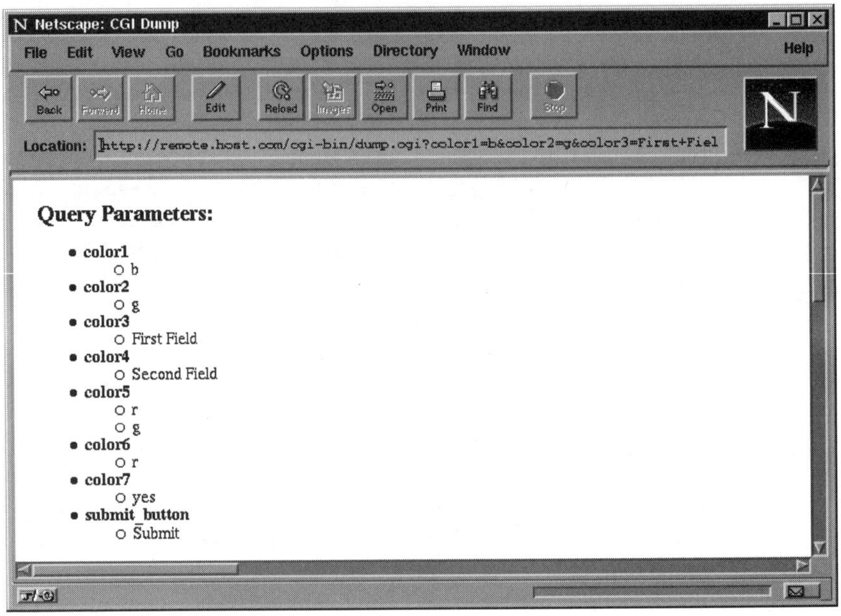

Figure 5.8 Output of form.pl.

——form.pl

```perl
#!/usr/bin/perl -w

use CGI qw/:standard :html3/;

%labels = ('r' => 'Red', 'b' => 'Blue', 'g' => 'Green');

$popup_menu = popup_menu(            ### popup menu
    '-name'    => 'color1',          # field name
    '-values'  => ['r', 'g', 'b'],   # individual values
    '-default' => 'r',               # preselected
    '-labels'  => \%labels);         # value -> displayed name

$radio_group = radio_group(          ### group of radio buttons
    '-name'    => 'color2',          # field name
    '-values'  => ['r', 'g', 'b'],   # individual values
    '-default' => 'r',               # preselected
    '-labels'  => \%labels);         # name -> displayed name

$textfield = textfield(              ### single-line text
    '-name'    => 'color3',          # field name
```

```
     '-default' => '');                    # initially empty

$textarea = textarea(                      ### multiline text
    '-name'    => 'color4',                # field name
    '-default' => '',                      # initially empty
    '-rows'    => 2,                       # two lines
    '-columns' => 20);                     # 20 characters wide

$scrolling_list = scrolling_list(          ### scrollable list
    '-name'     => 'color5',               # field name
    '-values'   => ['r', 'g', 'b'],        # selectable values
    '-default'  => ['r', 'g'],             # preselected
    '-size'     => 3,                      # height of box
    '-multiple' => 'true',                 # multiple selection OK
    '-labels'   => \%labels);              # name -> displayed name

$checkbox_group = checkbox_group(          ### group of checkboxes
    '-name'      => 'color6',              # field name
    '-values'    => ['r', 'g', 'b'],       # individual switch values
    '-default'   => 'r',                   # 1st switch pressed
    '-linebreak' => 'true',                # line up below each other
    '-labels'    => \%labels);             # name -> displayed name

$checkbox = checkbox(                      ### single checkbox
    '-name'    => 'color7',                # field name
    '-checked' => 'checked',               # preselected
    '-value'   => 'yes',                   # value if pressed
    '-label'   => 'Yes?');                 # displayed text

$submit = submit(                          ### submit button
    '-name'  => 'submit_button',           # field name
    '-value' => 'Submit');                 # legend and returned
                                           # value if pressed

$reset = reset(                            ### reset button
    '-value' => 'Reset');                  # legend

print header(),                            # output everything in HTML
    start_html('-title'   => 'Sample form',
               '-bgcolor' => '#e0e0e6'),

    start_form('-method' => 'GET', # start of form and action URL
               '-action' => '/cgi-bin/dump.cgi'),

    table({'border' => 1},                 # table of form elements
```

```
            TR(td(tt("popup_menu")), td($popup_menu)),
            TR(td(tt("radio_group")), td($radio_group)),
            TR(td(tt("textfield")), td($textfield)),
            TR(td(tt("textarea")), td($textarea)),
            TR(td(tt("scrolling_list")), td($scrolling_list)),
            TR(td(tt("checkbox_group")), td($checkbox_group)),
            TR(td(tt("checkbox")), td($checkbox)),
            TR(td(tt("submit")), td($submit)),
            TR(td(tt("reset")), td($reset)),
        ),
    end_form(),                     # end of form
    end_html();                     # end of HTML
```

form.pl

5.8.4 Hints and tips for CGI programming

Different standards apply to CGI scripts than to normal Perl scripts. The following sections provide some advice for their development.

The taint check

Since access to HTTP servers usually does not require any authentication procedure, CGI programs represent a considerable security risk for every Web server. Data entering a CGI script from outside must in no case be used in Perl commands such as `system` without being checked – too easily, unauthorized persons could otherwise gain control over the server.

Therefore, special precautions are advisable. The option `-T` traces the way of external parameters and lets `perl` howl (and abort) if their contents are carelessly used in precarious situations (a more detailed discussion of this subject can be found in the `perlsec` manual page). However, this method offers no guarantee; careful proceeding is called for.

Therefore, every good CGI program begins with the lines

```
#!/usr/bin/perl -Tw

use CGI;
use strict;
```

The `strict` option prohibits some additional unsafe constructs (see Section 1.14.3), thus giving one more degree of security.

Error handling

If a massive error occurs in a CGI script – so massive that one would like to chuck everything and abort the script – the problem arises that a CGI header is required before the error message as such; otherwise the browser displays an unsightly `Internal Server Error` that on the browser's side reads as: *Amateur at work!*

If the header output stands at the beginning, and the critical part of the script in the midst of an `eval` construct, nothing can go wrong: if the script runs into a `die` instruction, it jumps out of the `eval` block and *into* the subsequent `if` condition, because in this case `$@` holds the wording of the error message:

```
use CGI qw/:standard/;

print header();

eval {
    #...
    print p("Still going all right ...\n");
    #...
    die "Massive error!";
};

if ($@) {
    print h1("Error: $@");
}
```

If you prefer to do without the `eval` block, you can also intercept the pseudo signals `__DIE__` and `__WARN__`, and define a handler for the error case:

```
use CGI qw/:standard/;

$SIG{__DIE__} = $SIG{__WARN__} =
    sub { cgiprint(h1("@_")); exit 0 };

#...
cgiprint(p("Still going all right ..."));
#...
die "Massive error!";

sub cgiprint {
####################################################
# output text; header if required
####################################################
    print header() unless defined $header_printed;
    print "@_";
    $header_printed = 1;
}
```

This code routes all output through `cgiprint`, a `print` function that puts the header in front only at the first call. `cgiprint` 'remembers' this state in the global variable `$header_printed`.

Emergency brake

If, because of a programming error, a CGI script runs into an endless loop, this can significantly slow down the computer; several 'hanging' scripts can even paralyze the Web server. As a safety measure, an

```
alarm(60);      # initiate self-destruction after 60 seconds
```

called at the beginning of a script, terminates the corresponding CGI script after 60 seconds without mercy, thus getting potential 'hangers' out of the way. This is not what you would call a clean solution, but it certainly helps to guarantee smooth round-the-clock operation of a server.

5.8.5 Interaction-free CGI examples

A simple counter

Writing a CGI program that increments a permanent counter at each call and returns it as an HTML text is nothing special. It merely needs to store the current counter value in a file to have it ready for the next call.

But how do these tachometer-like contraptions get into a Web page that is not even a CGI script, but consists of standard HTML text?

The image tag of HTML can define not only a file, but also a CGI script as a data source:

```
<IMG SRC=cgi-bin/count.cgi>
```

Now, the task of the `count.cgi` script is to increment a permanent counter at each call and subsequently return its value as image information. Figure 5.9 shows the result.

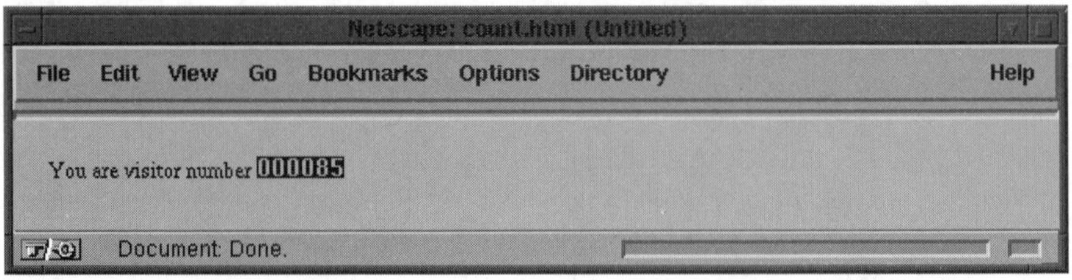

Figure 5.9   Counter in a document.

The HTML page shown defines an image tag whose data source is the CGI program `count.cgi`.

count.html

```
<HTML>
<BODY>
You are visitor number <IMG SRC=/cgi-bin/count.cgi>
<BODY>
</html>
```

count.html

count.cgi itself implements the permanent counter by means of the function inccounter, which opens a file specified as a parameter, reads a counter value (potentially) stored there, increments it, saves it, and finally returns it to the calling program.

The mileage counter lookalike originates from a design by Frans van Hoesel. The array @invdigits holds the digits from 0 to 9 stored as hexadecimally coded bitmaps. Each of the strings of the array contains ten hex codes separated by spaces that correspond to the horizontal pixel rows of the digits' bitmaps. Each hex code represents, interpreted as a bit sequence, the eight pixels of a bitmap row – thus 0xff corresponds to a row of black pixels because its binary representation is 11111111.

count.cgi

```perl
#!/usr/bin/perl

@invdigits = ("ff c3 99 99 99 99 99 99 99 99 c3 ff",  # 0
              "ff cf c7 cf cf cf cf cf cf cf c7 ff",  # 1
              "ff c3 99 9f 9f cf e7 f3 f9 f9 81 ff",  # 2
              "ff c3 99 9f 9f c7 9f 9f 9f 99 c3 ff",  # 3
              "ff cf cf c7 c7 cb cb cd 81 cf 87 ff",  # 4
              "ff 81 f9 f9 f9 c1 9f 9f 9f 99 c3 ff",  # 5
              "ff c7 f3 f9 f9 c1 99 99 99 99 c3 ff",  # 6
              "ff 81 99 9f 9f cf cf e7 e7 f3 f3 ff",  # 7
              "ff c3 99 99 99 c3 99 99 99 99 c3 ff",  # 8
              "ff c3 99 99 99 99 83 9f 9f cf e3 ff"); # 9

$count     = sprintf("%06d",
                 inccounter("/var/httpd/logs/counter.dat"));

$countlen = length($count);      # number of digits in the counter

$width  = $countlen * 8;         # width in bits
$height = 12;                    # height in bits

@bytes = ();                     # result array
```

```perl
for ($line=0; $line < $height; $line++) {
    for ($digit=0; $digit < $countlen; $digit++) {
        $field = substr($count, $digit, 1);
        $byte = substr($invdigits[$field], $line*3, 2);
        push(@bytes, $byte);
    }
}

print <<"EOT";                          # output bitmap
Content-type: image/x-xbitmap

#define count_width  $width
#define count_height $height

static char count_bits[] = {
EOT

for($i=0; $i<=$#bytes; $i++) {
    print "0x$bytes[$i]";
    print "," if $i != $#bytes;
    print "\n" unless ($i+1) % 7;
}

print "};\n";

######################################################################
# Increment permanent counter: inccounter($filename);
######################################################################
sub inccounter {
    my $file = shift;
    my $count = 0;

    if(open(FILE, "<$file")) {
        $count = <FILE>;
        close(FILE);
    }

    $count++;

    open(FILE, ">$file") || die "Cannot open $file";
    print FILE "$count";
    close(FILE);

    $count;
}
```

It is the task of the two `for` loops to combine the individual digits of the counter value as images in a large bitmap. The inner loop begins with the first row of the first digit and works its way down to the first row of the last digit. Subsequently, the outer `for` loop moves down row after row. Thus the bitmap of all represented digits develops row by row in the format

```
static char count_bits[] = { 0xff, 0xff, 0xff, ...
                             0xc3, 0xcf, 0xc3, ...
                             ...
                             0xff, 0xff, 0xff ...
                           };
```

Together with the prefixed height and width definition in the format

```
#define count_width  48
#define count_height 12
```

(where the width of `48` is calculated on the basis of a 6-digit number sequence of a width of 8 pixels each), this results in the typical C-language-like bitmap format that the browser can interpret and represent as graphics.

A fact not taken into account in `count.pl` is that the file in which the permanent counter resides represents a resource that can be accessed by only one process at a time. Since an HTTP server potentially processes several requests simultaneously, the file may become damaged under the influence of several writing processes. A method for handling *critical sections* introduced in Appendix F on page 415 efficiently prevents this catastrophe from happening.

Chart graphics with CGI

The Chart package presented in Chapter 3 is very well suited to pep up a Web page with graphics created *on-the-fly*. CGI scripts can transform dry data into well-structured color-coded bar and pie charts without requiring major programming efforts.

The illustration shown in the introduction to the Chart package (Figure 3.1 on page 152) has been created by means of the CGI script `chartcgi.pl` shown below.

The browser takes over the spatial arrangement of the individual graphics because if the script is not passed a CGI parameter named `graph` – which is the case in a call such as

```
http://localhost/cgi-bin/chartcgi.pl
```

the first `if` block is executed, which first outputs the HTTP header for an HTML document and the HTML start sequence, and then something like:

```
<IMG SRC="/cgi-bin/chartcgi.pl?graph=bars" ... >
<IMG SRC="/cgi-bin/chartcgi.pl?graph=stackedbars" ... >
<IMG SRC="/cgi-bin/chartcgi.pl?graph=pie" ... >
```

```
<IMG SRC="/cgi-bin/chartcgi.pl?graph=lines" ... >
<IMG SRC="/cgi-bin/chartcgi.pl?graph=points" ... >
<IMG SRC="/cgi-bin/chartcgi.pl?graph=linespoints" ... >
<IMG SRC="/cgi-bin/chartcgi.pl?graph=pareto" ... >
```

Thus chartcgi.pl outputs an HTML page that contains <IMG> tags. These in turn request GIF images, which are created dynamically – by no-one less than chartcgi.pl itself. The chartcgi.pl requests included in the tags pass the values for the graph parameter, following the GET method.

If graph for example holds the value "bars", chartcgi.pl jumps into the second if block, fetches the Chart::Bars package from the Chart collection, draws the corresponding graphics, outputs it together with a matching HTTP header and – says goodbye. The graphs for the other values of graph, thus for stackedbars, pie, lines, points, linespoints, and pareto, are also drawn by chartcgi.pl – and our illustration is ready to be shown.

chartcgi.pl

```perl
#!/usr/bin/perl

@days    = qw/Mo Tu We Th Fr Sa Su/;    # X value set
@sales_a = qw/ 3  4  3  6  8 10 15/;    # 1st Y value set
@sales_b = qw/ 5  5  5  6  6  7  7/;    # 2nd Y value set

use CGI qw/:standard/;

# called without parameters - output HTML page
if(!defined param("graph")) {

    print header, start_html(-title => 'Chart Test');
    for (qw/bars stackedbars pie lines points linespoints pareto/) {
        print img({src => "$ENV{SCRIPT_NAME}?graph=$_",
                   border => 3,
                   hspace => 3,
                   vspace => 3}), "\n";
    }
    print end_html;

} elsif(param("graph") eq "bars") {       ### bar chart

    use Chart::Bars;                        # include package
    my $g = Chart::Bars->new(200,200);      # create object
    $g->set('title' => 'Chart::Bars');      # set title
    $g->add_dataset(@days);                 # X data set
    $g->add_dataset(@sales_a);              # 1st Y data set
```

```perl
        $g->add_dataset(@sales_b);                  # 2nd Y data set
        $g->cgi_gif();                              # output gif

} elsif(param("graph") eq "stackedbars") {   ### stacked bars

        use Chart::StackedBars;                      # include package
        my $g = Chart::StackedBars->new(200,200); # create object
        $g->set ('title' => 'Chart::StackedBars');# set title
        $g->set('x_label' => "Week");               # legend X axix
        $g->set('y_label' => "Sales");              # legend Y axis
        $g->set('grid_lines' => "true");            # draw grid
        $g->set('max_val' => 30);                   # max. Y value
                                                    # colors: red and green
        $g->set('colors' => [[255,0,0], [0,255,0]]);
        $g->add_dataset(@days);                     # X data set
        $g->add_dataset(@sales_a);                  # 1st Y data set
        $g->add_dataset(@sales_b);                  # 2nd Y data set
                                                    # legend data sets
        $g->set('legend_labels' => ["Product A", "Product B"]);
        $g->cgi_gif();

} elsif(param("graph") eq "pie") {           ### pie chart

        use Chart::Pie;                              # include package
        my $g = Chart::Pie->new(200,200);          # create object
        $g->set ('title' => 'Chart::Pie');         # set title
        $g->add_dataset(@days);                     # share legends
        $g->add_dataset(@sales_a);                  # share values
        $g->cgi_gif();                              # output gif

} elsif(param("graph") eq "lines") {         ### lines

        use Chart::Lines;
        my $g = Chart::Lines->new(200,200);
        $g->set ('title' => 'Chart::Lines');
        $g->add_dataset(@days);
        $g->add_dataset(@sales_a);
        $g->add_dataset(@sales_b);
        $g->cgi_gif();                              # output gif

} elsif(param("graph") eq "points") {        ### points

        use Chart::Points;
        my $g = Chart::Points->new(200,200);
        $g->set ('title' => 'Chart::Points');
```

```
        $g->add_dataset(@days);
        $g->add_dataset(@sales_a);
        $g->add_dataset(@sales_b);
        $g->cgi_gif();                                  # output gif

                                                ### Lines with
} elsif(param("graph") eq "linespoints") {      ### anchor points

        use Chart::LinesPoints;                         # include package
        my $g = Chart::LinesPoints->new(200,200);       # create object
        $g->set ('title' => 'Chart::LinesPoints');      # set title
        $g->add_dataset(@days);                         # X data set
        $g->add_dataset(@sales_a);                      # 1st Y data set
        $g->add_dataset(@sales_b);                      # 2nd Y data set
        $g->cgi_gif();                                  # output gif


} elsif(param("graph") eq "pareto") {           ### pareto

        use Chart::Pareto;                              # include package
        my $g = Chart::Pareto->new(630,200);            # create object
        $g->set ('title' => 'Chart::Pareto');           # set title
        $g->set ('cutoff' => 3);                        # abort after 3 values
        $g->add_dataset(@days);                         # X data set
        $g->add_dataset(@sales_a);                      # 1st Y data set
        $g->cgi_gif();                                  # output gif
}
```

chartcgi.pl

5.8.6 Client-server interaction

Frequently, after a form has been sent, a dialog develops between client and server that may take several rounds of questions and answers. Thus, for example, the browser makes a request that the server answers with a dynamically generated Web page that contains a form with fields to fill in. After the user has obliged with this duty and forwarded the information to the server by pressing the submit button, the latter may find that the indications are incomplete. Therefore it transmits a Web page to the client that contains the form with the filled-in fields together with a note stating that one or more of the fields have not been filled in correctly and that therefore a repetition is required. After the necessary correction and a further click on the submit button by the user, the server confirms to the client that everything is now all right, for example by sending it an HTML page with a success message.

During these transactions, data accumulates that goes beyond the visible entries on the form. Thus the server might need to store information about the way the client arrived at the current form, and which data has already been transferred in this way and which data still needs to be requested.

The server has a number of possibilities for accomplishing this task:

1. It hides the collected information inside the forms that it sends to the client for further processing, so that the client unconsciously returns the data buffered in this way.

2. It buffers the accumulated information on the server's side and associates it to a transaction whose ID number the client transmits with each request.

Hidden fields

For the first method, HTML provides so-called *hidden fields* that – in the same way as the visible entry fields – store a value under an attribute name, but are not visible.

The HTML tag

```
<input type=hidden name="language" value="E">
```

defines a field of the name language that contains the value E. The language in which the user receives the requested Web pages is usually selected at the beginning of the communication by means of a CGI script. But the follow-up forms are also to be formulated in the same language: therefore client and server carry this information invisibly in the exchanged forms, so each of the communication partners always has the current status at their disposal without having to store local data.

Transaction IDs

In the second method, the server generates a hard-to-force number that is composed, for example, of the Internet address of the client, the current time, and a process number, and transmits this to the client.

If a client includes a valid transaction ID in a request, the server knows where to find potentially buffered data. If no such number is included in the request, the client obviously wishes to start a new transaction.

Again, there are two methods for the exchange of a transaction ID: either server and client exchange the ID number via hidden fields of transmitted forms, or they use the so-called *cookies*.

Originally, the Netscape browser came along with this mechanism without being asked. However, Microsoft's Internet Explorer followed soon, and today cookies are nearly a standard. With this method, the server invisibly transmits the generated unique ID to the browser, and the client includes it with each further request to the server without the user having to bother, or often without the user even knowing about it.

The clear advantage of this method is that, since the cookie used is invisible, the normal browser user cannot manipulate it (Perl programmers obviously can).

For this purpose, it is interesting to find out which header information is supplied by the WWW server of the Netscape company when a Netscape browser loads the document `http://www.netscape.com`. Since transfer of header data takes place prior to the transmission of the HTML page itself, this data is usually not visible. Therefore, the Perl script of Listing `netscape.pl` makes the server believe that it is a *Mozilla* agent (this is how the Netscape browser identifies itself), and outputs the header information supplied.

netscape.pl

```perl
#!/usr/bin/perl -w

use LWP::UserAgent;

$ua = LWP::UserAgent->new();  # create user agent
$ua->agent("Mozilla/3.04Gold (X11; I; Linux 2.0.30 i586)");

                              # create request
$request = HTTP::Request->new('GET',
                              'http://www.netscape.com');

                              # carry out network access
$response = $ua->request($request);

                              # error check
if($response->is_success) {
    print $response->headers_as_string();

} else {                      # error message
    print "ERROR code: ", $response->code(),
          " Message: ", $response->message(), "\n";
}
```

netscape.pl

The result shows that in this case not only the usual response header entry is supplied, but also a `Set-Cookie` instruction:

```
Date: Sat, 28 Mar 1998 23:21:29 GMT
Server: Netscape-Enterprise/2.01
Content-Type: text/html
Client-Date: Sat, 28 Mar 1998 23:17:27 GMT
Set-Cookie: NGUserID=cfc84949-24458-891127289-1; \
            expires=Wednesday, 09-Nov-99 23:12:40 GMT; \
            domain=.netscape.com; \
            path=/
```

Such IDs are generated by the server, and the Netscape browser stores them persistently in order to include them with the next access to a server of the same domain (domain entry) and a script under the same path (path entry). The server re-identifies the client via this ID and 'remembers' transactions that have possibly been carried out before.

A simple registration system

Listing regmp.pl shows a simple system for registration of users by means of their email addresses. Initially, it displays an entry form, submits entered addresses to a rudimentary syntax check, and stores them line by line in a text file. Previously registered users are rejected.

regmp.pl has two states that it recognizes on the basis of the passed CGI variable email: either a user arrives for the first time (email not set) or he/she attempts a registration (email set). In the first case, the script merely displays the registration form; in the second case it checks whether the entered address matches the pattern '_a_.__.'[7] In the positive case, it attempts a registration by means of the function register_email and, with both success and failure, outputs a message together with the repeated entry form. If the specified address does not match the pattern, the entry form is displayed again together with an error message.

If a script is activated by several browsers at the same time, many Web servers execute it in parallel processes (or *threads*) almost simultaneously in order to improve performance. If these parallel-running instances of a script do not negotiate access to a file processed by all of them, chaos breaks out and data may become corrupted. Therefore the function register_email secures itself exclusive access to the registry file by means of a file lock (for details of file locking see Appendix F).

_____*regmp.pl*

```
#!/usr/bin/perl -Tw

use CGI qw/:standard :html3/;     # standard CGI functions
use Fcntl qw/:flock/;             # define LOCK_EX etc.

my $efile = 'email.dat';          # address file

if(! defined param('email')) {    # no email entered (first
                                  # call?) => introductory page
    print_form("Please enter your email address.");

} elsif (param('email') =~ /\S\@.+?\...+/) {
```

_____

[7] Actually checking email addresses for authenticity is very laborious. The pattern specified above does not check the address syntax according to the official specification; a detailed solution is given in Friedl (1997). Moreover, even a 100% syntactically correct email address is not necessarily authentic. A solution to this problem is shown by the email registry on page 353.

```perl
                                    # valid email => store
    if(register_email(param('email'), $efile)) {
        print_form("Registration successful. Thank you.");
    } else {
        print_form("Error: $ERROR");
    }

} else {                            # nonsense entered; repeat
                                    # with error message
    print_form("Invalid email address - please try again.");
}


#####################################################################
sub print_form {                # output form together with message text
#####################################################################
    my ($message) = @_;

    print header,
          start_html('-title' => "Registration"),
          h2($message), start_form(),
          table(TR(td("Email:"),
                   td(textfield(-name => 'email',
                                -value => (param('email') || ""))),
                   td(submit(-value => "Register")))),
          end_form();
}


#####################################################################
sub register_email {                # include email in file
#####################################################################
    my ($email, $filename) = @_;
                                        # create file, if
                                        # not yet existing
    do {open(FILE, ">$efile"); close(FILE)} unless -f $efile;

    if(!open(FILE, "+<$efile")) {  # open for read/write access
        $ERROR = "Cannot open $efile (internal error).";
        return 0;
    }

    flock(FILE, LOCK_EX);           # protect agaist parallel access
    seek(FILE, 0, 0);               # move to beginning of file

    while(<FILE>) {                 # search for new email
        chomp;                      # strip newline
```

```
    if($_ eq $email) {
        $ERROR = "You are already registered.";
        close(FILE);
        return 0;
    }
}


seek(FILE, 0, 2);                # append email to end of file
print FILE "$email\n";
close(FILE);
return 1;
}
```

regmp.pl

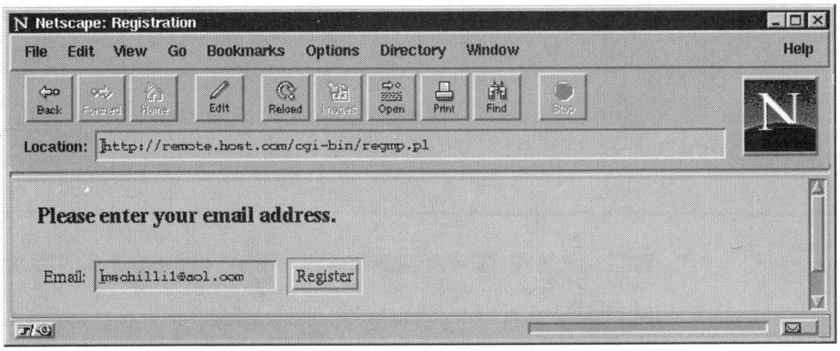

Figure 5.10   Registration form of the registration system.

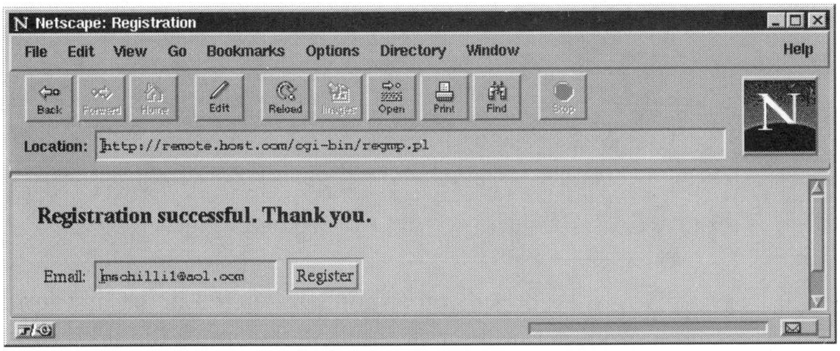

Figure 5.11   A successful registration.

A small online ordering system

The small online ordering system shop.pl accepts the customer number of the user (Figure 5.12) on the entry page. Once the user presses the submit button, shop.pl presents a range of available articles (Figure 5.13). If the user selects one or more of these and presses the submit button again, shop.pl displays a state of account including customer number and total sum, and appends the order data to a file for further processing (Figure 5.14).

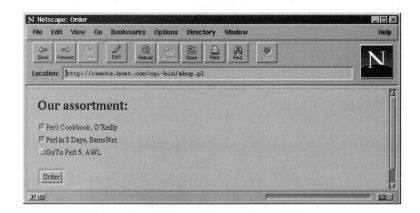

Figure 5.12   Registration with the online shop.

Figure 5.13   Selection from the product range.

How does the customer number entered in the first form, but not shown in the second form, get into the account statement of the third form? When the customer presses the submit button on the first page, param('customer_number') is true, and shop.pl executes the elseif block because the CGI parameter order is still undefined. Here, shop.pl displays the product range including the selection buttons and in addition smuggles the parameter customer_number in as a hidden field. This has

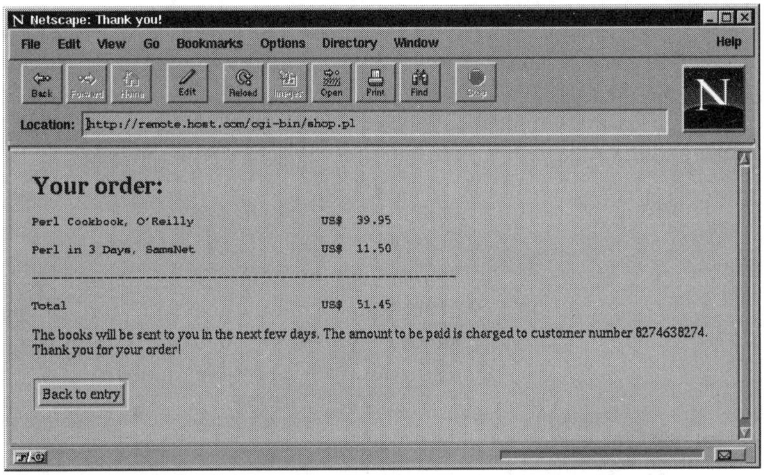

Figure 5.14   The order has been sent off.

the consequence that after issuing the order both `customer_number` and `order` are set and `shop.pl` can print a complete statement.

_____*shop.pl*

```perl
#!/usr/bin/perl -w

use CGI qw/:standard/;                          # CGI functions
use Fcntl qw/:flock/;                           # LOCK_EX

print header();                                 # output header

%products = (1 => ['Perl Cookbook, O\'Reilly', 39.95], # products
             2 => ['Perl in 3 Days, SamsNet', 11.50],
             3 => ['GoTo Perl 5, AWL', 38.90]);

%labels = map { ($_, $products{$_}->[0]) } keys %products;

eval {                                          # intercept errors

  if(!defined param('customer_number')) {       # no customer number?
    print start_html('-title', 'Welcome'),      # -> start page
          h1('Welcome to the Perl bookstore!'),
          start_form(), "Your customer number:",
          textfield(-name => 'customer_number'),
          submit(-value => "Go shopping!"),
```

```perl
                    end_form(), end_html();

    } elsif(!defined param('order')) {           # no order?
        print start_html('-title', 'Order'),     # -> ordering page
              h1("Our assortment:"), start_form(),
              checkbox_group(
                  '-name'      => 'order',
                  '-values'    => [keys %labels],
                  '-linebreak' => 'true',         # underneath each other
                  '-labels'    => \%labels),      # products
              p(), submit(-value => 'Order'),     # order button
              hidden(-name  => 'customer_number'), # forward
              end_form(), end_html();

    } else {                                      # store order
        @order = param('order');

        open(ORDER, ">>orders.txt") || die "Cannot open orders.txt";
        flock(ORDER, LOCK_EX);                    # set lock
        print ORDER "Customer number: ", param('customer_number'),
                    " Order: @order\n";
        close(ORDER);

        print start_html('-title', 'Thank you!'),  # thank you page
              h1("Your order: ");

        $sum = 0;

        foreach $order (@order) {
            $sum += $products{$order}->[1];
            print pre(sprintf "%-40s US\$ %6.2f",
                             $products{$order}->[0],
                             $products{$order}->[1]);
        }
        print pre("-" x 60);
        print pre(sprintf "%-40s US\$ %6.2f", "Total", $sum);

        print "The books will be sent to you in the next few days. " .
              "The amount to be paid is charged to customer number ",
              param('customer_number'),
              ". Thank you for your order!",
              start_form(), submit(-value => "Back to entry"),
              end_form(), end_html();
    }
};
```

```
if ($@) {                                          # error?
    print "Our system can currently not accept your order. " .
        "Please try again later.\n";
    open(ERRORLOG, ">>/tmp/errorlog");             # log error in file
    print ERRORLOG scalar localtime, "> $@";       # for analysis
    close(ERRORLOG);
}
```

_____*shop.pl*

Cookies with `CGI.pm`

How the cookies discussed in Section 5.8.6 can be created, sent out, and collected again by means of `CGI.pm` is shown in Listing `cookie.pl`. If it does not find a cookie, it creates a new one under the name `"cook_key"`, assigns it the value `"value!"`, and sends it to the browser. At the next call (even after a possible restart of the browser), the cookie is present, the `if` block is executed, and `cookie.pl` outputs the value of the cookie.

Additionally available options are:

- `-expires` specifies the point in time when the browser should forget the cookie. This indication is mostly made relative to the current date and time – for example, `+30m` (in 30 minutes), `+1d` (tomorrow), or `+1y` (next year) – but absolute time specifications in the format `Sunday, 03-Apr-98 01:30:10 GMT` are allowed.

- `-domain` specifies the name of a domain whose entire fleet of computers is served by the browser with the cookie.

- `-path` limits propagation of the cookie; only scripts under this path are served.

- If the `-secure` option holds a true value, the browser sends the cookie only to 'secure' servers (HTTPS protocol).

_____*cookie.pl*

```
#!/usr/bin/perl -w

use CGI qw/:standard/;

if(defined ($val=cookie(-name => 'cook_key'))) {

    print header();                    # cookie set,
    print h1("Cookie set: $val");      # output value
```

```
} else {
    $cookie = cookie(                      # cookie not set, create
        '-name'    => 'cook_key',          # name of the cookie
        '-value'   => "value!",            # value of the cookie
        '-expires' => '+1h',               # expires after 1 hour
        '-domain'  => '.scamp.com',        # valid for www.scamp.com,
                                           # host.scamp.com etc.
        '-path'    => '/cgi-bin',          # only for CGI scripts
        '-secure'  => 0                    # not only for HTTPS servers
    );
    print header('-cookie' => $cookie);
    print h1("Cookie transmitted!");
}
```

_____cookie.pl

The friendly doorman

Cookies can also hold several name/value pairs. Instead of a scalar, the `cookie` function of the `CGI` module also accepts a reference to a hash as a `-value` parameter and stores its name/value pairs in the created cookie:

```
$cookie = cookie(-name   => 'customer', -value => \%data);
```

From a received cookie, the call

```
%data = cookie(-name => 'customer');
```

extracts the data and stores it in the hash `%data`. Listing `doorman.pl` shows an application of this method in the form of a friendly virtual doorman who stands at the entry of an online shopping center and fills in the address form if he recognizes the customer.

At the very first call of `doorman.pl`, the browser has not yet set a cookie and the CGI parameter `go_shopping` holds no value either. Thus `doorman.pl` merely returns an empty address form. When the new customer fills it in and presses 'Go shopping,' `doorman.pl` grabs the form parameters, sticks them into a cookie, and shoves this over to the browser before the welcoming message of the shopping paradise appears.

At the next visit to the shopping paradise, the customer need not bother about the virtual paperwork: up to one year after the last visit, the browser remembers the cookie and sends it along if the customer selects the entry page again. `doorman.pl` extracts the name/value pairs from the cookie and puts them as preselections in the form fields, so the customer only needs to press 'Go shopping' if the address details have remained unchanged. If the customer changes the data, the browser is advised as well since `doorman.pl` sends a new cookie anyway before entering the shopping mall.

```perl
#!/usr/bin/perl -w

use CGI qw/:standard :html3/;        # standard and tables

if(defined param('go_shopping')) { # "Go shopping" pressed

                                      # form parameters -> cookie
    foreach $key (param()) { $data{$key} = param($key); }

                                      # send header with cookie
    $cookie = cookie(-name   => 'customer', -value => \%data,
                     -expires => "+1y");

    print header(-cookie => $cookie);

                                      # ... and here we go!
    print h1("Welcome to the shopping paradise!");

    # ... here we would proceed ...

} else {                              # obviously the first call
    if(cookie(-name => 'customer')) {        # cookie present?
        %cookie = cookie(-name => 'customer'); # receive cookie
        foreach $key (keys %cookie) {        # preset parameters
            param($key, $cookie{$key});
        }
    }

    print header();              # CGI header
    print_address_form();        # output address form
}

####################################################################
sub print_address_form {
####################################################################
    my $msg = (shift || "");

    print start_html(),
        tt(CGI::font({color => 'red'}, $msg)),
        start_form(),
        table(
            TR(td("Name:"),       td(textfield(-name => 'name')),
               td("First name:"), td(textfield(-name => 'prename'))),
```

```
        TR(td("Address:"),     td(textfield(-name => 'address'))),
        TR(td("City:"),        td(textfield(-name => 'city')),
          td("ZIP code:"),     td(textfield(-name => 'zip'))),
        TR(td("Method of payment"),
          td(popup_menu(-name =>'pay',
                    '-values' => ['Bill me later', 'Credit Card',
                                  'Check'])))),
      submit(-name => 'go_shopping', -value => "Go shopping"),
      end_form(), end_html();
}
```

doorman.pl

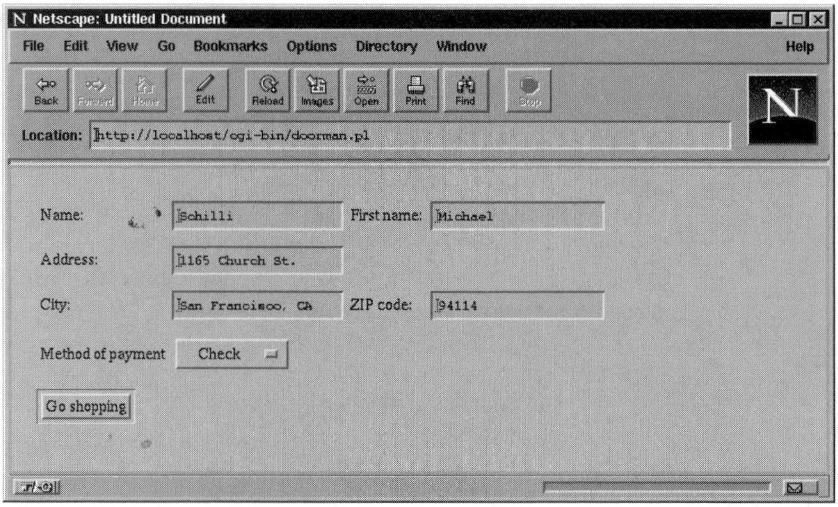

Figure 5.15   The friendly doorman has recognized the customer and filled in the address form.

Server storage with cookie support

When the data that accumulates during an electronic shopping spree no longer fits into one cookie or should not continuously be shoved back and forth, it is sensible to store intermediate states in a file on the server under a unique transaction ID.

To prevent the server from mixing up data from different customers, on the one hand, and to ensure, on the other hand, that malevolent fellow human beings cannot interfere with other people's transactions, the ID must

- uniquely identify a client, and

- be difficult to guess for outsiders.

The combination of current date and time, number of the current Web process and a random number used in our online shopper `cart.pl` should be sufficient for non-security-relevant applications.

Under this unique ID, a 14-digit hexadecimal number, the server stores address data and selected goods. A particularly practical way of doing this is the `save` method of the CGI package that stores all CGI data in a file:[8]

```
my $query = new CGI($in);          # read CGI data
$query->save($out);                # store CGI data in file
```

Here, `$in` and `$out` are references to new-generation file handles (see Section 3.1), and point to files opened for reading or writing.

When a new customer enters the virtual branch of the online store, the browser does not yet supply a cookie. For this reason, the server generates one and shoves it furtively over to the browser while it supplies an entry form (see Figure 5.16). After the customer has entered name and address and pressed the submit button, the server accepts the data and creates a new file under the transaction ID that the browser supplies this time as a cookie. The server intermediately stores all query parameters in this new file.

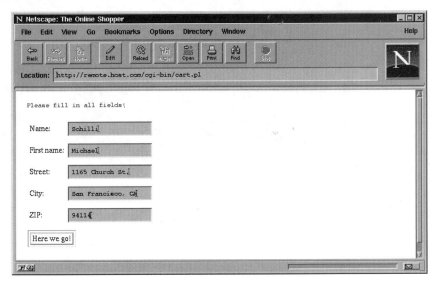

Figure 5.16   Enter address ...

The product range of the shop consists of 100 books, numbered from 1 to 100 for test purposes, 10 of which are shown per page. Customers can select individual

---

[8] While `CGI.pm` exports most of its methods also as functions and we have until now carefully avoided CGI objects wherever possible, loading and saving CGI data definitely require object-oriented syntax.

items and browse back and forth (Figure 5.17), until they finally decide to move over to the cash till and place their order (Figure 5.18).

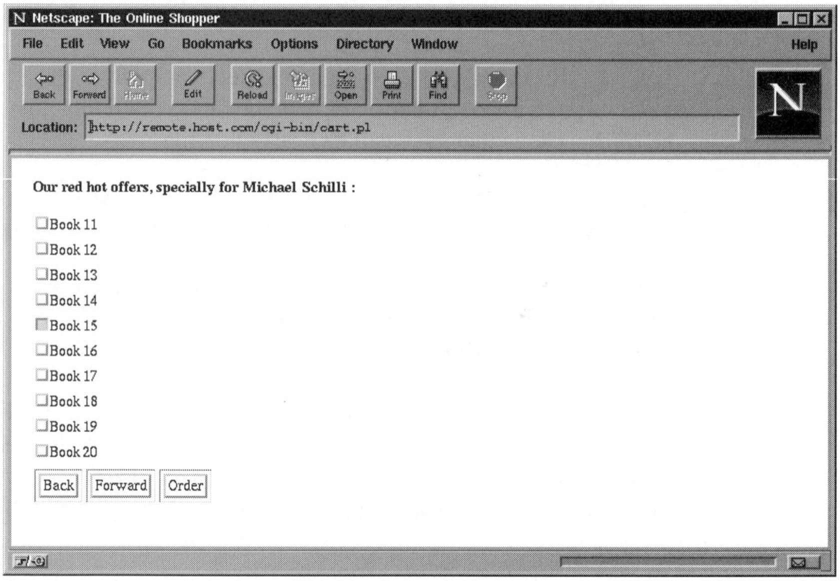

Figure 5.17   ... select products ...

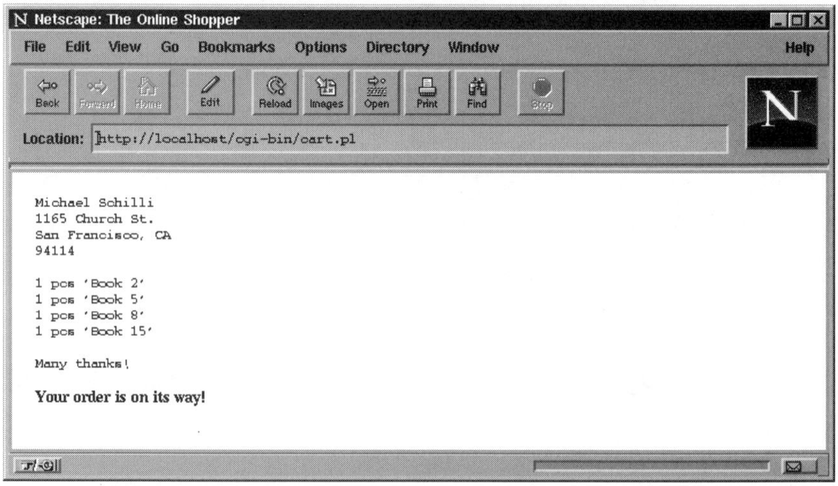

Figure 5.18   ... and to the till!

To make browsing work and selected items remain selected, the server must store the page that the customer was reading last (stored as item `offset`) and an array of numbers of selected items (stored as items) on top of the originally transmitted address data.

Each of the buttons 'Forward,' 'Back,' and 'Order' triggers the following actions on the server's side: on the basis of the incoming cookie, the server identifies the transaction file and uses it to generate a CGI object. This knows not only the address data of the customer, but also the numbers of the items selected up to now. cart.pl merges the items selected on the current catalog page into the existing order and stores the result again in the transaction file.

In the case of the 'Order' button, cart.pl displays a confirmation message and at the same time appends the following entry to the order file /usr/data/orders.dat:

```
Michael Schilli
1165 Church St.
San Francisco, CA
94114

1 pcs 'Book 2'
1 pcs 'Book 5'
1 pcs 'Book 8'
1 pcs 'Book 15'

Many thanks!
------------------------------------------------------------------
```

About the installation: the transactions directory under cgi-bin that accommodates the transaction files must already exist and be writable for the owner of the Web server. The same applies to the /usr/data directory, home of the file for executed orders.

cart.pl

```perl
#!/usr/bin/perl -wT
######################################################################
# cart.pl
######################################################################
# Perl Power! - Michael Schilli 1998
######################################################################

use CGI qw/:standard :html3/;      # CGI standard with tables
use Fcntl qw/:flock/;              # LOCK_EX
use IO::File;                      # new file handle generation
use strict;                        # strict conventions

my $TRANSDIR     = "transactions"; # directory for Temp files
my $ORDERFILE    = "/usr/data/orders.dat";  # file for orders
```

```perl
my $items_total   = 100;              # total number of items
my $items_perpage = 10;               # displayed per page
my %merchandise   = ();               # merchandise
my ($q, $i, $id);                     # variables

for($i=1; $i<=$items_total; $i++) {
    $merchandise{$i} = "Book $i";     # create test items
}

eval {                                # intercept errors

    if(!defined(my $id=cookie(-name => 'ID'))) {

        # create new cookie from time, process no. and random no.
        $id = unpack ('H*',
                   pack('Ncs', time, $$ & 0xff, rand(0xffff)));

        print header('-cookie' => cookie('ID' => $id));
        print_address_form();         # send cookie/address form

    } else {                          # cookie already exists
        print header();
        print start_html('-title'  => 'The Online Shopper',
                         -bgcolor => "white");

        ($id) = ($id =~ /([0-9a-f]+)/);       # percolate ID

        if(-f "$TRANSDIR/$id") {
            $q = restore_cgi($id);   # read old transaction data
            shop($q, $id);           # call shopper
        } else {                     # no transaction file? create
            $q = CGI->new();         # current CGI data
                                     # address information complete?
            if(grep { !$q->param($_) } qw/name first_name street
                                          city zip/) {
                print_address_form("Please fill in all fields!");
            } else {
                save_cgi($q, $id);   # create new transaction file
                shop($q, $id);
            }
        }
    }
};                                   # eval end;
```

```perl
if($a) {                                     # error occurred?
    print h1("Error: $a");
}


#####################################################################
sub shop { my ($q, $id) = a_;
#####################################################################
    my $item;
                                        # offset of visible section
    my $offset = ($q->param('offset') || 0);

        # store items selected up to now in @selected, but deselect
        # items shown in current window (will be inserted later)
    my @selected = grep {
                        $_ <= $offset || $_ > $offset+$items_perpage }
                    ($q->param('items'));

        # newly selected items to @selected
    foreach $item (param('newitems')) { push(@selected, $item); }

    $q->delete('items');             # store @selected in CGI
    $q->param('items', @selected);   # parameter 'items'
    save_cgi($q, $id);

        # 'Order' button pressed? Write invoice!
    if(param('Order')) {
        process_order($q, \%merchandise);
        $q->delete('items');         # order terminated,
        save_cgi($q, $id);           # reset shopping cart

    } else {                         # show item list

        if($offset >= $items_perpage) {
            $offset -= $items_perpage if param("Back");
        }
        if($offset < $items_total - $items_perpage) {
            $offset += $items_perpage if param("Forward");
        }

        $q->param('offset', $offset);
        save_cgi($q, $id);

        my @subset = sort {$a <=> $b} keys %merchandise;
        @subset = splice(@subset, $offset, $items_perpage);
```

```perl
                                       # new item list
         print b("Our red hot offers, specially for ",
                 $q->param('first_name'), " ", $q->param('name'), ":"),
                 start_form(),
                 $q->checkbox_group(
                      '-name'      => 'newitems',
                      '-values'    => [@subset],
                      '-default'   => [$q->param('items')],
                      '-linebreak' => 'true',
                      '-labels'    => \%merchandise),
                 submit('Back'), submit('Forward'),
                 submit('Order'),
                 end_form, end_html;
     }
}


#####################################################################
sub save_cgi {
#####################################################################
    my ($query, $id) = @_;

    my $out = IO::File->new(">$TRANSDIR/$id");  # write access
    die "Can't open $TRANSDIR/$id" unless defined $out;
    $query->save($out);
    close($out);
}


#####################################################################
sub restore_cgi {
#####################################################################
    my $id = shift;

    $id =~ s/[^0-9a-f]//g;          # protect against attacks

    my $in = IO::File->new("<$TRANSDIR/$id");  # read access
    die "Can't open $TRANSDIR/$id" unless defined $in;
    my $q = new CGI($in);
    close($in);
    return $q;
}


#####################################################################
sub print_address_form {
#####################################################################
    my $msg = (shift || "");
```

```perl
    print start_html('-title' => 'The Online Shopper',
                     -bgcolor => 'white'),
          tt(CGI::font({color => 'red'}, $msg)),
          start_form(),
          table(
            TR(td("Name:"), td(textfield('name'))),
            TR(td("First name:"), td(textfield('first_name'))),
            TR(td("Street:"), td(textfield('street'))),
            TR(td("City:"), td(textfield('city'))),
            TR(td("ZIP:"), td(textfield('zip')))),
          submit(-name => "Here we go!"), end_form(), end_html();
}


##################################################################
sub process_order {
##################################################################
    my ($q, $merchandiseref) = @_;
    my $item;

    my $order = sprintf "%s %s\n%s\n%s\n%s\n\n",
                        $q->param('first_name'), $q->param('name'),
                        $q->param('street'),
                        $q->param('city'), $q->param('zip');

    foreach $item ($q->param('items')) {
        $order .= sprintf "1 pcs '%s'\n", $merchandiseref->{$item};
    }

    $order .= "\nMany thanks!";

    my $out = IO::File->new(">>$ORDERFILE");
    die "Cannot open $ORDERFILE" unless defined $out;
    flock($out, LOCK_EX);                        # set lock
    print $out $order, "\n", "-" x 70, "\n";
    close($out);

    print pre($order),
          b("Your order is on its way!"), end_html();
}
```

Redirects

To send the requesting browser to a different place by means of a redirect command, two lines of CGI script are sufficient:

```
use CGI qw/:standard/;
print redirect('http://www.othersite.com');
```

The redirect function outputs a Location: header and thus causes the browser to veer round immediately to the new URL.

5.8.7 Apache and mod_perl

On heavily loaded Web servers, CGI scripts in Perl have to struggle against the so-called *start-up penalty*: each request starts the Perl interpreter, which must parse the corresponding script, check it for syntax errors, translate it into the internal byte code, and finally execute it. If the Perl script includes additional modules, but runs only a relatively short time, the proportion between load and execution time can at times reach more than 10:1.

The Apache Web server with the mod_perl distribution by Doug MacEachern puts an end to this waste of computing time: a Perl interpreter constantly active in Apache keeps CGI scripts in its memory and when needed enters them as subroutines – the gain in performance is tremendous.

To make the Apache server take over this task, the Apache distribution needs to be translated and installed together with the mod_perl distribution (see Appendix A.8).

The Apache module that executes Perl CGI scripts at such a blazing speed answers to the name of Apache::Registry and becomes active if an HTTP request is made for scripts located in specific directories.

The approach to keeping executable scripts in memory can, however, be a bit treacherous: global variables keep their values beyond the running time of the script. In addition, Apache branches HTTP requests in alternation to its child processes – and the value of a global variable remains constant in the address space of a child process. The script

```
use CGI;
my $query = CGI->new();
print $query->header();
print "globalvar=", $globalvar++, " (PID=$$)\n";
```

returns for each call the value of a global variable $globalvar together with the ID of the executing process ($$). Executed several times by the Apache plugin, the script returned the following output in a test run:

```
globalvar=0 (PID=29045)
globalvar=0 (PID=29046)
globalvar=0 (PID=29049)
globalvar=0 (PID=29054)
globalvar=1 (PID=29045)
globalvar=1 (PID=29046)
globalvar=1 (PID=29049)
globalvar=2 (PID=29045)
globalvar=2 (PID=29046)
```

The riddle's solution: if an HTTP request by chance gets the same child process again, the value of the global variable $globalvar is incremented by 1 with respect to the previous call. Thus global variables need to be handled with care when using mod_perl; use of use strict is recommended.[9]

Note that mod_perl does not only provide increased performance in executing CGI scripts (running unchanged), but also a universal interface to Apache: with simple Perl scripts it is possible to penetrate into the most varied areas of the Web server and control logging, authentication, redirects, and much more, adapting it to one's personal requirements.

5.8.8 Server push and client pull

There are two ways of making the browser not only fetch a Web document once, but also continuously reload and update it: client pull and server push.

While with client pull, the browser reconnects to the server at predefined intervals and simply reloads the document, with server push, server and client leave the connection open, so the server can continuously supply data to the client.

Server push

With server push, the browser expects from the server not only one document, but several consecutive ones, of which it displays only the most recent one, and simply overwrites it when new supplies arrive. The starting shot is fired by the response header entry multipart/x-mixed-replace for Content-type. At the same time, this specifies a string that uniquely defines the transition between two documents. It must begin with the character sequence '--' and be so unique that it occurs nowhere in any of the subsequent documents. The last separation string of the multipart document is in addition appended '--.'

To make the browser display a countdown of the form 2...1...Boom! with freshly overwritten information at each step, the following pushes are needed:

---

[9] When used on purpose, global variables allow all sorts of tricks to be realized – if they are really global, that is, accessible under transaction control by all instances of the server. The package IPC::Shareable, available via the CPAN, opens this road.

```
HTTP/1.0 200 OK
Content-type: multipart/x-mixed-replace;boundary=PartDocSeparator

-- PartDocSeparator
Content-type: text/html

<H1>2</H1>

-- PartDocSeparator                              <<<- ... wait 1 second ->>>
Content-type: text/html

<H1>1</H1>

-- PartDocSeparator                              <<<- ... wait 1 second ->>>
Content-type: text/html

<H1>Boom!</H1>

-- PartDocSeparator --
```

To ensure that the server does not buffer the output (this would lead to the consequence that the countdown would be displayed in quick-motion in the browser window at the end of the total time), but sends the data to the browser immediately after being available, not only $| must be set to a true value in the script. nph-boom.pl is – as the server recognizes from its name – an NPH (Non-Parsed Header) script that the server simply executes, sending its output to the browser, without – as with the usual CGI scripts – checking the headers sent by the script. However, besides Content-type and similar headers, an NPH script must also return the status of the request, which in the case of success takes the value HTTP/1.0 200 OK. This boring chore is however blocked off by the CGI module, which, with a -nph option of the header function set to a true value, supplies the requested data.

Since the sequence of headers and document separators in the server push is slightly unclear, nph-boom.pl abstracts the necessary actions in the ServerPush class. The constructor either accepts a specified document separator or, if this is omitted, uses PartDocSeparator. The server_push method accesses this via the instance variable separator and performs the necessary actions, including the multi-part header sent at the very beginning.

_____*nph-boom.pl*

```perl
#!/usr/bin/perl -w

package ServerPush;

use CGI qw/:standard/;                    # export header()
```

```perl
sub new {
    my ($class, $sep) = shift;              # $sp = ServerPush->new($sep)

    my $self               = {};           # instance variable hash
    $sep                   ||= "PartDocSeparator";
    $self->{separator}     = $sep;         # partial document separator
    $self->{header_sent}   = 0;            # first header sent?
    $| = 1;                                # debuffer output
    bless($self, $class);
}


sub server_push {
    my ($self, $content, $terminate) = @_;

    if(!$self->{header_sent}) {
        print header('-nph'  => 1,         # output header
                     '-type' =>
                "multipart/x-mixed-replace;boundary=$self->{separator}"
                    );
        print "\n--$self->{separator}\n";
        $self->{header_sent} = 1;          # set flag
    }

    print header(), "$content\n";
    print "\n--$self->{separator}",
        defined $terminate ? "--" : "", "\n";
}


#####################################################################
package main;

use CGI qw/:standard/;                            # export header()

$sp = ServerPush->new();                          # new server oush object

$sp->server_push(h1(2));                          # <H1>2</H1> with separator
sleep(1);
$sp->server_push(h1(1));                          # <H1>1</H1> with separator
sleep(1);
                                                  # <H1>Boom!</H1> with
$sp->server_push(h1("Boom!"), "terminate"); # terminating separator
```

_____*nph-boom.pl*

Client pull

The same problem is also solved by a CGI script that displays the counter value of a passed query parameter, decrements it, and calls itself after 1 second with the new value of the query parameter.

If, at the beginning of a document, the browser finds the sequence

```
<META HTTP-EQUIV="Refresh"
        CONTENT="1; URL=http://host/cgi-bin/clientpull.pl?count=2">
```

it will request the specified URL after the time lapse indicated in the CONTENT field (1 second). In the example, the URL refers to the CGI script that generated the page and which now calls itself using the GET method with a value of 2 for the count parameter. The task of the CGI script is then to generate a new page that replicates the tag represented above with a counter value decremented by 1 – and the countdown is running.

Alternatively, the server has the possibility of putting a refresh entry into the response header. For the reloading time 1s and the URL of the script, this has the following form:

```
Refresh: 1; URL=http://host/cgi-bin/clientpull.pl?count=2
```

The script clientpull.pl implements the required behavior. As long as the passed counter value is greater than zero, it puts the reloading instruction into the header before outputting the current counter value. The environment variable SCRIPT_NAME contains (according to server standards) the URL path of the executed script. When the counter reaches zero, clientpull.pl outputs a regular header before its last output, thus ending the reload rounds.

clientpull.pl

```perl
#!/usr/bin/perl -w

use CGI qw/:standard/;

$count = param('count');          # interrogate CGI parameters
$count ||= 3;                     # parameters not set? starting value
$count--;

if($count) {
    print header(-Refresh => "1; URL=$ENV{SCRIPT_NAME}?count=$count");
    print h1($count);
} else {
    print header();
    print h1("Boom!");
}
```

clientpull.pl

Appending data step by step

To avoid the browser display being constantly exchanged during the loading time of a document, as with the server push, but to have it instead append data continuously, it is sufficient to use a normal NPH script that debuffers its output and writes it step by step as in `nph-append.pl` (currently, this procedure works only with Netscape Navigator):

_____*nph-append.pl*

```perl
#!/usr/bin/perl -w

use CGI qw/:standard/;                   # export header()

$| = 1;

print header(-nph => 1);

print (h1("2"));
sleep(1);

print (h1("1"));
sleep(1);

print (h1("Boom!"));
```

_____*nph-append.pl*

5.8.9 Simulating forms with the user agent

Filling in and sending back WWW forms manually to launch a request is a boring thing when requests become more frequent. A Perl script carries out this repetitive work reliably and without laments.

First of all, the user agent needs to know the structure of the form in question to be able – like the browser – to send filled-in fields to the server and accept a response. Again, we refer to the HTML command set summarized in Appendix D.

HTML pages of WWW servers are not only present as formatted output of the browser, but their raw data source can be analyzed either directly in the browser (for example, via the `View source` menu entry in Netscape Navigator) or, after being stored in a file on the local hard disk, with any editor of your choice.

To mechanize a form request, the following parameters must be determined:

- the CGI program (as a URL) to which the form is sent (usually by activating the submit button),

- the method of parameter passing (GET or POST),
- the fields of the form as key/value pairs of field name and field content.

Let us have another look at the HTML form form.html discussed in the previous section:

———*form.html*

```
<HTML>
<BODY>
  <FORM METHOD=GET ACTION="http://remote.host.com/cgi-bin/dump.cgi">
    Name <INPUT TYPE=TEXT NAME=customer>

    Mastercard <INPUT TYPE=RADIO NAME=cc VALUE="mc" checked>
    Visa <INPUT TYPE=RADIO NAME=cc VALUE="visa">

    <INPUT TYPE=SUBMIT VALUE=Order>
  </FORM>
</BODY>
</HTML>
```

———*form.html*

The third line defines the form and specifies GET (and not POST) as the transmission method, together with the URL of the CGI program to be activated:

```
http://remote.host.com/cgi-bin/dump.cgi
```

The subsequent form fields bear the names customer and cc. These indications are already sufficient to write a Perl script that issues a request which for the receiving server is indistinguishable from the request of a browser and thus elicits the required information.

Listing formget.pl shows a simple implementation that forwards the data pairs customer => wesley and cc => visa to the server.

———*formget.pl*

```
#!/usr/bin/perl -w

use LWP::UserAgent;

$ua = LWP::UserAgent->new();

$request = HTTP::Request->new('GET',
    "http://localhost/cgi-bin/dump.cgi?customer=wesley&cc=visa");
```

```
                                  # format query
$response = $ua->request($request);

print $response->content();
```
_____*formget.pl*

formget.pl generates a user agent and a request object that selects the GET method and specifies the URL that contains the query string. The query string is separated by a question mark ('?') from the path of the associated CGI script. Key and value of a data pair are joined with an equals sign ('='), while the data pairs are separated by an ampersand ('&').

If the server expects parameters rolling in according to the POST method, this simple 'append to the URL' does not work (some servers do indeed insist on the POST method, while most servers accept GET *and* POST).

With the POST method, the client first sends the server a header with the content type application/x-www-form-urlencoded, and then includes the parameters in GET format in the message text.

Listing formpost.pl shows the procedure and in addition presents another method of parameter coding. Since the query string, no matter whether for GET or POST, is present in the format key1=val1&key2=val2..., neither keys nor values must contain characters such as '=', '&' or '?' in their packed state. The function list2query accepts a list of arguments, and combines these pairwise into a query string which it returns. Critical characters are coded according to the CGI protocol as hexadecimal numbers with a prefixed percent sign: thus a space, which bears the ASCII number 32 (hexadecimal 20), becomes '%20'. The while loop in list2query fetches the data pairs pairwise from the parameter array @_, and appends key[10] and coded value to the variable $querystring. Coding is carried out by means of ord(), which returns the ASCII code of a character, and sprintf("%%%20x", ...), which returns a percent sign ("%") followed by the corresponding 2-digit hexadecimal value ("20").[11] Thus, the value pairs

```
f1 => Why? & How?
f2 => A slash: /
```

are converted into the query string

```
f1=Why%3f%20%26%20How%3f&f2=A%20slash%3a%20%2f
```

which the receiving Web server automatically converts back into the original value pairs.

---

[10] If not only values, but also keys contain special characters, the latter need to be coded too. In practice, however, this rarely happens.

[11] More information on this procedure can be found in Section 1.10.8 on page 72.

formpost.pl

```perl
#!/usr/bin/perl -w

use LWP::UserAgent;

$ua = LWP::UserAgent->new();  # create user agent

                             # create request
$request = HTTP::Request->new('POST',
                    'http://localhost/cgi-bin/dump.cgi');

                             # declare form content
$request->content_type('application/x-www-form-urlencoded');

                             # set form content
@form = ('f1' => 'Why? & How?', 'f2' => 'A slash: /');

$querystring = list2query(@form);

$request->content($querystring);

                             # carry out network access
$response = $ua->request($request);

print $response->as_string();

######################################################################
sub list2query {
######################################################################
    my ($key, $value);
    my $querystring = "";

    while(($key, $value) = splice(@_, 0, 2)) {
        $value =~ s/[^\w-_]/sprintf "%%%02x", ord($&)/ge;
        $querystring .= "&" if $querystring;
        $querystring .= "$key=$value";
    }

    $querystring;
}
```

formpost.pl

Back to the POST method: the line

```perl
$request->content_type('application/x-www-form-urlencoded');
```

issues the header that tells the server that POST parameters will follow in the text of the request. The `content` method of the request object sticks the coded `$querystring` into the request text – and there we go!

The Caltrain server form

A practical sample application for automatic access to form-driven Web services is shown in Listing `caltrain.pl`. The Web page `http://www.transitinfo.org`, offers links to schedules of public transportation systems in the California Bay Area. Caltrain, which operates a train between San Francisco and the Silicon Valley, provides an easy-to-handle online timetable service that, for example, allows the user to find out the railway connections between two locations at a specific time. Now, if you need, for example, information on the same connection, but for the current time and day, it is sensible not to fetch a form from the server and fill it in every single time, but to use a Perl script to obtain the required information for the current date and the current time.

The script `caltrain.pl` passes the railway server the required parameters as a GET request, receives the HTML response and renders it to plain text on the standard output.

caltrain.pl

```perl
#!/usr/bin/perl -w

use LWP::UserAgent;
use URI::URL;
use HTML::FormatText;
use HTML::TreeBuilder;

$url  = 'http://www.transitinfo.org/cgi-bin/all_times';

foreach $time (time(), time() + 2*3600) {
    my($hour, $minute) = (localtime($time))[2,1];
    $am_pm = $hour >= 12 ? "pm" : "am";
    push(@times, sprintf("%d:%02d$am_pm", $hour, $minute));
}

@form = ('C'            => 'CT',                # form content
         'FromStation' => '22nd',
         'ToStation'   => 'Hillsd',
         'D'           => 'WD',
         'ALL'         => 'N',
         'TIME'        => $times[0],
         'ATIME'       => $times[1],
        );

$ua = LWP::UserAgent->new();                    # create user agent
```

```
                                                  # build query string
while(($key, $value) = splice(@form, 0, 2)) {
    $value =~ s/[^\w-_]/sprintf "%%%02x", ord($&)/ge;
    $querystring .= "&" if $querystring;
    $querystring .= "$key=$value";
}
                                                  # create request
$request = HTTP::Request->new('GET', "$url?$querystring");

$response = $ua->request($request);        # carry out network access

$tree = HTML::TreeBuilder->new()->parse($response->content());

$formatter = HTML::FormatText->new();          # formatter object

print $formatter->format($tree);               # output
```

_____*caltrain.pl*

How do the form parameters such as departure or arrival stations get into the @form array in Listing caltrain.pl, from where they are sent to the server? Or, in other words: how do you simulate filled-in form fields in Perl?

First, we need an analysis of the original HTML page, because the programmer needs to find out how the document transmits its form entries to the server. For this purpose, the page is loaded from the original server (http://www.transitinfo.org/Caltrain/) into the browser and saved locally by means of the 'Save As' menu entry. Subsequently, the definition of the form action in the document[12]

```
<form method=GET action="/cgi-bin/all_times">
```

is changed to

```
<form method=GET action="http://localhost/cgi-bin/dump.cgi">
```

If you now load the manipulated HTML file into the browser with 'Open File,' fill in the editable fields with easily recognizable data and press the submit button, the browser does not issue the request to the Caltrain server, but calls the analysis program dump.cgi (see page 299 for the listing) on the local computer.[13] The CGI pro-

---

[12] In the fast-paced Internet nothing is stable – not even the slow-paced Caltrain. It's to be assumed that the URLs mentioned will change over time, this example is just supposed to illustrate automatic extraction of Web content.

[13] For this purpose, the local computer must be configured as an HTTP server, and dump.cgi must be installed. If this cannot be done, the parameters and values needed for the transmission can also be deducted by studying the field definitions in the source code of the HTML page.

gram `dump.cgi` on the local WWW server promptly answers, as shown in Figure 5.19, with a list of received parameters.

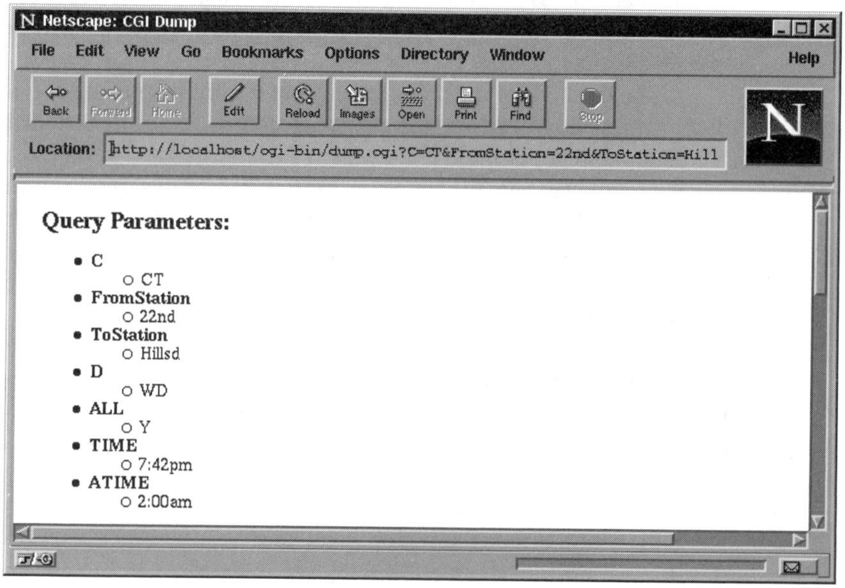

Figure 5.19   Parameter analysis of the Caltrain server.

Thus, for the parameter `FromStation` for example, `dump.cgi` shows the value `22nd` – this is the value of the selected item of the select box for the departure station. Listing `caltrain.pl` reflects this connection in the entry

```
'FromStation' => '22nd',
```

in the `@form` array. It also calculates the values of the fields `TIME` and `ATIME` to be the timeframe between the current time and two hours after that. After converting the HTML output of the Caltrain server to plain text, something like

```
...
       Train      22nd    Hillsd   Notes

          22      5:05a    5:38a
          24      6:05a    6:39a
          26      6:35a    7:08a
          30      7:05a    7:38a
...
```

will result from a call at around 5 a.m. in the morning.

5.9 Telnet

For simple routine work with computers on the network, it is often desirable to mechanize the ever-lasting *log in – issue commands – log out* procedure. The Net::Telnet module by Jay Rogers provides an easy-to-handle interface with a simple *send/expect* logic.

The methods of the module carry out the login procedure on remote computers, issue commands, wait for the returning command prompt, and receive the results output up to that point.

Listing telnet.pl creates a telnet object and sets its timeout value to 60 seconds and the expected command prompt to the dollar sign. A call of the quotemeta function masks out all critical special characters in the $prompt string, so that the new constructor in the given example receives '/^\$/m' as a regular expression for the command prompt: a dollar sign at the beginning of the line – and with the modifier m, '^' and '$' match the beginning and the end of *every* line in multiline strings.

With user ID and password as its arguments, the login method carries out the login procedure. Subsequently, the cmd method executes commands in the shell running on the remote computer and returns the result output lines as a list.

If errors occur, the routines simply 'die.' Improved error handling can be achieved via the value pair Errmode => 'return' in the constructor call: in this case, the routines return on error with undef.

telnet.pl

```perl
#!/usr/bin/perl -w

use Net::Telnet;

$host   = "localhost";                    # computer
$userid = "michel";                       # ID
$passwd = "nixgibts!";                     # password
$prompt = quotemeta('$');                  # prompt

$telnet = Net::Telnet->new(Host    => $host,
                           Timeout => 60,   # 60 seconds
                           Prompt  => "/^$prompt/m");

$telnet->login($userid, $passwd);          # login

@lines = $telnet->cmd("/bin/ls -l");       # issue command
print "@lines\n";                          # output result

@lines = $telnet->cmd("uptime");           # issue command
print "@lines\n";                          # output result
```

telnet.pl

5.10 Email

Electronic mail can easily be used with popular programs such as `elm`, `mail`, or the mail system of the Netscape Navigator: you specify the receiver's address in the format

```
user@remote.host.com
```

perhaps adding on some friends who should receive a copy, write the message text, and send it off.

The mail protocol SMTP (*Simple Mail Transfer Protocol*) controls transfer of electronic mail in the network. However, handling electronic mail at this level is extremely time consuming – if you have ever tried to edit the file `sendmail.cf` you will know what I mean.

The `Mail::Send` module by Tim Bunce and Graham Barr provides a simple interface, comparable to that of the UNIX programs `mail` or `mailx`.

The constructor of a new mail object processes parameter specifications of addressee (`To`), subject (`Subject`), and recipients of copies (`Cc` and `Bcc`[14]) in the standard `$param => $value` structure.

The `open` method of the mail object returns a file handle through which the message text is inserted by means of the usual `print` function. The `close` method closes the letter and starts the transmission operation.

If the `open` call does not contain any parameters, `Mail::Send` uses the UNIX `mail` program for data transmission to the recipient. With `"sendmail"` as a parameter, on the other hand, `Mail::Send` attaches itself directly to the locally installed sendmail daemon. It should be noted that, depending on the UNIX version, the UNIX `mail` program shows a very different behavior and does not recognize all the options offered by `Mail::Send`. The `sendmail` program, instead, reacts everywhere in the same way and handles the full set of options.

Listing `mail.pl` shows the application.

---
mail.pl

```perl
use Mail::Send;

$mail=Mail::Send->new(                        # new mail object
    Subject => "Important message!",          # subject
    To => 'user@remote.host.com',             # addressee
    Cc => 'anotheruser@site.com',             # copy to (optional)
    Bcc => 'yetanotheruser@site.com');        # blind copy to (optional)

$mail->set("From", 'me@there.com');           # sender (optional)
$mail->set("Reply-To", 'me@there.com');       # return address (optional)
```

---

[14] 'Blind carbon copy' recipients receive a copy, as do the `Cc` candidates, but do not appear in the 'Cc:' header of the mail.

```
$mailhandle = $mail->open("sendmail");    # start mail program

print $mailhandle <<EOT;                   # create text
Here comes the
message text.
EOT

$mailhandle->close();                      # close and send
```
                                                                    mail.pl

5.10.1 **Attachments**

Binary files that contain images, sounds, or compressed distributions are enclosed with emails as *attachments*. MIME headers announce parts coded with the *Base64* method, while delimiter strings subdivide the email file itself into sections:

```
Content-Type: multipart/mixed; boundary="_-----------=...
                                    ..._889858076314550"

MIME-version: 1.0
...
Content-Length: 2874

This is a multi-part message in MIME format.

--_-----------=_889858076314550
Content-Disposition: inline; filename="name.jpg"
Content-Transfer-Encoding: base64
Content-Type: image/jpg; name="name.jpg"

/9j/4AAQSkZJRgABAQAAAQABAAD//gBHQ1JFQVRPUjogWFYgVmVyc2lvbiAz
...
KMAAdBRRVRpRi+ZEyqykuVn/2Q==

--_-----------=_889858076314550--
```

The `MIME::Lite` module by Eryq helps to create emails with attachments and send them out into the world. The `new` constructor creates a new `MIME::Lite` object, which is already supplied with specifications of addressee, sender, etc. of the message. The `attach` method then includes documents of different MIME types in the mail text and encodes them, if the `Encoding` parameter is set to `base64`, following the Base64 method. Data may be present both as files (`Filename` parameter) and as scalars (`Data` parameter). The `send` method finally contacts the locally installed `sendmail` daemon and passes it the message together with all attachments for sending. Listing `attach.pl` packs clear text, a JPG image, and a binary file `data.tgz` into an email and sends it off.

At the recipient's end, provided the email system is capable of handling MIME messages, the mail is displayed as shown in Figure 5.20.

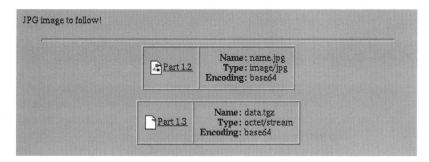

Figure 5.20 Email with attachments.

attach.pl

```
#!/usr/bin/perl -w

use MIME::Lite;

$msg = MIME::Lite->new(
    From       => 'sender@host.com',    # sender
    'Reply-To' => 'reply@host.com',     # return address
    To         => 'to@host.com',        # addressee
    Subject    => "The subject!",       # subject
    Type       => "multipart/mixed");   # announce attachments

$msg->attach(                           # include normal text
    Type    => 'text/plain',            # plain text
    Data    => 'JPG image to follow!'); # content

$msg->attach(                           # include image
    Type     => 'image/jpg',            # JPG image
    Path     => 'source.jpg',           # source file
    Encoding => 'base64',               # encoding scheme
    Filename => 'name.jpg');            # name after arrival

$msg->attach(                           # include binary
    Type     => 'octet/stream',         # binary type
    Path     => 'data.tgz',             # source file
    Encoding => 'base64',               # encoding scheme
```

```
           Filename => 'data.tgz');          # name after arrival

    $msg->send();                            # pass on to sendmail
```

_____*attach.pl*

5.10.2 **POP3 client**

The POP3 protocol is used by mail programs to interrogate a mail account. The `Net::POP3` module by Graham Barr provides an indispensable service for searching a mailbox for incoming mail by means of a Perl script instead of using Netscape Navigator, Eudora, `mail`, `elm`, or another client.

The `new` constructor creates a `Net::POP3` object that is immediately supplied with the name of the mail host. The `login` method logs the client in on the server and authenticates it by means of a user ID and password. If the server denies access, `login` returns the value `undef`; otherwise it returns the number of available messages. Listing `pop3.pl` shows an application that lists the sender and subject lines of available mail.

_____*pop3.pl*

```
#!/usr/bin/perl -w

use Net::POP3;
######################################################################
$host   = 'my.mail.host';          # mail host
$userid = 'huber';                 # login
$passwd = 'nixgibts!';             # password
######################################################################

                                   # contact host
($mail = Net::POP3->new($host)) || die "Could not open $host";

                                   # login
$nof_messages = $mail->login($userid, $passwd);
die "Userid/Passwd Error" unless defined $nof_messages;

if($nof_messages) {                # are there any messages?
                                   # for all messages
    foreach $mesgno (keys %{$mail->list()}) {
                                   # scour all header lines
        foreach (@{$mail->top($mesgno)}) {
            $subject = $1 if /^Subject: (.*)/;
            $from    = $1 if /^From: (.*)/;
```

```
            }

        printf "%02d %-30s %s\n", $mesgno, $from, $subject, "\n";
    }
}

$mail->quit();                        # exit mail program
```

_____*pop3.pl*

If there are new mail messages, pop3.pl signals, for example,

```
01 bgates@microsoft.com           Do you want to work for us?
02 peter@blaxxun.com              Golf on Thursday?
03 tomasw@addison-wesley.de       Faster! Faster!
```

When called with an empty argument list, the list method returns a reference to a hash that contains the message numbers as keys and the lengths of the corresponding messages as values.

When called with a message number as an argument, the top method returns a reference to an array that contains the header lines as elements. Similarly, the get method returns a reference to an array containing all header and body lines.

The delete method marks a mail message belonging to a given message number as deleted. When the session with the mail server is terminated by means of the quit method, the server 'forgets' all messages marked as deleted.

Email registry

Unfortunately, there is no simple procedure for checking the authenticity of email addresses as there is for verification of host names, where a simple call of gethost-byname shows whether the specified computer exists or not.

Whether we will really find the presumed addressee behind a syntactically correct email address can only be verified by actually sending an email to that address and waiting for the addressee to actively cooperate and send back a response.

The email registry system presented below carries out the following steps:

Registration
The user is asked to type his/her email address into a form and to press the submit button.

Initiate verification
The server generates an email message and sends it to the specified address. The message text asks the user simply to launch the mail program's reply function and to send the message back to the sender. Until this confirmation arrives at the server, it marks the registration status as 'pending'.

Activate

Once the answer arrives at the server, it identifies the sender, assigns it to the corresponding 'pending' entry in its data and activates the registry entry.

These tasks are carried out by the two scripts `emailreg.pl` and `emailregc.pl` shown below. The first one is a CGI script that works in a similar way to the `regmp.pl` script presented on page 319, except that it generates a unique identification number, which it stores in the address file in the format

```
mschilli@darkstar.schilli.com 35269b6be0
```

and at the same time puts it into the subject line of an email message that it forwards to the registering user:

```
Your registration (key: 35269b6be0)
```

A click on the reply button of the user's mail program sends in turn a message to the registration system, with the following subject line:

```
Re: Your registration (key: 35269b6be0)
```

Then, on the server side, the script `emailregc.pl` comes into play, which is called once a minute via a `cron` job and by means of the `Net::POP3` package checks the system's `register` mail account for incoming mail. If it finds a message, it extracts key and sender, looks for the corresponding entry in the address file, and activates it by overwriting the key with a simple `OK` and deleting the message from the mailbox:

```
mschilli@darkstar.schilli.com          OK
```

Both scripts secure their access to the address file by means of an exclusive lock. The unique ID, which more or less ensures that the incoming email message is effectively an answer to the issued control message, is combined by `emailreg.pl` out of the current time of day (`localtime`) and the number of the process executed by the CGI script (`$$`) by packing both values one behind the other with `pack` and unpacking the resulting value as a hexadecimal number.

emailreg.pl

```perl
#!/usr/bin/perl -Tw

use CGI qw/:standard :html3/;      # standard CGI functions
use Fcntl qw/:flock/;              # define LOCK_EX etc.
use Mail::Send;                    # mail functions

my $efile          = '/usr/data/email.dat'; # address file
                                   # email of registry system
```

```perl
    my $regsystem_email = 'register@registration.com';

    if(! defined param('email')) {        # no email registered (first
                                          # call?) => introduction page
        print_form("Please enter your email address.");

    } elsif (param('email') =~ /\S\@.+?\..+/) {


                                          # create unique ID
        $id = unpack ('H*', pack('Nc', time, $$ % 0xff));

                                          # store, verification mail
        if(register_email(param('email'), $efile, $id)) {
            print_form("Registration received. Please wait" .
                    "for incoming mail and answer this " .
                    "to confirm your registration.");
            send_mail(param('email'), $id, $regsystem_email);
        } else {
            print_form("Error: $ERROR");
        }

    } else {                              # nonsense entered, repeat
                                          # with error message.
        print_form("Invalid email address - please try again.");
    }


    ####################################################################
    sub print_form {                      # output form with message text
    ####################################################################
        my ($message) = @_;

        print header,
            start_html('-title' => "Registration"),
            h2($message), start_form(),
            table(TR(td("Email:"),
                    td(textfield(-name => 'email',
                                -value => (param('email') || ""))),
                    td(submit(-value => "Register")))),
            end_form();
    }


    ####################################################################
    sub register_email {                  # store email in file
    ####################################################################
        my ($email, $filename, $id) = @_;
```

```perl
                                    # create file if it
                                    # does not yet exist
    do {open(FILE, ">$efile"); close(FILE)} unless -f $efile;

    if(!open(FILE, "+<$efile")) {  # open read/write
        $ERROR = "$efile cannot be opened (internal error).";
        return 0;
    }

    flock(FILE, LOCK_EX);           # protect against parallel access
    seek(FILE, 0, 0);               # go to beginning of file

    while(<FILE>) {                 # search for new email
        chomp;                      # strip newline
        if($_ eq $email) {
            $ERROR = "You are already registered.";
            close(FILE);
            return 0;
        }
    }

    seek(FILE, 0, 2);               # append email to and of file
    print FILE "$email $id\n";
    close(FILE);
    return 1;
}


####################################################################
sub send_mail {
####################################################################
    my ($to, $key, $from) = @_;

    my $mail=Mail::Send->new(               # new mail object
        Subject => "Your registration (key: $key)", # subject
        To      => $to);                    # addressee

    $mail->set("From", $from);              # sender
    $mail->set("Reply-To", $from);          # reply address

    $mailhandle = $mail->open("sendmail"); # start mail program

    print $mailhandle <<EOT;                # create text
    Dear $to,

    in order to confirm your registration, please send
```

```
        this mail simply back to the sender by using the reply
        function of your mail program. Thank you!

        Virtually yours, your email registry
EOT

    $mailhandle->close();                # close and send
}
```

_____*emailreg.pl*

_____*emailregc.pl*

```perl
#!/usr/bin/perl -w

use Net::POP3;                   # mail interrogation handler
use Fcntl qw/:flock/;            # define LOCK_EX

my $efile = '/usr/data/email.dat'; # address file

my $activ = 0;                   # statistics

$host   = 'localhost';           # mail host
$userid = 'register';            # registration mail account
$passwd = 'topsecret!';          # password

$verbose = 0;                    # talkative?
@ARGV = grep { !(/^-v$/ && ($verbose = 1)) } @ARGV;

                                 # read mail
($mail = Net::POP3->new($host)) || die "Could not open $host";

$nof_messages = $mail->login($userid, $passwd);
die "Userid/Passwd Error" unless defined $nof_messages;

if($nof_messages) {              # are there any messages?
                                 # for all messages
    foreach $mesgno (keys %{$mail->list()}) {
                                 # scour all header fields
        foreach (@{$mail->top($mesgno)}) {
            $key = $1 if                 # key in subject field
                /Subject: Re: Your registration \(key: (.*)\)/;
            $from = $1 if(/From: (.*)/);    # find sender
        }
```

```perl
            activate_entry($from, $key) &&        # activate
                $mail->delete($mesgno) &&         # delete mail
                $activ++;                         # statistics
        }
    }


$mail->quit();                                    # exit mail program
print "Mailbox: $nof_messages Activated: $activ\n" if $verbose;

####################################################################
sub activate_entry {                    # activate selected entry
####################################################################
    my ($from, $key) = @_;          # sender, key

    open(FILE, "+<$efile") || die "Cannot open $efile";

    flock(FILE, LOCK_EX);           # protect against parallel access
    seek(FILE, 0, 0);               # go to beginning of file

    while(<FILE>) {                 # find sender
        ($cfrom, $ckey) = /(.*) (\S+)$/;
                                    # email and key must match
        if(index($from, $cfrom) && $ckey eq $key) {
            $len = length($ckey);
            seek FILE, -$len-1, 1; # go back by key length
            printf FILE "%${len}s", "OK";  # overwrite key with OK
            print "Activated $cfrom\n" if $verbose;
            close(FILE);
            return(1);              # activated
        }
    }
    close(FILE);
    return 0;                       # entry not found
}
```

emailregc.pl

5.11 Usenet news

With the general click-click euphoria in the World Wide Web, Usenet news, one of the most important services on the Internet, is often underestimated. And yet, millions of users utilize this institution to access highly up-to-date first-hand information, obtain support for freely or commercially available software products, or communicate their own developments and discoveries.

News gives every user the opportunity to write an article in the form of a question or a researched news item to a vast public, which can in turn publicly react to this or respond directly to the author. This electronic form of (offline) discussion is subdivided by subject areas. There are currently more than 25,000 newsgroups, each of which is devoted to a strictly delimited subject.

In all newsgroups, we can find dynamically growing *threads*: that is, series of articles that usually initiate with a question or an assertion and continue to grow with articles of reacting participants until, at some point, things calm down and the subject quietly goes away.

A *posted* article is accepted by a news server that distributes this and all other incoming articles to further news servers to which it is connected. Thus, within a few days, postings are distributed all around the world.

Newsreaders – that is, client programs that fetch Usenet articles from the server and display them – are of great help for the consumption of articles. They sort articles by subject areas, process the threads, and display them in an appropriately structured layout. Newsreaders present their users with a list of selected newsgroups in which new articles have arrived since the last interrogation. Within a newsgroup, the newsreader lists the threads and displays their headlines (`Subject` fields). After having selected a thread, the user can navigate back and forth through all of its articles (usually, however, beginning with the article that initiated the thread).

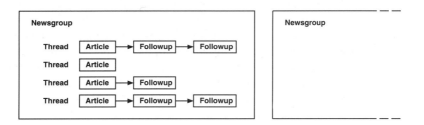

Figure 5.21 Newsgroups article structure.

Thus users always work their way from coarsely structured groups to finer-grained subdivisions. Given the multitude of articles on Usenet, this is extremely important in order to keep a clear overview and to be able to find interesting articles the way you can find a needle in a haystack. Moreover, the newsreader stores information on which articles have already been read and no longer displays them.

The NNTP protocol covers all kinds of communication for this service: whether a client communicates with a server or servers communicate with each other, the process is always governed by NNTP commands. The original specification of the NNTP protocol is set forth in RFC 997 (*Request for Comments*, see Appendix G.3), the mandatory format of a Usenet article in RFC 850.

Listing `article.txt` shows the header of a Usenet article.

article.txt

```
Path: lrz-muenchen.de!informatik.tu-muenchen.de!fu-berlin.de!
zrz.TU-Berlin.DE!franz.ww.TU-Berlin.DE!koenig
From: koenig@franz.ww.TU-Berlin.DE (Andreas Koenig)
newsgroups: comp.lang.perl.misc
Subject: Re: AUTOLOAD: Cannot delegate
Date: 14 Jul 1996 06:52:11 GMT
Organization: TU-Berlin
Lines: 38
Message-ID: <4sa5er$e3m@brachio.zrz.TU-Berlin.DE>
References: <4s8jf8$f6b@sunsystem5.informatik.tu-muenchen.de>
NNTP-Posting-Host: franz.ww.tu-berlin.de

38 lines of text to follow...
```

article.txt

The `Path:` entry shows the individual news servers that the article has already passed – in the opposite direction of their traversal. Somebody named Andreas Koenig has sent it from host `franz.ww.TU-Berlin.DE`, and after three intermediate stops it has finally been received by the news server `lrz-muenchen.de`. Such information is mainly used by the Usenet servers to prevent an article from going round and round in the widely branched network. No server would forward the article to a server whose name already appears in the `Path` entry.

The `Message-ID` field holds the worldwide unique identification string of the article. It is composed of the address of the posting computer and an ID unique to that computer. Each server that receives an article from another server for forwarding first uses the message ID to check whether it has already received the article in a different way. If this is the case, it rejects the article, thus preventing multiple distribution.

The `newsgroups` field contains the newsgroups in which the article is to appear, separated by commas. In the present case, only a single group, `comp.lang.perl.misc`, is specified. `Subject` specifies the subject of the article, which in the present case begins with the character sequence `Re:`. This marks the article as a *follow-up*, an answer to a question in a thread. And indeed: the `References` field contains the message ID of the question to which the article refers. A newsreader on the client side receives the articles from the server in the order in which the latter received them, thus potentially in a jumbled sequence. The information contained in the `Reference` field helps the newsreader to collect and order the threads by initiating article and follow-ups.

The `Lines` entry specifies the number of lines that the text of the article takes up, which, after all these header fields and an empty line, finally begins.

In addition to the worldwide unique message ID, each article is given by the current news server a running number that is unique per newsgroup and server. Clients may specify the articles also by using this number. When asked for available articles, the news server always answers with a number range that is defined by

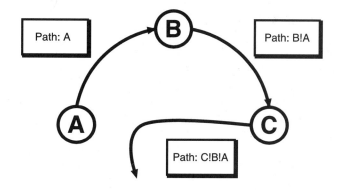

Figure 5.22   The path information prevents news server A from receiving the circulating article once again from C.

the running numbers of the first and the last current article. If the client specifies an article by means of a local running number, an additional *current article pointer* is set, which subsequently issued NEXT or LAST commands position to the next or previous article. A downloading instruction then automatically refers to the article pointed to by the *current article pointer*.

Table 5.4 shows the commands of the NNTP protocol and their meaning.

Many servers also support protocol parts that go beyond RFC 977. Table 5.5 shows the most important ones.

The Net::NNTP package provides an easy-to-handle client interface for Usenet news. An object of the Net::NNTP class represents a *newsagent* that is set to a news server and exchanges data with it.

5.11.1 The newsagent

The constructor of the newsagent also predefines a news server:

```
use Net::NNTP;

my $nntphost = "news.host.com";

        # check news host
gethostbyname($nntphost) || die "Unknown host $nntphost";

        # create newsagent and connect to NNTP host
$newsagent = Net::NNTP->new($nntphost) || die "Cannot connect
    to host";
```

To prevent the agent from getting desperate while searching for untraceable Internet addresses, a prior call of gethostbyname verifies that the specified host re-

Table 5.4 NNTP protocol commands.

LIST	Fetch list of available newsgroups
ARTICLE	Fetch article with header and body
BODY	Fetch article text without header
HEAD	Fetch header of article, but not article text
GROUP	Fetch article numbers of specified newsgroup
STAT	Mark article as 'current' article
NEXT	Fetch next article (after the current one)
LAST	Fetch previous article (before the current one)
POST	Send article to newsgroup(s)
NEWGROUPS	Newly created groups since timestamp
NEWNEWS	Newly arrived articles since timestamp
SLAVE	Client requires higher priority because it is no normal client, but a slave server
IHAVE	Slave server offers an article to a server
HELP	Fetch short help text
QUIT	Terminate NNTP conversation

Table 5.5 Some extended commands of the NNTP protocol.

ACTIVE	Lists active newsgroups that match a pattern
XGTITLE	Lists names of newsgroups that match a pattern, together with group and description text
XHDR	Returns a specified header field (for example Subject) of a range of articles

ally exists. The value returned by the newsagent constructor in case of success is a reference to an object of the NNTP class.

In the first place, the user obviously wants to find out which newsgroups are carried by the selected server. The list method of the newsagent object brings it to light:

```
        # interrogate groups - list() yields:
        # {"groupname" => [$last, $first, $flag], ...}
$groups = $newsagent->list();


        # extract all information
foreach $groupname (sort keys %$groups) {

    ($last, $first, $flag) = @{$groups->{$groupname}};
    print "$groupname: $last $first $flag\n";
}
```

The list method of the newsagent object returns a reference to a hash whose keys represent the group names and their value references to an array. The array contains the number of the last and the first available article of the group, together with a flag that specifies whether posting articles in this group is allowed. 'y' as flag value means that the group allows posting, whereas 'n' means that it prohibits posting. The above code fragment terminates with a loop that illustrates the evaluation of the return information of the list method.

A group can be selected for further analysis by means of the group method of the newsagent:

```
            # set group and fetch article numbers
($nof_articles, $first, $last, $groupname) =
                              $newsagent->group("news.answers");
```

The group method marks the specified group (news.answers in the example) as current and in addition returns information on the articles currently available. The return list contains the total number of available articles, the number of the first and last one, and once more the name of the selected newsgroup. Note that the difference between the first and the last article number does not necessarily correspond to the total number, because articles deleted for having expired do not appear.

All further requests to the newsagent refer to the group marked as 'current' by the group method.

In most cases, reading out all currently available articles of a group means unnecessary data transfer (for example, 1000 new articles of about 2 kbytes each correspond to 2 Mbytes of data that take more than 15 minutes to get through a 33,300 modem). Usually, an analysis of the header lines is sufficient to find out which articles are of interest and which are not.

The head method supplies the header lines of an article. As a parameter, it processes the current article number of the message ID. Called without parameters, head refers to the current article pointer, which after the group command issued above points to the first available article of the group. head returns a reference to an array, whose elements are the lines of the article header.

Thus the header lines of the current article are analyzed by

```
            # fetch header of current article
$head = $newsagent->head();

            # iterate through header lines
for (@{$head}) {
            # separate field name and content
    my ($fieldname, $content) = /^(\S+): (.*)/;

    print "FIELD $fieldname\n";         # output for testing
    print "CONTENT $content\n";
}
```

The pointer to the current article is moved forward or backward by the methods `next` and `last`. With `nntpstat`, it is possible to position the pointer to an article specified via the running article number. In addition, `next`, `last`, and `nntpstat` return the message ID of the current article.

```perl
        # position to first article
$msgid = $newsagent->nntpstat($first);
print "1st article: $msgid\n";

            # position to next article
$msgid = $newsagent->next();
print "Next article: $msgid\n";

            # position to previous article
$msgid = $newsagent->last();
print "Previous article: $msgid\n";
```

Listing `newssub.pl` uses the methods described above to read the `Subject` entries of all articles of the current group.

newssub.pl

```perl
#!/usr/bin/perl

use Net::NNTP;

        # news server from environment variable
my $nntphost = $ENV{NNTPSERVER};

        # check news host
die "Unknown host $nntphost" unless gethostbyname($nntphost);

        # create newsagent and connect to NNTP host
$newsagent = Net::NNTP->new($nntphost) || die "Cannot connect to host";

        # set group and fetch article numbers
($nof_articles, $first, $last, $groupname) =
                            $newsagent->group("news.answers");

        # iterate through all articles of the newsgroup
for($newsagent->nntpstat($first); $newsagent->next();) {
    ($subjectref) = grep { $_->[0] eq "Subject" }
                    map { [/^(\S+): (.*)/] } @{$newsagent->head()};
    print "Subject: $subjectref->[1]\n";
}
```

```
$newsagent->quit();
```

newssub.pl

The body of the `for` loop needs some explanation: the `head` method of the newsagent object returns an array reference that is dereferenced to an array by means of

```
a{ $newsagent->head() }
```

Since the elements contain the header lines in the format

```
...
Subject: Re: AUTOLOAD: Cannot delegate
Date: 14 Jul 1998 06:52:11 GMT
...
```

the preceding `map` operator converts the text lines into references to arrays that contain two elements each: the name of the header field (such as `Subject`), and its content. This array of array references is subsequently handed over (we are slowly working our way from left to right) to the `grep` command, which lets pass only those elements that contain the string `"Subject"` as a header field name. Thus the `grep-map` combination returns in `$subject` a reference to an array whose first element contains the text `"Subject"`, while its second element holds the subject text. The following `print` command shows how to access it.

We should also mention the body of the `map` command: the regular expression contains two pairs of brackets: that is, in an array context, it returns the two strings that have been found. The square brackets enclosing the regular expression do not only _force_ the array context, but also return a reference to the string array – and the `grep` command indeed expects an array of array references.

However, this method for analyzing the `Subject` lines of all articles of a newsgroup fetches far more information from the news server than is actually needed. Thus `newssub.pl` evaluates only a fraction of the transmitted header lines and practically transfers an amount of data over the network that is 10 times too large.

For the purpose of handling this typical newsreader task, more recent news servers therefore support the `XHDRS` command (not yet included in RFC 977), which transmits only selected parts of the article headers of a newsgroup. The call

```
$newsagent->xhdr('Subject', [$first, $last]);
```

returns a reference to a hash that contains the articles found in the (running) number range between `$first` and `$last`. As _keys_, the hash carries the article numbers, and as _values_ the content of the specified header field `Subject:`.

Listing `newsheaders.pl` outputs all `Subjects` of current articles of the newsgroup `comp.lang.perl.tk`.

```perl
#!/usr/bin/perl -w

use Net::NNTP;
                    # create newsagent
$newsagent = Net::NNTP->new($ENV{NNTPSERVER});


my ($total, $first, $last) = $newsagent->group("comp.lang.perl.tk");


                    # subject hash reference:
                    # keys:   article numbers of the newsgroup
                    # values: subjects as text
$subjects = $newsagent->xhdr('Subject', [$first, $last]);


                    # output all subjects sorted
                    # by article numbers
foreach $i (sort { $a <=> $b } keys %{$subjects}) {
    print "$i: $subjects->{$i}\n";
}


$newsagent->quit();
```

The output

```
7961: setting/using X resources
7963: Geometry of (not yet) visible windows?
7964: Tk with Safe.pm
7965: Re: Tk Module List
7967: Scrollbar bug
7968: mSQL patch for Radius?
7969: ANNOUNCE: Tk-Clock-1.03
7970: Re: setting/using X resources
7972: Re: setting/using X resources
```

shows that some articles are seemingly related to each other. The identical subjects of articles 7961, 7970 and 7972 let us suppose that article 7961 represents the original posting, while 7970 and 7972 are follow-ups (the definite proof is provided by an analysis of the Reference header fields of articles 7970 and 7972, which contain the message ID of either the starting article or a follow-up).

The text of an article, instead, is obtained via the method

```perl
$newsagent->body($msgnum);
```

which returns a reference to an array whose elements are the individual lines of text of the article body, including the newline characters.

The entire article inclusive of the header is supplied by the method

```
$newsagent->article($msgnum);
```

As with `head` and `body`, the return value is an array reference. If the running article number is omitted, `body`, `head`, and `article` refer to the article pointed to by the *current article pointer*.

5.11.2 Practice: freeing `news.answers` from periodical postings

As a practical sample, we are going to use Listing `wna.pl` (*Weed out news answers*), which searches the newsgroup `news.answers`[15] for new FAQs (*Frequently Asked Questions*). Since the articles of this newsgroup are posted periodically (every two weeks or once a month), the news user is often faced with the problem of the newsreader displaying lots of new articles of which only very few, however, really contain new information. `wna.pl` maintains a local database that identifies repeated articles on the basis of the `Subject` headers.

`wna.pl` cooperates with the newsreader under UNIX via the file `.newsrc` in the user's home directory. In `.newsrc`, the newsreader program stores the numbers of the articles the user has already read and thus does not wish to see in future, for each newsgroup. The task of `wna.pl` is now to compare newly appearing articles with its database and, if they have already been registered, mark them in `.newsrc` as read. Thus `wna.pl` makes the newsreader believe that the periodically posted articles have already been read, and saves the user the manual perusal.

The file `.newsrc` contains ranges of read article numbers ordered by newsgroups:

```
comp.databases: 1-4398,4403
comp.lang.perl.tk! 1-1234,1237,1240-1244,1250,1260
news.answers: 1-30783,30800
```

A colon after a newsgroup name marks an active newsgroup, whereas an exclamation mark at the same position indicates that the user currently does not wish to receive articles from this newsgroup. The number ranges consist of combinations of individual numbers and intervals. The excerpt from `.newsrc` shown above indicates for the `comp.databases` newsgroup that the articles with numbers 1 to 4398 have already been processed, while the articles in the missing range 4399-4402 up to the next entry 4403 are still unread.[16]

---

[15] The newsgroup `news.answers` contains summaries of the question-answer sequences of other newsgroups to prevent these from being submerged all over again by the same questions.

[16] The article numbers are assigned by the news server itself; thus they are not at all unique across the world, and a change of news server needs a new `.newsrc` file.

A user-friendly, object-oriented interface for manipulating the .newsrc file is provided by the News::Newsrc module by Steven McDougall.[17] It operates with Newsrc objects, which read .newsrc, permit all kinds of manipulation of its entries, and finally write .newsrc back to the disk. Newsrc objects can insert and delete groups in .newsrc, and mark and unmark specific articles.

Application of Newsrc.pm is as follows:

_____*Newsrc.pm*

```
use News::Newsrc;

$newsrc = News::Newsrc->new();     # create Newsrc object

$newsrc->load();                   # load ~/.newsrc
$newsrc->load($file);              # load $file as .newsrc

$newsrc->add_group($group);        # insert group
$newsrc->del_group($group);        # delete group

$newsrc->subscribe  ($group);      # activate group
$newsrc->unsubscribe($group);      # deactivate group

$newsrc->mark($group, $article);   # mark article in group

                                   # mark list of articles
$newsrc->mark_list($group, \@articles);

                                   # mark articles of a
                                   # number range
$newsrc->mark_range($group, $from, $to);

                                   # unmark article
$newsrc->unmark($group, $article);

                                   # unmark article list
$newsrc->unmark_list($group, \@articles);

                                   # unmark number range
$newsrc->unmark_range($group, $from, $to);
```

---

[17] Even regular CPAN visits do not protect against parallel development: for wna.pl, the author of these lines invested two nights' work in the original development of a module that, moreover, bore the same name: Newsrc.pm. When, by pure hazard, he bumped into Steven McDougall's module, he immediately binned his own. The words he uttered at that point are not fit to be printed – but they were *loud* and in *Bavarian*.

```
if($newsrc->exists($group)) {        # does group exist?
    print "$group exists!\n";
}


if($newsrc->subscribed($group)) { # group activated?
    print "$group active!\n";
}
                                     # article marked?
if($newsrc->marked($group, $article)) {
    print "Article $article in group $group marked!\n";
}


$newsrc->save();                     # store ~/.newsrc
$newsrc->save_as($file);             # store under different name
                                     # (both return 0!)
```

Newsrc.pm

wna.pl connects to the selected news server and then uses the group method of the newsagent to find out the numbers of the articles available on the server in news.answers. Articles in this range that have been read are removed, and a number range is built to include only numbers of current unread articles.

For each of the intervals found, wna.pl calls the newsagent's xhdr method, which fetches the Subject headers of the corresponding articles from the news server. Synchronization with the database, a persistent hash created with tie, subsequently shows whether an article with that header has already been analyzed. If this is the case, wna.pl marks it as read; otherwise it includes the Subject header in the database. Since the .newsrc file is subsequently written back to disk, a newsreader called after the run of wna.pl no longer displays the repeated articles of news.answers.

wna.pl

```
#!/usr/bin/perl -w

use Net::NNTP;                       # news communication
use POSIX;                           # for O_RDWRetc.
use SDBM_File;                       # persistent hash
use News::Newsrc;                    # read and write .newsrc
use Set::IntSpan;                    # additional range handler
use strict;

my $newsanswers = "news.answers";    # newsgroup
my $newshost    = "$ENV{NNTPSERVER}"; # news server from Env variable
```

```perl
my ($subject, %db);                           # local variables
my ($stat_new, $stat_archived, $stat_replay) = (0,0,0);


my $newsrc = News::Newsrc->new();             # new Newsrc object

print "Reading file .newsrc ...\n";
$newsrc->load();

print "NNTP with $newshost ...\n";
my $na = Net::NNTP->new($newshost);

    ### create or open persistent hash for subject lines
tie(%db, "SDBM_File", "$ENV{HOME}/.$newsanswers",
    O_CREAT|O_RDWR, 0644) || die "Persistency error";

    ### fetch newsgroup news.answers article numbers via NNTP
print "Group information $newsanswers ...\n";
my ($total, $first, $last) = $na->group("$newsanswers");

    ### build intervals of unread articles in a Set::IntSpan object
my $intervals = Set::IntSpan->new(
        join(',', $newsrc->unmarked_articles($newsanswers,
                                            $first, $last)));
print "Fetching subjects ...\n";

    ### store intervals of unread articles
for (split(/,/, $intervals->run_list())) {
    my ($from, $to) = split(/-/, $_);

        ### amend intervals ($to == $from means
        ### _all_ available articles for xhdr())
    $to = $from +1 if(!defined $to || $to == $from);

        ### fetch subjects of unread articles
    my $subjects = $na->xhdr('Subject', [$from, $to]);

    foreach $subject (keys %{$subjects}) {
        $stat_new++;                          # total no. of articles

                                              # already archived?
        if(defined($db{"$subjects->{$subject}"})) {
                                              # mark as read because,
                                              # already archived
            $newsrc->mark($newsanswers, $subject);
            $stat_replay++;
```

```
      } else {                          # not yet archived?
        $db{"$subjects->{$subject}"} = 1;
        $stat_archived++;
      }
    }
}

$na->quit();                          # close NNTP connection
print "NNTP connection closed.\n";

print <<"EOT";                        # output statistics
$total articles available
of which $stat_new unread ones analyzed
        $stat_replay repetitions eliminated
        $stat_archived new ones archived
EOT

$newsrc->save();                      # write back .newsrc
```

_____*wna.pl*

In addition to News::Newsrc, wna.pl also makes use of the Set::IntSpan module, which facilitates generation and manipulation of ranges of integer numbers. The constructor of Set::IntSpan accepts strings of the format

```
from-to,from-to,...
```

and stores the number ranges very efficiently. The run_list method outputs them again in the same format. As a matter of fact, Set::IntSpan provides the complete functionality to perform operations on the defined ranges of integers – but wna.pl employs Set::IntSpan only to extract the number ranges for the news.answers group from the Newsrc object. Newsrc itself does not provide such an interface, but can only return an array of numbers of unmarked articles. However, loading the article subjects individually from the server number by number would mean nullifying the performance gain achieved through xhdr. Therefore wna.pl feeds the values of the array into a Set::IntSpan object, and shortly after that uses the run_list method to read optimized number *ranges*.

5.11.3 Practice: checking newsgroups

Some interesting newsgroups, including comp.lang.perl.misc, suffer from too much traffic. No working person can keep up to date with a number of messages exceeding 100 per day.

If you set a question and then sit there waiting for incoming answers, there are – as usual – two possibilities: you can either browse on a daily basis through all of the new articles with a newsreader, or you can use the script `chknews.pl`, which scours the messages by subjects and notifies you of newly arrived messages. The command

```
chknews.pl comp.lang.perl.misc 'perl performance'
```

outputs all articles of the newsgroup `comp.lang.perl.misc` whose subject headers contain the character string `'perl performance'` in any possible combination of upper and lower case spelling (`'Perl Performance'` and so on). `chknews.pl` even supports (Perl-suitable) regular expressions. Thus, for example,

```
chknews.pl comp.lang.perl.modules '\btar\b'
```

looks for articles in the Perl modules newsgroup that contain new announcements of the 'Tar' module. The word boundaries inserted at the beginning and the end ensure that words such as `'start'` do not trigger a message.

    `chknews.pl` 'remembers' analyzed articles by means of the message numbers contained in the `data/news.dat` file in the user's home directory, in the same format as a newsreader would do.[18] Once again, we employ Steven McDougall's useful `News::Newsrc`, which abstracts the access to `.newsrc` files. However, since the functionality of `News::Newsrc` is not sufficient for the application, `chknews.pl` quickly defines a new class `MyNewsrc`, which inherits all methods of `News::Newsrc` and defines two new ones: `get_unmarked_articles()` returns a string of unmarked number ranges exactly as `get_marked_articles()` of the original `News::Newsrc` does the same with marked number ranges. `clear_old_ranges` kills off ancient fragmented number ranges marking all articles whose numbers go further back from the current state than `$article_limit`.

    To achieve the above inheritance, it is sufficient to define the `MyNewsrc` package with an `@ISA` entry of `News::Newsrc` (see Section 2.4.6). As in `wna.pl` (page 371), `Set::IntSpan` is employed, which processes number ranges efficiently.

    The variable `$newsserver` contains the name of the next reachable news server. The script reads it from the environment variable `NNTPSERVER`, which must hold the corresponding value prior to the start of the script.

    `chknews.pl` supports the option `-h`, which outputs a *usage* message, and the *re-check* option `-r`, which runs previously checked articles through an additional check. The `-d` option is used for debugging and starts outputting data while the script is still working.

    If you look for *several* terms in *one* newsgroup, these must be packed into one call. The call

```
chknews.pl comp.text.tex 'postscript|graphics'
```

searches for article titles in `comp.text.tex` which contain either `postscript` or `graphics`. The consequence of two consecutive calls of `chknews.pl` for the *same*

---

[18] If you set the original `.newsrc` file, instead, it will still function, except that both the newsreader *and* `chknews.pl` write to the file, with the consequence that the newsreader no longer displays articles processed by `chknews.pl`.

newsgroup is that the corresponding articles would have already been marked as 'read,' and the second call would not analyze them any longer. Searches in *different* newsgroups, however, pose no problems. The calls

```
chknews.pl comp.os.linux.announce 'kernel'
chknews.pl comp.os.linux.development.system 'kernel'
chknews.pl comp.os.linux.networking 'kernel'
```

search the three specified newsgroups for articles with the word 'kernel' in their title.

_____*chknews.pl*

```perl
#!/usr/bin/perl -w
######################################################################
# chknews.pl - search newsgroups for new titles
######################################################################


#*********************************************************************
# Extended Newsrc class
#*********************************************************************
package MyNewsrc;

use News::Newsrc;                       # manage Newsrc file
use Set::IntSpan;                       # additional range handler

@ISA = qw/News::Newsrc/;                # base class

######################################################################
sub get_unmarked_articles {             # fetch list of unmarked
    my ($self, $ng, $from, $to) = @_;   # articles; format: as Newsrc
######################################################################

    my $intervals = Set::IntSpan->new(  # create IntSpan object
        join(',', $self->unmarked_articles($ng, $from, $to)));
    $intervals->run_list();             # return string
}


######################################################################
sub clear_old_ranges {                  # limit ranges
    my ($self, $ng, $article_limit) = @_;
######################################################################
                                        # find last article
    my $articles = $self->get_articles($ng);
    my ($last_article) = ($articles =~ /(\d+)$/);
```

```perl
                                            # overwrite ranges before
    if($last_article > $article_limit) { # the last N articles
        $self->mark_range($ng, 1, $last_article-$article_limit);
    }
}


#*********************************************************************
# Main program
#*********************************************************************
package main;

my $newsrcfile    = "$ENV{HOME}/data/news.dat"; # "memory"
my $newsserver    = "$ENV{NNTPSERVER}";          # news server
my $article_limit = 10000;                  # length of monitored zone
                                            # at end of number range
$| = 1;                                     # do not buffer output

use Net::NNTP;                              # NNTP user agent
use Getopt::Std;                           # command line parameter

$opt_r = $opt_h = $opt_v = $opt_d = undef; # options -r, -h, -d, -v
getopts("rhvd");

my($ng, $pattern) = @ARGV;                  # command line parameter
usage("Argument Error") unless defined $pattern;
usage() if defined $opt_h;                  # -h set?

$newsrc = MyNewsrc->new();                  # create Newsrc object

if(-f $newsrcfile) {                        # read Newsrc file
    $newsrc->load($newsrcfile) || die "Cannot load $newsrcfile";
}

print "Scanning $ng for $pattern\n" if $opt_v;

                                            # create newsagent
print "Connecting to $newsserver\n" if $opt_d;
($newsagent = Net::NNTP->new($newsserver)) ||
    die "Cannot connect to $newsserver";
                                            # fetch numbers of available
                                            # articles from the server
(my ($total, $first, $last) = $newsagent->group($ng)) ||
    usage("Unknown newsgroup $ng");
                                            # define ranges of
                                            # unread articles
```

```perl
print "$total ($first-$last) articles in $ng\n" if $opt_d;
$unmarked = $newsrc->get_unmarked_articles($ng, $first, $last);
                                    # re-check option: all
$unmarked = "$first-$last" if defined $opt_r;

foreach (split(/,/, $unmarked)) {          # for each range:
    my ($from, $to) = split(/-/, $_);
                                    # amend interval
    $to = $from +1 if(!defined $to || $to == $from);

    print "XHDR $from $to\n" if $opt_d;  # fetch subject lines
    (my $subjects = $newsagent->xhdr('Subject', [$from, $to])) ||
        die "xhdr failed";

    while (($msgno, $subject) = each %$subjects) {
        $newsrc->mark($ng, $msgno);      # mark as 'read'
                                    # output if match
        if($subject =~ /$pattern/i) {
            print "    " if($opt_d || $opt_v);
            print "$ng: $subject\n";
        }
    }
}


$newsrc->clear_old_ranges($ng, $article_limit);  # limit ranges

$newsrc->save_as($newsrcfile);

$newsagent->quit();                      # release newsagent

#####################################################################
sub usage {                               # display usage
#####################################################################
    (my $program = $0) =~ s,.*/,,g;       # determine base name
    print "$program: @_\n";
    print "usage: $program [-rvhd] newsgroup subject\n";
    print "         -r: re-check all Articles\n";
    print "         -v: verbose on\n";
    print "         -h: print out this message\n";
    print "         -d: debug on\n";
    exit 0;
}
```

Installing Perl

A.1 Basic installation

To run Perl scripts on your computer, you need at least a functioning implementation of the Perl interpreter `perl`.

Perl is freely available and simply needs copying to the platform in question. Current UNIX systems (such as LINUX, HP-UX, Solaris, Irix, AIX, and so on) take the source code of the Perl distribution, compile it, and install the result. This procedure does not require any special knowledge and can easily be carried out even by beginners. Perl source code is also available for Windows 95 and NT, but since not all systems are equipped with a C compiler, installation is typically carried out on the basis of a readily compiled distribution.

A.1.1 Where do I get it?

One obvious possibility for getting hold of the current Perl distribution is the CD-ROM enclosed with this book. The UNIX distribution can be found in the `CPAN` directory. It is a compressed archive in `tar` format named `perl5.004_04.tar.gz`. The distribution for Windows 95 and NT, on the other hand, is stored as file `perl5.00402-bindist04-bc.tar.gz` in the `win32` directory. The CD-ROM content is described in more detail in Appendix H.

A second possibility for getting hold of a (possibly more up-to-date) Perl distribution is provided by those FTP servers on the Internet that mirror the data of the CPAN (*Comprehensive Perl Archive Network*). Besides the standard distribution, they also keep a large number of additional Perl modules available. More detailed information can be found in Section A.4.

Just copy the relevant files from the CD-ROM to your hard disk. Access to the CPAN is described in Section A.4.

A.1.2 Installation under UNIX

The command sequence

```
> gzip -d perl5.004_04.tar.gz
> tar xfv perl5.004_04.tar
```

unpacks the compressed `tar` archive and creates the directory `perl5.004_04`, where it builds the Perl source tree.

After unpacking, Perl needs to be configured to the local hardware environment and the current operating system. This process is carried out by means of the shell script `Configure`, which is located in the `perl5.004_04` directory. The commands

```
> cd perl5.004_04
> ./Configure
```

call the configuration tool, which asks various questions about the local environment and evaluates them. For the installer who is in a rush, `Configure` provides the option `-d`, which prepares a standard installation for all common systems by answering the relevant questions itself.

After configuration has been completed, it is followed by the compiler run, which is initiated by

```
> make
```

and which, depending on the computing power of the local hardware, may take up to an hour, but requires no more intervention. The installation of the finished Perl interpreter including a set of ready-made modules is finally triggered by the command

```
> make install
```

Depending on which directory has been set as the installation directory, this call may require `root` privileges.

A.1.3 Installation under Windows 95 and NT

A program such as `WinZip` unpacks the distribution (`Win32/perl5.00402-bindist04-bc.tar.gz`) into a temporary directory, maintaining the subdirectory structure. Subsequently, you enter this directory with the Explorer and double-click on the `install.bat` script, which starts the installation process in a DOS window. The following answers to the questions lead to a successful installation:

```
Where would you like Perl to be installed? [c:\perl]   ⏎
Ok to create 'c:\perl'? [y]                            ⏎
mkdir c:\perl
mkdir c:\perl\lib
Do you have a C compiler? [y]                         n ⏎
Install HTML documentation? (needs 4.5MB) [y]          ⏎
Where should HTML be installed? [c:\perl\html]         ⏎
...
Root of the perl HTML tree? [/c|/perl/html]            ⏎
...
Proceed? [y]                                           ⏎
...
Have a nice day.
```

Subsequently, the path `PATH` in the `AUTOEXEC.BAT` file must be modified to include the `bin` directory of the Perl installation (in the example, `c:\perl\bin`). After a system restart, the Perl interpreter `perl` should finally be available, which can be verified by running the 'Hello World' script (`hello.pl` on page 2) by means of the command line:

```
perl hello.pl
```

A.2 Installing Perl/Tk

The packed distribution of the Perl/Tk package can be found on the CPAN servers under

```
CPAN/modules/by-module/Tk/Tk800.010.tar.gz
```

or as `CPAN/Tk800.010.tar.gz` on the enclosed CD-ROM.

The Perl/Tk package is unpacked, installed, and tested in the same way as most other Perl modules. The next section shows how this is done.

For Windows 95 and NT, no installation of the Tk package is required, since the precompiled Perl version on the CD-ROM already includes the Tk package.

A.3 Installing additional modules

All modules used in the sample programs of this book are not only available from the CPAN, but are also included on the enclosed CD-ROM. The following list shows which distribution bundle in the `CPAN` directory of the CD is responsible for the modules in question:

```
Archive::Tar            # authors/id/SRZ/Archive-Tar-0.072.tar.gz
Benchmark               # Standard Distribution
CGI                     # authors/id/LDS/CGI.pm-2.42.tar.gz
CGI::Switch             # authors/id/LDS/CGI.pm-2.42.tar.gz
CPAN                    # authors/id/ANDK/CPAN-1.40.tar.gz
Carp                    # Standard Distribution
Chart::Bars             # authors/id/DBONNER/chart-0.93.tar.gz
Chart::LinesPoints      # authors/id/DBONNER/chart-0.93.tar.gz
Chart::Pareto           # authors/id/DBONNER/chart-0.93.tar.gz
Chart::Pie              # authors/id/DBONNER/chart-0.93.tar.gz
Chart::StackedBars      # authors/id/DBONNER/chart-0.93.tar.gz
Cwd                     # Standard Distribution
Data::Dumper            # authors/id/GSAR/Data-Dumper-2.09.tar.gz
Date::Manip             # authors/id/SBECK/DateManip-5.33.tar.gz
Fcntl                   # Standard Distribution
File::Basename          # Standard Distribution
File::Copy              # Standard Distribution
File::Listing           # authors/id/GAAS/libwww-perl-5.36.tar.gz
GD                      # authors/id/LDS/GD-1.18.tar.gz
GDBM_File               # Standard Distribution
Getopt::Std             # Standard Distribution
HTML::FormatPS          # authors/id/GAAS/HTML-Tree-0.51.tar.gz
HTML::FormatText        # authors/id/GAAS/HTML-Tree-0.51.tar.gz
HTML::Parse             # authors/id/GAAS/HTML-Tree-0.51.tar.gz
HTML::TreeBuilder       # authors/id/GAAS/HTML-Tree-0.51.tar.gz
HTTP::Daemon            # authors/id/GAAS/libwww-perl-5.36.tar.gz
HTTP::Status            # authors/id/GAAS/libwww-perl-5.36.tar.gz
IO::File                # authors/id/GBARR/IO-1.20.tar.gz
IO::Socket              # authors/id/GBARR/IO-1.20.tar.gz
LWP::RobotUA            # authors/id/GAAS/libwww-perl-5.36.tar.gz
LWP::Simple             # authors/id/GAAS/libwww-perl-5.36.tar.gz
LWP::UserAgent          # authors/id/GAAS/libwww-perl-5.36.tar.gz
MIME::Base64            # authors/id/GAAS/MIME-Base64-2.06.tar.gz
MIME::Lite              # authors/id/ERYQ/MIME-Lite-1.123.tar.gz
Mail::Send              # authors/id/GBARR/MailTools-1.11.tar.gz
Net::FTP                # authors/id/GBARR/libnet-1.0605.tar.gz
Net::NNTP               # authors/id/GBARR/libnet-1.0605.tar.gz
Net::POP3               # authors/id/GBARR/libnet-1.0605.tar.gz
Net::Telnet            # authors/id/JROGERS/Net-Telnet-3.01.tar.gz
News::Newsrc            # authors/id/SWMCD/News-Newsrc-1.06.tar.gz
POSIX                   # Standard Distribution
Proc::Simple          # authors/id/MSCHILLI/Proc-Simple-1.12.tar.gz
SDBM_File               # Standard Distribution
Set::IntSpan            # authors/id/SWMCD/Set-IntSpan-1.06.tar.gz
Socket                  # Standard Distribution
```

```
Term::ReadKey              # authors/id/KJALB/TermReadKey-2.12.tar.gz
Text::Wrap                 # Standard Distribution
Tk                         # authors/id/NI-S/Tk800.010.tar.gz
URI::URL                   # authors/id/GAAS/URI-0.09.tar.gz
Win32::Process             # authors/id/GSAR/libwin32-0.12.zip
```

Perl packages that are present in compressed form as `tar` archives are usually unpacked by the following command sequence (in the example, for the distribution of the `Proc-Simple-1.12.tar.gz` module):

```
> gzip -d Proc-Simple-1.12.tar.gz
> tar xfv Proc-Simple-1.12.tar
```

A subsquent change of directory to the freshly created source tree with

```
> cd Proc-Simple-1.12
```

and the call of

```
> perl Makefile.PL
```

create, with the aid of configuration files of the original Perl installation,[1] a Makefile, which is used by a subsequent

```
> make
```

to carry out the steps needed for localization. A subsequent

```
> make test
```

runs possibly included test routines. If these do not signal any errors, the module can be installed by means of

```
> make install
```

A possibility for mechanizing this installation process is shown in Section A.4.3.

A.4 The CPAN

For many day-to-day programming jobs there is already a solution in Perl. The only difficulty is to find out who developed this solution and through which channels it is accessible. For this purpose, the CPAN (*Comprehensive Perl Archive Network*) has been set up.

In the CPAN, committed Perl programmers make their reusable developments available to the general public. Since no single server would be able to satisfy the

---

[1] This task is usually carried out by `MakeMaker`, a standard Perl package by Andreas König.

module requirements of all Perl addicts across the world, the modules of the CPAN are stored on dozens of mirrored servers.

For ease of use, the enclosed CD-ROM includes all modules referred to in this book (see the previous section), but for more recent versions or additional modules it is always worth while checking the CPAN.

Which is the nearest CPAN server? A standard browser provides the reply: the CPAN dispatcher by Tom Christiansen,

```
http://www.perl.com/CPAN
```

presents a list of various CPAN mirrors in different countries. Once you have made your choice, the dispatcher puts it in a cookie, which is stored by your browser. A subsequent request for a file under the `http://www.perl.com/CPAN/` directory is automatically routed by the dispatcher to the selected CPAN mirror. Thus the request

```
http://www.perl.com/CPAN/CPAN.html
```

for the CPAN introductory document immediately becomes, for example,

```
ftp://ftp.demon.co.uk/pub/mirrors/perl/CPAN/CPAN.html
```

if you happen to live in the UK, reducing the amount of byte streams transferred over long distances.

Obviously, you may also access the CPAN FTP servers in the traditional way, by means of anonymous FTP. In the long run, however, it is easier to include your nearest CPAN URL in the 'Bookmark'/'Favorites' list of your WWW browser.

First of all, the CPAN contains the latest distributions of the Perl interpreter `perl` itself. In addition, a multitude of free modules is available. Figure A.1 shows (on the basis of the Perl distribution `perl5.004_04` and the module `Proc::Simple`) selected access paths under the `CPAN` directory of every CPAN server.

A.4.1 Perl distributions

Thus, as can be seen from the second path from the right of Figure A.1, the most recent Perl version is (always) located under `CPAN/src/latest.tar.gz` or (currently) `CPAN/src/5.0/perl5.004_04.tar.gz`, ready to be fetched.

Ported distributions for Windows or MacOS are located, as shown in the path at the extreme right, under `CPAN/ports/win32` or `CPAN/ports/mac`.

The subdirectories of the `win32` path had to be omitted from Figure A.1 for reasons of space. Under

```
win32/standard/x86/perl5.00402-bindist04-bc.tar.gz
```

you can find the current Windows distribution of March 1998, provided by Gurusamy Sarathy.

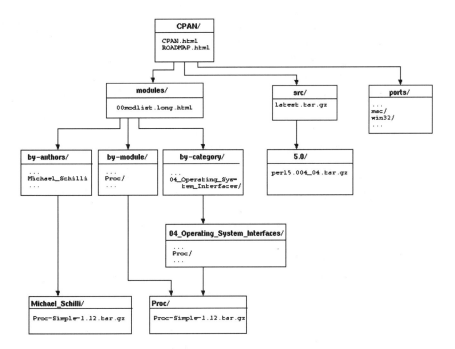

Figure A.1   Selected access paths in the CPAN.

A.4.2 Modules

The `Proc::Simple.pm` module presented on page 155 can now be searched for in the CPAN in various ways:

- If you know the author, `modules/by-authors/Michael_Schilli` leads you to your goal.

- The module list on page 379 shows that `Proc::Simple` is part of the distribution `Proc-Simple-1.12.tar.gz`, which is located, as shown in Figure A.1, in the `by-module` path, hierarchically classified under `modules/by-module/Proc`.

- The `by-category` path subdivides the modules into categories, such as `02_Perl_Core_Modules`, `03_Development_Support`, and so on, until `23_Miscellaneous_Modules`, each branching into the corresponding module hierarchy. `Proc::Simple` belongs to the operating system interfaces and is therefore located under the branch `04_Operating_System_Interfaces/Proc` of the `modules/by-category` hierarchy.

The following files lead users through the CPAN:

- `CPAN/ROADMAP.html`   gives an overview of the documents described below as well as several others. If you forget where to look for a specific document, this is the proper entry point.

- `CPAN/CPAN.html` provides a detailed introduction to the CPAN organization and lists the available modules. This is the main document of the CPAN, ideal for joining the crowd.

- `CPAN/modules/OOmodlist.long.html` is the list (also distributed via the newsgroup `comp.lang.perl.misc`) of all Perl modules available via the CPAN. Here, you can also find useful hints for developing your own modules.

A.4.3 Automatic updates

Thanks to the indefatigable creative urge of CPAN developers, new Perl modules appear every day. Now, the overworked system administrator must not only install these modules, but must also keep them up to date. However, remedy is at hand: the last module still to be installed manually is called `CPAN.pm` – after this, everything happens automatically.

A typical example: a Perl script uses

```
use LWP::UserAgent;
```

for WWW access and, instead of the expected Web pages, continues to display the error message:

```
Can't locate LWP::UserAgent.pm in @INC at ./t line 3.
BEGIN failed--compilation aborted at ./t line 3.
```

Obvious diagnosis: the module is not present on the local computer. It can certainly be downloaded from the CPAN – but from where, precisely?

Provided that the module `CPAN.pm` by Andreas König is properly installed,[2] this works automatically. The call

```
perl -MCPAN -e shell
```

displays a command line interpreter that upon the demand

```
cpan> i /agent/
```

outputs a whole range of hits in the form of a list of short descriptions:

```
Author        AGENTML (Mailing List For Perl5 Agents)
Distribution  SPURKIS/Agent-3.01a.tar.gz
Modules       Agent            (SPURKIS/Agent-3.01a.tar.gz)
Modules       Agent::Message   (SPURKIS/Agent-3.01a.tar.gz)
Modules       Agent::TCPIP     (SPURKIS/Agent-3.01a.tar.gz)
Modules       LWP::UserAgent   (GAAS/libwww-perl-5.21.tar.gz)
Modules       RPC::Simple::Agent (DDUMONT/RPC-Simple-0.5.tar.gz)
```

---

[2] The Perl distribution `perl 5.004_04` included on the enclosed CD-ROM already contains `CPAN.pm`; the necessary configuration steps are described in Section A.4.4.

The explicit search for the module `LWP::UserAgent`

```
cpan> i LWP::UserAgent
```

helps with more detailed information:

```
modules id = LWP::UserAgent
    DESCRIPTION  A WWW UserAgent class
    CPAN_USERID  GAAS (Gisle Aas)
    CPAN_VERSION 1.58
    CPAN_FILE    GAAS/libwww-perl-5.36.tar.gz
    DSLI_STATUS  Rmp0 (released,mailing-list,perl,object-oriented)
    MANPAGE      LWP::UserAgent - A WWW UserAgent class
    INST_FILE    (not installed)
```

Thus `LWP::UserAgent` is part of the `libwww` bundle by Gisle Aas, whose most recent version `5.36` is available in the CPAN. To install this module (on most systems, this requires `root` privileges; if in doubt, exit the CPAN shell with `'q'` and restart it as `root`), you type

```
cpan> install LWP::UserAgent
```

The CPAN shell checks whether there is already a version of `LWP::UserAgent` and, if this is obsolete or not present at all, installs the latest `libwww` bundle on the computer. It loads the distribution from the selected CPAN mirror, unpacks it, executes `perl Makefile.PL`, `make`, `make test`, and `make install` – and the module is ready for use.

In doing all this, `CPAN.pm` avoids unnecessary effort. A subsequent attempt to install the module `LWP::Simple` from the same distribution, for example, is immediately aborted by the CPAN shell, because `LWP::Simple` is already present in its most recent version:

```
cpan> install LWP::Simple
LWP::Simple is up to date.
```

In contrast,

```
cpan> force install LWP::Simple
```

forces the installation process, no matter whether it is needed or not. As a further gimmick, you can obtain information on the CPAN authors either by means of a regular expression

```
cpan> a /andreas/
Author id = ANDK
EMAIL a.koenig@franz.ww.TU-Berlin.DE
FULLNAME Andreas König
```

or, if the CPAN abbreviation of the developer is known, by means of

```
cpan> a MSCHILLI
Author id = MSCHILLI
EMAIL michael@perlmeister.com
FULLNAME Michael Schilli
```

To avoid unnecessary network traffic, `CPAN.pm` holds a cache of fixed maximum size, which stores fetched distributions and text files on the hard disk. Only if the latter turn out to be obsolete is a transfer carried out from the CPAN server.

The cache directory is set by the installation routine of `CPAN.pm`; default is `.cpan` in the home directory of the installing user. Here, in the `sources` directory, `CPAN.pm` creates a small CPAN mirror: current copies of the 'machine-readable' CPAN overview files `01mailrc.txt.gz`, `02packages.details.txt.gz`, and `03modlist.data.gz` can be found in the `authors` and `modules` subdirectories. In the `authors/id` directory, the original 'tarred' and compressed distributions are stored under the author shortcuts. `.cpan/build` houses the builds unpacked and potentially prepared for installation.

A.4.4 Configuration of the `CPAN.pm` module

The first call of the CPAN shell with

```
perl -MCPAN -e shell
```

leads to an installation dialog. If you do not use the enclosed Perl version `5.004_04`, but a previous version, the module must be downloaded from the CPAN directory `CPAN/modules/by-module/CPAN` and installed manually (see Section A.3).

Most of the questions can be answered by merely pressing the ⏎ key. At the question regarding the nearest CPAN server, the latest version 1.40 supplies a selection list, while the `CPAN.pm` version 1.24 included with the standard distribution just wants to know the name of a URL.

Once the CPAN shell is running,

```
cpan> install Bundle::CPAN
```

loads and installs additional modules from the CPAN to improve ease of handling for the `CPAN.pm` module.

A.4.5 Documentation

The documentation of Perl modules is usually contained directly in the module code: the POD (*Plain Old Documentation*) command set introduced with Perl 5 (see Appendix E) allows hiding of manual information in functioning Perl code. The `make install` command sequence usually triggers extraction of this information, uses it to create manual pages, and copies these to a specific location, where the `perldoc` command finally looks for them.

A.4.6   If the system administrator refuses ...

If Perl is present on the local system, but the responsible system administrator refuses to install new CPAN modules continuously, you can also store additional modules in a local directory.

A Perl script that includes one of these locally installed modules with

```
use FancyModule;
```

should, however, know in which directory it must carry out the additional search. Usually, this search path is set only to the current directory and the directory of the standard installation. By means of a prefixed use lib instruction, an additional path is defined. Thus, to make the interpreter find the module FancyModule.pm in the directory /users/spock/perl,

```
use lib "/users/spock/perl";
```

must be placed at the beginning of the script.

A.5   Legal questions

Perl is freely available. The call of the Perl interpreters perl with the option -v shows it quite clearly:

```
This is perl, version 5.004_04 built for i586-linux

Copyright 1987-1997, Larry Wall

Perl may be copied only under the terms of either the Artistic License
or the GNU General Public License, which may be found in the Perl 5.0
source kit.
```

Perl is *free software*. In clear text, this means that the author keeps all rights to his/her sources, but makes them freely available even for commercial use. Thus *free software* must not be confused with *public domain*: the rights of the author are protected.

Persons intending to modify the sources and subsequently make them available again must observe some rules described in the Artistic License that is part of every Perl distribution. These are simply restrictions that are in any case dictated by the rules of fairness towards developers of freely available software.

Commercial use of user-developed scripts and modules is explicitly allowed. Bundling them with a Perl distribution is in this context completely unproblematic.

A.6 Installing the SSL library for libwww

To enable the user agent of the libwww (page 263) to handle URLs in the format https://..., two elements must be installed on the computer: the module Net::SSLeay.pm by Gisle Aas, which can be found under

```
CPAN/modules/by-module/Net/Net_SSLeay.pm-0.04.tar.gz
```

in the CPAN, and the SSL library of the Australian Eric Young, which can be obtained as source code under

```
ftp://ftp.psy.uq.oz.au/pub/Net/SSL/SSLeay-0.6.6.tar.gz
```

Both distributions are also included on the enclosed CD-ROM in the directories CPAN and misc. Young took advantage of a gap in the otherwise watertight RSA company: one fine day, an anonymous article appeared in the newsgroup sci.crypt, whose author was never identified. The article showed an implementation of the secret RSA encryption algorithm, with which Young re-implemented the SSL protocol of Netscape and made it freely available on the Internet. He thumbed his nose not only at RSA, who otherwise demand $25,000 for a license, but also at the USA with their dubious export prohibition for hard-to-break encryption algorithms (see Garfinkel and Spafford, 1997).

Unpacking, configuring, compiling, and installing is as usual done with

```
gzip -dc SSLeay-0.6.6.tar.gz | tar xfv -
cd SSLeay-0.6.6
./Configure SYSTEM
make
make install
```

where SYSTEM is to be substituted with one of about 20 system configurations: you will find everything, from solaris-sparc-gcc via linux-elf to hpux-gcc (a list is displayed via ./Configure). After this installation, we will tackle the corresponding Perl module:

```
gzip -dc Net_SSLeay.pm-0.04.tar.gz | tar xfv -
cd Net_SSLeay
perl Makefile.PL
make
make test
make install
```

Ready! – from this moment on, the LWP::UserAgent automatically processes 'https://...' URLs.

A.7 Installation of a Web server

The Apache Web server available on the enclosed CD-ROM in the `misc` directory can be installed without problems on any standard UNIX platform (the Windows NT distribution is located in the same directory, named `apache_1_3_1.exe`). For our installation we assume that Apache will end up in the directory `/services/http`. For this purpose, unpack, compile and install the distribution somewhere with

```
tar zxfv apache_1.3.1.tar.gz
cd apache_1.3.1
./configure --prefix=/services/http
make
make install
```

In the configuration directory of Apache, `/services/http/etc/apache`, update the port setting in the file `httpd.conf` from `Port 8080` to `Port 80`. For CGI scripts, the entry

```
ScriptAlias /cgi-bin/ /services/http/share/apache/cgi-bin/
```

must be uncommented, then we can proceed (as `root`) with

```
/services/http/sbin/apachectl start
```

and the server starts. An

```
http://localhost/index.html
```

via a browser subsequently fetches the HTML file

```
/services/http/share/apache/htdocs/index.html
```

via the HTTP protocol, while the CGI script `test.cgi` under `/services/http/share/apache/cgi-bin` is executed by the call

```
http://localhost/cgi-bin/test.cgi
```

Apache is provided with extensive documentation in the form of HTML documents; once it is installed so far, a browser that calls

```
http://localhost/
```

will display the title page, which refers to the online documentation that you may use to delve deeper into Apache details.

To make the server start automatically when booting the computer, it is recommended that the above start command line is included in the start-up script of the computer (under LINUX, for example, in `/etc/rc.d/rc.local`).

A.8 Installing the Apache CGI accelerator

For installation, unpack `mod_perl-1.15.tar.gz` from the CPAN directory of the enclosed CD-ROM (or from `CPAN/modules/by-module/Apache`) and `apache_1.3.1.tar.gz` from `misc` (or, for example, from `http://www.apache.org`) into the same directory:

```
gzip -dc apache_1.3.1.tar.gz | tar xfv -
gzip -dc mod_perl-1.15.tar.gz | tar xfv -
```

The preparation of `mod_perl` is accomplished by

```
cd mod_perl-1.15
perl Makefile.PL \
    APACHE_PREFIX=/services/http \
    APACHE_SRC=../apache_1.3.1/src \
    DO_HTTPD=1 \
    USE_APACI=1 \
    EVERYTHING=1
make
```

This does not only prepare the installation of `mod_perl`, but also compiles the Apache distribution and configures the server for use with `mod_perl`. Installation of the `mod_perl` modules is then carried out by

```
make install
```

Adapting the server port and starting the server are (if not already accomplished) done as described in the previous section.

Especially for the `mod_perl` configuration the following rule applies: to make an Apache server installed underneath the `/services/http` directory recognize Perl scripts stored under `/services/http/share/apache/perl` as CGI scripts, whose execution is taken over by the `mod_perl` handler, the following entry must be inserted in the Alias section of `/services/http/etc/apache/srm.conf`:

```
Alias /perl/ /services/http/share/apache/perl/

<Location /perl>
SetHandler perl-script
PerlHandler Apache::Registry
options ExecCGI
<Location>
```

Equipped in this way, we only need to start the server, which is done by

```
/services/http/sbin/apachectl start
```

Since Apache immediately after start creates a number of child processes, and it is cumbersome in this test phase to terminate them one by one, the server stores its own process ID in the file `/services/http/var/apache/run/httpd.pid`. Thus to terminate the server together with all its children it is sufficient to issue a `kill` command with this PID. Thus

```
kill `cat /services/http/var/apache/run/httpd.pid`
```

stops the current HTTP daemon together with its children.

A script `scriptname.pl` in `/services/http/share/apache/perl` can subsequently be called with a browser via the HTTP interface as

```
http://servername/perl/scriptname.pl
```

Further modules required for the installation are: `libwww-perl-5.36.tar.gz` and `CGI.pm-2.42.tar.gz`, both of which can be found in the CPAN directory of the enclosed CD-ROM.

Starting scripts

B.1 UNIX

Two things are required to start a Perl script under UNIX: the script itself, and the Perl interpreter `perl`. The explicit call of the interpreter from the command line with the script as an argument works reliably on all systems:

```
> perl myscript.pl
```

However, this is relatively impractical, since most Perl scripts behave like shell scripts or compiled C programs, and are supposed to hide the fact that `perl` has been used for their execution as far as possible. It therefore seems sensible to supply the information on which the interpreter is to be used with the script itself. Thus, in analogy to shell scripts, the first line of a new Perl script `myscript.pl` contains the somewhat cryptical notation

```
#!/usr/bin/perl
```

which causes the UNIX kernel to delegate execution of the script not to the shell, but to the `perl` interpreter. A necessary condition is, however, that the file in question is executable (which can be achieved by means of `chmod +x filename`, if required).

The length of the first line should not exceed 32 characters; otherwise, some systems might produce completely baffling errors. If the system administrator does not allow Perl to be installed in `/usr/bin` or `/usr/local/bin`, and the next reachable path is already too long, remedy can be brought – if allowed – by a symbolic link from `/usr/bin/perl` to the interpreter in the actual installation directory.

Some shells, however, do not even understand the `#!` notation. Or, even worse: what happens if the Perl interpreter is not installed in `/usr/bin`, but for example in the `/usr/local/bin` directory? An error message appears. Often enough, this is

```
myscript.pl: No such file or directory
```

which does not immediately lead you to the conclusion that the Perl interpreter is only located in the wrong directory.

With these problems as the background, some smart developers designed a portable solution. The information on the interpreter used is meant to

- satisfy both shell and Perl syntax,
- cause the interpreting shell to call `perl`,
- let `perl` itself keep cool.

The sequence

```
eval 'exec perl -S $0 ${1+"$@"}'
        if $running_under_some_shell;
```

at the beginning of a script forces exactly this behavior. First, the shell tries to understand the new syntax. Execution of the `eval` command starts the Perl interpreter – wherever it is located. The only condition is that the directory where `perl` is installed is included in the `PATH` environment variable of the shell, meaning that `perl` can be started from the command line without a path specification. The `exec` command overloads the current process with the Perl interpreter. Thus the shell never reaches the incomprehensible second line.

The shell syntax `perl -S $0 ${1+"$@"}` needs some additional explanation. The option `-S` causes `perl` to search for the script specified as the next parameter not only in the current directory, but in all paths included in the shell variable `PATH`. This comes into play when the script (this time interpreted as a shell script) is called from a foreign directory without explicit path specification, and the script variable `$0` does not include the entire path – a bad habit still found on many systems.

The construct `${1+"$@"}`, instead, merely expands all arguments passed to the current script. One might think this could be done more easily with `$*`; however, special cases such as spaces within file names would not be handled correctly.

Back to Perl: the Perl interpreter started from within the shell script subsequently sees the `eval` command, but does not execute it, since the following condition `if $running_under_some_shell` is false because of the non-initialized variable. The rest of the script is processed as usual.

But even this portable solution does not work in all cases: for example, when started from within a C shell. A solution does exist for this case too, but it is so complicated that nobody can be asked to disfigure each and every script with it:

```
eval '(exit $?0)' && eval 'exec /usr/bin/perl -S $0 ${1+"$@"}'
& eval 'exec /usr/bin/perl -S $0 $argv:q'
    if 0;
```

In fact, the portable syntax is seldom used – the most popular solution still remains `#!/usr/bin/perl`. In the end, there is no 100% solution, but only one adapted to the actual application.

B.2 Windows 95 and NT

Unfortunately, the Windows operating systems do not recognize the #! notation. Thus, apart from modifying the registry in such a way that *.pl files are opened with the Perl interpreter, there is nothing better than the traditional call:

```
perl script.pl
```

This can, however, only work if the bin path of the Perl distribution is included in the PATH variable set in AUTOEXEC.BAT.

B.3 Important command line options

If it is not worth while to create a separate file for a short Perl script, the Perl code can simply be passed to perl via the die command line:

```
perl -e 'print "Howdy, World!\n"'
```

The option -e accepts Perl code line by line; several instructions may also be distributed across several -e options:

```
perl -e '$a = 42; print "a=$a\n"'       # outputs both times a=42
perl -e '$a = 42' -e 'print "a=$a\n"'   # with line breaks
```

B.3.1 Line-by-line manipulation

To ensure that perl does not fall behind UNIX tools such as sed and awk with regard to writing short filters, the options -n and -p set Perl to a mode which subjects incoming files line by line to a treatment defined by the string belonging to the -e option. Thus the command line

```
who | perl -n -e 'print $_ if /kirk/;'
```

takes the output of the who command

```
mccoy    tty1     Apr 18 19:02
spock    ttyp0    Apr 18 21:15 (:0.0)
spock    ttyp1    Apr 18 23:04 (:0.0)
kirk     ttyp2    Apr 18 19:17 (:0.0)
mccoy    ttyp3    Apr 19 00:28 (:0.0)
```

and extracts only the line

```
kirk     ttyp2    Apr 18 19:17 (:0.0)
```

because the option −n wraps the Perl code `print $_ if /kirk/;` in the following construct:

```
while (<>) {
    print $_ if /kirk/;
}
```

As already explained in Section 1.8.7, this loop processes the files specified on the command line one after the other, line by line, or, if no files are specified, the data stream of the standard input.

The option −a causes `perl` to separate incoming lines at each space into individual fields, which it stores in the array `@F`. Thus

```
who | perl -a -n -e 'print "$F[0]\n"'
```

for example, outputs

```
mccoy
spock
spock
kirk
mccoy
```

while, in order to eliminate duplicates,

```
who | perl -a -n -e 'print $_ unless $user{$F[0]}++'
```

creates a hash `%user` with the user names as keys and outputs

```
mccoy   tty1    Apr 18 19:02
spock   ttyp0   Apr 18 21:15 (:0.0)
kirk    ttyp2   Apr 18 19:17 (:0.0)
```

If the individual fields are separated not by whitespace, but by another character sequence, this must follow the −F option:

```
perl -n -a -F: -e 'print "$F[0]\n"' /etc/passwd
```

This example takes a UNIX password file in the format

```
mschilli:8KYC67g9n4tsI:501:100:Michael Schilli:
    /home/mschilli:/bin/bash
```

extracts the first field (the user name), and prints it out.

One-line scripts, which process, manipulate, and output their input, are better off using the −p option instead of −n. If a file `file` contains the circular letter

```
Dear Kirsty,
you are my sunshine.
```

the following one-liner outputs the text adjusted to the personal requirements:

```
perl -p -e 's/Kirsty/Shelley/g' file
```

If the file itself is to be changed, and the text of the original file is to migrate to `file.bak`, the following construct does the job:

```
perl -p -i.bak -e 's/Kirsty/Shelley/g' file
```

B.3.2 Determining the version

One can identify the version of the Perl interpreter that is installed via the call `perl -v`:

```
This is Perl, version 5.004_04 built for i586-linux
Copyright 1987-1997, Larry Wall
Perl may be copied only under the terms of either the Artistic License
or the GNU General Public License, which may be found in the Perl 5.0
source kit.
```

To communicate friendly helpers in case of problems over which system configuration is installed on the computer in question, the output of `perl -V` is used, which reveals not only the exact version of the Perl interpreter, but also the versions of compiler, operating system, and all libraries involved:

```
perl -V
Summary of my perl5 (5.0 patchlevel 4 subversion 4) configuration:
  Platform:
    osname=linux, osvers=2.0.30, archname=i586-linux
    ...
  Compiler:
    cc='cc', optimize='-02', gccversion=2.7.2.3
    ...
    ...
Characteristics of this binary (from libperl):
  Built under linux
  Compiled at Dec 15 1997 23:53:59
  ...
```

B.3.3 Syntax check

You may check a script `script.pl` for syntax errors, without actually executing it, by calling

```
perl -c script.pl
```

B.3.4   Loading additional modules

Freely available Perl modules can also be used in Perl one-liners. The option `-M`, directly followed by a module name, includes the corresponding module in the same way as `use` *modulename;* would do in the code:

```
perl -MLWP::Simple -e 'getprint "http://remote.host.com"'
```

The above one-liner is probably the quickest way to fetch a Web page from the Net (details on `LWP::Simple` can be found on page 260).

B.3.5   Warning mode

The option `-w` switches `perl` into a mode that, strictly speaking, should be active by default: if you use variables without initializing them, write to reading file handles, redefine subroutines, or perform some other type of silly action, `perl` issues warnings. Thus

```
perl -w -e 'print $i'
```

signals that the variable `$i` was accessed without having being initialized:

```
Name "main::i" used only once: possible typo at -e line 1.
Use of uninitialized value at -e line 1.
```

A summary of all available command line parameters can be found on the manual page `perlrun` (which can be viewed by calling `perldoc perlrun`).

Troubleshooting

The following sections point out errors that typically occur with incorrectly installed Perl scripts or with an incorrectly configured or missing Perl interpreter, and are intended to help beginners to get going without problems. Section C.4 discusses errors appearing in applications under Perl/Tk.

C.1 UNIX

When a Perl script `test.pl` is started under UNIX by means of the command

```
test.pl
```

a running `bash` shell may signal the following errors (other shells, such as `ksh`, `csh`, `tcsh`, or `zsh`, react in the same or a very similar way):

- **bash: test.pl: command not found**
  The specified file does not exist, or the path (environment variable `PATH`) does not include the current directory. Solution: create the file in the current directory and append '.' to `PATH` (for example, by means of `PATH=$PATH:.` in the Bourne/Korn/Bash shells).

- **bash: ./test.pl: No such file or directory**
  The intepreter specified in the first line of the script does not exist (see Appendix B). Check whether the correct path for the Perl installation is specified and, if needed, correct the value. If the command `perl ./test.pl` works, you can use `which perl` to find out where the Perl interpreter is actually located and amend the path specification accordingly.

- **bash: ./test.pl: Permission denied**
  The user has no execution rights for the script file. Solution: set execution privileges, for example by means of `chmod +x test.pl`.

C.2 Windows

If the call of

```
perl test.pl
```

under Windows does not lead to the expected result, the command interpreter evidently does not find the Perl interpreter `perl`:

```
Bad command or file name
```

indicates that `perl` is not included in the search path of the interpreter. Remedy is brought by an entry in the `AUTOEXEC.BAT` file, which appends the installation path of the Perl distribution (default is `C:\PERL\BIN`) to the existing `PATH` variable:

```
PATH=C:\WINDOWS;C:\WINDOWS\COMMAND;...;C:\PERL\BIN
```

C.3 External help

If a script does not run even after a longer reflection about possible causes, it is always a good idea to consult the FAQ (see page 4). If this too does not lead to the desired result, friendly people might be of help who read the newsgroup `comp.lang.perl.misc`. However, if you ask a question that could have been solved by reading the FAQ, be prepared to receive masses of nasty email messages and follow-up articles. To let the friendly helpers know how to help, your posting should include the following items:

- a precisely formulated question;
- a piece of the suspect code that produces the error;
- the output of the command `perl -V`, which shows details about your current Perl installation.

Normally, you will get what you deserve: if you ask a polite question, you usually get a friendly answer. If, however, it is quite obvious that someone merely shuns longer thinking and tries to scrounge a free, ready-to-use solution, reactions will be mockery and disdain.

C.4 Error diagnostics for Perl/Tk applications

Applications under the X Window system, including all Perl/Tk scripts, require a properly set environment. Precondition is a running X server on the computer responsible for the display. This program is usually called `xdm` or simply `X`, and runs automatically on X terminals, but must often be set up first on 'normal' computers. The client computer, on which the application itself is running, uses a TCP/IP network connection to the server.

C.4.1 Setting up the display server

First of all, the application must know which X server takes on the representation of its interface. This is defined by the DISPLAY environment variable on the client computer. It specifies the host and, because a server machine can provide several X server programs with several screens, their numbers in the format [host]:server[.screen]. If the DISPLAY variable is not set, the X application usually signals the error

```
appname: Xt error: Can't open display:
```

In the Bourne shell,

```
DISPLAY=myhost:0.0
export DISPLAY
```

sets the responsible display server to the computer myhost, where X server number 0 together with screen number 0 will be the right choice in most cases.

C.4.2 Conferring X server privileges

Only selected clients on the network are allowed to represent their interfaces on a server provided with an X server. The privilege to do so is conferred by the server itself. With the command

```
xhost +myhost
```

the server includes the client myhost in the elite circle of those that are allowed to use its X server. The command xhost -myhost divests the client of this privilege.

HTML
quick reference

This appendix intends to provide a minimal overview of the most important HTML commands. Figure D.1 shows Netscape Navigator with the HTML document `struct.html` loaded. The file `struct.html`, whose source code is printed below, defines fundamental HTML structures such as

- headlines and highlights;
- bulleted, glossary, and numbered lists;
- hyperlinks with and without image information;
- editable form fields;
- check and radio buttons;
- listboxes;
- submit and reset buttons.

The visual representation in connection with the source code should suffice to convey the minimal knowledge of HTML required in this book. For deeper insight, we would like to refer you to the specialized literature (for example, Spainhour and Quercia, 1966) and documents freely available on the Internet (see Appendix G).

struct.html

```
<HTML>

<!-- Page header -->
<HEAD>
<TITLE>IMPORTANT HTML TAGS</TITLE>
</HEAD>
```

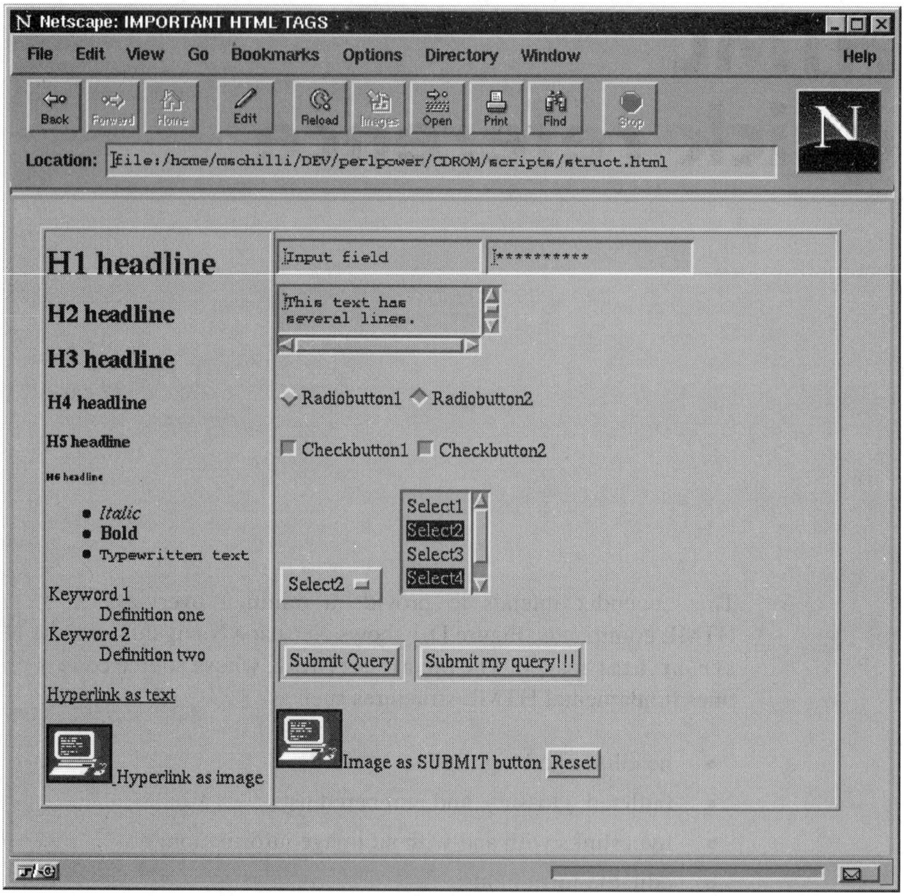

Figure D.1 Browser representation of the HTML file `struct.html`.

```
<!-- Page contents (body) -->
<BODY>
<!-- Two-column table (separation via td tag) with margin width 1 -->
<table border=1>
<td>

<!-- =========================================================== -->
<!-- Fonts and sizes -->
<H1>H1 headline </H1>
<H2>H2 headline </H2>
<H3>H3 headline </H3>
<H4>H4 headline </H4>
<H5>H5 headline </H5>
```

```
<H6>H6 headline </H6>


<!-- ============================================================ -->
<!-- Bulleted list -->
<UL>
<LI><I>Italic</I>
<LI><B>Bold</B>
<LI><tt>Typewritten text</tt>
</UL>


<!-- ============================================================ -->
<!-- Glossary list -->
<DL>
<DT>Keyword 1
<DD>Definition one
<DT>Keyword 2
<DD>Definition two
</DL>


<!-- ============================================================ -->
<!-- Hyperlinks -->
<A HREF="http://remote.host.com"> Hyperlink as text</A>


<p>
<A HREF="http://remote.host.com">
<IMG SRC=../../gif/term.gif ALT="Alternative text"> </A>
Hyperlink as image

<!-- Column separator for table -->
<td>


<!-- ============================================================ -->
<!-- Form definition with actions in case of SUBMIT -->
<FORM NAME=formname METHOD=GET
      ACTION="http://remote.host.com/cgi-bin/dump.cgi">


<!-- Input field, single line -->
<INPUT TYPE=text NAME=textfield VALUE="Input field">


<!-- Password entry field, two lines -->
<INPUT TYPE=password NAME=password VALUE="MyPassword">


<!-- Multi-line text field -->
<TEXTAREA ROWS=2 COLS=20 NAME="area1">
This text has
```

```
several lines.
</TEXTAREA>

<!-- Radio buttons --> <p>
<INPUT TYPE=radio NAME=radio VALUE="Radiobutton1">
    Radiobutton1
<INPUT TYPE=radio NAME=radio VALUE="Radiobutton2" checked>
    Radiobutton2

<!-- Checkbuttons --> <p>
<INPUT TYPE=checkbox NAME=check VALUE="Checkbutton1" checked>
    Checkbutton1
<INPUT TYPE=checkbox NAME=check VALUE="Checkbutton2" checked>
    Checkbutton2

<!-- Select menu --> <p>
<SELECT NAME="select" >
<OPTION VALUE=1 > Select1
<OPTION VALUE=2 SELECTED> Select2
<OPTION VALUE=3 > Select3
</SELECT>

<!-- Multi-line select box with multiple choice -->
<SELECT NAME="select" SIZE=4 MULTIPLE>
<OPTION VALUE=1 > Select1
<OPTION VALUE=2 SELECTED> Select2
<OPTION VALUE=3 > Select3
<OPTION VALUE=4 SELECTED> Select4
<OPTION VALUE=5 > Select5
</SELECT>

<!-- Submit and reset buttons --> <p>
<INPUT TYPE=submit NAME=submit>

<INPUT TYPE="submit" VALUE="Submit my query!!!"
        NAME="submitButtonName">

<p>
<INPUT TYPE="image" SRC="../../gif/term.gif" NAME="imgn"
        VAL="imgv">Image as SUBMIT button

<INPUT TYPE=reset>

<!-- End of form -->
</FORM>
```

```
<!-- End of table -->
</table>

<!-- End of document -->
</BODY>
</HTML>
```

_____*struct.html*

D.1 Foreign language special characters

Common HTML browsers usually understand accented letters and umlauts as defined in ISO-8859-1, but the official representation of accents and umlauts follows the pattern shown below:

```
Ä => &Auml;
ä => &auml;
Ö => &Ouml;
ö => &ouml;
Ü => &Uuml;
ü => &uuml;
à => &agrave;
é => &eacute;
```

Documentation

No 'true' programmer likes to write documentation. Therefore, with the POD (*Plain Old Documentation*), Perl 5 provides a means that allows creation of manual pages in parallel with program development. Since POD format commands may be inserted anywhere in the Perl code, comments to module or function headers, for example, can immediately flow into the documentation.

If you send a Perl script written in this manner through an appropriate filter, the output can be a ready manual page, a LaTeX document, or even an HTML page.

This procedure is by now used by the majority of modules provided by the CPAN. Thus you do not look for the manual page for a sample module `Mymod.pm` somewhere outside, but extract it by calling the filter

```
pod2man Mymod.pm | nroff -man | more
```

The `pod2man` formatter searches the script for POD commands and uses the UNIX-typical `nroff` command to create a manual page. The `nroff` program accepts the `pod2man` output and formats it for the screen using the `man` macro package. The pager `more` displays the manual information page by page – in the same way as if you had called the `man` command.

This procedure is usually carried out by the installation program included with the module (usually `MakeMaker`), which does not only copy the new module to the correct location in the Perl search path, but also extracts the manual pages and stores them in the `Man` directories. Thus a subsequent call of

```
man Mymod
```

supplies information on the `Mymod.pm` module in the usual layout of the UNIX manual pages. The command

```
perldoc Mymod
```

works in a platform-independent way also on non-UNIX systems.

E.1 POD commands

The number of POD commands has been kept small on purpose. The aim was not to create yet another powerful text formatting language, but rather a simple tool. Thus POD is not suited for writing a book, but turns the daily creation of program code documentation into a pleasure instead.[1]

POD recognizes the following commands, which must always be placed at the beginning of a line to be recognized as such:

```
=pod                    # start of POD
=cut                    # end, followed by Perl code

=head1 heading          # first-order heading
=head2 heading          # second-order heading

=over N                 # indent by N columns
=item text              # list entry
=back                   # back to no indent
```

After an introductory =pod (or any other POD command), the formatter arranges unmarked text in paragraphs.[2] Indented text is automatically interpreted as program code and represented in typewriter style without automatic line breaking.

The most important formatting commands in the running text are:

```
I<text>     # italic (for example, to denote variables)
B<text>     # bold (programs and enumeration points)
S<text>     # no line breaking in spaces
C<code>     # typed text (for example, source code)
L<name>     # link to another section on the same page or
            # to another manual page
F<file>     # file names
E<char>     # special characters (such as E<lt> = '<', E<gt> = '>')
```

Listing `Mymod.pm` shows how with POD the documentation can become part of the production code.

Mymod.pm

```perl
#!/usr/bin/perl -w

package Mymod;
```

---

[1] Well, not entirely.

[2] While the pod2man formatter justifies the text pieces, the result of pod2html in HTML is a left-ranged sequence of lines.

```
=head1 NAME

Mymod - brief description

=head1 SYNOPSIS

    use Mymod;

    Mymod::func1($par1);
    Mymod::func2($par1, $par2);

=head1 DESCRIPTION

Extensive description of C<Mymod>

=head1 METHODS

=head2 func1

Here comes the function description

    $ret = func1($par1);

=cut

######################################################################
# Perl code starts
######################################################################
sub func1 {
    my($par1) = @_;

    # ...
}

=head2 func2

Here comes the function description

    $ret = func2($par1, $par2);

=cut

######################################################################
# Perl code starts again
######################################################################
```

```
sub func2 {
    my($par1, $par2) = @_;

    # ...
}

=head1 AUTHOR

Michael Schilli I<michael@perlmeister.com>
```

Mymod.pm

E.2 Filters

POD-formatted text can be converted by means of the filters

- pod2man into nroff/troff manual page format,
- pod2text into clear text,
- pod2html into HTML pages,
- pod2latex into LATEX documents.

The filters are included with the Perl standard distribution and convert the file, whose name they are passed as the first argument, either to the standard output or into an appropriate file.

Listing Mymod.txt shows the clear textversion, Figure E.1 the manual page processed with nroff, and Figure E.2 the HTML version in a browser.

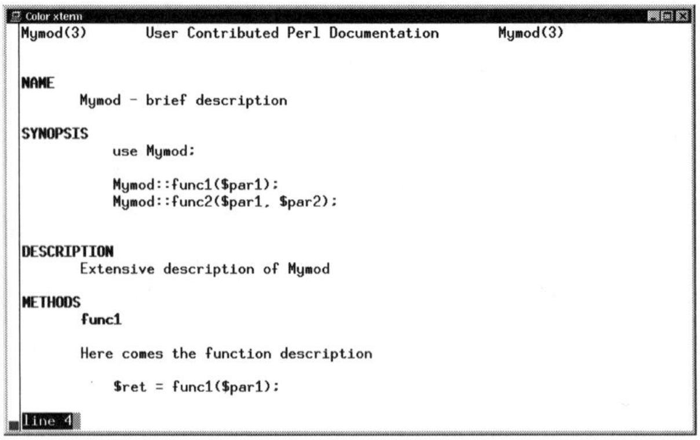

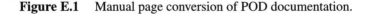

Figure E.1   Manual page conversion of POD documentation.

Mymod.txt

```
NAME
    Mymod - brief description

SYNOPSIS
        use Mymod;

        Mymod::func1($par1);
        Mymod::func2($par1, $par2);

DESCRIPTION
    Extensive description of `Mymod'

METHODS
  func1

    Here comes the function description

        $ret = func1($par1);

  func2

    Here comes the function description

        $ret = func2($par1, $par2);

AUTHOR
    Michael Schilli *michael@perlmeister.com*
```

Mymod.txt

E.2.1 Filter-specific POD commands

Some things, however, are treated differently by the different POD filters: while an HTML document can include an illustration in GIF or JPG format without problems, the corresponding text or manual page document must do with clumsy character scribbling. The =for directive allows you to supply the processors for clear text, HTML code, and manual pages with different instructions for the representation of a text element. The pod code of Listing switch.pod defines an image like Figure E.3 for the resulting HTML code, while the corresponding manual pages and clear text representations will show a character sequence of the kind

```
file 1  <-  directory  ->  file 2
```

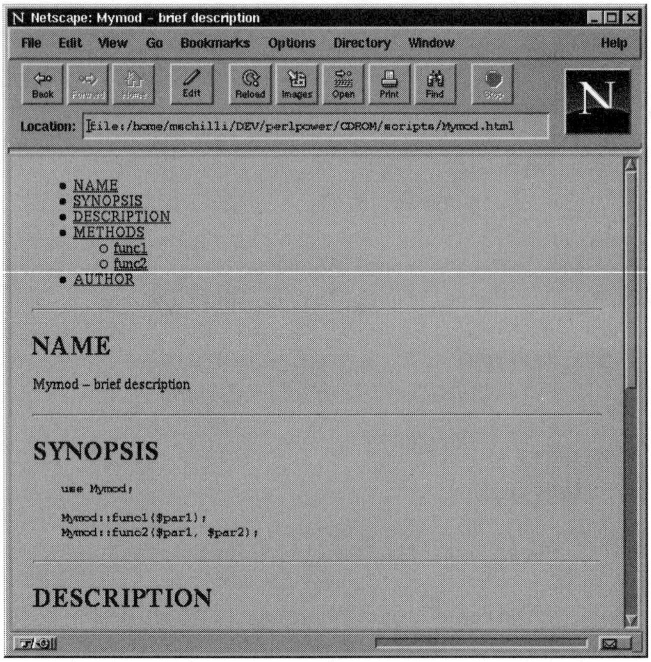

Figure E.2 HTML conversion of POD documentation.

Figure E.3 Graphics as a JPG image.

switch.pod

```
=for html
<IMG SRC=pod.jpg>
<I>Figure 1</I>

=for text
file 1  <-  directory  ->  file 2

=for man
file 1  <-  directory  ->  file 2
```

switch.pod

Synchronization of parallel processes

Although Perl does not (yet) support multi-threading, the much-feared *race conditions* can occur all the same, if several processes simultaneously access resources that can serve only *one* process at a time.

A CGI script (Section 5.8) that reads, modifies, and stores the contents of a file can be interrupted during this process by another process that potentially also manipulates the file. The result of such an action is unpredictable: depending on which process gains control at which time, the file may contain different data – or be entirely destroyed.

In this chapter, we present two methods for synchronization of processes: file locking with `flock`, and semaphores.

The so-called *critical sections*, in which a process must have exclusive control over a resource, are enclosed in commands that as atomic instructions (that is, single instructions that cannot be interrupted by the operating system) set a lock and release it again.

F.1 Exclusive `flock`

The `flock` command is used to set a lock on a file. Although files on which an exclusive lock is set can still be read and even written, no further process can set an exclusive lock on this file too.

The `LOCK_XX` macros included by means of

```
use Fcntl qw/:flock/;
```

are used to set an exclusive lock on the file opened with the file handle `FILE` by means of the command

```
flock(FILE, LOCK_EX);          # exclusive lock
```

The lock expires if

```
flock(FILE, LOCK_UN);          # release lock
```

is executed, or the file is closed explicitly, or if it is automatically closed at program termination. This means that, during execution of the critical section, the opened file must not be closed even temporarily.

Listing `race.pl` shows how *race conditions* come into being. It generates three child processes, which nearly simultaneously enter a critical section that contains a sleep process of a 1 second duration. During this time, the operating system carries out so many task switches that it is completely unpredictable which process wins the 'race' and leaves the critical section first.

_____*race.pl*

```perl
#!/usr/bin/perl -w

my $pid;

foreach $i (1..3) {

    if(!defined ($pid = fork())) { # fork error
        die "fork error";
    } elsif($pid == 0) {           # child
        critical($i);
        exit 0;
    } else {                       # parent
    }
}

while(wait() > 0) { ; }            # wait for termination
                                   # of the child processes

sub critical {
    my $number = shift;

    print "$number enters critical section\n";
    sleep(1);
    print "$number leaves critical section\n";
}
```

_____*race.pl*

The `race.pl` script generates the following output (which is completely random):

```
1 enters critical section
2 enters critical section
3 enters critical section
2 leaves critical section
1 leaves critical section
3 leaves critical section
```

However, if it is to be guaranteed that no process 'overtakes' another process in the critical section (that is, that only one process at a time is present in that area), synchronization measures must be taken. Listing `raceflock.pl` shows how these are realized by means of the `flock` command.

raceflock.pl

```perl
#!/usr/bin/perl

use Fcntl qw/:flock/;              # predefine lock parameters

open(FILE, ">lockfile");

foreach $number (1..3) {

    if(!defined ($pid = fork())) { # fork error
        die "fork error";
    } elsif($pid == 0) {           # child
        critical($number);         # execute section
        exit 0;                    # terminate child
    } else {

                                   # parent
    }
}

close(FILE);                       # parent closes lock file

while(wait() > 0) { ; }            # wait for termination
                                   # of the child processes

sub critical {
    my $number = shift;

    flock(FILE, LOCK_EX);          # set exclusive lock
```

```
        print "$number enters critical section\n";
        sleep(1);
        print "$number leaves critical section\n";

        flock(FILE, LOCK_UN);              # release lock
    }
```

raceflock.pl

Correspondingly, the output of `raceflock.pl` is:

```
1 enters critical section
1 leaves critical section
3 enters critical section
3 leaves critical section
2 enters critical section
2 leaves critical section
```

As the output shows, the processes may enter the critical section in a random order, but while one process is present in that area, no second process enters it.

The fact that `flock` needs an opened file handle to obtain exclusive write privileges for a file sounds somewhat of a paradox, since an

```
open(FILE, ">file");
```

would destroy a potentially present file content, before an `flock` could identify a conflict. For this reason, two parallel processes that enter data in a file open the resource in read/write mode by means of

```
open(FILE, "+<file");
```

and subsequently maneuver back to the beginning with a `seek` command. This does not overwrite anything, but returns a writable file handle `FILE`.

Listing `exfile.pl` shows the function `exwrite()`, which makes use of this technique. In addition, it defines a function `exread()`, which uses `LOCK_SH` to set only a *shared lock* on the file. Although several processes can obtain a *shared lock*, the operating system still prevents a single *exclusive lock* to be set while a *shared lock* is set, which means that the affected file can be either read simultaneously by any number of processes, or written by only one single process.

exfile.pl

```
use Fcntl qw/:flock/;

$lockfile = ".lockfile";
```

```perl
sub exwrite {
    open(WFILE, "+<$lockfile") ||
        die "Error opening $lockfile";

    flock(WFILE, LOCK_EX);      # start of critical region

    seek(WFILE, 0, 0);          # jump to beginning
    truncate(WFILE, 0);         # ... and truncate

    print WFILE "test\n";

    close(WFILE);               # end of critical region
}

sub exread {
    open(RFILE, "<$lockfile") ||
        die "Error opening $lockfile";

    flock(RFILE, LOCK_SH);      # start of critical region

    my @file = <RFILE>;         # read file

    close(RFILE);               # end of critical region

    join('', @file);
}
```

_____*exfile.pl*

F.2 Semaphores

With semaphores, operating systems provide systemwide counters that can be set and checked *atomically* and block a process until the semaphore reaches a specified value.

A mutex semaphore – that is, a semaphore that only one process can 'own' at any time – therefore represents a block for processes also wishing to access a resource that, however, can serve only one process at a time. When a semaphore is created, it has the value 0. When a process fetches the semaphore, it must wait until the semaphore carries the value 0. Without the operating system being able to put another process in between, the process 'fetches' the semaphore and increments its counter by 1.

Other processes, which also want to obtain exclusive possession of the semaphore, must now wait until the semaphore again carries the value 0, which is achieved when the first process releases the semaphore and decrements its value by 1.

The UNIX interface to semaphores is not very user-friendly: thus, for example, the commands `semop` and `semctl` are supplied command sequences in the form of numerical values, which then run guaranteed without being interrupted. Here we need a simplified access: the `Mutex.pm` module presented below makes use of methods of object-oriented programming. To understand the implementation, a basic knowledge of Perl's object-oriented constructs is indispensable. Unacquainted readers should refer to Chapter 2.

The `Mutex.pm` module abstracts the semaphore interface to a class `Mutex`, which provides only the methods

```
$sem = Mutex->new($key);   # create semaphore ($key: numerical value)
$sem->lock();              # set lock
$sem->release();           # release lock
$sem->delete();            # delete semaphore
```

and is thus supposed to facilitate the use of semaphores. The variable `$key`, which is passed to the constructor as a parameter, is an (arbitrary) numerical value that identifies the semaphore throughout the entire system. `Mutex.pm` is designed in such a way that it releases a semaphore as soon as the corresponding process terminates, but the semaphore itself remains known to the system under its ID `$key`, until `$sem->delete()` definitely deletes it.

Mutex.pm

```perl
#!/usr/bin/perl -w

package Mutex;

use strict;

# flags for semaphore

my $IPC_CREAT  = 0001000;   # create semaphore
my $IPC_EXCL   = 0002000;   # create fails if key exists
my $IPC_NOWAIT = 0004000;   # error if blocked

my $SEM_UNDO   = 0100000;   # release semaphore if
                            # process terminates
# semaphore commands

my $IPC_RMID = 0000000;   # remove
my $IPC_SET  = 0000001;   # set
my $IPC_STAT = 0000002;   # interrogate
```

```perl
##########################################################################
sub new {
##########################################################################
    my $class = shift;
    my $key   = shift;

    my $self = {};

    $self->{'semid'}  = semget($key, 1, 0644|$IPC_CREAT);

    die "Create failed" unless defined($self->{'semid'});

    bless($self, $class);
}


##########################################################################
# Set semaphore lock: $sem->lock();
##########################################################################
sub lock {
    my $self = shift;

    my $semnum  = 0;    # first semaphore of list
    my $semflag = 0;

    # wait until semaphore is zero
    my $semop     = 0;
    my $opstring1 = pack("sss", $semnum, $semop, $semflag);

    # increment semaphore counter by 1
    $semop      = $IPC_SET;
    $semflag    = $SEM_UNDO;  # release semaphore when
                             # process ends
    my $opstring2 = pack("sss", $semnum, $semop,  $semflag);

    semop($self->{'semid'}, $opstring1 . $opstring2) ||
                                       die "Lock failed";
}


##########################################################################
# Release semaphore lock: $sem->release();
##########################################################################
sub release {
    my $self = shift;
```

```
    my $semnum  = 0;    # first semaphore of list
    my $semflag = 0;

    # count down
    my $semop = -1;
    my $opstring = pack("sss", $semnum, $semop, $semflag);

    semop($self->{'semid'},$opstring) ||
                            die "Release failed";
}


####################################################################
# Delete semaphore: $sem->delete();
####################################################################
sub delete {
    my $self = shift;

    semctl($self->{'semid'}, 0, $IPC_RMID, 0) ||
                            die "Delete failed";
}


1;
```

_____*Mutex.pm*

At the beginning, `Mutex.pm` defines several constants, which are UNIX-dependent and derive from the headers `ipc.h` and `sem.h` of the `/usr/include/sys` directory.

Listing `racesem.pl` shows once again the test sample `race.pl`, which is persuaded by a `Mutex` object to respect the critical section. As in `raceflock.pl`, the individual processes pass the bottleneck separately and one after the other.

_____*racesem.pl*

```
#!/usr/bin/perl

use Mutex;

$sem = Mutex->new(123);

foreach $number (1..3) {

    if(!defined ($pid = fork())) { # fork error
        die "fork error";
    } elsif($pid == 0) {           # child
```

```
        critical($number);          # execute section
        exit 0;                      # terminate child
    } else {

                                     # parent
    }
}


while(wait() > 0) { ; }               # wait for termination
                                      # of the child process


$sem->delete();                       # delete semaphore


sub critical {
    my $number = shift;

    $sem->lock();                     # set semaphore lock

    print "$number enters critical section\n";
    sleep(1);
    print "$number leaves critical section\n";

    $sem->release();                  # release semaphore lock
}
```

_____*racesem.pl*

Addresses

G.1 The Perl 5 module list

More or less regularly, about every two weeks, the newsgroups

```
comp.lang.perl.modules
comp.answers
news.answers
```

publish 'The Perl 5 Modules List', a list of all currently available CPAN modules compiled by Andreas König. Besides short descriptions of the modules, it contains quite a lot of hints and tricks for Perl 5 programming and development. It is also available on the World Wide Web under the URL

```
http://www.perl.com/CPAN/modules/00modlist.long.html
```

G.2 Quick Reference cards

The CPAN also provides Quick Reference cards for both Perl and Tk in the form of Postscript files. Once printed out, they are indispensable helpers. Relative to the CPAN directory, they are stored in

```
Perl Reference
doc/perlref-5.004.1.tar.gz

Tk Quick Reference
authors/id/LUSOL/ptkref-402.003.0.tar.gz
```

A quick overview of Perl is also available as a printed book (Vromans, 1996).

G.3 RFCs

The specification of an Internet protocol is always published as an RFC (*Request for Comments*). With an RFC, the author of a protocol asks the Internet community for comments on a new development that is extensively described in the RFC itself.

RFCs that describe components that have successfully established themselves are kept in archives, and are used as a reference. A good address for all important RFCs is

```
http://www.isi.edu/rfc-editor/categories/rfc-standard.html
```

This archive also includes RFCs 850 and 977 quoted in Section 5.11, which describe the format of Usenet articles and the NNTP protocol.

G.4 Additional addresses

```
Rules for Internet robots
http://info.webcrawler.com/mak/projects/robots/norobots.html

Development of another Perl NT port
http://www.ActiveState.com

HTML specification
http://www.w3.org/hypertext/WWW/MarkUp/

Client Pull/Server Push
http://www.netscape.com/assist/net_sites/pushpull.html

Practical HTML overview
http://vzone.virgin.net/sizzling.jalfrezi
```

G.4.1 More information on Perl on the WWW

- **Official Perl Homepage** The Web page `http://www.perl.com` supervised by Tom Christiansen is the Number One Perl page on the Internet. News about the Perl scene, references to the CPAN, book reviews, FAQs – and all of this with the official – *Bang!* – stamp of the Perl committee.

- **Randal Schwartz's homepage** A true bonanza for all sorts of Perl tricks by a master of the matter. Under `http://www.stonehenge.com/merlyn` you will find, amongst others, links to Randal's monthly columns in the magazines *Web Techniques* and *Unix Review*.

- **Michael Schilli's homepage** Yes, even the author of this book occasionally writes magazine contributions. On the Web page `http://www.perlmeister.com` (run from San Francisco) you will find links to his articles in *iX* and in the *Linux-Magazin*.

- **Effective Perl Programming**   The Web page for Joseph N. Hall's book *Effective Perl Programming* under `http://www.effectiveperl.com` contains additional links to all sorts of things you should know about Perl.

- **Malcolm Beattie's Perl page**   Malcolm Beattie develops the Perl compiler and important modules such as `Safe`. He will be responsible for Release 5.005, which is expected for the end of 1998. `http://users.ox.ac.uk/~mbeattie/perl.html` informs about the current state of his research.

- **The Perl Journal**   `http://www.tpj.com` is the exclusive Perl magazine; here writes the crème de la crème. *Subscription highly recommended!*

- **Perl for Win32 systems**   `http://www.netaxs.com/~joc/perlwin32.html` gives hints and tips for running Perl on Windows 95 and NT systems.

- **FAQ for Perl/Tk**   `http://w4.lns.cornell.edu/~pvhp/ptk/ptkFAQ.html` holds the FAQ for Perl/Tk.

- `libwww-perl`   `http://www.ics.uci.edu/pub/websoft/libwww-perl` informs about the omnipresent `libwww`.

G.4.2 Newsgroups

- `comp.lang.perl.misc`   First address for Perl questions. Very high data rate (about 100 articles/day) despite drastic control measures (as an answer to your first posting, you are automatically sent a small Perl FAQ), but little information in proportion to the volume. Larry Wall, Randal L. Schwartz, and Tom Christiansen, together with a dozen of high-carat people read the articles and answer questions, as long as these are not too daft. If they are, or if questions are asked about CGI without reference to Perl, some grumbling will be heard.

- `comp.lang.perl.modules`   Questions and answers about extension modules.

- `comp.lang.perl.announce`   Moderated announcements forum for new Perl releases, modules or forthcoming events.

- `comp.infosystems.www.authoring.cgi`   Newsgroup for CGI-relevant questions, not only referring to Perl.

- `comp.lang.perl.tk`   Forum for Perl/Tk questions.

Contents of the CD-ROM

The CD-ROM enclosed with this book contains:

- all code samples included in the text of the book,
- the Perl source distribution for most UNIX variations,
- the Perl binary distribution for Windows 95 and NT,
- the Perl/Tk distribution.
- additional selected modules of the CPAN.

The CD-ROM directories contain the following files:

- **scripts** The named Perl scripts and modules and the HTML files printed in the book.
- **CPAN** The Perl distribution for UNIX, `perl5.004_04.tar.gz`, together with the freely available modules for scripts used in the book (for installation see page 378). Also, an experimental version of `perl5.005` can be found here.
- **misc** The distributions of two versions of the Apache Web server (1.2.6 and 1.3.1; for installation see page 389) together with the freely available SSL implementation by Eric Young (see page 388).
- **exercises** The solutions to the exercises of Chapters 1 and 3, sorted by exercise numbers.
- **win32** The Perl distribution for Windows 95 and NT. Several modules for the Windows world.

References

Booch G. (1994). *Object Oriented Analysis and Design with Applications*. The Benjamin/Cummings Publishing Company Inc.

Chapman N. (1997). *Perl: The Programmer's Companion*. Wiley

Christiansen T. and Torkington N. (1988). *The Perl Cookbook*. O'Reilly & Associates, Inc.

Eriksson H. E. and Penker M. (1998). *UML Toolkit*. Wiley

Friedl J. (1997). *Mastering Regular Expressions*. O'Reilly & Associates, Inc.

Gamma E., Helm R., Johnson R. *et al.* (1995). *Design Patterns*. Addison-Wesley

Garfinkel S. and Spafford G. (1997). *Web Security & Commerce*. O'Reilly & Associates, Inc.

Gundavaram S. (1996). *CGI Programming on the World Wide Web*. O'Reilly & Associates, Inc.

Hall J. N. and Schwartz R. L. (1998). *Effective Perl Programming*. Addison-Wesley

Herrmann E. (1996). *Teach yourself CGI programming with Perl in a week*. Sams Net

Krol E. (1994). *The Whole Internet*. O'Reilly & Associates, Inc.

Libes D. (1995). *Exploring Expect*. O'Reilly & Associates, Inc.

Nye A. (1990). *Xlib Programming Manual*. O'Reilly & Associates, Inc.

Ousterhout J. K. (1994). *Tcl and the Tk Toolkit*. Addison-Wesley

Patchett C., Wright M., and Holfelder P. (1997). *The Cgi/Perl Cookbook*. John Wiley & Sons

Patwardhan N. and Irving C. (1997). *Programming with Perl Modules* (Part of the Perl Resource Kit). O'Reilly Software

Quercia V. and O'Reilly T. (1990). *X Window System User's Guide*. O'Reilly & Associates, Inc.

Rumbaugh J., Blaha M., Premerlani W. *et al.* (1991). *Object-Oriented Modeling and Design*. Prentice-Hall

Schilli M. (1996). *Effektives Programmieren mit Perl 5*. Addison-Wesley

Schwartz R. L. (1997). *Learning Perl* 2nd edn. O'Reilly & Associates, Inc.

Schwartz R. L., Olson E., and Christiansen T. (1997). *Learning Perl on Win32 Systems*. O'Reilly & Associates, Inc.

Siever E. and Futato D. (1997). *Perl Module Reference* Vol. 1 & 2 (Part of the Perl Resource Kit). O'Reilly Software

Spainhour S. and Quercia V. (1996). *Webmaster in a Nutshell*. O'Reilly & Associates, Inc.

Srinivasan S. (1997). *Advanced Perl Programming*. O'Reilly & Associates, Inc.

Stevens W. R. (1990). *UNIX Network Programming*. Prentice Hall

Stevens W. R. (1994). *TCP/IP Illustrated*, Vol. 1. Addison-Wesley

Vromans J. (1998). *Perl 5 Pocket Reference*, 2nd edn. O'Reilly & Associates, Inc.

Wall L., Christiansen T., and Schwartz R. L. (1996). *Programming Perl 5*. O'Reilly & Associates, Inc.

Wong C. (1997). *Web Client Programming*. O'Reilly & Associates, Inc.

Index